The Poetics of Iblīs

Narrative Theology in the Qur'ān

HARVARD THEOLOGICAL STUDIES
62

HARVARD
THEOLOGICAL
STUDIES

CAMBRIDGE, MASSACHUSETTS

The Poetics of Iblīs

Narrative Theology in the Qur'ān

Whitney S. Bodman

DISTRIBUTED BY

HARVARD UNIVERSITY PRESS

FOR

HARVARD THEOLOGICAL STUDIES

HARVARD DIVINITY SCHOOL

The Poetics of Iblīs
Narrative Theology in the Qur'ān

Harvard Theological Studies 62

Managing Editor: Margaret Studier

Copy Editors: Richard Jude Thompson, Kynthia Margaret Taylor
Typesetters: Richard Jude Thompson, Kynthia Margaret Taylor
Proofreaders: Kynthia Margaret Taylor, Chan Sok Park

Indexer: Whitney S. Bodman

Foreign language fonts: Arabic transliteration font used was TranslitArabicALC; Hebrew font was New Jerusalem available from Linguist's Software, Inc., PO Box 580, Edmonds, WA 98020-0580; tel: (425) 775-1130. Website: www.linguistsoftware.com

Bodman, Whitney S., 1950–
The Poetics of Iblīs : Narrative Theology in the Qur'ān / Whitney S Bodman.
p. cm. — (Harvard theological studies; 62)
Includes bibliographical references and index.
ISBN 978-0-674-06241-2 (alk. paper)
1. Devil—Islam—Koranic teaching. 2. Koran—Theology. 3. Koran stories—History and criticism. I. Title.

BP134.D43B63 2007

297.2'16—dc23

2011021309

To my parents,

who did not live to see this final publication,

but whose blessings follow it;

and to my wife, Betty,

who tolerated long absences.

Table of Contents

Acknowledgments

It is said that many hands make light work. While I hope this work will be illuminating, it has certainly not been light. Many hands have shaped its production.

I must start with Wadi Haddad. In his Qur'ān course at Hartford Seminary I first discovered and wrote about Iblīs, who (to the consternation of some) has been my constant companion for years since.

Certainly among the most important guides in this project has been my lead adviser, Bill Graham, who has also been a family friend for decades (and my father's student). Wolfhart Heinrichs, who shares my interest in Iblīs, was also there, always. Another central figure was Selīm Barakāt, of blessed memory, who patiently led me through *tafsīr* after *tafsīr* in Damascus.

Dr. Angelika Neuwirth also has a special place in this project. Under her guidance I produced an article that was the first effort to organize my thoughts on the diversity of interpretations of Iblīs.

Jane Hobler helped with German texts. Jean Butler organized a conference in Denmark at which Iblīs was one topic of conversation, especially in regards to the chronology of the Qur'ān.

Dr. Peter Machinist at Harvard gave good guidance throughout the process of rewriting the dissertation into a book. Austin Presbyterian Theological Seminary graciously allowed me time off from teaching to finish the revisions.

The text has been edited time and again over the months and years, not least by my father. Students Lisa Straus and Katie Muzos spent hours editing the text. Thanks also go to the production staff in Massachusetts: to managing editor Margaret Studier for her tireless efforts, to Richard Jude Thompson for his attentive copyediting and typesetting, to Kynthia Margaret Taylor for further copyediting and superb proofreading, and to Chan Sok Park for his detailed proofreading of the bibliography.

A host of conversation partners—students, scholars, and others—has also enriched this work: Ṣādiq al-'Aẓm in Damascus, and the following in

Egypt: Maryam Sharief, Salma Anwar, Rasha Disūqī and Dahlia Sabry—and students here at the seminary in the "Murder, Mayhem and Betrayal" class on scriptural stories. That class demonstrated perfectly how those with no knowledge of the Qur'ān can read a text and see something that I have missed, even though I have been reading the text for years.

These are a few who have had a hand in this project. There are many more, and I worry that I have missed someone or something important. That is an error of deficient memory, not of deficient gratitude.

Whitney S. Bodman
Austin Presbyterian Theological Seminary
Austin, Texas; August 2011

Introduction

This study began as an attempt to describe the understanding of theodicy in Islam. In light of a commonly heard claim that Islam does not accept the concept of "original sin," I sought to understand how Islam accounts for the manifest evil(s) in the world. Islam does not have a single theodicy—like other religious traditions, it encompasses a diversity of opinion and perspective through the ages and throughout its geographical range. Nevertheless, certain dogmas have come to be dominant, such that one can speak of a normative tradition.

The study subsequently took me into some unexpected realms of exploration, probing the nature and place of narrative in Islam, specifically in the Qur'ān. The two endeavors, narrative and theodicy, are connected. Certain interpretations of evil are best communicated and investigated through the medium of story. It is narrative that captures the tragic dimensions of life: the ambiguities of fate, the confusion of flawed characters, noble intentions with ruinous outcomes. Any reduction of these realities to divine sovereignty and human evil belies the truth of human experience.

Dogmatic theology is more comfortable with binary oppositions of evil and good. As Elaine Pagels has pointed out with respect to early Christianity, social and political conflict can also lend its support to the simplicity and comfort of assertions of the goodness of "us" against the evil of "them."[1] This conflict generally finds its way into theological justifications.

Theology itself does not occupy a prestigious seat at the Islamic table.[2] Philosophy and jurisprudence are more prominent. Sadly, even the rich tradition of Islamic philosophy finds little popular appeal in the modern age. When one comes to the problem of evil, jurisprudence may well teach us

[1] Pagels, *Origin of Satan*, 35–62.

[2] Van Ess, "Beginnings."

how to deal with the consequences of evil, but it does not say much about its source, pervasiveness, or essential nature.

To answer the question of the source of evil in Islam, we must first, of course, turn to the Qur'ān. There we—at least we who are weaned on the Western corpus of religious texts—find a familiar story. We find Satan (al-Shayṭān) tempting Adam in the garden and causing Adam and his partner to be cast out into the world. We also find, joined to this story, a prior event—the refusal of Iblīs to bow down to the form of Adam.

This story is close to unique to the Islamic scriptural tradition. The personage of Iblīs (often traced to the Greek *diabolos*[3]) is generally unfamiliar to the non-Muslim community. Heb 1:6 has a brief reference to angels bowing down to Christ,[4] and the basic story appears in the apocryphal *Gospel of Bartholomew* and *Life of Adam and Eve*, as well as the pseudepigraphical *Cave of Treasures*.[5] It does not take much further reading in the Islamic tradition to find that Iblīs takes on characteristics that may remind a reader of Milton's Lucifer, a romantic and tragic character, or of Goethe's Mephistopheles, or of Prometheus, or even of Judas Iscariot in some more sympathetic treatments. This last comparison is particularly worthy of further consideration.

My original intention had been to explore this diverse Islamic interpretive tradition surrounding Iblīs. I intended to do the requisite chapter on the story in the Qur'ān, then move on to the interpretation of Iblīs by Abū Nuwās, to the legends recorded in mystical Sufi literature, in al-Jāḥiẓ, Majlisī, and other medieval authors, and finally, in some modern novels.

But the Qur'ān proved to be unexpectedly complex and rich. The Iblīs story, in its seven recensions, provoked more questions, so I had to seek

[3] It is mainly non-Muslim scholars who make this connection. See Bell, *Introduction*, 118; Carter, *Foreign Vocabulary*, 136; Katsh, *Judaism and the Koran*, 33; Rippin, "Iblis"; and Wensinck and Gardet, "Iblis," in EI^2 (*Encyclopaedia of Islam*, 2nd ed.), 668–69. In Muslim commentaries, the term is often regarded as a variant of the fourth form (*if'īl*) of the root *b-l-s*, with the meaning "to feel remorse, to despair of the good," because he has nothing to expect from the mercy of God. See Al-Ṭabarī, *Tafsīr*, 1:227 (vol. 1); Butler, *Iblīs*, 30–38.

[4] Bateman, *Jewish Hermeneutics*; Fletcher-Louis, "Divine Humanity"; Patton, "Adam"; Schenck, "Enthroned Son"; Steenburg, "Worship of Adam"; and Zwemer, "Worship of Adam." Bateman does not mention the Qur'ānic story of the angels prostrating themselves to Adam in his discussion of Heb 1:6. Current thinking among New Testament scholars seems to connect this passage more to Psalm 8 and Ps 2:7 than to midrash concerning the veneration of Adam.

[5] Anderson and Stone, *Synopsis*; Budge, *Book of the Cave of Treasures*; and Elliott, *Apocryphal New Testament*, 652–72.

the tools to give it adequate study. At first, I thought the tools of mythic analysis, such as the structuralism of Lévi-Strauss, would do the trick, but these were not adequate, as they could not catch the nuances in the variants of the same story. Gradually I was drawn to the diversity of approaches in the disciplines of literary studies, discourse analysis, and, a term new to me, "narratology." Some of these tools have been applied to the literature of the Bible (especially the Old Testament, or Tanakh) by such scholars as James Kugel,[6] Meir Sternberg,[7] Mieke Bal,[8] and Robert Alter.[9] This analysis proved a far richer trove and has helped me see dimensions of the text that had eluded me before.

The result has been a study largely focused on the Qur'ānic text, and which, I hope, will offer not only a way to ground the Iblīs of legend in the Iblīs of the Qur'ān but also a test of some new ways of approaching the text of the Qur'ān itself—ways that build on the work of Stefan Leder,[10] Anthony H. Johns,[11] and Angelika Neuwirth.[12]

Approaches

The organization of the chapters seeks to follow in some way the development of this approach. The first three chapters (part 1) explore the methodology. In these three chapters, I try to develop an argument for the legitimacy of a narratological approach both on the basis of the tools of the discipline itself and on the basis of Muslim understandings of the Qur'ān.

In chapter 1, I begin where I started ten years ago when I discovered Peter Awn's book on Sufi psychology in the library of Hartford Seminary in preparation for a paper for a Qur'ān course with Professor Wadi Haddad.[13] In this chapter, I give a brief rendition of Awn's findings and then go on to raise what is for me the central question: What is the difference between Iblīs and al-Shayṭān? Conventional Muslim theology treats the two as functionally the same, with Iblīs being the proto-Shayṭān, but some Muslim literature

[6] For example, Kugel, *In Potiphar's House*.

[7] Sternberg, *Poetics of Biblical Narrative*.

[8] Bal, *Narratology*.

[9] Alter, *Art of Biblical Narrative*.

[10] Leder, *Story-Telling*.

[11] Johns, "Joseph."

[12] Neuwirth, "Negotiating Justice (Part I); idem, "Negotiating Justice (Part II)."

[13] Awn, *Satan's Tragedy and Redemption*.

treats the two quite differently. I explore this difference, building on Awn's evidence of a more sympathetic treatment of Iblīs than is ever meted out to al-Shayṭān, in the Qur'ān and elsewhere.

The basic difference between Iblīs and al-Shayṭān is that the former is a narrative character. Hence, Iblīs is best approached utilizing narrative analysis. The rest of this chapter explores the tools of narratology, especially the approaches developed by Wolfgang Iser.

Iser is a leader of the modern reader-response trend in narrative interpretation or narratology. He asserts that literary meaning is created by the interaction between a fixed text and a reader. The text defines a range of meaning and interpretive possibilities that are bounded by the text itself. In its production, the author has in mind an implied reader, a set of suppositions about the range of knowledge and abilities of expected readers. However, these authorial suppositions do not describe the actual reader. The actual reader brings to the task of reading his or her own particular experience, insights, prejudices, commitments, and imagination. In the interaction between the text with its interpretive range and the reader with a repertoire of mental formations, meaning is generated. This approach allows me to investigate the range of meaning of each telling of the Iblīs story in the Qur'ān, as well as some possible repertoires brought to the reading/hearing of the Qur'ān by its early or original audience.

Chapter 2 raises the question of the basis for such narrative analysis in terms of the Qur'ān's understanding of itself. Does the Qur'ān lend itself to such an approach? Does the Qur'ān itself, or classical interpretation of the Qur'ān, indicate that a reader may read stories as stories rather than as illustrations of divine exhortations?

Muslim theology and Qur'ānic hermeneutics have generally spurned fiction, grudgingly approved *isrā'īliyyāt* (tales from Jewish and Christian sources) only for purposes of support for what is already established by other means, and tried to keep a firm wall between factual history and fictional literature. But the Qur'ān does contain narrative. Even if we do not call it fiction, we can at least recognize that it has fictive elements, or a fictive character, if we keep in mind the distinction that Iser proposes between the fictive and the imaginary. In fact, only by treating narrative as narrative can the multiplication of narratives of the Iblīs story—and the variations among them—begin to make sense.

This does, of course, raise a multitude of questions about the construction of the stories, their placement in their respective *sūrahs*, and the design of the *sūrahs* themselves (who? how? why?). Hence chapter 2 raises methodological issues with specific reference to the Qur'ān.

Chapter 3 may seem an unwelcome diversion. After two chapters on methodology, one ought to get on with the project, into the substance of the story. However, the mythic or legendary background of the Iblīs story has provided important insights into interpretive possibilities and thus becomes a necessary background without which some of the interpretive forays of later chapters would be less comprehensible.

Since the Qur'ān sees itself in continuity with the biblical tradition, and Iser has emphasized the importance of "repertoire" in the interpretation of texts, it made sense to explore the diverse narratives concerning the origin of evil in the biblical tradition. The helpfulness of this is that it alerts us to an established range of interpretation intimately related to the texts of our concern. It was only when I realized that the Cain and Abel story was also a story of the origin of evil that I began to see how some versions of the Iblīs story set Iblīs and Adam in a similar sibling-like relationship of contention, similarly mediated by God.

The biblical repertoires may also form part of the repertoire of the implied reader. To this may be added other legendary traditions, such as the pre-Islamic tradition of *jinn*. This latter source does not figure in this chapter but emerges in later chapters, ad hoc, when it is called into play by a specific version of the Iblīs story.

The *Sūrahs*

Part 2 leads us to the text of the Qur'ān itself: *sūrah* by *sūrah*. Each of the seven *sūrahs* examined includes a version or citation of the Iblīs story. Each one directs our attention to a different aspect of the story. Chapter 4 examines Sūrah ṬāḤā, which has a short—one verse—citation of the Iblīs story. The *sūrah* is dominated by a lengthy cycle of stories following Moses from his birth to the episode of the golden calf. Here we try to understand the message of the Iblīs story by looking carefully at the dominant narrative of the *sūrah*, believing that the inclusion of the Iblīs story must be designed to contribute to the message of the *sūrah* as a whole. The Moses story emphasizes Moses' individual incapabilities but then shows that he succeeds due to the watchful eye and care of God. The Iblīs story contributes to this theme by showing Iblīs's own incapacity to follow God's command.

Chapter 5 considers a similar construction in Sūrat al-Kahf which also has a brief narration of the Iblīs story, though a bit longer than that of Sūrah ṬāḤā. Sūrat al-Kahf contains several sustained narratives: the seven sleepers, Moses and Khiḍr, Dhū al-Qarnayn, and the parable of two men and a garden. These stories contain a common theme that I then apply to the Iblīs story itself. Here my main intent is to examine the narrative in the light of the implied reader's repertoire of knowledge. Since Iblīs is identified as a *jinn*,[14] we can ask what that might have meant to various communities of readers of the text. We cannot know what the term meant to the revealer of the text, but we can survey, in various ways, the contemporary associations with the idea of *jinn* and relate that to the interpretation of the Iblīs passage.

In chapter 6 one comes to a longer narration of the Iblīs story in Sūrat al-Ḥijr. Here one has the opportunity to examine in detail the internal dynamics of a particular narration of the Iblīs story. I note a particular similarity between the way the Iblīs story is told here and the sibling rivalry myth familiar from the Bible, particularly in the Cain and Abel story in the book of Genesis. I do not, however, neglect to set the narrative in the context of the whole *sūrah* and look for consistent themes. I find such a theme in the idea of destiny, the knowledge that God has of the future, which knowledge has been denied to humans, and now also to the *jinn*. This relates some of the content of Sūrat al-Ḥijr to the Azazel story of the watcher myth that I have described in chapter 3.

Chapter 7 examines a version of the Iblīs story in Sūrah Ṣād that is similar in many respects to that in Sūrat al-Ḥijr. The major theme of the *sūrah* is disputation, which also appears in the Iblīs story at the end. In this chapter I look at the way the narrative of the Iblīs story has changed in particular ways from that in Sūrat al-Ḥijr to yield a significantly different message. I will argue in the conclusion that this shift occurs not only because of the contrasting themes of the two *sūrah*s but also because of the development of the Iblīs story in successive revelations. In Sūrah Ṣād, the narrator takes a more active role in interpreting the character of Iblīs than is evident in Sūrat al-Ḥijr. Here Iblīs is haughty and an unbeliever, and the conflict—the disputation—between Iblīs and God is sharpened through subtle changes in the dialogue in the narrative.

[14] In 18:50 and implied in 15:27.

Chapter 8 examines the story in Sūrat al-Isrā'. Here Iblīs is depicted in full assault on humanity with military imagery, and humanity is warned not to take Iblīs as a protector. God alone is the trustee of human interests: *al-Wakīl*.

Chapter 9 investigates the Iblīs story in Sūrat al-'Arāf, a well-developed version of the story that joins it to the Qur'ānic garden story.[15] The issue of shame and the covering of shame are motifs in the story that merge in complex ways, as covering is both a mechanism for hiding shame, which disobedience has exposed, and also an adornment, a positive description.

Finally, the version of the Iblīs story in Sūrat al-Baqarah is, by consensus of both Muslim and non-Muslim scholars, the latest telling in terms of the order of revelation, but it is the first encountered in the bound (*muṣḥaf*) order of the Qur'ān. In the commentarial tradition it receives the bulk of attention. In our analysis we situate the Iblīs story as the third in a primordial cycle of four stories that relate the position of humanity to that of the angels. The Iblīs narrative follows stories of the objection of the angels to the creation of humanity and God's instruction to Adam about the names of all things. The garden story of the successful temptation of Adam follows it. Iblīs's own role in the larger narrative is minor, and his story receives little attention. Nevertheless it is important in the larger narrative.

Conclusion

This study has two conclusions. On the one hand, I have tried to demonstrate the value of reader-response narratology as a method for analyzing stories in the Qur'ān, especially stories that appear in multiple places and forms. In the first two chapters, I describe and defend this approach. One conclusion summarizes the results of this application.

The second conclusion pertains to the theme of the nature of evil and the range of interpretation allowed by the Qur'ān. After some comments on the theology of tragedy based on my analysis of the Iblīs story, I move to four modern literary works—a poem, two novels and a short story—to demonstrate that the range of interpretation that the various renditions of the Iblīs story in the Qur'ān permit includes the tragic Iblīs. I am suggesting here that the diversity of interpretation of Iblīs found in these modern works

[15] In the Genesis narrative this is, of course, the garden of Eden. The Qur'ān makes no mention of the name, nature or place of the garden, except that it is above the earthly sphere. It is not necessarily to be identified either with "heaven" or with "paradise."

is foreshadowed in the diversity of the Qur'ānic story itself. The Qur'ān does not tell a simple story of Iblīs but weaves a complex and suggestive narrative that allows for a range of diverse and divergent interpretations. Muslims through the ages have found within that range the opportunity to explore various nuances of the age-old issue of theodicy. The Qur'ān indeed not only allows this exploration but also invites and encourages it.

CHAPTER 1

The Nature of Narrative

More than twenty years ago, Peter Awn published a revision of his Harvard dissertation as *Satan's Tragedy and Redemption: Iblīs in Sufi Psychology*,[1] a study of the treatment of Iblīs in various Sufi texts. He began his work, however, by exploring some of the legends of Iblīs contained in *tafsīr*, the commentarial literature appreciated by most Muslims, such as the *tafsīr* of Abū Ja'far al-Ṭabarī and that of 'Abdallah Ibn 'Umar al-Bayḍāwī. He then points out parallels with pre-Islamic material such as the *Gospel of Bartholomew* and the *Life of Adam and Eve*. With this prehistory Awn roots the Iblīs story in a long tradition of legend and mythology[2] that concerns itself with the origin and nature of human evil.

Islamic responses to the question of evil are no less complex than responses in other traditions. The key to understanding a religious tradition may lie not in its construction of divinity or ultimacy but in its anthropology, its assessment of the nature, limitations, and potentialities of the human being. An important component in this assessment of the human is an evaluation of the nature and source of evil. To understand the nature of evil is to understand the nature of humanity, and to understand the nature of humanity, in a given

[1] Awn, *Satan's Tragedy and Redemption*.

[2] Though traditionally "myth" has been defined as narrative of primordial times and non-terrestrial environments, while "legend" has been taken to mean narrative within historical time and earthly place, these distinctions are less tenable now. However much it is stressed that "myth" does not mean "false," the stain of that association remains for many not familiar with the discourse in the discipline of the history of religion. While generally maintaining the traditional division in usage of the two words, I will also occasionally use both for the same story.

religious tradition, is to understand the heart of that tradition. Indeed, it is to understand claims about the nature of God.

The Nature of Evil

Gustav von Grunebaum asserted the importance of anthropology to religion as the first of four principles in his description of the Muslim concept of evil in a 1970 article.[3] His second principle was that, unlike Christianity, in Islam the concept of evil does not have a primary role in the structure of the religion. It is not constitutive of the faith. In Christianity, the role of Christ as Savior resolves the primal disorder of the fall, the evil brought into the world by the act of Adam. In Islam, the similar act of Adam is simply an example of human fallibility, not its cause. A corollary to this idea is that Islam rejects the Augustinian Christian idea of evil as the absence of good. It also rejects the idea that things are good and evil in themselves and that human analysis could determine such a thing. This view was the Mu'tazilite "error," rejected in the early tenth century by, among others, Abū al-Hasan al-Ash'arī.[4] He suggested that things are good and evil because God has encouraged or prohibited them for God's own secret reasons. This has been the prevailing notion in Sunni Islam since the tenth century.[5]

The third principle that von Grunebaum identifies is that there is a tension in Islam between individual responsibility for individual actions and a collective sense of pollution. Sins within a community, although imputed eschatologically to the individual who will stand alone before the judging angels, nevertheless have an impact on the community. One definition of evil, as "that which deserves blame," assumes a communal definition.

The fourth principle that von Grunebaum asserts is that of a thoroughgoing predestination. Islam does not shy away from holding God responsible for the evil in the world as Christianity does.[6] In Islam all that occurs is determined by God's will, no matter how unfair it may appear by human standards.

[3] Von Grunebaum, "Observations."

[4] In making this judgment, von Grunebaum is articulating not a Muslim consensus, but the theology of the Ash'arite school, which became dominant in Sunni theology. Shi'a Muslims, for instance, posit a more rational basis for the nature of evil, closer to the Mu'tazilite position.

[5] Watt, *Formative Period*, 238–42.

[6] The issue of theodicy is complex, especially when approached comparatively. Wiser authors would let this comment pass without elaboration. My assertion that Christianity is less willing (although not absolutely unwilling) to associate evil with God can be briefly

This description falls short of an actual definition of evil. The Ash'arite synthesis in which we are not to ask what is evil but only what is prohibited holds sway. In this system, al-Shayṭān performs the function as a representation of the evil inclination in humanity. Al-Shayṭān is not the cause of evil; God ultimately causes evil and mortals immediately cause it. Al-Shayṭān serves only to lure us to the many attractive alternatives to the straight path (*ṣirāṭ-al-mustaqīm*). Since good and evil cannot be discerned by reason and cannot be examined in those terms (again, the Mu'tazilite "error"), the only question is that of rightly perceiving what God has commanded in any situation. In essence, in this view, there is no fundamental theology of evil in Islam. Instead, there is a theology of submission.

But this vastly oversimplifies the picture given in the Qur'ān. The mortal is not simply a determined puppet in God's world but one who has the choice, and the responsibility, for choosing between the straight path and other paths. The human condition has not so much the character of mechanical determination as one of tragic potential. Nobly made, but weakly empowered, each mortal struggles to live a life ordered according to God's *shari'ah* (design; law) against all temptations that might lead one astray. Although all humans are born "muslim," in the sense of being naturally in accord with God's order until human interaction changes this, the Qur'ān also states that the mortal is created weak.[7] Vulnerability to temptation is a part of human nature that makes submission to God an act that requires consistent effort. In

---

indicated by two observations. First, the Qur'ān asserts that Satan is the enemy of humanity (35:6), while in the New Testament, Satan is the enemy of both humanity (Matt 13:39) and God (Revelation 12 and 13). In the Revelation to John, Satan's authority still derives from God ("he is given authority") but his power on earth is one of dominion, capable of massive destruction. There is a tendency toward dualism in Christianity. In Christian theology, God's "goodness" is ontological, the fundamental characteristic of God's nature. In Islam, God's goodness is everywhere manifest, but it is manifest as acts of God not as the essence of God's being. For Christians it is more difficult to reconcile evil in the world with the fundamental goodness of God. This reconciliation has often been effected by rejecting the world in favor of the kingdom of God, variously defined. However, the association of God with love as the expression of God's fundamental goodness, especially through Christ, means that Christian theology makes intimacy rather than obedience as the ideal of divine-human relationship.

[7] S. 4:28: *khuliqa al-insān ḍa'īf*[an] (humanity was created weak), and S. 70:19: *inna al-insān khuliqa halū'*[an] (humanity was created impatient); see also S. 21:37. Note that in all three instances the passive tense of the verb is used, which diminishes the sense, if not the actuality, of God's agency in this aspect of human nature. See also Mohamed, "Interpretation of Fitrah," 129–51.

this demanding labor, the character of Iblīs appears in some versions to be the clear adversary: the proto-Shayṭān. But as Awn demonstrates, the character of Iblīs is more complex than this, to the point that sometimes Iblīs is even a helper in the effort toward faithfulness. Whereas al-Shayṭān is always the evil adversary, Iblīs has a multitude of other dimensions. Iblīs emerges in many Sufi formulations, and as I will show, in other contexts, as a character in a story, not merely a representative of evil.

The story of Iblīs is short. A composite of the seven versions in the Qur'ān that I will discuss might read like this: God tells his angels that he will create a human from hardened, "ringing" clay. The angels worry that this human will corrupt the earth. God reassures them, then shapes Adam and blows divine breath into him. God then commands the angels to bow down to Adam, which they do, except Iblīs, a *jinn*, who refuses. God questions Iblīs about this refusal. Iblīs says, "I am better than he. You created me from fire, but him from putrid clay." God evicts Iblīs from heaven, rejecting him, but before Iblīs leaves, he asks for respite until the day of resurrection. God gives him respite until "an appointed time." Iblīs then promises to lead humanity astray, all but God's faithful. In three versions the Adam and Eve story in paradise immediately follows this story.

Iblīs and the Sufis

Awn's aim was to explore the various twists, meanings, and usages that Sufis have discovered in the Iblīs story. In Sufi renditions Iblīs often represents the various earthly temptations by which mortals are seduced and which those who seek the divine must studiously avoid—such studiousness requiring careful analysis of the myriad ways the material world and grosser human appetites might invade the pure spirit. Iblīs is here the wily tempter, the adversary with many disguises and ruses. He uses subterfuge to gain access to the human spirit, as in this tale told by the thirteenth century Persian Sufi Farīd al-Dīn 'Aṭṭār:

> [One day Adam went off to work and Iblīs came to visit Eve, bringing along his little son, al-Khannās.] Iblīs said, "Something important has come up. Please watch my son until I come back." Eve agreed and Iblīs went on his way. When Adam came back, he asked, "Who is this?" She said, "It is the child of Iblīs; he has been left in my care." Adam reproached her, "Why did you agree?" He flew into a

> rage, killed the child, chopped him into pieces, and hung each piece from the branch of a tree. Iblīs came back and asked, "Where is my child?" Eve told the whole story: "He has been cut into pieces and each piece has been hung from the branch of a tree." Iblīs called out to his child and he was joined back together. Alive once again, he stood before Iblīs.
>
> Another time he addressed Eve: "Here, take him; I have something else important to do." Eve refused. He kept after her with entreaty and lament until she agreed. Then Iblīs went on his way. Adam returned and asked her, "Who is this?" Eve told the whole story. Adam berated her and said, "I do not know what the secret is in this affair. My order you reject, but the one from God's enemy you accept, and you are beguiled by his words!" Thereupon he killed the child and burned him. Half of his ashes he threw into the water and half he flung to the winds; then he left.
>
> Iblīs returns and the same scenario is acted out once again. He resurrects his son from the ashes and asks Eve to watch over him; she refuses, for now she fears Adam's wrath even more: "He will destroy me!" she pleads. But Iblīs reassures her, and she capitulates, unable to resist his power. Adam returns and is both baffled and furious. He wonders how long this will go on. At wit's end, Adam resolves to devise a permanent solution.
>
> Adam killed Khannās and fried him; he ate half himself and gave Eve the other half to eat. . . . When Iblīs returned and asked for his child, Eve recounted the whole tale: "He killed him and fried him; I ate half and Adam half." Iblīs said, "This was exactly my intention, in order that I might have access to man's interior! Since his breast is now my abode, my goal is achieved."[8]

Here Iblīs is conjoined with the human spirit, a view that comes close to a recognition of a natural, if not original, human disability, perhaps the human weakness to which the Qur'ān often refers (as in 4:28). But Sufis do not uniformly hold that the human soul (*nafs*) should be identified with Iblīs. Often the *nafs* is simply the instrument of Iblīs, the arena of human vulnerability.

In other Sufi accounts, Iblīs represents particular human liabilities, such as the danger of pride that inhibits true vision. Iblīs is the "One-Eyed":

[8] 'Aṭṭār, *Tadhkirāt*, 529–31, quoted in Awn, *Satan's Tragedy and Redemption*, 63.

See in everyone's face a wondrous moon.
When you have seen the beginning, see the end
so that you do not become like Iblīs, one-eyed.
Half he sees, half not, like some defective.
He saw Adam's clay, but his faith he saw not;
he saw this world in him, but his other-worldly eye
he saw not.[9]

Any attraction to the world (*al-dunyā*) becomes an opportunity for Iblīs, since Iblīs is the master of this world as the story below makes clear. Jesus comes to represent the ideal Muslim ascetic, one who has given up all attachment to the things of this world, but even he is vulnerable, not by his will or lack of piety, but rather by inadvertence:

Jesus, son of Mary, had fallen asleep,
and had put half a brick under his head.
When Jesus opened his eyes after his restful sleep,
he saw the accursed Iblīs above his head.
He cried, "O accursed one, why stand you there?"
He replied, "Because you have placed my brick
under your head!
The whole world is like my domain;
it is clear that this brick belongs to me.
You are appropriating goods in my kingdom;
you have trespassed in my territory.'
Jesus hurled that thing from beneath his head;
he resolved to sleep with his face on the ground.
When he (Jesus) flung that half brick away, Iblīs said,
'Now that I leave your presence, sleep well!"[10]

In this story Iblīs is not simply challenging Jesus but also teaching him. The temporal world belongs to Iblīs, and the spiritual world belongs to the believers. A longer version in Sanā'ī's *Ḥadīqah* clarifies that the issue of the story is the proper assignment of worlds. God has assigned the temporal world to Iblīs as his legitimate domain. Here in 'Aṭṭār's version, the last line is almost a blessing, now that Jesus, the spirit of God, is no longer encroaching on the material world that belongs to Iblīs. A parallel version of the same story in Abū Ḥamīd al-Ghazzālī's *Iḥyā 'Ulūm al-Dīn* in the section on renunciation (*zuhd*) identifies the adversary as al-Shayṭān and does not

[9] Rūmī, *Mathnawī*, quoted in Awn, *Satan's Tragedy and Redemption*, 90.

[10] 'Aṭṭār, *Conference of the Birds*, quoted in Awn, *Satan's Tragedy and Redemption*, 158–59..

include the last line. Other texts contain similar versions.[11] Al-Ghazzālī's version removes any suggestion that Iblīs might be the legitimate owner of the stone or might actually be clarifying the spiritual path of asceticism for Jesus. ʿAṭṭār's version is an indication of the difference between Iblīs and al-Shayṭān that we will explore further.

There are, however, a multitude of stories and texts that present Iblīs in a more sympathetic manner even than ʿAṭṭār describes. One of the best known is the encounter between Iblīs and the caliph Muʿāwiya recounted by Rūmī in the *Mathnawī*.[12] Iblīs awakens Muʿāwiya in the palace, urging him to prayer. Under questioning by the caliph, Iblīs recounts how he used to be an angel who was faithful and obedient to God, indeed, a lover of God. Now that he has been separated from God, he knows all the more the value of union with God, and even now, "During the short while since He drove me from His presence, mine eye hath remained (fixed) upon His beauteous face." Iblīs acknowledges his envy of Adam but argues that envy arises from love. Muʿāwiya replies that since this error, Iblīs has waylaid thousands and recounts numerous examples from history. Iblīs replies that he serves God as the touchstone that distinguishes the true from the false: "To the good I act as guide, the dry branches I rip off." But Muʿāwiya still dismisses him and complains to God about this night visit. Finally Iblīs confesses that he has urged Muʿāwiya to perform his prayer because his anguish of regret, had he missed the prayer, would have been far more valuable to God than the prayer itself. Although Iblīs is exposed as a deceitful character, the clear impact of the story is to clothe him with tragic sympathy. As Awn points out, Muʿāwiya comes across as stiff and common while Iblīs is passionate, nuanced, and engaging.[13]

While the animosity of Iblīs toward humanity is clear, so also, here and in other texts, is his abiding love for God. In a sense, Iblīs exemplifies a distorted but nevertheless admirable faithfulness to God. In his devotion, Iblīs can still hope for God's mercy:

> My heart was filled with His glory;
> I was a confessor of His unity.
> Nevertheless, without cause, in spite of all this devotion,
> He drove me from His threshold without warning.

[11] See Khalidi, *Muslim Jesus*, 18.

[12] Rūmī, *Mathnawī*. 1.356–66 (Book 2, lines 2604–2792); Kappler, "Le dialogue d'Iblis."

[13] Awn, *Satan's Tragedy and Redemption*, 87.

No one of the creatures of the threshold had the courage
to ask, 'Why did You banish him so suddenly?'
So if He should, without cause, accept me back again,
it would not be strange, for it cannot be fathomed.
Since without cause I was driven away by Him,
I can also, without cause, be called back by Him.
Since in God's actions there is no how and why,
it is not right to abandon hope in God.
Since His anger decreed my being driven off,
it would not be strange if His grace called me back.
I do not know; O God, I do not know!
You know; You know what You will.
One You call with a hundred caresses,
another You drive away with a hundred blows.
. . . .
Since, without cause, You bestow great wealth,
now, too, without cause, grant me this favor.
Since, without cause, You bestowed the gift of existence,
in the same way, without cause, drown me in Your generosity.
Since Your repose depends not on my suffering,
Your liberality depends on no cause.[14]

Iblīs holds out hope that he might indeed be redeemed at some point. But other Sufis dismiss this possibility:

> There is a report that it was said to him [Iblīs] by God, "Bow down to the grave of Adam and I will accept your repentance and I will forgive your disobedience." But he said, "I would not bow down to his form and his corpse, so how can I bow down to his grave and his cadaver?"[15]

A more famous narrative is found in the *ṬāwāSīn* of Ibn Manṣūr al-Ḥallāj, who is best known for claiming, "I am the Truth," in Baghdad and being crucified for heresy (and perhaps for political reasons as well). The *ṬāwāSīn* is a set of eleven compact and complex essays and narratives. In the sixth chapter, we find this description of Iblīs:

[14] 'Aṭṭār, *Ilāhīnāma*, 376 1.18–377 1.7, and 377 1.18–378 1.2, quoted in Awn, *Satan's Tragedy and Redemption*, 176–77.

[15] Al-Bursawī, *Tafsīr*, 1.105 (translations mine for all al-Bursawī quotations).

6. Among the inhabitants of heaven, there was no affirmer of unity like Iblis,
7. When Iblis was veiled by the *'ayn*, and he fled the glances and gazed into the secret, and worshipped his deity stripped of all else,
8. Only to be cursed when he attained individuation and given demands when he demanded no more.
9. He was told, "Bow down!" He said, "[to] no other!" He was asked, "Even if you receive my curse?" He said, "It does not matter. I have no way to an other-than-you. I am an abject lover."[16]

Here Iblīs is the ultimate monotheist, who will bend the knee to none other than God, even if such a determination means disobedience to that same God. He disobeys the *command* of God to bow to Adam in order to obey the *will* of God to worship none other than God. He is also one who discreetly approaches the "secret," perhaps the key to total, "naked," devotion. Al-Ḥallāj does not present Iblīs in the *ṬāwāSīn* as purely pious. The evil tempter is there as well, and Ḥallāj makes no attempt to reconcile the two.

From the evidence that Awn has gathered, it is clear that Iblīs is a complex character. In this he stands in contrast to al-Shayṭān, who is never (to my knowledge) depicted with sympathy. In many accounts, to be sure, the names "Iblīs" and "al-Shayṭān" are used interchangeably, but one may discern a significant distinction between the referents. Iblīs is primarily a narrative figure, one whose domain is the story. Al-Shayṭān often appears in stories as well but not in a central role. This raises an important issue that will become a key aspect of this study. Iblīs is presented in the story of his encounter with Mu'āwiya, and in many other stories and legends, as a narrative figure, a character. This follows naturally from his origin in the Qur'ān, where his story is told, not once but seven times, each narrative being somewhat different.[17] Beyond this particular story of his refusal to bow down

[16] Sells, *Early Islamic Mysticism*, 274. The full *ṬāwāSīn* is translated, with notes, in Massignon, *Teaching of al-Hallāj*, 3:282–307. The Arabic word *'ayn* can be translated as *essence*, or *eye*, perhaps the eye of God, or *source*, as of a stream. Its meaning here is, perhaps deliberately, mysterious.

[17] I use "story" here to refer to the basic plot and "narrative" to refer to a specific telling or rendering of that plot. Hence, in the Qur'ān there is one story of Iblīs, in seven different narratives. In the field of narratology, there is a confusion of alternate terminologies, including Mieke Bal's usage, which uses "fabula" for a sequence of events, and "story" for a particular version or telling of the fabula. See Bal, *Narratology*, 5.

to the form of Adam, the Qur'ān mentions Iblīs only twice.[18] The Qur'ān does not refer to Iblīs as a representation of evil. In fact, in some versions of the Qur'ānic story, most likely early ones, Iblīs is not characterized as evil at all. The portrayal of evil beyond the creation story is almost exclusively represented by al-Shayṭān, who is the adversary of humanity, but never, in the Qur'ān, the subject of a story.

The relationship between Iblīs and al-Shayṭān is nowhere clearly explained in the Qur'ān, but the presumption of the relationship is clear enough. When Iblīs is evicted from heaven, he becomes, somehow, al-Shayṭān, the tempter of humanity. Hence the relationship between the two may be chronological. Apart from the garden story, al-Shayṭān makes regular appearances as the scourge of all of the descendents of Adam and Eve. In this way, as Fazlur Rahman points out, the careers of Adam, Eve, and al-Shayṭān entwine.[19]

Even though Iblīs disappears from the Qur'ānic descriptions of life in the world after the creation, he does not disappear from the textual tradition of Islam. We see this most clearly in the Sufi tradition, as exemplified above. Outside the Qur'ān we continue to read of al-Shayṭān, a thoroughly evil character, and of Iblīs, also an evil character—except when he is not, or not quite. Why, or how, or in what situations does Iblīs show such versatility of character that is not evident in al-Shayṭān? This difference may be described in two ways, both as that between a character and an actor, and as two discrete discourses on the nature of evil.

Iblīs and al-Shayṭān

The discipline of the study of narrative, or narratology, helps us distinguish between various kinds of roles in narrative discourse. Mieke Bal makes a distinction between an actor and a character.[20] In these terms al-Shayṭān is an actor, a participant in a story, who plays a role but never develops. He is a consistent representative of the force of evil.

Iblīs, on the other hand, is commonly a character, the focal point of a story, who develops a personality that evolves and responds to shifting situations.[21] Bal defines the difference as follows. An actor could be a dog

[18] 26:95 and 34:20. Both citations are brief.

[19] Rahman, *Themes*, 18.

[20] Bal, *Narratology*, 114–32.

[21] Other narratologists use different terminology, distinguishing a "flat character" (Bal's

or a machine as well as a person. When an actor is invested with distinctive human characteristics, it becomes a character. The dog Lassie, in the television show by that name, comes close to being a character, while many of the humans in that drama are simply actors.

Iblīs shows the marks of a character in stories such as Rūmī's narrative of his encounter with Mu'āwiya. In that story, Mu'āwiya is an actor, one who represents, consistently and without development, resistance to Iblīs. Iblīs himself, however, draws the focus of the story to himself and shows several dimensions of character—passion, anguish, joy, cleverness, forethought, and regret. In these ways he is more human than the caliph Mu'āwiya, which is why we are drawn to him, since we mortals can sympathize with such human passions and experience. A basic element of narrative is the development of character through various devices, descriptions, and encounters, and, as we shall see, Iblīs shows such development even in the Qur'ān.

A second way of describing the difference between Iblīs and al-Shayṭān is that they signify two distinct discourses about the nature of evil. These discourses are not antithetical but complementary. The *shayṭānī* discourse locates the source of evil outside the individual. In terms we will expand upon later, the figure of al-Shayṭān comes primarily out of the combat myth of the ancient Near East in which good and evil are symbolized, even incarnate, in figures in perpetual opposition to each other. In the case of al-Shayṭān, he is the permanent opponent of humankind. His personification of evil is generally without qualification or countervailing virtue. He is wholly evil, wholly dark, and wholly cursed. He has always been evil. He always will be.

This is not the case with Iblīs, who conveys a more human demeanor. Some of the legends that we will explore recall a primordial time when Iblīs was a model citizen of heaven and a pious, worshipful being. He then changed, although the reason for the change is a subject of debate. There was no al-Shayṭān for Iblīs, no tempter, and no demon whispering in his ear. His emergence as the first to disobey God is without precedent and without external cause. He changed. Why? How?

Further, since Iblīs is by many accounts a *jinn*, who by nature can be either good or evil, Iblīs has a certain degree of comparability with the human condition. He went astray as humans change. Is this changeableness a part of Iblīs's essential nature? Could he change back? This question, raised in Christian circles as the question of apocatastasis, is clearly uncomfortable

---

actor) from a "round character" (Bal's *character*). I will be following Bal's usage.

for many of the authors we will examine and unavoidable for some.[22] We have seen it raised by ʻAṭṭār, Sanā'ī, and al-Bursawī. The changeable nature of Iblīs can become, and does become for some commentators, a mirror in which to see human inconstancy. The story of Iblīs places this inconstancy not in some corner of the vast world of humanity but right at the feet of God. In Iblīs's disobedience, contained as it is in a story with only two primary characters—Iblīs and God—all the difficult theological issues of human disobedience are present: Why do we disobey? How do we turn from obedience to disobedience and back again, with such ease? What roles do God's power and foreknowledge play in this human inconstancy? In the heat of these questions, Iblīs emerges not so much as an evil character but as a tragic figure. This is not to say that tragedy can replace evil as the notation under which we examine human shortcomings. It is to say that God has indeed created us weak (*ḍaʻīf*, 4:28), and that Iblīs may represent this weakness, the tragic flaw. Therein lies the struggle of humanity.

It is also the narrative dimension of Iblīs that makes him the subject of a whole cycle of stories or myths. As followers of the *Star Wars* movies—or any other narrative—know, stories are expandable. Sequels and prequels, as well as expansions of minor characters and explorations of subplots, are endlessly possible.

This study will explore these flexings of the character of Iblīs. The ways in which the character of Iblīs develops do not indicate uncertainty as to the identity of Iblīs so much as a creative effort to discover meaning in the character of Iblīs. They are also, I will argue, a theological attempt to wrestle with the nature of evil. Al-Shayṭān shows us evil in stark opposition to good. The fixity of this opposition does not allow al-Shayṭān to participate in narrative except as a fixed point in the human drama. Iblīs, however, regularly participates in narrative as a central character in his own right, not only as a foil for another.

The twin foci of this book are, then, an exploration of the tragic character of Iblīs in the Qur'ān and narrative as a mode by which such an exploration takes place. To set the stage, we must define our terms carefully. What do we mean by a tragic character, and what is the structure of narrative?

[22] Patrides, "Salvation of Satan," 467–78.

Tragedy

Tragedy is notoriously difficult to define and has spawned a sizeable literature of debate about its nature. Richard Palmer's *Tragedy and Tragic Theory*, in which he outlines classical, psychological, romantic, ritual, existential, dualistic, and a host of other approaches, summarizes much of this theory.[23] As he describes it, theories about the nature of tragedy fall into three broad categories: those that focus on audience response, those that focus on the individual tragic hero, and those that set the tragic individual or situation in the context of a cosmic structure that is somewhat dualistic. Most definitions of tragedy will include elements of all three categories but will privilege one.

Discussions of tragedy usually begin with Aristotle's definition, which, in brief, defines tragedy in terms of its effect upon an audience: "through pity (*eleos*—empathic suffering) and fear (*phobos*—dread) it achieves the purgation (*catharsis*—sobering emotional relief) of such emotions."[24] The purgation leaves the audience with a sense of pleasure in that balance—both in the world and in their own psyches—has been restored. Good tragedy produces similar responses across vast time periods, as Greek tragedy does in modern times.

Audience response is itself mixed and conflicted. It combines sympathy and terror, attraction and revulsion. Northrope Frye defines it as "a paradoxical combination of a fearful sense of rightness (the hero must fall) and a pitying sense of wrongness (it is too bad that he falls)."[25] Not only the engendering of contrary emotions but also the tension between them is complex and filled with ambiguity. Dissenting from Aristotle's goal of balance and purgation, Frye asserts that the audience does not come away with a clear sense of right and wrong, or good and evil. Tragedy confounds such easy categories.

The second group of theories, often characterized as anthropocentric, places the tragic hero at the center of the drama of tragedy. Palmer identifies several proponents of these theories. For Ferdinand Brunetière, "Tragedy depicts insurmountable obstacles that produce a corollary greatness in the responding human will."[26] David D. Raphael sees the hero self-consciously

[23] Palmer, *Tragedy and Philosophy*.

[24] See the discussion of Aristotle's definition in Kaufmann, *Tragedy*, 33–54; also, Palmer, *Tragedy and Philosophy*, 20–26.

[25] Frye, *Anatomy of Criticism*, 214.

[26] Palmer, *Tragedy*, 88.

battling against power, referred to as "necessity." The hero loses but gains in greatness of spirit.[27] Henry Alonzo Myers focuses on justice, which ultimately can only be found as a virtue in the individual amidst an unjust world.[28] Finally, Oscar Mandel, in *A Definition of Tragedy*, gives this characterization:

> A work of art is tragic if it substantiates the following situation: *A Protagonist who commands our earnest good will* is impelled in a given world by a purpose, or undertakes an action, *of a certain seriousness and magnitude*; and by that very purpose or action, subject to that same given world, necessarily and inevitably meets with *grave* spiritual or physical suffering.[29]

The third class of theories sets the tragic hero within a dynamic relationship with a metaphysical structure. Richard Sewall focuses on the situation of humanity in the face of a contrary, indifferent, or even hostile universe. He quotes Paul Tillich saying, "Tragedy combines 'Guilt and Necessity' and the response of the hero is neither to yield to fatalism nor to humble himself in total guilt but to press on in his action to find by experience the truth of his own nature and of the nature of man."[30] The tragic heroes—the Antigone, the Oedipus, the Hamlet—have a rebellious quality. They strive against plots human and divine, against fate, uncertainty, and even themselves, to make some sense, rational or otherwise, of the cosmos:

> The Greek plays and Job presented a view of the universe, of man's destiny and his relation with his fellows and himself, in which evil, though not total, is real, ever threatening, and ineluctable. They explored the area of chaos in the human heart and its possibility in the heavens. They faced the facts of cruelty, failure, frustration, and loss, and anatomized suffering with shocking thoroughness but with tonic honesty. The Greeks affirmed absolutes like justice and order, but revealed a universe which promised neither and often dealt out the reverse.[31]

There is good in the world and it is distinguishable from evil, but few people and few choices are clearly one or the other. Because of this complex situation,

[27] Ibid., 89.

[28] Ibid., 93.

[29] Quoted in Palmer, *Tragedy*, 99 (italics in the original).

[30] Sewall, *Vision of Tragedy*, 72.

[31] Ibid., 46.

tragedy spurns simple judgments of right and wrong, leaving the audience squirming and struggling with emotional complexity and moral doubt. The hero acts, even if wrongly, to force the issue and to protest, even if fruitlessly, against the dark.

The ambiguity presented by the tragic leaves open the question of whether the universe is ordered, sensible, and comprehensible, or, on the contrary, disordered and indifferent. Can mortals discern a reasoned mind and justice, however ethereal, behind the perils of life? Or do no such mind and no such justice exist? If there is no reliable justice, is there nevertheless requital for injustice? George Steiner claims:

> Tragedy would have us know that there is in the very fact of human existence a provocation or paradox; it tells us that the purposes of men sometimes run against the grain of inexplicable and destructive forces that lie "outside" yet very close. To ask of the gods why Oedipus should have been chosen for his agony or why Macbeth should have met the Witches on his path, is to ask for reason and justification from the voiceless night. There is no answer. Why should there be? If there was, we would be dealing with just or unjust suffering, as do parables and cautionary tales, not with tragedy. And beyond the tragic, there lies no "happy ending" in some other dimension of place or time. The wounds are not healed and the broken spirit is not mended. In the norm of tragedy, there can be no compensation. The mind, says I. A. Richards, "does not shy away from anything, it does not protect itself with any illusion, it stands uncomforted, alone, and self reliant. . . . The least touch of any theology which has a compensating Heaven to offer the tragic hero is fatal."[32]

Albert Camus sees tragedy as emerging during civilizational shifts, such as Periclean Greece and Elizabethan Europe, when increasing individualism challenges an accepted religious order of the universe.

> Tragedy occurs when man, by pride . . . enters into conflict with the divine order, personified by a god or incarnated in society. The more justified this revolt, and the more necessary this order, then the greater the tragedy which stems from the conflict. . . . The hero rebels and rejects the order which oppresses him, while the divine power, by its oppression, affirms itself exactly to the same extent as it is denied.[33]

[32] Steiner, *Death of Tragedy,* 128–29 (ellipses in the original).

[33] Camus, "Lecture," 182.

Camus notes that "if the divine order cannot be called into question and admits only sin and repentance, there is no tragedy."[34] Those who question stand alone, having left the consensus of society, defiant not only of the heavens but also of the norms of the community. They are proud, independent, and solitary.

When one regards God as completely sovereign, and the duty of all creatures is but to submit, there can be no tragedy. In such a universe, there can be al-Shayṭān but no Iblīs; there can be revolt but no justified revolt. Iblīs becomes a tragic figure once we grant to him some justification for his refusal to bow down to Adam and his refusal of God's direct command.

In Sūrat al-Ḥijr such a justification is provided. The narrator, God, and Iblīs all describe Adam as being formed from stinking, decayed mud (the one thing upon which they agree). Adam is literally the scum of the earth. It is to this mess that God commands Iblīs to give reverence. Iblīs refuses such a command as being contrary to common sense. He uses the cognition with which he has been endowed by God to determine that such reverence, even if it be not worship, is nevertheless neither logical, nor just, nor warranted on the evidence.

God never refutes this argument. God rejects a universe in which the divine one's judgments are subject to rational inquisition. Such a universe would make God penultimate in power, subject to reason that alone would be truly omnipotent and universal. Naturally God refuses to assent to the premise of Iblīs's argument, which is that Iblīs has any standing at all before God to make an argument.

Iblīs, in turn, does not accept God's terms and does not accept that he has erred. In three versions of the story, those in Sūrah Ṣād, Sūrat al-Baqarah, and Sūrat al-'Arāf, he is described as being haughty or proud. He defiantly declares in Sūrat al-'Arāf, "Because you have put me in the wrong, I will lay out enticements for them on earth and I will surely lead them all astray" (15:39). "Because *you* have put me in the wrong . . ." The "wrong" of Iblīs is God's doing, God's fault. Iblīs will demonstrate to God that this new creature and his descendents are not worthy of reverence. They will show themselves to be fickle, temptable, and contemptible—not even capable of the rational discernment that Iblīs himself has demonstrated. He will prove God wrong.

[34] Ibid.

The audience knows that such an effort may be successful in the short run—Iblīs will indeed tempt many to stray—but that ultimately it will fail. Iblīs cannot prevail against God. For all the righteousness of his stance and the integrity of his reasoning, he will never force God to subject divine sovereignty to a higher standard of reason. Yet Iblīs, asserting his own free will—that which makes him, and any of us, free individuals before God—cannot yield to God such a prerogative.

We find a similar dynamic in our examination of Sūrat al-Baqarah where it is the angels who point out to God that the creatures he is about to create will sow corruption and shed blood on earth. Again, God does not refute this observation, and Iblīs, who has sown no corruption and shed no blood, has good reason to refuse to give reverence to those who will.

This tragic Iblīs is one whose reasoning ability, an ability given to him by God, is exactly that which removes him from God. His reason enables him to determine what is fair and just, and certainly God, one of whose names is al-ʿAdl (the Just), should epitomize justice. Yet here it is God who seemingly sustains injustice and unfairness. Rightfully, in the name of justice, Iblīs must disobey the Just.

The use of such reasoned argument (*qiyās*) in Islam is controversial. Muḥammad Ibn Idrīs al-Shāfiʿī, writing in the eighth century, defends *qiyās* as an important foundation of Islamic law.[35] Al-Ṭabarī, writing a century later, comments that Iblīs is the first to use *qiyās*, and this is his error.[36] Ibn Kathīr, writing in the fourteenth century, echoes this rebuke.[37] Iblīs's use of *qiyās* is widely condemned in the Qur'ānic commentarial tradition, but *qiyās* as a legitimate tool of law has had wide, although not unanimous, support.[38] As understood by al-Shāfiʿī, however, *qiyās* was always subservient to divine revelation (interpreted as Qur'ān).[39] In Iblīs's case, his *qiyās* is contesting revelation.

Similarly, we have seen earlier in this chapter that, in Rūmī's description of the encounter of Iblīs and Muʿāwiya, Iblīs is condemned by God—in his own mind without cause—and yet he is the most passionate lover of God. He is the loyal servant of God who divides the sincere devotees from those who

[35] Majid Khadduri, *Risālā*, 288–94.

[36] Al-Ṭabarī, *Jāmiʿ*, 8.130–131 (vol. 5).

[37] Ibn Kathīr, *Tafsīr*, 2.248.

[38] Kamali, *Islamic Jurisprudence*, 197–228; Weiss, *Search for God's Law*, 551–664.

[39] Hallaq, *Islamic Law*, 113–19.

are not counted among the faithful, the "dry branches." Yet for this service and this love, he is nevertheless condemned. He, the lover, is commanded to bow before Adam, whose faithfulness toward God is questionable and fickle. In the *ṬāwāSīn* of al-Ḥallāj, we have seen an Iblīs who both obeys (in worshipping no other) and disobeys (in refusing to bow to Adam). For this absolute devotion, or in spite of it, he is severely punished. For Rūmī and al-Ḥallāj, it is not the logic of reason that precipitates the tragedy of Iblīs; it is the logic of love.

Is Iblīs admirable in his devotion or condemnable because of his arrogance? In the accounts of Rūmī and al-Ḥallāj, he is both and neither. Is he justified in his reasonable argument or despicable in his rebellion? Iblīs is a tragic character who does nothing to clarify issues of good and evil. He is both rebellious, a characteristic that Sewall and Camus see in the tragic, and paradoxical, a feature that Frye emphasizes. Iblīs pries open the ambiguities that lie hidden within the oft-repeated Qur'ānic command to obey God and to worship none other than God.

Every comment here about Iblīs is also a comment about God. Is God reasonable? Is God just (a question that vexed the Mu'tazilites)? Did God create a world full of moral ambiguities? Are God's commands comprehensible?

Iblīs, like other tragic characters, plays to an audience. As Aristotle noted, ultimately it is the audience—in this case the reader—who decides what is tragic. The character of Iblīs and the meaning of his story will be determined by the reader's response to it, which is why a consideration of the nature of narrative and the enterprise of reading becomes so critical to an understanding of Iblīs.

Narrative

The second issue that requires careful consideration is the nature of narrative. By narrative we are essentially speaking of storytelling. The practice of telling stories hints of an element of fiction in this art. Islam has generally resisted the idea of fiction. Just as invention in religion (*bid'ah)* is heresy, so invention in literature is regarded with suspicion.[40] But as Stefan Leder and others have pointed out, a fictive aspect of Islamic historiography is readily discernible. One can approach this from two angles. One is the purely

[40] See Leder, "Conventions." 34; also von Grunebaum, *Medieval Islam*, 287.

historiographic, which notes that Islamic history writing tends to be highly stylized and programmatic, characterized by a limited package of stylistic tropes, and often written without reliable sources.[41] A more important critique, from our perspective, is that the act of telling a story requires choices of acts, contexts, and interpretations that inevitably introduce creativity into the activity.[42] Leder draws on Wolfgang Iser's helpful expansion of the typical contrast of real and fictional to the triad of real, fictive, and imaginary. The fictive is the meeting place of the real and the imaginary. An example might be the parable, an imagined story used to describe the real. Another example, one explored in depth by Iser, is philosophical construction in which a thinker designs imaginary models of logic and thought in order to describe the nature of the real.

This assertion of a fictive character of narrative is founded on a complex evolution of thought about the nature of language, of interpretation, and even of thinking itself, beginning perhaps with Friedrich Nietzsche, or with Martin Heidegger who argues against the existence of objective historical knowledge. Interpreters and the interpreted are similarly conditioned by their location in time and space. Language is the means through which individuals, conditioned by their place in history, seek understanding of the present and future. Heidegger's student, Hans-Georg Gadamer, adds that language itself shapes thinking, both making it possible and limiting its possibilities. The world is linguistic in nature. Gadamer does not believe that language limits thought absolutely, but rather that language mediates the intersubjectivity of the world, the interaction among humans, and the relationship between humans and the world.

As a mode of expression, narrative describes or reflects this intersubjectivity in two ways. First, it represents the human activity of living in the world, or an interpretation of human living in the world. In so doing, it reflects our subjective experience, since we live our lives narratively, as a sequence of events that we interpret backwards in memory and forwards in anticipation. In this sense, it is narrative that most directly addresses religious anthropology, including, of course, the anthropology of evil. Secondly, in the act of reading in which the reader encounters the presentation of the narrative—both reader and narrative being shaped by history, experience,

[41] Humphreys, "Qur'anic Myth," 271–90. See also Duri, *Historical Writing*; Khalidi, *Historical Thought;* Noth, *Historical Tradition*; and Waldman, *Historical Narrative*.

[42] White, *Tropics of Discourse*.

other texts, and the structure of language itself—the reader engages in a dialogical process. Gadamer describes it as follows:

> Whenever someone wants to understand a text, he always formulates a projection. He projects before him a meaning of the whole as soon as the initial meaning is indicated. Such an intimation occurs only because one is already reading with certain expectations of a determinate meaning. In working out such a preliminary projection—which is, of course, continually revised as there is a further penetration into the meaning—consists the understanding of what is there.[43]

Wolfgang Iser is a representative of the Konstanz School (based at the Universität Konstanz in Germany) that developed the "aesthetics of reception," a reorientation of critical focus toward the reader as the constructor of the meaning(s) of texts. This approach—not a unified theory—rejected Formalism and New Criticism, both of which asserted that the structure and characteristics of the text itself determine its meaning. We will return to consider Iser's approach specifically in the following pages.

Another representative of this school, Hans Robert Jauss, stresses that a long history of response and analysis, reflecting various trends and historical contexts, affects the meaning of a text. At any given time, readers are shaped by a "horizon of expectations," a mindset shaped by the events of that period, other contemporary literature, the culture of the reader, and critical theories in fashion at the time. As time and place shift, so does the horizon of expectations.

In Iser's construction, this is the repertoire of the reader. Iser's approach also shifts attention away from the text toward the recipient of the text, the reader. This is especially significant in this case because, as we have already seen, one aspect of the nature of tragedy involves the reader/audience response.

The most radical proponent of reader-response criticism is Stanley Fish. Fish argues that the ultimate source of meaning is not in the text but in interpretive communities that shape the manner and context in which a word or sentence is understood. Although texts may be stable, in that the printed words of, say, Shakespeare's *Romeo and Juliet,* are the same today as they were a hundred years ago (but not necessarily!), the meaning of the text is a product of the contemporary context in which it is read—the current

[43] Gadamer, *Truth and Method,* 236–37.

meanings of words, familiarity with styles, the reputation of Shakespeare, the politics and sociology of our time, and a host of other factors. This context has to do with the reader, not the text itself. In Fish's view, it is the reader who makes the meaning. The text matters little. "The objectivity of the text is an illusion, and moreover, a dangerous illusion because it is so physically convincing. The illusion is one of self-sufficiency and completeness."[44] Elsewhere Fish elaborates:

> [Meanings] do not lie innocently in the world; rather, they are themselves constituted by an interpretive act. The facts one points to are still there (in a sense that would not be consoling to an objectivist) but only as a consequence of the interpretive (man-made) model that has called them into being. The relationship between interpretation and text is thus reversed: interpretive strategies are not put into execution after reading; they are the shape of reading, and because they are the shape of reading, they give texts their shape, making them rather than, as is usually assumed, arising from them.[45]

So argues Stanley Fish. In the more balanced theory developed by Iser, the focus is on both the reader and the text. The reader interprets, but the text shapes and guides that interpretation through a combination of schema and conditions. The result is an aesthetic response or realization, individual to each reader, but conditioned by the common text.

It is helpful here to make a distinction between the text and the literary work. The literary work has two dimensions—two poles. The author who produces a text represents the artistic pole. The aesthetic pole is the reader's reception and realization of the text but not only of that particular text.[46] The reader brings to the encounter with the text a host of other elements, all of which become part of the response to the text, the creation of meaning and significance. In this way the literary work, the product of both the artistic pole and the aesthetic pole, is a virtual work.

Thus the Qur'ān exists as a written text or perhaps as a remembered text. When articulated in recitation (*tajwīd*), it becomes something else. The particular inflection of a reciter adds an interpretive layer. Absent from any particular recitation are other possible inflections that represent the unchosen interpretations. Further, that presentation has a virtual nature because as soon

[44] Fish, "Literature in the Reader," 82.

[45] Fish, *Text*, 13.

[46] Iser, *Act of Reading*, 20–21.

as it is articulated in sound, it disappears into memory, a memory then shaped by the next articulation, by thought, and by association. It is that dynamic reception and interpretation on the part of the hearer that becomes the Qur'ān at that moment. The range of interpretation is limited both by the text itself, which is determinate, and by the rules of *tajwīd* that do not allow for every possible recitation but rather serve to establish acceptable forms.[47] Even within these fairly strict constraints, the literary work of the Qur'ān, in Iserian terms, becomes something different from, and more than, the text itself.

The artistic pole, the production of text itself, contains an array of devices and structural features—metaphor, character development, poetic stylizations, parallelisms (chiastic and otherwise), allusive language, etc.—that the Formalists and New Critics of the early part of the twentieth century investigated in depth. Beyond this, the Qur'ānic text has as its background a repertoire of allusions and relationships to previous literature and to the surrounding Meccan and Medīnan culture. Thus the Qur'ān includes as its repertoire the previous Scriptures to which it makes overt allusion (and those to which it does not), the Arab milieu that shaped the language and culture of Muḥammadan Arabia, and the specific historical contexts into which it was revealed.

This repertoire gives some indication of what Iser calls the "implied reader." This reader is not the "real" reader, a description of what specific readers have found in the text in the past, nor is it a hypothetical reader, a creation of the critic. The implied reader is one for whom the effects of the text seem to be designed. But designed by whom?

Iser gives this description:

> If, then, we are to try and understand the effects caused and the responses elicited by literary works, we must allow for the reader's presence without in any way predetermining his character or his historical situation. We may call him, for want of a better term, the implied reader. He embodies all those predispositions necessary for a literary work to exercise its effect—predispositions laid down, not by an empirical outside reality, but by the text itself. Consequently, the implied reader as a concept has his roots firmly planted in the structure of the text; he is a construct and in no way to be identified with any real reader.
>
> It is generally recognized that literary texts take on their reality by being read, and this in turn means that texts must already contain

[47] Nelson, *Reciting*, 14–18; Rasmussen, *Women*, 74–124.

> certain conditions of actualization that will allow their meaning to be assembled in the responsive mind of the recipient. The concept of the implied reader is therefore a textual structure anticipating the presence of a recipient without necessarily defining him: this concept prestructures the role to be assumed by each recipient, and this holds true even when texts deliberately appear to ignore their possible recipient or actively exclude him. Thus the concept of the implied reader designates a network of response-inviting structures, which impel the reader to grasp the text.[48]

The reader also has a repertoire. This will, of course, be different for every reader. Part of the durability of a text through time is the degree to which it can accommodate, or speak to, a broad diversity of reader repertoires. If the Qur'ān required knowledge of the Muḥammadan milieu to be understood, it would have less appeal to peoples other than Muḥammad's contemporaries and no appeal to modern non-Arabs. But every reader brings a repertoire of expectations, cultural characteristics, literary awareness, and personal experience to the reading, and the Qur'ān can accommodate them.

In chapter 5 we will investigate the meanings of the name "*jinn*" in Sūrat al-Kahf, which contains the only instance where Iblīs is called a *jinn*. How might the original hearers of the Qur'ān have understood the meaning or referent of that word? What was a *jinn* in their mind? We cannot assume that the interpretive repertoire of readers in the seventh century is the same as the repertoire of later readers.

Unlike a painting, which is present in full at every moment, the process of reading is diachronic. At each moment the reader forms expectations as to what will happen next and revises previous expectations, now memories, of what has happened in the past. This process Iser calls the "wandering viewpoint."[49] It is an element of the dynamic of reading. The textual mechanisms seek to direct this movement but proceed on the basis of an implied reader, not an actual reader.

The control is greater with certain kinds of texts. The "response-inviting structures" are more complex in certain texts. In the Qur'ān, the parænetic elements call for a response, but it is not a response that gives much latitude to the reader. The span of interpretation is narrow. These passages tend to be cast in the authorial first person, as in the following passage:

[48] Iser, *Act of Reading*, 34.

[49] Ibid., 108–29.

> O children of Israel, remember my favor which I bestowed upon you and fulfill your covenant with me as I fulfill my covenant with you, and fear none but me. And believe in what I reveal, verifying what is with you, and do not be the first to disbelieve in it, and do not sell my signs for a small price, and fear none but me. (Sūrat al-Baqarah 2:40–41)

In this passage the text puts the reader in the position of a passive recipient of instruction—do this and do not do that. This reception requires an element of interpretation, as expressed in the question: How do I fulfill the covenant? But the reader remains outside the text as the addressee. Here the artistic pole is set opposite an ethical pole, not an aesthetic pole. There is clearly artistry in the text, but the text calls for an ethical response, not an aesthetic response. Iser quotes Robert Kalivoda on the nature of the aesthetic, "In our eyes the paramount discovery of scientific aesthetics is the recognition of the fact that the aesthetic value is an empty principle, which organizes extra-aesthetic qualities."[50] Where the parænetic direct address fills the reading space with clarity, the aesthetic narrative frames an empty space that the reader fills with images drawn from the reader's own mind and experience.

Where the ethical is conceptual, inviting rules and formulations for right action, aesthetics is preconceptual, or perceptual. The Greek *aesthesis* (αἴσθησις) refers to sense perception, which Kant differentiates from the realm of knowledge and the realm of action, both of which are dependent upon concepts. "Intuition" also derives from the idea of sense perception. Ernst H. Gombrich uses the term "illusion" to the same end. It is, as he writes:

> not an error, a matter of deception; it is rather how and what we see. And the arts function by helping us to shape what we see, to help us apprehend the "reality" in which we experience our living. And with far more complex antecedents and consequences, Iser's sense of the "imaginary" is in many ways consonant with this tradition.[51]

This discussion becomes particularly relevant as we explore the difference between Iblīs as a proto-Shayṭān (or Iblīs in his *shayṭānī* mode) and Iblīs in his tragic dimension—what I am calling his *iblīsī* mode. The *shayṭānī* Iblīs is associated with parænetic address, with the reading space, the range of interpretation afforded the reader, narrowed. The *iblīsī* character, with its

[50] Kalivoda, *Der Marxismus*, 29, quoted in Iser, *Act of Reading*, 70.

[51] Quoted in Krieger, "Imaginary," 135.

tragic dimension, amplifies the reading space, affording the reader a wider range of interpretation. The reading space is less determined—we might say "open to interpretation"—which invites and even requires more involvement in the formation of meaning on the part of the reader. We are freer to wander among possibilities of interpretation and meaning that will be shaped by our own repertoire of experience. We will have the opportunity to explore this in detail in the context of the Iblīs passages themselves.

The wandering viewpoint provokes a desire to create consistency and to draw the mosaic of perspectives into some coherence or synthesis.[52] This is a continuing process, as reading is a continuing process. Much of the synthesizing practice is hidden in that it is not a product of conscious thought. The wandering viewpoint divides the text into separate events, but the reader's need for consistency and coherence splices and reorganizes the events as they unfold into the reader's own viewpoint—what Iser calls the "Gestalt." The basic element of passive synthesis is image-building. The images the reader builds in his or her mind are inspired and provoked by the text or by the "response-inviting structures" of the text, but they are equally a product of the reader's own repertoire. The image, which is meaning-making, is a joint production of the text with its devices, both those intended by the author and those unintended, and the reader with his or her own devices, both passive and active, conscious and unconscious.

The normative interpretation of Iblīs in the Islamic commentaries that we will examine is to create a Gestalt that combines the seven renderings of the Iblīs story into one consistent, combined narrative. This study, on the contrary, treats each of the seven narratives separately, as each one can allow for a distinct range of meaning that is obscured when the seven Iblīs stories are merged into a single story. I argue that Sufi, legendary, and modern interpretations of Iblīs that depart from traditional interpretations do so because readings of individual Iblīs stories can produce interpretations that counter the common, combined narrative.

A final element in this process, particularly important for understanding the ways by which the reader enters into the text to make meaning, is what Iser calls the "blank." A narrative can never tell the whole story. The author chooses what to tell and what to leave up to the reader's imagination. In some places, the detail may be exorbitant; in other places years and miles may be left unaccounted for. One person may be described in detail, with

[52] Iser, *Act of Reading*, 113–25.

even odors and intuitive assessments provided for the reader; another person may not even be named. The blanks in the story are intentional devices that invite, or even require, the reader to supply the missing information from his or her own store of experience and imaginative resources. Iser also refers to "gaps" as the unintentional counterparts to blanks. Gaps in the story are not, in the author's eyes, significant to the plot. The reader nevertheless fills them in through the process of assembling the story in his or her mind. For example, mention of a tree becomes, in the reader's mind, a particular kind of tree, although the actual species is unimportant to the story. A blank may be redressed later in the story, just as the murderer is revealed at the end of a mystery but hidden until then.

Both gaps and blanks call upon the activity of the reader to fill the space. The content of the reader's additions is shaped by the reader's own repertoire. Each reading differs from other readings. The meaning of the story also differs, since the meaning is shaped as much by the gaps and blanks—what is absent—as by the text itself.

Not only gaps and blanks but also negations appear, where what we might expect to be true is negated. Our norms may be rejected or violated. What we believe may be held to be false, and what we understand as false may be held to be true.

To participate in the process of reading requires us to accept the norms of the story and go along with the premises of the story. Thus, although we may not believe that *jinn* exist, for the purposes of the story we have to enter into a world in which *jinn* not only exist but even recite Qur'ān to each other (Sūrat al-Jinn, 72:1, 13). The reader may also need to imagine not only what is between the elements of the story but also what is behind the story—the reality that forms its own background.

The transformative power of reading lies in this multifaceted activity of response to blanks, gaps, and negations. The reader not only draws upon his or her own repertoire to participate in the generation of coherence in the story, the reader also abandons certain presumptions, expectations, and experiences in order to accept the terms laid down by the text. In short, the reader abandons the self and becomes someone, or something, else. The familiar world of the reader surrenders in order to enter a new world framed by the text and its devices. By allowing the reader to bring familiar repertoire into the blanks and gaps, the text is inviting. By requiring readers to leave behind certain elements of their repertoires, providing replacements (or not) through the structure of the text, the literary work is transformative.

Conclusion

If Iblīs is essentially—both in the Qur'ān and perhaps because of the Qur'ān, in subsequent texts—a narrative character, and if narrative by its nature involves the reader in the construction of meaning, then we find ourselves confronting, at least in a portion of the Qur'ān, a significantly different hermeneutic for Qur'ānic texts.

If Iblīs is essentially—both in the Qur'ān and perhaps because of the Qur'ān, in subsequent texts—a tragic figure, and if tragedy by its nature and definition shows a heroic, proud, and in certain ways admirable figure, who, in the name of love or justice, calls the divine order to account, then we find ourselves confronting a theological understanding of evil significantly different from a simple binary opposition of right and wrong. The common Muslim aphorism, so clear and powerful in its simplicity, that Muslims are a community of discernment—"they enjoin the right and they forbid the wrong" (*ya'murūna bi-l-ma'rūfi wa-yanhawna 'ani l-munkar*)[53]—is confounded by Iblīs in whom right and wrong are, if not quite confused, at least complicated.

The seven versions of the Iblīs story in the Qur'ān give slightly different accounts of the basic story. When analyzed closely using literary tools, these differences emerge as significant, provoking different potential responses from the reader. The variations of meaning are not only interesting from a narratological point of view, they also are theologically consequential. The literary and the theological cannot be separated here. When we speak of different meaning produced by different literary constructions of the story, or a different range of interpretation, we are speaking of different theologies of the nature of evil. While some interpreters will say that the tragic is missing from Islam, our readings of particular renderings of the Iblīs story indicate that the tragic is indeed present—present in the Qur'ān, no less, and therefore within the parameters of Islamic theology.

Tragedy requires narrative to reveal the murky dimensions of human experience through time. Iblīs reveals this murkiness. In the multiplicity of his presentation in the Qur'ān, he holds up for the reader's contemplation the human struggle to discern what is *ma'rūf* (virtuous)—a recognized act

[53] 3:104.

of goodness—and what is *munkar* (false)—a recognized act of wrong-doing. In contrast to *shayṭānī* clarity, Iblīs exposes what all humans know: that while religious texts might wish to pose the moral and ethical choices facing mortals daily as simple binary opposites, experience knows the ambiguity of so many human choices. We live not so much in a *shayṭānī* world in which good and evil are clear and opposed as in an *iblīsī* world in which evils contain more than a shadow of good, and goods are tinged, if not laden, with darker dimensions. The Qur'ān knows this and shows this in the seven tales of Iblīs. Given that anthropology reflects theology, what we conclude about the nature of good and evil in the world says a great deal about the nature of God.

In this chapter we have explored the general nature of narrative as a particular genre that makes particular demands upon the reader. In the next chapter we ask whether the Qur'ān itself will allow such an understanding of narrative and the act of reading/listening as we have posed in this chapter. How might one sustain—either on its own internal evidence or, barring that, on the basis of Muslim understandings of the Qur'ān—a reader-response approach to the Qur'ānic text?

CHAPTER 2

Hermeneutics

Normative Muslim understanding holds the Qur'ān to be the verbatim word of God, and this study will operate within that understanding or, at least, not dismiss it arbitrarily.[1] This study will develop a method of analyzing stories that will accommodate, and perhaps even expand, an understanding of the Iblīs stories as Scripture. One may pose the question this way: Why does God present the Iblīs story in the particular way(s) that it occurs in the Qur'ān? Or, perhaps better, since to ask a "why" question of God is more than a little pretentious, one may pose the question this way: What can we make of the particular way the Iblīs story is told—told and retold—in the Qur'ān? Does it generate meanings beyond the simple moral of the story—"don't disobey God"—through its narrative mode and multiple versions, which seem to encourage mortals to get in on the storytelling act and to tell more stories? To continue the problem, how then should one understand the post-Qur'ānic stories of Iblīs, where mortals have indeed taken up that invitation?

Since Iblīs is himself fundamentally a Qur'ānic figure, having no source prior to the Qur'ān,[2] every tale of Iblīs is in some sense a commentary on the Qur'ān that takes the initial story and, in true literary fashion, expands

[1] William Graham formulates an effective argument for a common approach to the study of the Qur'ān that respects both Western and Muslim academic traditions. He argues that scholarship must recognize the fact of Muslim belief and exercise humility about the limits of reason and historical study. He calls this "humane scholarship." See Graham, "Those Who Study," 9–29.

[2] As mentioned in the previous chapter, the story of one who refuses to bow down to Adam exists in several pre-Qur'ānic texts, such as the *Life of Adam and Eve* and the *Gospel of Bartholomew*, but in none of these texts is there a character named Iblīs who is distinct from Satan.

upon it. But how is that valid? In what sense is this interpretation? What is the hermeneutical principle operating here? Do the stories that Awn has collected from Sufi sources tell us only about Sufis, or do they interpret the Qur'ānic story of Iblīs and, hence, interpret the Qur'ān?

Commentaries on the Qur'ān—the classical standard works of al-Ṭabarī, al-Zamakhsharī, al-Bayḍāwī, Ibn Kathīr, and al-Qurṭubī, and their more modern successors, al-Bursawī, Ṭabāṭabā'ī, Sayyid Quṭb, Rashīd Riḍā, and others—for the most part do not treat Iblīs as a narrative figure. Some commentators, al-Ṭabarī and Ibn Kathīr in particular, give some attention to the *isrā'īliyyāt* (tales derived from Jewish and Christian sources) but not to the narrative nature of the Qur'ānic stories themselves. The histories of al-Ṭabarī, Ibn Kathīr, and al-Diyārbakrī, as well as the *qiṣaṣ al-anbiyā'* (tales of the prophets) literature, add to the corpus of stories of Iblīs. Are these works commentaries? If a line of connection extends from storytelling within the Qur'ān to storytelling beyond the Qur'ān, all dealing with, in some fashion or another, an essentially Qur'ānic story, then to what degree do such elaborations of the story function as interpretation or as the discovery of meaning—not just any meaning but Qur'ānic meaning? In other words, when God tells stories, and mortals expand upon those stories, is that legitimate interpretation? Is it, in some sense, canonical?

This study will extend these questions to their most extreme extent beyond Sufi stories and early legends to four modern literary contributions: *A Message from the East* by Muḥammad Iqbal, *Jannah wa Iblīs* (The Innocence of the Devil) by Nawal al-Saadawi, *Awlād Ḥāratinā* (The Children of Gebelaawi) by Naguib Mahfouz, and *The Martyr*, a short story by Tawfīq al-Ḥakīm. Do these works also constitute commentary on the Qur'ān by virtue of their exploration of the meaning of the Qur'ānic story within a hermeneutic suggested by the Qur'ān itself?

The Qur'ān as Literature

In recent years, increasing attention has been given to the literary character of the Qur'ān and its stories. We have only to point to the recent volumes edited by Issa Boullata,[3] Stefan Leder,[4] and Stefan Wild,[5] and the numerous

[3] Boullata, ed., *Literary Structures*.

[4] Leder, *Story-Telling*.

[5] Wild, *Qur'an as Text*.

articles therein and elsewhere by Angelika Neuwirth,[6] Uri Rubin,[7] and others. Particularly enduring in this area has been the work of Anthony H. Johns, recently celebrated in a Festschrift dedicated to him by Peter Riddell and Tony Street.[8]

In 1993, Johns spoke broadly of the literary character of the Qur'ān, suggesting that seeing it in this light may provide fertile ground for understanding between Muslims and Christians. He states:

> The centrality of storytelling in the Qur'ān is often overlooked by non-Muslim students of Islam, even by Arabists, for much the same reasons as the Qur'ān itself may make little appeal: in part because of the internal arrangement of the book, in part because of the rhetoric of their presentation, and in part because the literary *imaginaire* of those living in the European tradition is so dominated by the biblical presentation of such stories.[9]

This evaluation may appear a bit harsh, as Johns admits elsewhere. The Qur'ānic style of storytelling is lean and subservient to its larger hortatory purpose. Fred Donner asserts:

> The characters that populate the Qur'ān's narrations are bleached out, because its focus on morality is so intense. The only judgment about a person that really matters, in the Qur'ānic view, is whether he or she is good or evil, and most characters presented in the Qur'ānic narratives fall squarely on one side or other of that great divide. More often than not, it gives us "ideal types," with little suggestion that a single personality might be a mixture of good and evil impulses in constant tension. Moreover, it conveys no sense that the tension itself, being uniquely human, is of special interest. That is, there is little appreciation of the human moral struggle in its own right; there is only concern for its outcome. Hence one finds in the Qur'ān no sympathy for the sinner as someone succumbing, against his own best interest in the long run, to all-too-human impulses in the face of overwhelming temptation, despite the valiant efforts to

[6] Neuwirth, "Du Texte de Récitation," 194–229; idem, "Negotiating Justice (Part I)," 25–41; idem, "Negotiating Justice (Part II)," 1–18; idem, "Qur'ānic Literary Structure," 388–420; idem, "Referentiality and Textuality," 143–72.

[7] Rubin, *Eye of the Beholder*.

[8] Riddell and Street, *Islam: Essays on Scripture*. Among other major articles that Anthony H. Johns has written on narrative aspects of the Qur'ān, see the following: "Narrative, Intertext and Allusion in the Qur'anic Presentation of Job."

[9] Johns, "Common Ground," 193–209.

> resist temptation. Rather, the Qur'ān portrays humanity in a strictly polarized way.[10]

This opinion, too, is harsh, but as Johns points out, when Qur'ānic stories are set alongside and compared to the more elaborate and comprehensive stories of the Tanakh, they do seem stark and almost barren by comparison. But this is an unfortunate comparison, as Marilyn Waldman reminds us. She asserts that while comparison among stories (in this case the popular comparison of the Joseph narratives in the Qur'ān and the Bible) is appropriate and healthy, too often the presumption is that the biblical version is the original version and all others, including the Qur'ānic, must be judged according to that standard.[11] Although the Qur'ān specifically acknowledges the existence of other, prior, renditions, it gives no quarter on the revelatory primacy of its own. The issue of primacy is not our concern, nor need we evaluate the literary character and quality of the Qur'ān in comparison to that of the Bible or any other text. The Qur'ān has its own qualities that we will do our best to discern. Johns gives a general description of these literary qualities as follows:

> Its stories are presented in a sequence of vivid scenes, compact and full of tension, played out by dramatic dialogue. The relationship between such scenes is often to be inferred; there may appear to be gaps or silences that the hearer has to fill from his or her imagination; events that are part of the motivation of the movement of the story are only alluded to, dialogue is often elliptic, and names are rarely used to identify the *dramatis personae* in any episode.[12]

With such challenges, it is no wonder that Donner and others would find the Qur'ānic narrative so flat. But this brief description by Johns invites just the kind of Iserian approach that we have outlined in chapter 1: the need for the reader to infer relationships, to fill in gaps and silences from his or her own imagination, to test the range of interpretation, and to attend to the subtleties of the art of storytelling. We will need, however, to be a bit more explicit about the ways in which a reader-response analysis might assist in, and be legitimately applied to, a hermeneutics of the Qur'ān.

[10] Donner, *Islamic Origins*, 75–76.

[11] Waldman, "New Approaches," 1–16.

[12] Johns, "Common Ground," 204.

The Repertoire of the Qur'ān

Donner claims that stories are secondary to the parænetic purpose of the Qur'ān. The Qur'ān presumes that the stories of old—the narratives of Moses, Abraham, Joseph, and others—are important confirmations of the truth of the Islamic message. In the light of these earlier stories, the Qur'ān can affirm that its revelation is not entirely new, perhaps not new at all in substance but only in form and audience. Some stories, such as the Joseph narrative in Sūrat al-Yūsuf, even require awareness of their biblical precedents in order to understand some of the details and references.[13] The audience, initially Arab, is presumed to be familiar with the basic story. The formula, "Has the story of Moses reached you?" introduces the Moses story in Sūrah Ṭa Hā (20:9) with the presumption that it has reached the Arabs, or ought to have, and that it is important for that story to have reached the audience of the Qur'ān. The story of Moses is part of the expected repertoire of the reading community, the implied readers.

The unbelievers are regularly chastised for failing to attend to the stories to which they are heir and for dismissing them as "fables of the ancients" (*asāṭīr al-awwalīn*; see 6:25, 8:31, 16:24, 23:83, 25:5, 27:68, 46:17, 68:15, 83:13). In Sūrat al-Furqān (25:5), the unbelievers accuse Muḥammad of having had these tales written down, and this accusation clarifies that the stories in the Qur'ān are the reference, although not necessarily an exhaustive collection, of these fables. In several *sūrah*s the tales concern resurrection of the dead at the end of historic time (27:68, 46:17, 68:15, 83:13).

It is not accidental at all that the word predominantly used to refer to the message or warning that Muḥammad brings, and which is the subject of the Qur'ān, is *al-dhikr* (the reminder). The overall message of the Qur'ān is not new but a reminder of what has already been revealed in other circumstances, in other forms, and to other peoples. The audience of the Qur'ān does not so much need to be informed of the message as to be reminded of it. Thus the constant reference to the past is quite in keeping with the essence of the Qur'ānic message. In a sense, this is only natural. Narrative, being reflective of direct experience, is prior to parænesis. The hortatory message of the Qur'ān presumes the narrative life to which it gives correction and direction.

The stories found in al-Ṭabarī, Ibn Kathīr, and the *qiṣaṣ al-anbiyā'* literature are categorized as *isrā'īliyyāt* (stories that come from Jewish-

[13] Waldman, "New Approaches," 1.

Christian sources) and considered suspect, but also necessary, for the understanding of Islam.[14] Islamic tradition renders support for both attitudes. Meir J. Kister reports serious disagreement about the appropriateness of reading the Torah:

> Reading the Torah was made lawful by the Prophet's permission. 'Abdallah b. 'Amr b. al-'Āṣ told the Prophet about his dream. He saw that he had on one of his fingers honey and on the other one butter. The Prophet explained the dream and said: "You will read the two Books: the Torah and the Furqān (i.e., the Qur'ān — K)." He read in fact both these Books. This tradition, transmitted by Ibn Lahī'a, was vehemently attacked by al-Dhahabī in the eighth century AH: nobody was allowed to read the Torah after the Qur'ān had been revealed. The Torah, argues al-Dhahabī, had been changed and tampered with; truth and falsehood are mixed in this book. It is permissible to read this book for one purpose only: to answer the Jews. But opinions about the study of the Torah were quite different in the first century. Ibn Sa'd records a story about 'Āmir b. 'Abd Qays and Ka'b sitting in a mosque: Ka'b read the Torah and explained some interesting passages to 'Āmir. Abū l-Jald al-Jaunī used to read the Qur'ān and the Torah. He used to celebrate each conclusion of reading of the Torah (he read it during six days) summoning people (for this purpose) and used to quote a saying that Mercy descends at each conclusion of the reading of the Torah.[15]

Kister's entire essay traces the tortuous history of a *ḥadīth* that says, with many variations, "Transmit on my authority, be it even one verse (from the Qur'ān), narrate (traditions) concerning the children of Israel, and there is nothing objectionable (in that); he who tells a lie on my authority—let him take his place in hell."[16] Some variations even manage to reverse the apparent meaning of the *ḥadīth,* further indicating the controversial nature of the issue.

[14] There is some debate as to whether *isrā'īliyyāt* is a proper collective category, including creation legends and stories of the prophets, as Vadja claims (in *EI*[2] [*Encyclopaedia of Islam*, 2nd ed.] s.v. *isrā'īliyyāt*), or whether *qiṣaṣ al-anbiyā'* is the general category and *isrā'īliyyāt* is a subcategory referring to legends of the people of Israel but not the prophets or the creation stories, as Nagel takes it. See Adang, *Muslim Writers*, 8–10, for discussion. We follow Vadja here. The literature on *isrā'īliyyāt* gives some attention to the issue of their legitimate use in Islam. See Albayrak "Isrā'īliyyāt"; Barker, *Great Angel*; Firestone, *Journeys in Holy Lands*; and Stuckenbruck, *Angel Veneration and Christology*. Butler, *Iblīs*, 27–30.

[15] Kister, "Ḥaddithū," 231–32.

[16] Ibid., 215–16.

The issue is not settled by various Qur'ānic verses, such as in Sūrat al-Yūnus (10:94), which seem to entrust Jews and Christians with special knowledge of the revelation of God: "If you are in doubt about what We have revealed to you, then ask those who recited the Book before you; the Truth has indeed come to you from your Lord."[17] While these verses attribute experience with the revelation to Jews and Christians, they do not specifically identify the Torah (*tawrāt*) and the Gospel (*injīl*) as the reliable record of those experiences. Ma'mar b. Rāshid, in his *Jāmi'*, cites a contrary *ḥadīth*: "The Prophet said: Do not ask the people of the Book about anything, because they will not show you the right path having already led themselves astray. We asked: O Messenger of God, may we not narrate (stories) concerning the Children of Israel? The Prophet answered: Narrate, there is nothing objectionable (in that)."[18] Here it is acceptable to tell the stories but not to consult with the people. The repertoire is more formally confined.

Which biblical texts the early Muslims read, or to which they referred—the Pentateuch, the whole Tanakh, or the Christian New Testament—is far from certain. References in the Qur'ān seem to reflect apocrypha, pseudepigrapha, and midrashim rather than canonical Scripture. The paucity of New Testament stories and the inclusion of events recorded only in pseudepigrapha, such as Jesus' miracle of bringing clay birds to life as a child,[19] suggest that the literature on which early Muslims drew was not the Gospels themselves, but other oral or written tradition.

An exception may be Wahb b. Munabbih (d. 728 or 732), who seems to be the source of much *isrā'īliyyāt*.[20] His writings indicate familiarity with the Tanakh, the Gospels, and other Christian writings, and perhaps even the Talmud. That any of these were available in Arabic in his time is much in doubt, hence he may well have been familiar with Hebrew and Syriac.[21] An alternative explanation is that he heard oral transmission of biblical texts and tales; his records of texts are often at variance with the texts in the Tanakh or Gospels.

Since Islamic tradition sees these stories against the background of Jewish and Christian traditions, chapter 3 will give a brief account of those traditions

[17] See also 21:7, 16:43, 25:59, 2:211.

[18] Kister, "Ḥaddithū," 219.

[19] Sūrat al-'Imrān (3:49). See comparison with *Infancy Gospel of Thomas* in Elliott, *Apocryphal New Testament*, 75–76.

[20] Khoury, *Wahb b. Munabbih*.

[21] Duri, *Historical Writing*, 124–25.

and some of the developments of the myths prior to their Islamic appearance. These connections do not assert a direct historical descent. One cannot trace any particular pattern of diffusion, but by calling these stories *isrā'īliyyāt*, Muslims themselves call attention at least to a context, and probably more, a general origin. As we read through the Iblīs stories, we will pay attention to places in which the pre-Islamic tradition(s) seems to be evident. If the implied reader is one familiar with pre-Islamic tradition, then the nature of those traditions bears on the interpretation of the Qur'ānic passages.

The Aesthetic of the Qur'ān—*Muḥkam* and *Mutashābihāt*

Fred Donner, cited above, asserts that the narrative dimension of the Qur'ān is subservient to the parænetic dimension. At first glance, this assertion would seem to be true. But the Qur'ān itself admits to two categories of content, to be interpreted in two ways.

The *locus classicus* of the Qur'ān's guidance for its own interpretation is Sūrat al-'Imrān 3:7, which states:

> It is he who has sent down the Book to you, in which are verses *muḥkamāt*; they are the mother (or foundation) of the Book, and others are *mutashābihāt*. As for those in whose hearts is deviation, they follow what is ambiguous (*tashābaha*) among them, striving for divisiveness and striving for its explanation (*ta'wīl*), and none know the explanation of it except God, and those well-grounded in knowledge, who say, "We believe in it; all is from our Lord and none remembers except those of intellect."[22]

The key words at issue are left untranslated. The *muḥkamāt* are usually understood to be verses that are clear, "categorical" (Ahmed Ali), or "perspicuous" (Azad). The word often has judicial connotations—Ahmad Zaki Hammad has "clearly decisive." *Mutashābihāt*, on the other hand, has been translated as "ambiguous" (Arberry, Bell, Hammad), "parabolic" (Kinberg, Sale), "of not well-established meaning" (Yūsuf 'Alī), "open to interpretation" (Bewley), "like one another" (Jones), "Metaphorical" (Qara'i), and "allegorical" (Ahmed Ali, Pickthall).[23] The root meaning

[22] Shī'a interpreters do not put a break between "except God" and "those well-grounded in knowledge," claiming that the latter refers to the Imams who do have full knowledge of Qur'ānic interpretation.

[23] Ahmed Ali, *Al-Qur'ān*; 'Yūsuf 'Alī, *Meaning*; Arberry, *Koran Interpreted*; Assad,

of the word can be either "similar" or "ambiguous." Commentary on these verses has been analyzed by Leah Kinberg,[24] Jane McAuliffe,[25] and Sahiron Syamsuddin.[26]

The range of interpretation of the *muḥkamāt* is not as large as that of the *mutashābihāt*. Syamsuddin summarizes five interpretations given by al-Ṭabarī: 1) the *muḥkamāt* are the abrogating verses; 2) they are pronouncements on that which is permitted and forbidden; 3) they are verses permitting only one interpretation; 4) they are verses and stories of the previous prophets in which God affirms his message; 5) they are those verses whose meanings can be understood by the scholars.[27] Kinberg, in her broader survey, adds other meanings: they are the verses that contain the fundamentals of Muslim life, such as Sūrat al-An'ām 6:151–153 and Sūrat al-Isrā' 17:23–25; they are those commandments of God that never change through time and place (al-Rāzī); they are the majority of the verses of the Qur'ān;[28] they are commandments that apply to all religious communities, not just the Muslim community (al-Rāzī);[29] and they are verses that cannot be distorted.[30] The predominant interpretation relates them to the parænetic passages.

The *mutashābihāt* admit of an even greater range of interpretations. Al-Ṭabarī defines them as passages "similar in wording but different in meaning," or passages that cannot be clarified from other sources in the Qur'ān or Sunnah, or verses that have been abrogated, or the "mysterious letters" (*muqaṭṭa'āt* or *al-fawātih*), and the time of the day of judgment—things known not even by Muḥammad, but only to God.[31] The word *mutashābihāt* can have implications of similarity as well as of ambiguity. Kinberg describes a group of interpretations that focus on this aspect: verses that are similar in meaning, in wording, or various combinations of these. Further suggestions

Message; Bell, *Qur'ān*; Bewley, *Noble Quran*; Hammad, *Gracious*; Jones, *The Qur'ān*; Pickthall, *Meaning*; Qara'i, *The Qur'an*; and Sale, *Koran*.

[24] Kinberg, "Muḥkamāt," 283–312.

[25] McAuliffe, "Qur'anic Hermeneutics," 46–62.

[26] Syamsuddin, "Muḥkam and Mutashābih," 63–79.

[27] Ibid., 63–64.

[28] This is based on a variant meaning of *muḥkam* (majority). This also correlates with their designation as the *umm al-kitāb*.

[29] In this understanding the *muḥkam* would be similar to the Noahide commandments in Gen 9:3–6.

[30] This interpretation provides opportunity to critique Mu'tazila, Christian, Jewish, "infidel," and polytheist understandings.

[31] Syamsuddin, "Muḥkam and Mutashābih," 67–68.

are that they deal with all nonjuridical aspects; that they are groups that require careful interpretation by scholars; that they allow of multiple interpretations; that they are easily misinterpreted and distorted, creating dissent; or that they are subject to no interpretation at all.

A final interpretation of *mutashābihāt* particularly relevant to our approach, is that they are part of the *'ijāz al-qur'ān* (the inimitability of the Qur'ān). Al-Rāzī argues that the *mutashābihāt* provide a flexibility of interpretation that allows the Qur'ān to speak to different people at different times. They are still commandments, still guidance, but the applications will vary. Al-Rāzī further asserts that the *muḥkam* and the *mutashābihāt* should not be considered opposing categories of verses, but rather complementary verses, or even complementary aspects of the same verses, speaking to different kinds of religious duties, some immutable, others adaptable. This is a demonstration of the *'ijāz al-qur'ān*.

But why should the Qur'ān have *mutashābihāt* at all? Ibn Qutaybah answers that the *mutashābihāt* require observation, examination, and a science of interpretation of the Qur'ān, and demonstrate the different abilities of people. Furthermore, the efforts of scholars to understand these verses and to harmonize them with the *muḥkamāt* "train them intellectually, strengthen their belief, and eventually lead to a blessed Afterworld."[32] Here the *mutashābihāt* enable a different quality of engagement with the Qur'ān. While the *muḥkamāt* may ensure correct behavior, the *mutashābihāt* shape the spirit.

These last definitions begin to move us into a different kind of epistemology in which knowledge imparted by the Qur'ān is not simply discursive and directive, but also intuitive or even aesthetic. In this sense we may regard the stories with which we are concerned not only as didactic, intent upon conveying a clear (*muḥkam*) lesson, but also as intent upon creating an environment in which more "parabolic" (to use Kinberg's translation) truths are conveyed.

This environment is the aesthetic aspect of the Qur'ān that shapes perception. Such literary qualities have been cited as proof of the authenticity of the Qur'ān as sacred writ, but here it is not imprimatur, but an essential element of the substance of its message. This message is not only communicated in the words but, as Johns points out, in "silences [that] are, as it were, caskets in which a variety of stories and significances lie hidden,

[32] Kinberg, "Muḥkamāt," 302–3.

waiting to be discovered."[33] He cites Erich Auerbach, who compares the Homeric description of the homecoming of Odysseus and the biblical story of the sacrifice of Isaac. I quote Auerbach directly:

> It would be difficult, then, to imagine styles more contrasted than those of these two equally ancient and equally epic texts. On the one hand, [in the *Odyssey*] externalized, uniformly illuminated phenomena, at a definite time and in a definite place, connected together without lacunae in a perpetual foreground; thoughts and feeling completely expressed; events taking place in leisurely fashion and with very little of suspense. On the other hand, [in the Bible] the externalization of only so much of the phenomena as is necessary for the purpose of the narrative, all else left in obscurity; the decisive points of the narrative alone are emphasized, what lies between is nonexistent; time and place are undefined and call for interpretation; thoughts and feeling remain unexpressed, are only suggested by the silence and the fragmentary speeches; the whole, permeated with the most unrelieved suspense and directed toward a single goal (and to that extent far more of a unity), remains mysterious and "fraught with background."[34]

De-Familiarizing the Story

Texts so "fraught with background" require a variety of tools with which to excavate possible structures of meaning. Reader-response approaches describe tools that readers use instinctively. Although literary theoreticians elaborate complex descriptions of the various intricacies of a text and the process of reading, the ultimate goal is not to make reading itself complex but to understand the interaction, conscious and subconscious, between the reader and the text.

At a pragmatic level, readers have at least six means by which to derive meaning from texts.[35]

First, intertextually, readers relate texts consciously or unconsciously to other texts or to other parts of the same texts. The text itself will often make reference to other texts, as we have already pointed out in the Qur'ān. In similar fashion, the Qur'ān will shape the reading of other texts and form a matrix of interpretation.

[33] Johns, "Common Ground," 204.

[34] Auerbach, *Mimesis*, 11–12.

[35] I draw this outline from Thistelton, *New Horizons*, 38–51.

Second, situationally, texts often describe specific situations located in a particular time and space. Our familiarity with the *Sitz im Leben* of the narrative, or our misconstrual of it, will affect our reading of it. Muslim research into the "occasions of revelation" (*asbāb al-nuzūl*) of the texts recognizes this principle. But it is not uncommon to find passages of text, especially scriptural texts, which are memorable in ways quite different from their actual original context. For instance, the moving expression of devotion in Ruth 1:16–17 is popular at weddings and applied to the devotion of husband and wife, although its original context is the relationship between Ruth and her mother-in-law.

Third, horizontal factors refer to the kinds of assumptions that readers bring to the text that affect the reception of the text. If one believes, for instance, that Iblīs and al-Shayṭān are one and the same, then one will read the text with that expectation and usually find it confirmed. However, one can understand horizons in two ways. They are limitations of vision, but they are also capable of movement as one's stance shifts—an important aspect of the image. As Waldman points out, if we read the Qur'ānic text from a biblical background and evaluate the depiction of Jesus or Joseph in that light and with that normative expectation, our reception of the Qur'ānic text will be affected. But if we read the text without that background, without that normative expectation, and find new insights into either of those narratives, our horizons shift.

Fourth, semiotic theory raises questions about the uses of language to encode particular social structures and cultural presumptions about which the reader may be, or ought to be, suspicious. This system of signs may not express the intention of the author, but does allow for various political, cultural, countercultural, and sociological readings of the text.

Fifth, the hermeneutical model is important to interpreting the text. What makes it possible to understand a text written so long ago? What barriers inhibit that understanding, and what constitutes a legitimate approach to comprehension and reception?

Finally, the textuality of the medium as a physical object resulting from a process of creation by an author is conveyed in a particular form to a reader. The orality of the Qur'ān would be an issue here, as well as the involvement of the early Muslim community in its formation and transmission. How does the format of the Qur'ān (that is, the ordering of the *sūrah*s, the composition of the longer *sūrah*s, the intonations of *tajwīd*, and the translation or rendering of the text into different languages for the vast majority of Muslims—and, of course, non-Muslims—who are not schooled in Qur'ānic Arabic) affect the understanding or reality of the text? And what is the role of the reader? Does the reader simply receive the counsels of the text, or does reading the Qur'ān require a more active engagement, an entry into a Qur'ānic vision, as al-Rāzī and Ibn Qutaybah seem to suggest is the purpose of the *mutashābihāt*?

Intertextual Issues

What questions will the intertextual nature of the Qur'ān raise? Three levels of intertextuality warrant consideration: first, the relationship within the texts of the Qur'ān, between identifiable pericopes of a *sūrah*, and then between the *sūrahs* themselves, called "its inner-textuality";[36] secondly, the relationship between the text of the Qur'ān and pre-Qur'ānic literature, both biblical and extrabiblical, an area that has received a great deal of attention;[37] and thirdly, the relationship between the Iblīs story and subsequent literature against which background the reader encounters the Qur'ānic story. This intertextuality includes the whole breadth of literature mentioned above—commentary, legend, poetry, and novel, as well as theological analysis and preaching.

As we have mentioned, the Iblīs story is told seven times in the Qur'ān. How do these texts relate? When the story is told differently and how are we to regard those differences? When God asks Iblīs why he did not bow down to Adam, and we have one answer in Sūrat al-Ḥijr and a different answer in Sūrah Ṣād, what are we to make of these variations? Is the multiplicity of renderings indicative of the way stories function in Islamic discourse? Does the story serve a different purpose in each placement? Is the lesson of the story different in some way in different versions? Can we see any sort of development or change as the Qur'ān unfolds over its twenty-two-year history of revelation?

The common approach of Muslim commentators is to merge all seven stories into one and comment upon the composite story. In other words, the commentators address the story, but not the individual versions of the story. The Iblīs story is read horizontally, compiled with other Iblīs stories. Thus the

[36] The term is discussed in Sailhamer, *Old Testament Theology*, 201–12. The concept traces back to Michael Fishbane, who discusses "inner-biblicality" in Fishbane, *Biblical Interpretation*, 7.

[37] Most notably, Katsh, *Judaism in Islām*; Schwarzbaum, *Biblical and Extra-Biblical Legends*; Speyer, *Die biblischen Erzählungen*. More recently, Uri Rubin has contributed to this area in Rubin, *Between Bible and Qur'ān*.

commentary on each telling does not address its distinctiveness as a telling, but rather its contribution to a composite story. From the perspective of the reader of the canon of the Qur'ān, who may well have in mind the other versions of the story, thus makes each telling a reminder (*dhikr*) of the whole story.

This approach, however, diminishes, if not eliminates, any purpose to God's telling the story in a particular way. Each narrative is simply a mnemonic device, designed to call to mind the composite story that is scattered in its seven locations throughout the Qur'ān.

Associated with this composite approach is the practice of most Muslim commentaries of approaching the text in a linear fashion. Although generally the Qur'ān, like many other Scriptures, is not read in strict page, or *muṣḥaf*, order, front to back, but selectively, almost all Muslim commentaries address the text in *muṣḥaf* order, beginning with the first *sūrah* and ending with the last. This means that the commentarial energies are largely expended on the first two instances of the story in order of pagination, which happen to be, most likely, the later revelations of the story chronologically. If the chronological order of revelation is meaningful, this order means that, not by intention, most commentary is directed largely to the late Meccan and early Medīnan versions of the story. The chronologically earlier versions receive little, if any, further comment, and thus their unique characteristics do not receive the attention they deserve.

An alternative approach, pursued by some modern academic scholars of the Qur'ān, is to attempt to read the seven stories in the chronological order of their revelation. Since the Qur'ān was revealed over a twenty-two- to twenty-three-year period, it is possible to postulate a chronological sequence of versions in order of revelation. In this way one can trace the development of Qur'ānic theology from the earliest through the latest revelations. With such an approach, differences between the Iblīs of the earliest *sūrah*s and the Iblīs of the later *sūrah*s become evident.

Alford Welch has suggested that the Qur'ān speaks of the supernatural realm (to which Iblīs belongs) differently in the earlier revelations than in the later revelations.[38] He points out that in the earliest parts of the Qur'ān, numerous and diverse supernatural beings, all of whom have distinct identities, populate the universe. Toward the latter part of the Qur'ān, in the Medīnan *sūrah*s, the distinctiveness of these beings, angels and *jinn* in the main, fades. It is not that the angelic world disappears, but rather that angels have less personality

[38] Welch, "Allah," 733–58.

and become more like mechanical extensions of the divine act and message. They become actors rather than characters. In his own words:

> In pre-Badr contexts the major roles of the angels involve their service to Allah in a variety of celestial, Last Judgment, and infernal scenes; in post-Badr contexts the major roles of the angels involve their relationship or assistance to man in current, historical events. Angels are thus brought down closer to people. Significantly, this development occurs at the same time that *jinn*, demons, and Iblis and his "hosts" (*junūd*) cease to be mentioned in further revelations, which happens also to be the time when emphasis on the "oneness" of Allah and the nonexistence of other deities reaches its zenith in the development of major themes in the revelation. The Qur'an thus portrays, in late Meccan and early Medinan revelations, an increasing polarization of supernatural powers for good and evil in the lives of people. Whereas a profusion of supernatural forces appear in Meccan revelations, with their exact identity and relationships not clearly defined, in Medinan (or post-Badr, to be more precise) portions of the Qur'an all supernatural, but non-divine, power for evil or misfortune is focused in a single being, Shayṭān. As is seen regarding the angels in the Qur'an, Shayṭān also undergoes a gradual transition from the realm of the mythical to that of the mundane. The vivid personalities of Iblīs, the fallen-angel, and Shayṭān, the sly tempter who portrays the characteristics of the serpent in the story of the fall of Adam, are fused into a single being by the time of the final Qur'anic account of the two stories in 2.34–38.[39]

In his unpublished dissertation, Welch generates his own chronology of the Iblīs stories, taking an approach influenced by Richard Bell. Bell's chronology goes further than those of Nöldeke and Blachère in his willingness to regard *sūrah*s as composites of elements revealed at different times. Nöldeke accepts that most *sūrah*s are complete, revealed units and orders the *sūrah*s primarily on the basis of style and the use of certain expressions, such as *al-Rahmān* as a name for God and *qul!* (Say!) as an introductory formula.[40] His ordering of the Iblīs stories is: 20, 15, 38, 17, 18, 7, and 2. He locates the first five texts in his "Middle Meccan" period, with Sūrat al-ʿArāf (7) in the Late Meccan and Sūrat al-Baqarah (2) as the first Medīnan revelation (pre-Badr). The two other mentions of Iblīs, in Sūrat al-Shuʿarā (26) and Sūrah Saba' (34), are also Middle and Late Meccan respectively. Régis Blachère, in his

[39] Welch, "Allah," 748–49.

[40] Nöldeke, *Ursprung des Qorāns*. See also Watt, *Bell's Introduction*, 108–20.

French translation of the Qur'ān, follows the main contours of Nöldeke's chronology.[41] His ordering of the Iblīs passages, however, is significantly different than that of Nöldeke: 38, 7, 20, 17, 15, 18, and 2.

Bell attempts to recognize component parts of longer *sūrahs* but does not try to assign a precise ordering of *sūrahs* and their components. He assumes that in Medīna, Muḥammad engaged in a more conscious compilation of a Book, and thus stories in earlier revelations were revised and rewritten with later *āyahs* amending earlier ones without actually replacing them. Variations in rhyming patterns give some evidence of this revision. Much of Bell's approach is premised on the popular report, attested by numerous *ḥadīth*, that the Qur'ān was first recorded on palm leaves, pieces of papyrus, flat stones, leather, etc., and sometimes on both sides, with, presumably, no indication as to which side or object came first.[42]

Welch, in his study of the supernatural figures in the Qur'ān, including Iblīs, proposes an ordering of the seven Iblīs stories based on Bell's theory of progressive revision of the stories. He distinguishes the story of Iblīs's refusal to prostrate himself before Adam and his consequent eviction, from the al-Shayṭān story of the temptation in the garden, which occurs only three times (*sūrahs* 7, 20, and 2). These three versions of the al-Shayṭān story are attached to the latest three versions of the Iblīs story and give the beginnings of a chronological sequence. The earliest Iblīs story, according to Welch, is in Sūrah Ṣād 38:71–85 where it immediately follows a reference to the high council in heaven. His sequence of revelation is thus: 38, 15, 18, 17, 7, 20, and 2. Welch's approach is attractive as a way to understand the narrative in that he pays careful attention to the precise content of each story without reading into it elements that are found only in other versions. Welch determines that the Iblīs story is earlier than the al-Shayṭān story, which leads him to put all instances where the two are joined (7, 20, and 2) later. The earliest account, in Sūrah Ṣād, associates the story with mention of the "high council." The version in Sūrat al-Ḥijr (15) is second in sequence because of its similarity to the first version in Sūrah Ṣād, in length and content—neither mentions Adam and both mention the *rūḥ* of God.

Angelika Neuwirth has recently suggested a different chronology based on a theory of the development of a canon from early ritual elements toward a

[41] Blachère, *Le Coran*.

[42] Bell, *Commentary on the Qu'ran*, 8–15.

written text.[43] She begins with Sūrat al-Ḥijr in which Iblīs is simply included as part of the variety of creation without clear condemnation, building on concepts mentioned already in Sūrat al-Raḥmān (55). The mention of the *qur'ān* in the first verse refers to liturgical elements not yet conceived as a book. *Kitāb* refers to the scriptural stories of Abraham. Sūrah Ṣād (38) builds on the core element of the previous version. Iblīs is still not condemned, but his disputation becomes the archetype of communal disputation in Mecca. By Sūrat al-Isrā' (17) *qur'ān* and *kitāb* are of equal rank. Liturgy is becoming codified into a Book, or a Scripture, that makes the Meccan community closer in nature to Christians and Jews. Iblīs's nature becomes progressively more evil. By Sūrat al-Kahf he has become a *fāsiq* (ungodly one).

The chronology reveals a development from liturgical elements to parænetic elements of debate. The characters become encoded with specific associations. God is omniscient, Iblīs is arrogant, and Adam is, in the last version, vice-regent on earth. Homiletic replaces narrative, and ambiguity is reduced to the minimum. This also tracks the development of the community from one in which liturgical elements are shared among a small group of believers to a more ordered community in which authoritative and codified exhortations are given to the community by God and his messenger.

Neuwirth's chronology adds several dimensions to Welch's earlier effort. She not only looks at characteristics in the larger *sūrah* in which each Iblīs story is located but has also developed a narrative of community and canonical development that tracks the changes in the text. This chronology marks tremendous progress in our understanding of the construction of the Qur'ān, which should yield fruit in applications to other *sūrah*s. It does, however, presume the early integrity of the *sūrah*s. In Sūrah Ṣād the Iblīs story appears to interrupt a series of three *qul!* pericopes, which suggests that it may be a later insertion into a preexisting composition. Such evidence of compilation over a period of time weakens Neuwirth's approach. The following chart shows the seven *sūrah*s with Iblīs narratives (plus the two other mentions of Iblīs in italics) with various chronological orderings.

[43] Neuwirth, "Negotiating Justice (Part I)." See also Neuwirth, "Du Texte de Récitation," 194–229; and idem, "Referentiality and Textuality," 143–76.

Sūrah	Nöldeke	Egyptian	Blachère	Welch	Neuwirth
2 al-Baqarah	91-7 First Medīnan	91-7	87-7	7	7
7 al-'Arāf	87-6 Third Meccan	87-6	39-2	5	6
15 al-Ḥijr	57-2 Middle Meccan	57-2	54-5	2	1
17 al-Isrā'	67-4 Middle Meccan	67-4	50-4	4	5
18 al-Kahf	69-5 Middle Meccan	69-5	69-6	3	4
20 ṬāHā	55-1 Middle Meccan	55-1	45-3	6	2
26 al-Shu'arā	*56 Middle Meccan*	56			
34 Saba'	*85 Third Meccan*	58			
38 Ṣād	59-3 Middle Meccan	59-3	38-1	1	3

As indicated by the chart, Neuwirth's chronology is not greatly different from the traditional Egyptian ordering or from that of Nöldeke (but differs significantly from that of Blachère), but in each case, small differences in ordering have theological implications that have not been explored. Charting the progression of Iblīs stories shows a theological movement from the tragic Iblīs to the evil, *shayṭānī* Iblīs.

The *Sūrah* as a Unit

Although Muslims commonly regard the Qur'ān as the verbatim word of God with no human artifice in its writing, there is considerable debate concerning the process of collecting and arranging the *sūrah*s and even of groups of *āyah*s within *sūrah*s. In the early *ḥadīth* literature, some traditions support the collection of the Qur'ān of Ibn Mas'ūd as the complete and authoritative *muṣḥaf* received directly from Muḥammad. Others invest authority in the 'Uthmānic codex collected by Zayd Ibn Thābit well after the death of Muḥammad. Later Muslim tradition united behind the 'Uthmānic tradition as the Qur'ān revealed to Muḥammad and preserved without error or change to the present day.

The story that has come to be widely accepted in Muslim literature is that the Qur'ān was at first recorded in the memories of the early Muslims and written on palm leaves or thin stones. These were not the complete text, but small or large portions of it. Then Abū Bakr, 'Umar, or 'Uthmān collected these parts together to establish the first complete written text of the Qur'ān. Variant versions tell the story of this collection. The process of collection might have begun at the initiative of Abū Bakr and been completed by ʿUthmān, who also reconciled and eliminated variant versions that had come to be used in Kufa, Basra, and other parts of the Islamic empire to produce a single authoritative text of the Qur'ān. John Burton, who has examined these and other traditions in great detail, surprisingly concludes that it was Muḥammad who collected the Qur'ān.[44] This idea has not been widely accepted among scholars.[45]

The various accounts of the collection of the Qur'ān still leave the essential question open for argument. Is the collection of the *sūrah*s by ʿUthmān, or Ibn Masʿūd, or even Muḥammad, also an authoritative ordering of the *sūrah*s? Did some divine guidance dictate the particular progression of *sūrah*s in the Qur'ān? In some traditions Gabriel recites the Qur'ān in its totality to Muḥammad, during the month of Ramadan, according to Sūrat al-Baqarah (2:185), or in a single night, according to Sūrat al-Dukhān (44:3). This implies, but does not require, some sort of organization of the recitation. If a complete recitation at one sitting is the model of revelation, then the *sūrah*s could have been ordered prior to revelation, in heaven, or at least in the process of revelation. On the other hand, Sūrat al-Furqān (25:32) clearly states that the Qur'ān was not sent down all at once, but in ordered installments. Clearly Muslim tradition affirms the latter, gradual revelation, but gives various explanations for the tradition that the Qur'ān was sent down wholesale in Ramadan. Some say that the whole Qur'ān was revealed in Ramadan but it was also sent down in portions. Others argue that "Qur'ān" here refers not to the whole but to a part, or that it refers to the portion for that year.[46]

The text itself, and modern treatments of it, assumes that it was sent down in portions. The literature examining the occasions of revelation (*asbāb al-nuzūl*) confirms this. Editions of the Qur'ān often indicate whether *sūrah*s were revealed in Mecca or Medīna and sometimes the exact order of revelation as well. Sometimes particular verses within a *sūrah* are specified as being revealed at a time different from the rest of the *sūrah*. The *muṣḥaf* is not ordered by time of revelation, which remains largely speculative. The result is a text in which some of the larger units, and occasionally smaller units, seem awkwardly joined.

[44] Burton, *Collection of the Qur'an*.

[45] See Shnizer, "Sacrality and Collection," 159–71, for a good summary. Burton, *Collection*, 1:351–61; Motzki, *Alternative Accounts*, 59–75.

[46] See Ayoub, *Qur'an*, 191–92, for a summary of views from a variety of commentators.

Modern interpreters must guess at the logic that governed the arrangement. That the text has such a logical arrangement—that it was not haphazard—must be assumed. This was and is, after all, sacred text, not to be handled carelessly or frivolously. If the text does seem awkwardly joined, this could be an indication first of all of the distance between the modern reader and the ancient compiler. Secondly, it may be evidence of the care given to assemble fixed texts without altering the texts themselves to make the joins smoother. Thirdly, one might theorize that the ordering was in some way dictated without regard for smooth transition. However one attempts to explain it, we should not take this seemingly awkward assembly as an indication of carelessness on the part of the ancient compiler(s), even if the results are puzzling to us.

Is this sense conveyed by the construction of the *sūrah*s itself a part of divine revelation? Herein lies a difficulty. If the collection and ordering of the *sūrah*s is itself a product of divine revelation, then why is there no commentary on the meaning of the ordering? Daniel Madigan notes this problem. He notes that al-Suyūṭī, quoting the Qādi Abū Bakr, argues that the ordering of both *sūrah*s and *āyah*s were given by God, but that commentary pays no attention to the ordering, which indicates that the claim of divine ordering is likely a claim on principle with no empirical foundation.[47]

Muslims claim divine authorship of the organization of the Qur'ān but without then exploring any significance to that ordering. Further, the approach of most interpreters—an analysis of individual *āyah*s without examination of larger sections of text as whole units—seems to give no revelatory significance to the larger structure.

Even shorter *sūrah*s that are clearly revealed as units receive this atomistic treatment from the commentators. Some commentators, such as the Shī'a commentator Ayatollah al-Sayyid Abū al-Qāsim al-Khū'ī, claim that Muḥammad designed the ordering of the Qur'ān.[48] Al-Khū'ī, however, does not go on to assert that this ordering is itself revelatory or worthy of attention in the process of interpretation. Rather, al-Khū'ī argues the point as part of the *'ijāz* (inimitability) of the Qur'ān. But if he is right (and Burton as well) that Muḥammad ordered the Qur'ān, is this the same as saying that the order itself is part of the revelation of the Qur'ān? Even if it is Muḥammad who ordered the verses and the *sūrah*s, this implies that such order is meaningful, and if meaningful, then itself a subject of interpretation

[47] Madigan, *Self-Image*, 47–48.

[48] Al-Khū'ī, *Prolegomena*, 163–77.

of the Qur'ān. Any act of ordering requires some thought process and some basis for decision.[49] Given this logic, it would be appropriate to interpret the verses of the Qur'ān not atomistically, in isolation, but contextually.

But how shall we determine this context? This impinges upon the interpretation. For instance, we could look at the Iblīs stories horizontally, comparing each story to other narratives of the story. This approach pays no attention to the particular ordering of the *sūrah*, but does attend to the context of the full story of Iblīs of which each telling is only a part.

On the other hand, we might see the context as the full *sūrah* in which the Iblīs story is placed. As we shall see in the cases of Sūrah Ṣād and Sūrah ṬāHā, the context of the story in the larger *sūrah* may shift the meaning of the story. In this approach the reader understands each narrative version of the story to be designed specifically for its immediate textual context. The features of the story included in each location have a purpose, and the absence of other features is equally purposeful. The Iblīs story is not simply one story, but seven narratives, each with a specific meaning attuned to and contributory to the meaning of its *sūrah*. We must pay close attention to the way the story is told in relation to passages before and after, as well as to the overall structure of the *sūrah*. This becomes more challenging in the later, larger *sūrahs*, where an overall structure is more elusive, but in the earlier Meccan *sūrahs*, it yields some surprising insights.

The value of this reading is that it leaves open the boundaries of story. The only sure boundaries in the Qur'ān are those of the *sūrahs*. Through what knowledge could we decide that a particular pericope or story begins or ends at a particular line? A more important yield of this approach is that meanings of particular narratives of the Iblīs story will be suggested by their context, not by homogenizing them with other Iblīs narratives. This allows each version of the Iblīs story to be understood in its own context.

This also follows the recent work by Mustansir Mir, who describes the approach of Amīn Aḥsan Iṣlāhī, a twentieth century Pakistani scholar who based his eight-volume commentary on the Qur'ān, *Tadabbur-i-Qur'ān,* on the concept of *naẓm* (a coherent organization).[50] In Iṣlāhī's view, there is indeed a coherent structure to every *surāh* that can be discerned through careful

[49] One may note here the theological import of the fact that the books of the Jewish Tanakh are ordered differently from the chapters of the Christian Old Testament, the former expressing a theology of exile and return, the latter a theology of messianic expectation.

[50] Mir, *Coherence in the Qur'ān*.

analysis of the flow of the arguments and determination of the *'amūd* (center pole) of each *sūrah*. Iṣlāḥī then goes on to demonstrate such an approach in every *sūrah*, including the difficult and long Medīnan *sūrah*s.

Mir argues that the commentarial treatment of *sūrah*s as unified compositions is a twentieth-century phenomenon.[51] The effect of this use of *naẓm* is, in some instances, to direct commentators such as Sayyid Quṭb away from reliance on determination of the *asbāb al-nuzūl* for explanation and toward explanation of an *āyah* through its context. This is not yet a literary approach, but such approaches cannot proceed without such an awareness of larger contexts and themes.

Western scholars have attempted to apply other methods to uncover schemes of unity within the longer *sūrah*s. Richard Martin, a pioneer in this effort, applies a programmatic approach to Sūrat al-Shu'arā (26).[52] His approach is based on structuralist symbolic analysis that attempts to identify parallel surface and deep structures in the text. This is a rather rigid approach, not promising in itself, but quite suggestive of the kinds of resources in anthropology, semiotics, and literary theory that are helpful. Other recent attempts, such as the analysis of Sūrat al-Baqarah by David Smith, show increasing interest in such approaches but do not yet show the way that one can understand elements within the *sūrah* as contributing to an overall theme.[53] It is this element that we will explore through the Iblīs stories.

This study will bring in other aspects of literary analysis as needed in the following chapters. In the next chapter, it will fill in some of the repertoire of pre-Islamic narratives of the origin of evil, both so the emergence of similar themes in the Islamic corpus will be apparent and also to train our ears for nuances of story and interpretation that others have explored in the past.

[51] Idem, "Sūra as a Unity," 211–24.

[52] Martin, "Structural Analysis," 665–83.

[53] Smith, "Structure of al-Baqarah," 121–36.

CHAPTER 3

The Mythic Repertoire

The story of Iblīs comes to Islam with a venerable and rich heritage. The myth of Iblīs must be seen, as the commentators see it, against the tapestry of Jewish and Christian legend, Scripture, and thought that comes into Islam under the category of *isrā'īliyyāt*. We cannot trace the actual flow of specific tales from Jewish and Christian (and other?) sources to the Islamic writers. Such a path of transmission will probably never be reconstructable. We cannot know for certain which traditions and what sources were familiar to the commentators or the *muḥaddithīn*. We must, however, describe what was there in the background, in terms both of the specific myth of, for instance, the fallen angel that is a logical parallel, and of other related strategies for the explanation of the nature of evil. These myths help us discern alternative meanings and implications of specific elements of the story. The fallen angel story often comes mixed with elements drawn from other specific mythic streams.

Mythic Strategies

Typologies of myth are often helpful but inevitably clumsy. Just as the Islamic myth of Iblīs melds almost (but not quite) seamlessly into the character of al-Shayṭān, so ancient stories of watcher angels, the heavenly prosecutor, and Leviathan also tend to commingle and assume various shapes and forms. Nevertheless, the effort to distinguish story themes helps us to ask the right questions and discern nuances that might otherwise escape our notice. Five particular themes will be helpful. The combat myth sets good against evil, often in a creation story, in fairly absolute terms. The heavenly prosecutor story appears primarily as the *śāṭān* of the Tanakh, mainly in the book of Job. The watcher angels are described in Genesis 6 and the book of *Enoch*. The fallen angel story appears in Isaiah 14 and in later pseudepigrapha. Finally, narratives of sibling rivalry such as the Cain and Abel story in Genesis 4 appear to have a powerful role in the origin of evil.

There are typologies that we will not pursue, chief among them being the rich literature of the gnostics and of neoplatonic philosophy where evil is associated with materiality and emerges through the progressive, or rather regressive, emanation of the spheres. This is colorful literature, but it is not primarily narrative in nature. Our focus here, specifically, is on narrative explanations and accounts for the existence and nature of evil. The neoplatonic literature is generally descriptive of certain complex cosmologies and does not figure greatly in interpretations of the Iblīs story. We will, however, find neoplatonic elements that do mingle with the five myths, which we will outline and note.

The Combat Myth

The combat myth opposes good and evil in a somewhat absolutized form.[1] It often appears in a creation story. In the Babylonian *Enuma Elish*, Marduk defeats the chaos monster Tiamat. Out of the remnants of her body, Marduk forms the world. Marduk becomes the first king of Babylon and the archetype of kingship.[2] In the Canaanite account, Baal defeats Yamm, the sea-monster, prefiguring the battle between Yahweh, the God of Israel, and Leviathan, also apparently a sea-monster (Isa 27:1). In another narrative, Mot kills Baal, or swallows him, and for seven years that follow, the earth is barren until Anat, Baal's sister, finds his body, buries it, and kills Mot, which then revives Baal and sets in motion a continuous combat between the two.[3] Here the combat is not only between Baal and Mot but also involves Anat, whose destructive power is not always in service to humanity.

As Jon Levenson points out, the tension between Yahweh and a persistently present but opposing force of chaos is sometimes veiled but ever-present in the Tanakh.[4] Contrary to the conventional view of God's supreme mastery

[1] See Forsyth, *Old Enemy*, and Russell, *Devil*. Russell has written a series of five books tracing the concept of Satan through Western history; this book serves as the first volume.

[2] Heidel, *Babylonian Genesis*, 18–60.

[3] Gibson, *Canaanite Myths*; Whitney, *Two Strange Beasts*, 6–10.

[4] Job 3:8, 41:1; Ps 74:14, 104:26; and Isa 27:1. See Levenson, *Creation*, 3–13, and Whitney, *Two Strange Beasts*, for a detailed discussion of the tradition in the Second Temple

over all, the Tanakh presents a God who is ever struggling to maintain the order of creation against forces of disorder. Gen 1:1–23 does not describe the banishment of evil, but instead its restriction through God's orderly separations and categorizations. Psalm 44 shows a God whose everlasting attention is required to keep the ever-present forces of evil at bay:

> 22 Because of you we are being killed all day long, and accounted as sheep for the slaughter. 23 Rouse yourself! Why do you sleep, O LORD? Awake, do not cast us off forever! 24 Why do you hide your face? Why do you forget our affliction and oppression? 25 For we sink down to the dust; our bodies cling to the ground. 26 Rise up, come to our help. Redeem us for the sake of your steadfast love. (NRSV)

Many scholars also see *śāṭān* in 1 Chr 21:1 as an enemy of God, instigating David to call for a census against God's will. This *śāṭān*, rendered without the definite article, is, in this view, a later development of the concept of *śāṭān* in Job and Zechariah (to be discussed below).[5] Dissenters from this view will be discussed below in the section on the heavenly prosecutor motif.

The combat myth is also the defining myth of the sectarian community at Qumran. In particular, the War Scroll (1QM) describes in great detail the battle at the end times between Belial with the "spirits of his lot," the "sons of darkness," against the angel Michael, leading the "sons of light." The dualism here is between two mutually exclusive communities. In the Qumran materials, one is either among the "sons of light" or the "sons of darkness"; there is no third option.[6]

Scholars debate whether the extreme dualism of the Qumran sect derives from an expansion of apocalyptic passages in the Tanakh, or whether it develops from the Persian dualist tradition of Zoroastrianism and its derivatives.[7] The sources of the latter are fragmentary—most of the *Avesta* is lost.[8] In the original

period and early rabbinic Judaism.

5 Supporting this view are Dirksen, *1 Chronicles*, 257; Forsyth, *Old Enemy*, 119–21; Klein, *1 Chronicles*, 418–19; and Nielsen, *Prodigal Son*, 100–5.

6 Davidson, *Angels at Qumran*. Beliar is, in other texts, rendered as "Belial," but seems to be the same figure.

7 Davidson, *Angels at Qumran*, 232–34.

8 Tradition has it that much of the Avestan literature was destroyed when Alexander the Great burned the library at Persepolis in 331 B.C.E. and killed many of the priests. This is impossible to confirm, one way or another. Boyce, however, notes that the "Great Avesta" canon, established during Sassanian times, was destroyed in subsequent invasions—by Arabs,

teaching of Zarathushtra,[9] a single god, Ahura Mazda, rules all spirits, evil *daevas* and good *ahuras*. Ahura Mazda produces twins, Angra Mainyu, and Spenta Mainyu, who later becomes identified with Ahura Mazda.[10] After Zarathushtra's death the priestly caste develop the doctrine in a more dualistic direction.

The later Mazdaist interpretation is that two spirits, Ahura Mazda and Angra Mainyu, are locked in battle.[11] They are equal in power except that Angra Mainyu, the evil spirit, is limited in space and by the certainty of his eventual destruction. Another interpretation, put forth by the Zurvanites in Sassanian times, posited an *ur*-principle, Zurvan, who is hermaphroditic and produces Ahura Mazda and Angra Mainyu, in that order, to the horror of the parent.[12] The Zurvanite interpretation draws from neoplatonic influences, articulating a series of levels of creation from Ahura Mazda through six Amesh Spentas to four manifestations in the material world, including Gayomart, the ideal man.

Rabbinic thought never developed in the direction of the combat myth.[13] The Talmud gives some attention to the notion of opposing tendencies within the human: the bad inclination (*yēṣer hā-ra'*) and the good inclination (*yēṣer ṭôb*), both of which are natural tendencies within the human spirit, but these are never personalized to the extent of becoming external adversaries.[14] Two

---

Turks, and Mongols—such that no copy survives and perhaps a quarter of the original text is extant (Boyce, *Textual Sources,* 3).

[9] "Zoroaster" is a Westernized form of the name, drawn from Greek. "Zarathushtra" is the Avestan, or Old Iranian, articulation of the priest/prophet whose name is attached to this tradition.

[10] Angra Mainyu (in the Avestan language; *Ahriman* in Pahlavi) is the evil opponent of Ahura Mazda (*Ohrmazd* in Pahlavi) in the Pahlavi book the *Bundahishn* (Original Creation), but they are described as twins in *Yasna* 30 of the Avestan Gathas. The exact relationship between the two is constructed differently among different sects within the Zoroastrian historical tradition, which includes Zurvanism and Mazdaism.

[11] Mazdaism emerged as a development of the Zoroastrian tradition in Sassanian times, roughly the early sixth century C.E., influenced by Manichean ideas.

[12] The Zurvanites were later viewed as heretics, since their ideas seemed to demote Ahura Mazda to a secondary position in the pantheon.

[13] But the combat myth is not absent. See Whitney, *Two Strange Beasts*, concerning rabbinic commentary on Behemoth and Leviathan.

[14] There is no clear reason why "the evil inclination" is rendered with the definite article, *yēṣer hā-ra'*, and "good inclination," *yēṣer ṭôb,* is rendered without the *ha,* but that is the clear tradition. See Hirschberg, "Eighteen Hundred Years," 130; more generally, see Bulka,

gestures in that direction deserve to be noted, however. The first is a solitary but well-known passage from the Babylonian Talmud:

> In bB.B. 16a Resh Lachish said, "Satan, the evil yetzer, and the angel of death are all one. He is called Satan as it is written, 'And Satan went forth from the presence of the Lord.'" Job 2.7 He is called the evil yetzer (we know this because) it is written in another place, (every yetzer of the thoughts of his heart) was only evil continually' Gen 6.5 And it is written here (in connection with Satan) "only upon himself put not forth thine hand" Job 1.12. The same is also the angel of death since it says, "only spare his life" Job 2.6 which shows that Job's life belonged to him.[15]

This is, however, a single reference that has not had much impact on rabbinic thought.

A second form in which the combat myth emerges is in the eternal presence of Amalek. Amalek is a human enemy, a tribe dedicated to Israel's destruction, preying on the weak, but at times assuming an extra-human dimension. In Exodus 17 we read:

> 14 Then the LORD said to Moses, "Write this as a reminder in a book and recite it in the hearing of Joshua: I will utterly blot out the remembrance of Amalek from under heaven." 15 And Moses built an altar and called the name of it, The LORD is my banner. 16 He said, "A hand upon the banner of the LORD. The LORD will have war with Amalek from generation to generation." (NRSV)

The passage contains a tension between the promise to "utterly blot out" Amalek and even the remembrance of Amalek from existence and a contrary implication that the war with Amalek, a war engaged in by God, will continue from generation to generation.[16] Although the adversarial relationship between Israel and Amalek continues to be remembered through the Purim

"To Be Good or Evil," 53–71; Murphy, "*Yēṣer*," 334–44; Rosenberg, *Good and Evil*; and Sokol "Is There a 'Halakhic' Response," 311–23.

[15] Cohen Stuart, *Struggle*, 36.

[16] See also 1 Sam 15:7 and Deut 25:17–19, in which Amalek is attacking the weak laggards among the Israelites; Judg 10:12 where they oppose the Israelites' entrance to the Promised Land; and Ps 83:7, in which Amalek is part of a conspiracy against Israel.

holy day, it seldom becomes apotheosized into an opposition on a cosmic scale, as is found at Qumran and in other apocalyptic literature.[17]

The combat myth became the central Christian understanding of evil. Elaine Pagels, who traces the emergence of the theology of Satan in the early church, attributes this to an apocalyptic character of early Christian thought. According to Pagels, apocalyptic thought addresses the primary question, "Who are God's people?"[18] In practice, though, the question becomes, "Who are not God's people?" since the questioners inevitably assume their own inclusion among the righteous. This question invites an answer with reference to the combat myth.

Many of the early Christian texts reflect an oppositional approach that is not manifest in the Tanakh, with the exception, perhaps, of Daniel. It does, however, reflect the situation of the early church, opposed by the Sadducees and especially the Pharisaic sect of Judaism and later by the dominant Romans. In Pagels's reading, the evolution of the Christian combat myth reflects this oppositional social milieu in which real enemies contested the legitimacy of the church and its claims on the Israelite heritage. She calls this the "intimate enemy," who shares enough of one's own heritage to be a real danger to one's own authenticity.

The position of Satan as the opponent of Christ and the Christian was significant enough for Celsus to criticize Christianity to Origen, citing its blasphemous belief in the devil, which leads it into dualism.

What makes the Christians' message dangerous, Celsus writes, is not that they believe in one God, but that they deviate from monotheism by their "blasphemous" belief in the devil. For all the "impious errors" that the Christians commit, Celsus says, they show their greatest ignorance in "making up a being opposed to God, and calling him 'devil,' or, in the Hebrew language, 'Satan.'" . . . All such ideas are nothing but human inventions, sacrilegious even to repeat: "it is blasphemy . . . to say that the greatest God . . . has an adversary who constrains his capacity to do good." Celsus is outraged that the Christians, who claim to worship one God, "impiously divide the kingdom of God, creating a rebellion in it, as if there were opposing factions within the divine, including one that is hostile to God!"[19]

[17] On Amalek in Judaism, see Lee, "In the Shadow of Amalek," 44–49; Sagi, "Punishment," 323–46; and Sosevsky, "Sha'ul and Amalek," 37–56.

[18] Pagels, *Origin of Satan*, 51.

[19] Ibid., 143; quoting from Origen, *Contra Celsum* 6:42.

Origen responds that the victory of the demons is only immediate and apparent. In the long run, the death of martyrs results in their own resurrection and the destruction of the demonic. This in turn strengthens the faith of the Christian to resist oppression and accept torture and martyrdom. The opposition in heaven between Christ and Satan is a reflection of the opposition on earth between Christians and the Roman oppression. Origen had the opportunity to experience this in his own arrest and torture in which he refused to renounce his faith.

In later history, the combat myth is represented not only in the terminology of God and Satan but also as Christ and antichrist.[20]

The combat myth yields perhaps the simplest of theodicies. There is good and there is evil—separate, distinct, and utterly opposed. Much of the Qur'ānic "*shayṭānī*" discourse is of this nature. As Welch points out, the later Medīnan passages of the Qur'ān tend to depict an utterly evil al-Shayṭān opposed to humanity.[21]

For the most part, the opposition set up in the Qur'ān is between al-Shayṭān and humanity, specifically the believers:

> *Yā'ayyuhā al-ladhīna āmanū udkhulū fi-l-silmi kāffat*[an]
> *wa-lā tattabi'ū khuṭuwāti al-shayṭāni innahu lakum 'aduwwun mubīn*[un]
>
> O you who believe, enter into the peace completely
> And do not follow the footsteps of Satan as he is, to you, a clear enemy.[22] (2:208)

Throughout the Qur'ān, al-Shayṭān, as a rebel (19:44) and as an ingrate (17:27), opposes God, but he is never regarded as a coequal opponent or rival to God. Al-Shayṭān, and Iblīs in his *shayṭānī* aspect, fall somewhere between the combat myth and the heavenly prosecutor archetype, less empowered in the grand scheme of God's world than the former, and more earthly than the latter.

[20] McGinn, *Antichrist*.

[21] Welch, "Allah."

[22] See also 4:38; 6:142; 12:5; 17:53; 18:50; 35:6; 43:62 (among other places).

The Heavenly Prosecutor

Most Christian literature, and some Jewish writings, interpret the name "Satan" to refer to the opponent of God/Christ/Michael. This is a development from the *śāṭān* of the Tanakh, but the *śāṭān* has quite a different role from that of the apocalyptic Satan and must be kept distinct.

In most places in the Tanakh, *śāṭān* refers to a human adversary. Several passages (1 Sam 29:4; 2 Sam 16:5–8; 1 Kgs 5:2–6; and 1 Kings 11) use the term with regard to human adversaries in a military context.[23] Some commentators believe that *śāṭān* in 1 Chr 21:1 is also an earthly accuser.[24] In Ps 109:6 the *śāṭān* is also a mortal adversary, but the context is forensic; he is one who brings charges against the psalmist. In the Balaam story in Numbers 22, the context is also forensic, but the *śāṭān* is a messenger from heaven sent to accuse and redirect Balaam from a task for which he had received no divine sanction.[25] In all of these examples, *śāṭān* is rendered as an indefinite noun. In the forensic contexts of both Job and Zechariah, however, *śāṭān* is definite (*haś-śāṭān*).

The *locus classicus* for *śāṭān* in the role of divine prosecutor is Job 1–2, where *haś-śāṭān*, rendered with a definite article, has returned to heaven from roaming to and fro upon the earth.[26] He is identified in 2:1 as one of the *běnê hā-'ĕlōhîm*, "sons of God." The predominant understanding of this term, as supported by documents discovered at Ugarit, is that it refers to the members of the heavenly court, the angels and servants of God, who assist the divine in the maintenance and judgment on earth.[27] The *śāṭān* is the prosecutor in that heavenly court.

A close examination of the text indicates that God is being accused, not Job. The *śāṭān* challenges God on God's assumption that Job is a righteous person, suggesting that Job would not behave so purely if he were not so blessed and protected by God. At no time does the *śāṭān* deceive or lie. Nor does the *śāṭān* demonstrate any animosity toward Job. Indeed, Job is

[23] Day, *Adversary in Heaven*, 25–43.

[24] Beentjes, *Satan*, 46–47; Japhet, *Chronicles*, 116; and Jarick, *1 Chronicles*, 125.

[25] Beentjes, *Satan*, 45–67; Stokes, "Devil."

[26] Day, *Adversary in Heaven*, 69–106; Wilson, *Job*, 54–99.

[27] Wilson, *Job*, 54–61. Wilson argues that since the *śāṭān* is singled out here, he is not one of the *běnê hā-'ĕlōhîm*. In his view, *śāṭān* is both *Doppelgänger* and peer for Yahweh, an emanation of God's darker side, making the dialogue of Job 1–2 a device to illustrate tensions within the persona of God.

an unwitting pawn in a wager between the *śāṭān* and God. Even this wager reveals no sign of animus, but Job, of course, is not aware of this wager at his expense. The ultimate import is that the *śāṭān* wishes freedom to examine and possibly prosecute anyone on earth, but Job is being protected by God.

Zech 3:1–4 is the latest of the passages mentioning the *śāṭān* and therefore key, for it shows an evolution in the concept. Here the accuser is a heavenly figure, accusing a human, although not necessarily falsely.[28] The passage in chapter 3 reads as follows:

> [1] Then he showed me the high priest Joshua standing before the angel of the LORD, and Satan standing at his right hand to accuse him.
> [2] And the LORD said to Satan, "The LORD rebuke you, O Satan! The LORD who has chosen Jerusalem rebuke you! Is not this man a brand plucked from the fire?" [3] Now Joshua was dressed in filthy clothes as he stood before the angel. [4] The angel said to those who were standing before him, "Take off his filthy clothes." And to him he said, "Behold, I have taken your guilt away from you, and I will clothe you in festal apparel." (NRSV)

The issue at hand is an evaluation of the Zadokite priesthood after the return from exile. Those Israelites who had remained in the land resisted the Zadokite plan to reestablish the temple and the authority of its priesthood. Here Satan is a forensic accuser, although the nature of his accusation is not revealed. There is no indication that Satan lies, but Satan is at odds with the will of God. In this passage the emergence of a Satan who opposes God's will, and whom God not only refutes but rebukes, begins to be apparent. This *śāṭān* is a prosecutor, but there are shadows of the divine combat myth here.

The notion of a heavenly prosecutor emerges slowly from the Tanakh. Only in Zechariah does this image begin to take shape, and here it is still far from the Satan figure of the New Testament that rules the earth in resistance and opposition to God as in the combat myth. It is, however, important and helpful to maintain the unique characteristics of this story as distinct from the various other stories we have described. The heavenly prosecutor acts as a servant of God; he is one of *bĕnê hā-'ĕlōhîm* not an opponent of God. Although God, out of mercy, may choose to rule in opposition to the *śāṭān*'s allegations, that choice does not mean that God rejects the *śāṭān* himself, or vice versa. The heavenly prosecutor acts in opposition, not to human beings,

[28] Day, *Adversary in Heaven*, 107–26.

but to human sin, as the harsh investigator who leaves mercy to others. But there is no hint of lying, malice, or enmity in the depiction of the *śāṭān*.

We will examine later whether Iblīs, considered in isolation from al-Shayṭān, can be considered guilty of lying or of malice in his own right, but here we consider the corollary—whether al-Shayṭān, as well as being a "clear enemy" of humanity and a rebel against God, is also God's servant, a tester of human hearts. No passage in the Qur'ān clearly presents him so, but the following passages come close:

> And when al-Shayṭān made their deeds alluring to them, he said, "No people can overcome you this day for truly I am near you." But when the two groups saw each other, he retreated on his heels and said, "I am blameless of you; I see what you do not see; I fear God, and God is powerful in punishment."[29] (8:48)

> And al-Shayṭān will say when the issue is decided, "Truly God promised a true promise to you, and I promised you [as well]; then I failed you, as I had no authority over you, except that I called to you and you responded to me. So do not blame me, but blame yourselves.
> I am not a helper for you, and you are not helpers for me. Truly I reject your associating me with God in times past.
> Truly the wrongdoers will have a severe torment." (14:22)

Here, and in similar passages, al-Shayṭān's recognition of God's sovereignty is manifest, and he conducts his temptation of humanity within that awareness. No passage, however, gives al-Shayṭān any sort of standing in heaven. More commonly, al-Shayṭān is identified with a path that is contrasted with that of God.

Unlike the *śāṭān*, who is counted among *běnê hā-'ĕlōhîm*, al-Shayṭān himself has no association with heaven or with the angels. In some texts, including that of the Qur'ān, angels can function as critical consultants to God. In Sūrat al-Baqarah (2:30), the angels resist the idea that God would consider making humans, who would corrupt the earth and shed blood. In Jewish literature, such as b. San. 38b in the Talmud, God creates a particular group of angels and then consults with them about the creation of Adam. They quote Ps 8:5: "What is man that you mention him, the son of man that you take thought of him"—and are destroyed for their objection. To their successor angels, God quotes Isa 46:4—"Until old age I am he, even until

[29] See a similar construction in 59:16–17.

I am gray I will bear with them." The angels comprehend justice, but God comprehends mercy. A roughly parallel story describes angelic complaint about the giving of the Torah to Moses.[30]

This (mildly) critical role of angels stands in contrast to other texts that affirm that angels always obey their Lord, such as, "they fear their LORD above them and they do what they are commanded" (16.50), prompting commentary about the difference between angelic disobedience and fallibility.[31] As Welch points out, the earlier Meccan revelations accommodated more disorder in heaven than the later Medīnan passages.[32] This accommodation appears more clearly in the analysis of Sūrah Ṣād. The tension remains between the clear evidence of angelic dissent and a Muslim commitment to regard angels, according to the Qur'ān (2:177), as reliable, perhaps infallible, servants of God.

Although no direct parallel to Job's *śāṭān* wagering with God appears in the Qur'ān, the story is told in the *qiṣaṣ al-anbiyā'* literature. In the narrative of al-Kisā'i, Iblīs assails Job. Iblīs, however, is not in heaven, but on earth, hearing only the voice of God both cursing him and empowering him to test Job.[33] He is not one of *bĕnê hā-'ĕlōhîm*. Rather, this is Iblīs in a *shayṭānī* role.

The Qur'ān's image of al-Shayṭān is much in the character of one who tests human righteousness. In this regard, he could be considered a servant of God, performing an important function in the divine plan. The Islamic corpus, however—Qur'ān, *ḥadīth*, and subsequent literature—puts much greater distance between God and al-Shayṭān. He is not portrayed as a heavenly figure at all, but as an earthly denizen: a foe and enemy of all that is close to God.

[30] Schultz, "Angelic Opposition," 89–99.

[31] See, for instance, al-Bayḍāwī, *Tafsīr al-Bayḍāwī*, 1:50; al-Ṭabarī, *Jāmi' al-Bayān*, 14:117–18 (vol. 8). See also discussion in Jadaane, "La place des anges"; Murata, "Angels"; Waugh, "Jealous Angels," 56–72; Webb, "Angel," 84–92; and Wensinck, *Muslim Creed,* 198–202.

[32] Welch, "Allah," 749.

[33] Al-Kisā'ī, *Tales of the Prophets*, 192–204.

The Watcher Myth

The distinct myth of the watcher angels[34] emerges from a curious passage in Genesis 6:

> [1] When people began to multiply on the face of the ground, and daughters were born to them, [2] the sons of God saw that they were fair; and they took wives for themselves of all that they chose. [3] Then the LORD said, "My spirit shall not abide in mortals forever, for they are flesh; their days shall be one hundred twenty years." [4] The Nephilim were on the earth in those days—and also afterward—when the sons of God went in to the daughters of humans, who bore children to them. These were the heroes that were of old, warriors of renown. [5] The LORD saw that the wickedness of humankind was great in the earth, and that every inclination of the thoughts of their hearts was only evil continually. [6] And the LORD was sorry that he had made humankind on the earth, and it grieved him to his heart. (NRSV)

The Tanakh neither elaborates upon nor refers to this story anywhere else. The "watcher" angels, sometimes called "guardian angels," are assigned to watch over cities. Later, in the first three chapters of the Revelation to John, letters concerning each of the seven churches in Asia Minor are written to the angels of those churches.

In the Pseudepigrapha, however, we find extensive elaboration in the Enochic literature. The books of Enoch date to the third century before Christ. The *Ethiopic Book of Enoch* contains two stories about the watcher angels in chapters 6 through 11.[35] In the first, the angel Shemihazah leads two hundred watcher angels from heaven, lusting after human women. The angels marry them and beget children. The angels are aware that this is a "great sin," but they express no intention other than to satisfy their own desires. The giants (*han-nĕpīlîm* of Gen 6:4) resulting from this union devour the food of the people and attack both humans and beasts. The higher-order angels, the archangels led by Michael, turn the giants against each other, resulting in their annihilation, but from their corpses evil spirits issue forth and continue to plague the earth. Hence the origin of evil derives ultimately from the lust of the watcher angels, but immediately from the evil spirits issuing from the

[34] See Barker, "Some Reflections," 7–29; Hanson, "Rebellion in Heaven"; Newsom, "Development," 310–29; Nickelsburg, *1 Enoch*, 165–250; and VanderKam, *Enoch*.

[35] Charlesworth, *Old Testament Pseudepigrapha*; see also Davidson, *Angels at Qumran*.

giants' corpses. The two hundred watcher angels are taken by Michael and his minions into captivity and thrown into the abyss, but the demons remain loosed upon the earth.

A second story, conflated with the Shemihazah text in *Enoch*, is that of Asael or Azazel, who descends from heaven to teach metallurgy and mineralogy to humanity.[36] From these arts come all manner of specialized knowledge:

> And Azaz'el taught the people (the art of) making swords and knives, and shields, and breastplates; and he showed to their chosen ones bracelets, decorations, (shadowing of the eye) with antimony, ornamentation, the beautifying of the eyelids, all kinds of precious stones, and all coloring tinctures and alchemy. And there were many wicked ones and they committed adultery and erred, and all their conduct became corrupt. Amasras taught incantation and the cutting of roots; and Armaros the resolving of incantations; and Baraqiyal astrology, and Kokarer'el (the knowledge of) the signs, and Tam'el taught the seeing of the stars, and Asder'el taught the course of the moon as well as the deception of man. And (the people) cried and their voice reached unto heaven.[37] (8:1–4)

Here knowledge and craft are the cause of sin in the world, an idea with parallels in the myth of Prometheus as well as being suggestive of the tree of knowledge in the Eden story of Genesis. There is, however, no reference at all in *Enoch* to the Eden story. The response to the cry of the people comes in the following chapter (*Enoch* 9) in which Michael and other heavenly angels observe the oppression and bloodshed upon the earth. Later, the knowledge taught by Azazel is characterized as "eternal secrets, which are performed in heaven (and which) man learned" (9:6), a concept with compelling parallels to stories of the *jinn* in Islam, which we will explore in reference to Sūrat al-Ḥijr.

The watcher myth largely disappears from Christian and Jewish sources after the intertestamental period except for a few passing mentions of the story. For instance, Athenagoras in his "Plea for the Christians," chapter 24, notes the free will of the watchers, who "fell into impure love of virgins, and were subjugated by the flesh, and . . . became negligent and wicked in the

[36] The name Azazel appears in Leviticus 16 as the recipient of the scapegoat in the wilderness.

[37] Charlesworth, *Old Testament Pseudepigrapha*, 1:16.

management of things entrusted to [them]."[38] But the point of Athenagoras's remark is to show that free will exists among angels and therefore must also exist among mortals, not to make any point about the origin or nature of evil. Other examples, like that of Athenagoras, tend to focus on the lust of the watchers but not on the Azazel variant of transfer of secret or heavenly knowledge.

The key point of the watcher myth, then, is the willful descent of angels to consort among mortals from which, somewhat accidentally, evil originates upon the earth. The angels themselves do not continue to roam at large but are confined, which distinguishes this myth from the combat myth where Belial/Satan continues to exert evil power on earth. The demons that erupt from the bodies of giants do not have the stature of a Satan and do not organize in willful defiance of God. Another key point of the watcher myth, in its Azazel form, is the transference of knowledge. This is not the form mentioned by most of the scholars of the early church. In Tertullian, Lactantius, and *The Clementine Homilies*, the Shemihazah myth of lust is featured, but nowhere does it form a foundation for a theology of evil.[39]

The implicit theology of the Shemihazah story is that great evil can emerge as an unexpected consequence of sinful acts. In the Genesis story, not only are the watcher angels not condemned, but also their giant progeny come to be considered the heroes of old. In the Enochic expansion, the angelic lust is clearly indicated as sin, rebellion against God, but not malice against humanity. [40] Evil is an unintended byproduct of the birth and death of the giants.

The Fallen Angel Myth

The fallen angel myth, which most closely matches the Qur'ānic story of Iblīs, has few parallels in the Tanakh and New Testament. In the Tanakh, Isa 14:12 is sometimes cited as a reference to the fallen angel: "How you are fallen from heaven, O Day Star, son of Dawn (*hêlēl ben-šāḥar*)! How you are cut down to the ground, you who laid the nations low!" The context indicates a taunt aimed at the dead Babylonian king, with reference to the Canaanite deity Shaḥar, the god of the dawn, whose son is the morning star (*hêlēl*). An

[38] Roberts and Donaldson, *ANF* 2:142.

[39] Bamberger, *Fallen Angels*, 74–76.

[40] Hanson, "Rebellion in Heaven," 198–99.

Ugaritic myth describes the failed effort of the lesser god, the morning star, to become head of the heavenly pantheon.[41] Isaiah draws the parallel between the Canaanite god and the king of Babylon. Jerome's Vulgate renders *hêlēl ben-šaḥar*, the "morning star," in Latin as Lucifer.

Later interpreters found an alternate reference to the fallen angel story in Ezekiel 28, a prophecy against the king of Tyre:

> [12] Mortal, raise a lamentation over the king of Tyre, and say to him, Thus says the LORD God: You were the signet of perfection, full of wisdom and perfect in beauty. [13] You were in Eden, the garden of God; every precious stone was your covering, carnelian, chrysolite, and moonstone, beryl, onyx, and jasper, sapphire, turquoise, and emerald; and worked in gold were your settings and your engravings. On the day that you were created they were prepared. [14] With an anointed cherub as guardian I placed you; you were on the holy mountain of God; you walked among the stones of fire. [or: You are the great shielding cherub who overshadows, and I have placed you on the holy mountain.] [15] You were blameless in your ways from the day that you were created, until iniquity was found in you. [16] In the abundance of your trade you were filled with violence, and you sinned; so I cast you as a profane thing from the mountain of God, and the guardian cherub drove you out from among the stones of fire. [or: I have destroyed you, O shielding cherub, from amid the fiery stones.] [17] Your heart was proud because of your beauty; you corrupted your wisdom for the sake of your splendor. I cast you to the ground; I exposed you before kings, to feast their eyes on you. [18] By the multitude of your iniquities, in the unrighteousness of your trade, you profaned your sanctuaries. So I brought out fire from within you; it consumed you, and I turned you to ashes on the earth in the sight of all who saw you. [19] All who know you among the peoples are appalled at you; you have come to a dreadful end and shall be no more forever. (NRSV)[42]

Origen, followed by other interpreters, applied this prophecy not to the mortal king of Tyre, but to the guardian angel of the city, in effect taking a fallen angel story (signified by "hurled to the earth") and transforming it into something closer to a watcher story (to whom the souls of the Tyrians were entrusted):

[41] This is the rebellion of Athtar within the Baal-Mot cycle. See Forsyth, *Old Enemy*, 130–32; Mullen, *Divine Council*, 7–110.

[42] Alternate translations in brackets are from Anderson, *Synopsis*, 138–39.

> We have shown then, that what we have quoted regarding the prince of Tyre from the prophet Ezekiel refers to an adverse power, and by it is most clearly proved that that power was formerly holy and happy; from which state of happiness it fell from the time that iniquity was found in it, and was hurled to the earth, and was not such by nature and creation. We are of [the] opinion, therefore, that these words are spoken of a certain angel who had received the office of governing the nation of Tyrians, and to whom also their souls had been entrusted to be taken care of.[43]

The Ezekiel 28 passage, if applied to Satan, would establish not only his fall but also his prior splendor as an archangel of the highest stature, "the signet of perfection, full of wisdom and perfect in beauty" (v. 12). It would also describe the absolute condemnation of Satan by God and associate him with fire. Christian interpreters were unwilling to apply this passage to Adam, as they were anxious to show that the mercy of God would not make the punishment of Adam and Eve so unrelenting.[44]

In this study, the watcher story will be kept distinct from the fallen angel story. In many analyses the two are conflated—understandably so, since such conflation, as noted in Origen's interpretation, was common in pseudepigraphical and early Christian sources. The value of maintaining a distinction is that there are clear differences in the traditions. The essential difference is that the fallen angel story usually involves a crime against God, a heavenly dispute, resulting in the banishment of a once-respected angel. Thus the Day Star, who says, "I will make myself like the Most High" (Isa 14:14), asserts equivalence with God and is cast down for such arrogance. Similarly, the sin of the king of Tyre in Ezekiel 28 is pride in his own perfections. The result is the same—he is cast down.

In the watcher story, the crime is against human beings, at least directly and immediately (in one sense all crime is ultimately against God). In fact, a careful reading of Gen 6:1–6 indicates no actual condemnation of the descent of the angels, only a recognition that the consequence of their actions is the unleashing of evil in the world through the procreation of giants. The watchers are never banished from heaven in the early accounts. A further

[43] Origen, *De Principiis*, 1.5.4, quoted in *ANF* 4:259 (brackets in original). I have relied on Anderson, *Synopsis*, 133–47, which gives a more comprehensive discussion of this passage and its early Christian exegetical uses.

[44] Charlesworth, *Old Testament Pseudepigrapha*, 2: 262.

difference is that the watcher angels descend of their own volition. They are not evicted from heaven.

In the New Testament, only one brief reference, in Luke 10:18, attests to the fallen angel story: "[Jesus] said to them, 'I watched Satan fall from heaven like a flash of lightning.'" No further explanation or reference is given. This indicates that Luke was familiar with a fallen angel story that had already been conflated with the Satan combat myth, but which fallen angel story remains a mystery.

A possibly contemporaneous work is the enigmatic *Slavonic Apocalypse of Enoch*, or *2 Enoch*, of undetermined provenance and date. In recension J, chapter 31 reads:

> And the devil understood how I wished to create another world, so that everything could be subjected to Adam on earth, to rule and to reign over it. The devil is of the lowest places. And he will become a demon, because he fled from heaven; Sotona, because his name was Satanail. In this way he became different from the angels. His nature did not change, (but) his thought did, since his consciousness of righteousness and sinful things changed. And he became aware of his condemnation and of the sin which he sinned previously. And that is why he thought up the scheme against Adam. In such a form he entered paradise, and corrupted Eve. But Adam he did not contact.[45] (31:3–6)

The primary sin here is resistance to God and God's plan to create another world. The sin does not include direct disobedience. The text describes the change in terms of a gradual change of awareness or disposition. No action occurs except the flight from heaven. As Francis I. Andersen explains in his note to this passage, the Satan here that becomes a demon is still a far distance from a dualistic ruler of hell or prince of darkness of the Qumran texts. The nature and exact reason for the resistance are unexplained here, but the J recension of *2 Enoch* 29:4 gives further detail:

> But one from the order of archangels deviated, together with a division that was under his authority. He thought up the impossible idea that he might place his throne higher than the clouds which are above the earth, and that he might become equal to my power.
> And I hurled him out of the height, together with his angels. And he was flying around in the air, ceaselessly, above the Bottomless.[46]

[45] Andersen, *1 Enoch*, 1:154.

[46] Charlesworth, *Old Testament Pseudepigrapha*, 1:148.

Here the cause of the eviction of the unnamed angel is the arrogance of power. The angel already has a throne but seeks a higher position.

The addition to the account of Satan's eviction from heaven of a cause—the refusal to worship Adam—is known from several accounts: the *Life of Adam and Eve*, the *Gospel of Bartholomew*, the Syriac *Cave of Treasures*, *3 Baruch* and the Armenian *Penitence of Adam*.

The *Life of Adam and Eve* exists in five recensions: Greek, Latin, Slavonic, Armenian, and Georgian, with some Coptic fragments, all of which derive from an original Greek version not equivalent to the surviving Greek text. The extant Greek recension, *The Apocalypse of Moses*, does not include the story of the revolt of Satan; nor does the Slavonic account include it. The Armenian recension, called the *Penitence of Adam*, is similar to the Latin version in length and has the same general plot but with variations in detail. The chart below compares the Latin and Armenian recensions. I have highlighted significant variations in italics:

Latin[47]	Armenian[48]
11. [Eve said to the devil,] "What have you to do with us? What have we done to you, that you should pursue us with deceit? Why does your malice fall on us? Have we stolen your glory and made you to be without honor? Why do you treacherously and enviously pursue us, O enemy, all the way to death?"	11:2. He was sad and called out great lamentation and said to Satan, "Why have you engaged in such a great conflict with us? What are our sins against you, that you have brought us out of our place? 11:3. Did we take your glory from you? Did we reject you from being our possession, that you fight against us unnecessarily?"
12. And the devil sighed and said, "O Adam, all my enmity and envy and sorrow concern you, since because of you I am expelled and deprived of my glory which I had in the heavens in the midst of angels, and because of you I was cast out onto the earth."	12:1. Satan also wept loudly and said to Adam, "All my arrogance and sorrow came to pass because of you; for, because of you I went forth from my dwelling; and because of you I was alienated from the throne of cherubs who, having spread out a shelter, used

[47] Ibid., 2:262

[48] Anderson and Stone, *Synopsis*, 9–13.

Latin	Armenian
	to enclose me; because of you my feet have trodden the earth."
Adam answered, "What have I done to you, and what is my blame with you? Since you are neither harmed nor hurt by us, why do you pursue us?"	12:2. Adam replied and said to him, 12:3. "What are our sins against you, that you did all this to us?"
13. The devil replied, "Adam, what are you telling me? It is because of you that I have been thrown out of there. When you were created, I was cast out from the presence of God and was sent out from the fellowship of the angels.	13:1. Satan replied and said, "You did nothing to me, but I came to this measure because of you, on the day on which you were created, for I went forth on that day.
When God blew into you the breath of life and your countenance and likeness were made in the image of God, Michael brought you and made (us) worship you in the sight of God, and the LORD God said, 'Behold Adam! I have made you in our image and likeness.'	13:2. When God breathed his spirit into you, you received the likeness of his image. Thereupon, Michael came and *made you bow down before God*. God said to Michael, 'Behold I have made Adam in the likeness of my image.'
14. And Michael went out and called all the angels, saying, '*Worship the image of the LORD God, as the LORD God has instructed*.'	14:1. Then Michael summoned all the angels, and *God said to them,* 'Come, *bow down* to *god whom I made*.'
And Michael himself worshiped first, and called me and said, '*Worship* the image of God, Yahweh.'	14:2. Michael bowed first. He called to me and said, 'You too, *bow down* to Adam.'
And I answered, 'I do not *worship* Adam.' And when Michael kept forcing me to worship, I said to him, 'Why do you compel me? I will not worship one *inferior and subsequent* to me. I am prior to him in creation; before he was made, I was already made. *He ought to worship me*.'	14:3. I said 'Go away, Michael! I shall not *bow down* to him who is *posterior* to me, for I am former. Why is it proper for me to bow down to him?'

15. When they heard this, other angels who were under me refused to worship him. *And Michael asserted, 'Worship the image of God. But if now you will not worship, the LORD God will be wrathful with you.'* And I said, 'If he be wrathful with me, I will set my throne above the stars of heaven and will be like the Most High.'	15:1. The other angels, too, who were with me, heard this, and my words seemed pleasing to them and they did not prostrate themselves to you, Adam.
16. And the *LORD* God was angry with me and sent me with my angels out from our glory; and because of you, we were expelled into this world from our dwellings and have been cast onto the earth.	16:1. Thereupon, God became angry with me and commanded to expel us from our dwelling and to cast me and my angels, who were in agreement with me, to the earth: and you were at the same time in the Garden.
And immediately we were made to grieve, since we had been deprived of so great glory. And we were pained to see you in such bliss of delights.	16:2–3. When I realized that because of you I had gone forth from the dwelling of light and was in sorrows and pains,
So with deceit I assailed your wife and made you to be expelled through her from the joys of your bliss, as I have been expelled from my glory."	16:4 then I prepared a trap for you, so that I might alienate you from your happiness just as I, too, had been alienated because of you."
17. Hearing this from the devil, Adam cried out with great weeping and said, "O Lord, my God, my life is in your hands. Remove far from me this my opponent, who seeks to destroy my soul, and give me his glory which he himself has forfeited." And immediately the devil disappeared from him. But Adam persisted forty days standing in repentance in the water of the Jordan.	17:1. When Adam heard this, he said to the Lord, "Lord, my soul is in your hand. Make this enemy of mine distant from me, who desires to lead me astray, I who am searching for the light that I have lost." 17:2. At that time Satan passed away from him.

Some key differences between the Latin and Armenian texts are that the Armenian version ascribes to Satan (not "the devil") arrogance rather than enmity and envy, and his initial description is not of eviction, but of a more voluntary "leaving." The Armenian version includes the surprising statement of "bowing down to *God*" (13.2) rather than "worshipping the image of God." In the Islamic material, bowing down is explicitly dissociated from worship. Further, in the Armenian version God issues the command to bow down to Adam, not Michael, as in the Latin version. In the Latin version, Michael has a slightly more prominent position than in the Armenian.

The Life of Adam and Eve has clear parallels with the Islamic story that is the subject of this study. Both describe the command that Satan/the devil bow down to Adam after God has breathed life into him. In both accounts Satan/the devil refuses, citing Adam's inferiority. In both, the result of that refusal is expulsion from heaven. Not every aspect here is in each Qur'ānic narrative, and there are significant differences in other details; those differences are the subject of later chapters.

Here in the *Life of Adam and Eve*, Satan is arguably in a tragic mode, victim as well as perpetrator of Adam's downfall. In the Latin version, Michael cites an instruction of God that is nowhere in the text. Michael commands worship to "the Image of the Lord God." Satan does not refuse to worship the image; he refuses to worship Adam. In the Armenian version, God commands worship, not to Adam, but to "god whom I made." In either case, the command given violates the fundamental ipseity of God. On those grounds, Satan's refusal is justified, but those are not the grounds that he gives. Rather he justifies his refusal on the basis of prior creation and, in the Latin version, superiority. In Satan's eyes these are convincing arguments, unrefuted by God or Michael, and supported by his minions. As is common in tragic figures, rationally defended justice cannot stand against the majesty of God.

The intent of the story may be to show Satan trying yet another deception on Adam by weeping false tears of anguish, yet through the rest of the text Satan is significantly absent. Adam does refer to Satan as his "opponent," but the text does not frame Satan in terms of the combat myth, but rather as a pitiful, if not pitiable, character.

The *Gospel* (or *Questions*) *of Bartholomew* gives a somewhat different account. The general tenor is much in the form of the combat myth, in contrast to the milder vision in *The Life of Adam and Eve*. Beliar is described in fearsome aspect—he is "1600 yards long and 40 yards broad. His face was like lightning of fire and his eyes like sparks, and from his nostrils came a stinking smoke."[49] In *The Gospel of Bartholomew* 4:25, Beliar informs us that Satanael became Satan when he rejected "the image of God." Later, in verse 28, he describes himself as the first angel created, formed by God from a handful of fire from the heavens before Michael, Gabriel, and the other archangels. Later he describes his downfall thus:

> 52. But the devil said: Allow me to tell you how I was cast down here, and how God made man.
> 53. I wandered to and fro in the world, and God said to Michael: Bring me earth from the four ends of the world and water out of the four rivers of paradise. And when Michael had brought them to him, he formed Adam in the east, and gave form to the shapeless earth, and stretched sinews and veins, and united everything into a harmonious whole. And he showed him reverence for his own sake, because he was his image. And Michael also worshipped him.
> 54. And when I came from the ends of the world, Michael said to me: *Worship the image of God which he has made in his own likeness. But I said: I am fire of fire, I was the first angel to be formed, and shall I worship clay and matter?*
> 55. And Michael said to me: Worship, lest God be angry with you. I answered: *God will not be angry with me, but I will set up my throne over against his throne, and shall be as he is*. Then God was angry with me and cast me down, after he had commanded the windows of heaven to be opened.
> 56. When I was thrown down, he asked the 600 angels that stood under me, whether they would worship (Adam). They replied: As we saw our leader do, we also will not worship him who is less than ourselves.
> 57. After our fall upon the earth we lay for forty years in deep sleep, and when the sun shone seven times more brightly than fire, I awoke. And when I looked around, I saw the 600 under me overcome by deep sleep.
> 58. And I awoke my son Salpsan, and took counsel with him how I could deceive the man on whose account I had been cast out of heaven.
> 59. And I devised the following plan. I took a bowl in my hand, and scraped the sweat from my breast and my armpits, and washed myself in the spring of water from which the four rivers flow. And Eve drank of it, and desire came upon her. For if she had not drunk of that water, I should not have been able to deceive her.[50]

[49] Hennecke, *New Testament Apocrypha*, 1:497; Nielsen, *Prodigal Son*, 79–105. See also Byrne, *Sons of God*; Cooke, "Israelite King," 22–47; Fossum, "Son of God," 128–37; Mullen, "Divine Assembly," 214–17; and Zimmermann, "Observations," 175–90.

[50] Hennecke, *New Testament Apocrypha*, 1:500 (italics mine).

Although the text describes Satan in fierce terms, the account of his fall is given in a rather matter-of-fact tone. A surprising twist here is Satan's expectation that God will not be angry with him (v. 55) and that God will allow him to set up his own throne as a counterpart to God. Satan here gives four reasons why he should not worship Adam: he is fire; he is first; Adam is only clay; and Adam is only matter. Three of these reasons are found in the Iblīs texts of the Qur'ān. The theme of a following of angels, who make their own decision not to worship, is also found in the Latin and Armenian Adamic books. The device used to awaken desire in Eve is a surprising twist.

The Cave of Treasures is a Syriac text that describes the history of the world from creation to the resurrection of Christ. The fall of Satan receives brief attention. God creates Adam from the four elements—earth, water, wind, and fire—and God announces to Adam, overheard by the angels, that Adam is created to be king, priest, prophet, governor, and lord of all creation. The angels respond by bowing the knees and worshipping him. But Satan responds differently:

> And when the prince of the lower order of angels saw what great majesty had been given unto Adam, he was jealous of him from that day, and he did not wish to worship him. And he said unto his hosts, "Ye shall not worship him, and ye shall not praise him with the angels. *It is meet that ye should worship me, because I am fire and spirit; and not that I should worship a thing of dust, which hath been fashioned of fine dust.*" And the Rebel meditating these things would not render obedience to God, and of his own free will he asserted his independence and separated himself from God. But he was swept away out of heaven and fell, and the fall of himself and of all his company from heaven took place on the Sixth Day, at the second hour of the day. And the apparel of their glorious state was stripped off them. And his name was called "Sâṭânâ" because he turned aside [from the right way], and "Shêdâ" because he was cast out, and "Daiwâ" because he lost the apparel of his glory. And behold, from that time until the present day, he and all his hosts have been stripped of their apparel, and they go naked and have horrible faces. And when Sâṭânâ was cast out from heaven, Adam was raised up so that he might ascend to Paradise in a chariot of fire.[51]

Here Satan is not the first formed of the angels but a prince of the lower orders. There is no command to the angels to worship Adam; it is a spontaneous

[51] Budge, *Book of the Cave of Treasures*, 55–56 (italics mine).

reaction to Adam's newly acclaimed role as lord over all creation. The reason for Satan's refusal is jealousy based on the superiority of fire and spirit over dust. As in the *Gospel of Bartholomew*, he instructs the legions under him not to worship and asserts his independence from God. There is no association given with Beliar and no references to any biblical texts. Two new names, "Shêdâ" and "Daiwâ," are given etiological explanations, as is the name "Sâåânâ." The text briefly describes the transfiguration of Satan, then the glorification of Adam, and finally the creation of Eve.

The *Greek Apocalypse of Baruch*, or *3 Baruch*, describes the heavenly journey of Baruch, the scribe of Jeremiah, through five heavens. There are two manuscript families, Greek and Slavonic, which diverge at points. In both, an angel (Samael in the Greek, Satanael in the Slavonic) plants the vine in the garden of paradise by which he later deceives Eve and Adam. The fallen angel narrative is not included, but Harry Gaylord has noted the following passage in a group of Russian manuscripts:

> And he said to Michael, Sound the trumpet for the angels to assemble and bow down to the work of my hands which I made. And the angel Michael sounded the trumpet, and all the angels assembled, and all *bowed down to Adam order by order. But Satanael did not bow down and said, To mud and dirt I will never bow down. And he said, I will establish my throne above the clouds and I will be like the highest.* Because of that, God cast him and his angels from his face just as the prophet said, These withdrew from his face, *all who hate God and the glory of God.* And God commanded an angel to guard Paradise. And they ascended in order to bow down to God. Then having gone, Satanael found the serpent and he made himself into a worm. And he said to the serpent, Open (your mouth), consume me into your belly. And he went through the fence into Paradise, wanting to deceive Eve. But because of that one I was cast out from the glory of God. And the serpent ate him and went into Paradise and found Eve and said, What did God command you to eat from the food of Paradise? And Eve said, From every tree of Paradise we eat; from this tree God commanded us not to eat. And having heard, Satanael said to her, God begrudged the way you live lest you be immortal; take and eat and you will see and give it to Adam. And both ate and the eyes of both were opened and they saw that they were naked.[52]

[52] Gaylord, "How Satanael," 303–9 (italics mine).

In this short passage, a surprising number of elements of the angelic prostration story are present. The angels are explicitly commanded to bow down to Adam, but the word "worship" is not used. Satan (Satanael) refuses because Adam is (mere) mud and dirt. Satan intends to establish his throne and seeks to be "the highest." Because of this intention, not his direct refusal to bow, God casts him and his angels out of heaven. Satan, in turn, blames Adam for his loss. Note here that Satanael and his followers "hate God and the glory of God." This is a strong element of the combat myth.

Concerning dates, all of these texts may well have been extant in some form or other prior to the Islamic period. Michael Stone and other scholars, however, support a date of the Latin *Life of Adam and Eve* translation in the early to mid-eighth century and the original Adam books, most likely in Greek, at a date earlier than the fifth century and most likely in the first to third centuries.[53] Whether a Christian or a Jew wrote them is unclear, since the imagined earliest form contains neither clear Christian references nor a clear connection to rabbinic material. *The Cave of Treasures* draws on this initial Adam book and therefore must be dated marginally later, but not later than 500.

Unlike the watcher and the heavenly prosecutor myths, which, although biblical, disappear from most later commentary, the fallen angel story has found a narrative life of its own. Although the story has minimal roots in the canon of the Tanakh or New Testament, it is elaborated in the extrabiblical tradition in multiple languages. The story grows and develops narrative emendations and alternative versions. Does Satan hate God? In a Russian manuscript of *3 Baruch* he does, but not in most other versions. Is Satan the first angelic creation? Yes, according to the *Gospel of Bartholomew,* but other accounts have no mention of this. Did Satan aspire to heavenly power? Yes, in *2 Enoch* and *2 Baruch*, but not in the *Life of Adam and Eve*. In *The Cave of Treasures*, he is already the "prince of the lower order of angels."

In several of these texts, Satan asserts his superiority over Adam as prior, superior, and of "fire" rather than "dust." These comparisons bring us to the last theme related to the Iblīs story: that of sibling rivalry.

[53] Stone, *History*, 53–58.

Sibling Rivalry

The literature on the Adam and Eve story as the origin of sin in the world is voluminous in Christian theological writing, but the issue here is not the origin of sin per se, but the origin of evil. Most renditions of the Adam and Eve story understand their error not as one of intentional malice, but rather of vulnerability, misjudgment, and even naïve innocence. They are expelled from paradise not because they intentionally defy God (as does Satan in many renditions of the fallen angel motif), but because they believe the serpent's interpretation of God's command. The innocence of Eve's action and Adam's replication of that action allow Jewish tradition (in contrast to Christian tradition) to interpret the story in a positive light, for instance, as humanity coming of age.

Malice comes to light in the story after the expulsion from Eden, the story of Cain and his murder of Abel.[54] There is no possibility of any positive interpretation of the Cain and Abel story.

While Christian theology identifies the Adam and Eve story as the origin of sin understood as distance or separation from God, both Christian and Jewish accounts interpret the Cain and Abel story as the origin of evil understood as malicious actions toward others on earth.

The story is complex and subject to many different interpretations. The text in Genesis 4 is as follows:

> 1 Now the man knew his wife Eve, and she conceived and bore
> Cain, saying, "I have produced a man with the help of the LORD."
> 2 Next she bore his brother Abel. Now Abel was a keeper of sheep,
> and Cain a tiller of the ground. 3 In the course of time Cain brought
> to the LORD an offering of the fruit of the ground, 4 and Abel for
> his part brought of the firstlings of his flock, their fat portions. And
> the LORD had regard for Abel and his offering, 5 but for Cain and
> his offering he had no regard. So Cain was very angry, and his
> countenance fell. 6 The LORD said to Cain, "Why are you angry, and
> why has your countenance fallen? 7 If you do well, will you not be
> accepted? And if you do not do well, sin is lurking at the door; its
> desire is for you, but you must master it."[55] (NRSV)

[54] A good overview of the story from a narrative perspective can be found in Van Wolde, "Story," 25–41.

[55] The middle part of this verse, *lap-petaḥ ḥaṭṭā't rōbēṣ*, is a difficult clause to sort out: literally "at/to the door—sin—crouching." It is grammatically unorthodox and not the expected sequel to the first clause.

> 8 Cain said to his brother Abel, "Let us go out to the field."[56] And
> when they were in the field, Cain rose up against his brother Abel,
> and killed him. 9 Then the LORD said to Cain, "Where is your
> brother Abel?" He said, "I do not know; am I my brother's keeper?"
> 10 And the LORD said, "What have you done? Listen; your brother's
> blood is crying out to me from the ground! 11 And now you are
> cursed from the ground, which has opened its mouth to receive your
> brother's blood from your hand. 12 When you till the ground, it will
> no longer yield to you its strength; you will be a fugitive and a
> wanderer on the earth." 13 Cain said to the LORD, "My punishment
> is greater than I can bear![57] 14 Today you have driven me away from
> the soil, and I shall be hidden from your face; I shall be a fugitive
> and a wanderer on the earth, and anyone who meets me may kill
> me." 15 Then the LORD said to him, "Not so![58] Whoever kills Cain
> will suffer a sevenfold vengeance." And the LORD put a mark on
> Cain, so that no one who came upon him would kill him.
> 16 Then Cain went away from the presence of the LORD, and settled
> in the land of Nod, east of Eden. (NRSV)

The text itself is full of gaps and blanks, and invites, and receives a great deal of often contradictory interpretation and commentary. What help did Eve receive from the LORD? Why was Cain's offering not accepted? Why did God have difficulty understanding why Cain was downcast? Why did Cain take his anger out on Abel? Why did an omniscient God ask Cain where his brother was? From whom did Cain fear retribution, since he was now the only man on earth, save his father, Adam? What is the sevenfold vengeance and what is the mark? For each of these questions, and many others as well, there is much speculation, but the question of the source and nature of Cain's anger leads to the subject of the source and nature of evil.

Louis Ginzberg introduces his summary of rabbinic interpretation as follows:

> Wickedness came into the world with the first being born of woman, Cain, the oldest son of Adam. When God bestowed Paradise upon the first pair of mankind, He warned them particularly against carnal intercourse with each other. But after the fall of Eve, Satan, in the guise of the serpent, approached her, and the fruit of their union was

[56] Cain's invitation to go out to the field is not included in the Hebrew Masoretic Text but is found in all Greek, Latin, Syriac, and Samaritan texts.

[57] Or: "My guilt is too great to be forgiven" (*gādôl ʿăwônî min-nĕśōʾ*).

[58] Or: "Therefore" (*lākēn*).

> Cain, the ancestor of all the impious generations that were rebellious toward God, and rose up against Him. Cain's descent from Satan, who is the angel Samael, was revealed in his seraphic appearance. At his birth, the exclamation was wrung from Eve, "I have gotten a man through an angel of the Lord."[59]

The idea that Cain was the fruit of a union between Eve and the serpent derives from a variant reading of Gen 5:3, noting that Seth was in the likeness and image of Adam (see parallel with Gen 1:26), but this is not said of Cain. This story is found in *Pirke de Rabbi Eliezer* 21, *Targum Pseudo-Jonathan* Gen 4:1, and in the New Testament in 1 John 3:12 and perhaps John 8:44.[60] There are further allusions to such an idea in several of the early church texts. This divine or semidivine origin of Cain puts him in the position of being, as Ginzberg suggests, the origin of wickedness in the world.

Even texts that do not cite this particular legend tend to see the world as divided between the children of Cain and the children of Abel. Josephus tells the story this way:

> 52. There were born to them [Adam and Eve] two male children. The first of them was called Cain (J: *Kais*) and this name, being interpreted, signifies "acquisition"; and the second was called Abel (J: *Abelos*), and it signifies "nothing."[61] Daughters were also born to them. 53. Now the brothers rejoiced in different pursuits. Abel, the younger, had regard for righteousness and, believing that God was present in all the things that were done by him, looked after virtue; and his life was that of a shepherd. On the other hand Cain was both most wicked in other respects and, looking only to gain, was the first to think of ploughing the earth; and he killed his brother for the

[59] Ginzberg, *Legends*, 1:107. The last comment from Eve forms the first verse of the Cain story (Gen 4:1).

[60] Maher notes that "B. Shabbat 146a, Yebam 103b and Abod. Zar. 22b say that the serpent copulated with Eve, and/or infused her with lust, but they do not say that he fathered Cain" (Maher, *Targum Pseudo-Jonathan*, 31 n. 2). Bowker adds that the legend is recorded more fully in the *Kitāb al-Majāl* 94b-95a: "Satan retained his envy of Adam and Eve because of the favor which the Lord conferred upon them. And he contrived to enter into the serpent, which was the reason why Iblīs, the cursed, hid in the serpent was his ugliness. . . . And if Eve had seen him without his being hidden in the serpent when she spoke with him, she would have fled from him" (Bowker, *Targums*, 126).

[61] Feldman uses the transliteration of Josephus's Greek renditions of the names. I have relegated these to parentheses and used the more familiar names: Cain, Abel, and later on, Nod and Enoch. Otherwise I have reproduced Feldman's translation.

following reason.
54. It seeming best to them to sacrifice to God, Cain offered fruits from the cultivation of the soil and plants, while Abel offered milk and the first-born of the grazing animals. God took greater pleasure in this latter sacrifice, being honored by things that grow automatically and in accordance with nature but not those things that grow by the force of grasping man with craftiness.
55. Consequently, Cain, provoked that Abel had been more highly valued by God, killed his brother and rendering his corpse unseen, supposed he would escape unnoticed. But God, being aware of the deed, came to Cain, inquiring about his brother, whither he had gone, since He had not seen him for many days, whereas at all other times He had beheld him in His company.
56. Cain, being at a loss and not having anything to reply to God, kept answering at first that he too was perplexed at not seeing his brother, but angered by God's persistent pressuring and detailed examination, he said that he was not the guardian and custodian of him and his deeds.
57. God thereupon now accused Cain of being his brother's murderer and said, "I am amazed that you are unable to say what has happened to a man whom you yourself have destroyed."
58. However, He exempted him from penalty for the murder, since he had offered a sacrifice and through this had supplicated Him not to devise too harsh an anger against him; but He made him accursed and He threatened that he would punish his descendants during the seventh generation, and He cast him out of that land together with his wife. . . .
61. And increasing his property through a great quantity of possessions acquired through robbery and force, enticing to pleasure and robbery those who crossed paths with him, he became a teacher to them of wicked activities. And then by invention of measures and weights he transformed the simple life with that men had previously lived, leading into knavery their life, that had been guileless and magnanimous owing to their ignorance. . . .
66. And while Adam (J: *Adamos*) was still alive, it happened that the descendants of Cain became most villainous, in succession and in imitation each one ending up worse than the other. They entered into wars without restraint and they rushed headlong into robbery. And if someone was hesitant about butchering he showed his boldness in another form of recklessness through being insolent and greedy.[62]

[62] Josephus, *Judean Antiquities*, 18–23.

In Josephus's account, Cain and Abel prefigure the opposition between those who choose good and those who choose evil, or between the farmer and the shepherd, and between the "natural man" and the city dweller. Here there is no concept of Cain being the child of Satan—in fact both Cain and Abel are introduced as the children of Adam and Eve. No explanation for his turn to greed is given; his greediness is self-generated and is the cause of all other evil.

Philo also uses Cain and Abel to describe contrary human attitudes.[63] The New Testament Epistle of Jude warns, "Woe to them, for they go the way of Cain and abandon themselves to Balaam's error for the sake of gain and perish in Korah's rebellion." The "way of Cain," which is clearly not restricted to murder, needs no explanation here. David Kevin Delaney describes it as "continuous and contagious disobedience."[64]

In early Christian commentaries, Abel comes to symbolize both Christ and the church, making Cain the representative of the scribes and Pharisees and of the Roman persecutors.[65] Following a tradition found in the *Testament of Abraham,* Rec. B, Abel comes to be the heavenly judge of souls, the sympathizer for all martyrs.[66]

Five aspects of this story and its interpretation are worthy of note in this study. The first is that Cain is often given a somewhat supernatural origin as the child of Eve and the serpent (or the fallen angel in the serpent), or some other genesis. Yet Cain is not himself regarded (apart from gnostic literature) as in any way divine. Rather he is the firstborn of humanity, the archetypal human in some ways. This parallels the ambiguous status of the *jinn* and particularly of Iblīs as a *jinn* among angels. Muslim commentators discuss at length whether *jinn* are a species of angel or a more terrestrial sort of being. This topic will be discussed further in chapter 5.

The second point is that the actual cause of Cain's anger, or of the rejection of his sacrifice, is never clear in Genesis 4. The secondary literature—Jewish, Christian and gnostic—is replete with explanations and tends to expand the nature of his sin from a single event to Delaney's "continuous and contagious disobedience." Whatever Cain's error, for all of its ambiguity, it becomes the source of all error.

[63] Philo, *On the Sacrifices of Abel and Cain*. See discussion in Delaney, "Sevenfold," 58ff.

[64] Ibid., 64–65 n. 24.

[65] Glenthøj, *Cain and Abel*, 26.

[66] In the *Testament of Abraham*, Rec. A 11:9, the judge is Adam, but in the parallel passage in Rec. B 12:2, it is Abel. See Charlesworth, *Old Testament Pseudepigrapha*, 1:871–902.

Thirdly, there is a tradition that after his sacrifice was refused, Cain sought to climb the holy mountain and take up his case with God. The mountain refused to allow this access to the divine precincts, driving Cain to seek another outlet to "grieve God." This outlet was Abel.[67] In this story, the object of Cain's anger was God, and the murder of Abel was simply a means to express that anger, having been denied a more direct route. This construction of events is triangular, directly involving not simply the siblings, but also God. Similarly, the Iblīs story triangulates, in various ways depending on the version, himself, Adam, and God. This raises the question as to the degree to which human events are offenses against other humans or against God, and what the relationship between those two dimensions might be.

Fourthly, as in the Iblīs story, Cain receives respite from his punishment. The explanation for this is the subject of a great deal of speculation.[68] It is incongruous that God would spare him, especially since one of the fundamental holy laws applying to all of humanity is that the penalty for murder is death.

Finally, although the Cain and Abel story fits into the sibling rivalry pattern, it also upsets the pattern, since it is not the younger, Abel, who confidently emerges the victor. Ultimately, however, Seth replaces Abel. Seth becomes the son made in the image of Adam (who himself is made in the image of God, Gen 5:3, 1:26). Although Western Christian interpretation tends to move the characters of Cain and Abel into typologies of good and evil, similar to Jewish sources such as the writings of Philo and Josephus, later Jewish interpretation and Eastern Christian interpretation resist the tendency toward such binary opposition. In other words, Latin Christian interpretation moves to absorb the Cain and Abel story into the combat myth, but Jewish and Syrian Christian interpretation, in parallel with other sibling rivalries in the Scriptures, move in a different direction. Eastern Christian interpretation tends to emphasize free will to a greater extent and to de-emphasize the power of original sin. It de-emphasizes, if not totally ignores, any implication that Cain is a child of Satan.

The Jacob and Esau narrative (Genesis 27), the rejection of Saul in favor of David (1 Samuel 15), the rejection of Leah (Genesis 29), and the story

[67] This story is recorded in Ephrem Graecus, *Homily on Cain and the Murder of Abel* (see Glenthøj, *Cain and Abel*, 38).

[68] See Eichhorn, *Cain*, 85–104; LaCocque, *Onslaught against Innocence*; and Mellinkoff, *Mark of Cain*. See also Quinones, *Changes of Cain*, for treatments of the story in literature.

of the prodigal son (Luke 15:11–32) in the New Testament all repeat the sibling rivalry theme. Northrop Frye notes that literature carries the theme of passing over the firstborn to the relationship between Lucifer and Christ particularly in the fifth chapter of Milton's *Paradise Lost*.[69]

Kristen Nielsen has argued that the idea of sibling rivalry between Satan and various mortals beloved of God can be found in biblical texts themselves.[70] She points out that the *śāṭān* in the Book of Job is one of the "sons of (the) God" (*bĕnê hā-'ĕlōhîm*; 1:6), and Job is likewise treated as a "son" in the particular way that close relationships of humans to God are often described in terms of father-son relationships.[71] She treats the conflict between Job and the *śāṭān* as a sibling rivalry and notes that the story is related in Jewish tradition to the Jacob and Esau story through Job's marriage to Dinah, a daughter of Jacob, and his own descent from Esau.[72]

Nielsen follows the same theme in the temptation narrative in Matt 4:1–11, where Satan, the inheritor of the temporal world,[73] challenges the new "king" and tests his acumen and awareness of divine prerogatives (and Satan's own prerogatives). A similar interpretation can be induced from the "Parable of a Father and Two Sons" (the "Prodigal Son" story) in Luke 15:11–32.

That there is a rivalry here is undeniable. To call it "sibling" stretches the point a bit. In the encounter between Satan and Jesus in the desert, both are answerable to God, and both inherit dominion over the earth. In the *śāṭān*/Job narrative, although *śāṭān* is numbered among the sons of God, Job is not. On the other hand, God protects Job in a special way—one might say, "like a son."

Of all the sibling rivalries in the biblical tradition, the extended narrative of the conflict between Jacob and Esau (Genesis 25–35) tends to be paradigmatic. It is a complex story, beginning with the struggle between the twins to emerge first from the womb. Esau sells his birthright to Jacob for a mess of pottage, and Jacob tricks his father Isaac into giving him the blessing meant for Esau. In all of this, the machinations of Rebecca favor the younger Jacob. After the theft of the blessing, Jacob flees. He comes into his

[69] Frye, *Great Code*, 180–81.

[70] Nielsen, *Prodigal Son*.

[71] See Byrne, *Sons of God*; Cooke, "Israelite King"; idem, "Sons of (the) God(s)"; Fossum, "Son of God"; Mullen, "Divine Assembly"; and Zimmermann, "Observations."

[72] Nielsen, *Prodigal Son*, 89. See also Ginzburg, *Legends*, 2:225.

[73] It is natural to relate the Christian understanding that the temporal world is ruled by Satan to the common Muslim assignment of Iblīs to the lowest heaven: *al-samâ' al-dunyā*.

own only after reconciling with Esau years later, a scene in which Esau calls Jacob "my brother" (Gen 33:9), but Jacob calls himself "his servant" (Gen 33:24). As well as providing great fodder for psychological explorations of the reconciliation of opposites and politico-historical explanation of the relationship between Israel (Jacob) and Edom (Esau), the story highlights the paradigm that Israelite history repeats throughout: that God may favor the younger over the elder and upset tribal norms for divine purposes.[74]

The most productive comparison to the Iblīs story, however, remains the narrative of Cain and Abel. In a sense, just as the Iblīs story represents the bifurcation of good and evil prior to the Adamic expulsion from paradise, so the Cain story represents a similar bifurcation after the expulsion. Iblīs, a creation of God "from fire," is in direct competition with Adam, a subsequent creation of God from clay. When the younger Adam is preferred to the elder Iblīs, the latter turns to a life of crime, tempting Adam and all of his descendents.

In keeping with the various biblical sibling rivalries described above, which do not devolve into a polarity of good and evil sons, the Jewish tradition focuses its attention on the concept of a good and an evil "impulse." Explanations of "the evil impulse" (*yēṣer hā-ra'*) commonly draw on verses of the Cain and Abel story.[75]

> The Holy One, blessed be He, spoke unto Israel, "My Children, I created the evil yetzer, but I created the Torah as its antidote. If you occupy yourselves with the Torah, you will not be delivered into his hand, for it is said, 'If thou doest well, shalt thou not be exalted.' (Gen 4.7) but if ye do not occupy yourselves with Torah, you shall be delivered into his hand, for it is written, 'Sin croucheth at the door.' Moreover, he is altogether preoccupied with thee (to make thee sin) for it is said, 'And unto thee shall be its desire.' Yet if thou wilt, thou canst rule over him, for it is said, 'and thou shalt rule over him.'"[76]

[74] A good overview of the sibling rivalry motif and its various interpretations can be found in Fox, "Stalking the Younger Brother," 45–68. On the other hand, Frederick E. Greenspahn has questioned whether any "rule" of primogeniture existed in Israelite society ("Primogeniture in Ancient Israel," 69–80).

[75] Bulka, "To Be Good or Evil"; Cohen Stuart, *Struggle*; Hirschberg, "Eighteen Hundred Years"; Leaman, *Evil and Suffering*; Lowry, "Dark Side," 88, 100; Porter, "Yecer Hara"; and Rosenberg, *Good and Evil*.

[76] Cohen Stuart, *Struggle*, 61. The quotation comes from bQid. 30b. (Babylonian Talmud [Bavli] tractate Qiddushin). Another verse that figures importantly is Gen 8:21, from the

Jewish interpretations of the story increasingly come to give more positive interpretations of Cain, perhaps in response to decidedly negative interpretations in the early Christian tradition.[77] The *yēṣer hā-ra‘* comes to be understood not simply as an inclination to evil balanced by a *yēṣer ṭôb* (inclination to good) but also as a necessary part of human nature:

> The idea that the evil yetzer is indispensable is found in bSan. 64a. A variant reading is the following: "Three good conditions the Holy One, Blessed be He, created in this world. They are the evil yetzer, envy, and mercy. If there is no evil yetzer, no man occupies himself with the duty of propagating the human race. If there is no envy, no man occupies himself with planting. If there is no mercy, the world does not endure."
> Gen. R. 9.7 "R. Nachman said, in R. Samuel's name, 'Behold, it was very good' Gen 1.31 refers to the good yetzer, and 'And behold, it was very good.' to the evil yetzer. Can the evil yetzer be very good? That would be extraordinary. But for the evil yetzer, however, no man would build a house, take a wife and beget children. And thus said Solomon, 'Again I considered all labor and all excelling in work, that it is man's rivalry with his neighbor.' Eccl. 4.4."[78]

Christian interpretation is less sanguine about any virtues of Cain and prefers a clearer typology that associates Cain with Satan or even with Judas Iscariot[79] and Abel with Christ. But the diptych of Cain and Abel is still, or even more so, a paradigm of the nature of good and evil. Various commentaries on the story show remarkable parallels with the Iblīs story in Islam. There is no indication at all of any historical connection, but what we seek, and see here, are typologies: narrative patterns of stories. So we find in a Syriac poem from the fifth century an echo of Iblīs's argument to God for his primogeniture. Cain says to Abel:

> I am the eldest, and so it is right that He should accept me, rather than you; but He has preferred yours [sacrifice], and mine He has abhorred,[80]
> and:
> Cain: He would have accepted me rather than you had you not done

Noah story: "For the *yēṣer* of a man's heart is evil from his youth."

[77] Glenthøj, *Cain and Abel,* 14.

[78] Cohen Stuart, *Struggle*, 19.

[79] Brock, "Two Syriac Dialogue Poems," 333–75.

[80] Ibid., 351.

> me this wrong: you are younger in both age and intelligence. Yet you took first place with the first fruits.[81]

In the story of Iblīs, particularly in Sūrat al-Ḥijr (ch. 6), echoes of sibling rivalry between Iblīs and Adam occur. A similar tendency to absorb the rivalry into the combat myth with elements of the heavenly prosecutor, also emerges in later *sūrahs*, as in the Latin Western tradition of Christianity. The story retains enough elements of the sibling rivalry to allow future commentators to build upon those aspects and to de-emphasize the binary opposition of mortals and al-Shayṭān.

Patristic Literature

The four mythic streams described earlier are all the inheritance of the early theologians of the Christian church.[82] The Gospels had placed the combat myth in a central position in Christian thought with a passing mention of a fallen angel in Luke 10:17 and no mention of the watcher myth. The divine prosecutor, *haś-śāṭān*, had fully cast off his judicial robes and become the enemy of Christ. Early literature, such as the *Shepherd of Hermas*, imagined two angels within the human soul, or speaking to the soul, one urging good and the other evil, with other angels sent by Christ to assist the weary Christian. But even the righteous angel chastises, as the *Sixth Similitude* explains,[83] which does recall the role of the *śāṭān* of Job.

All four mythic streams freely mixed in patristic literature with themes from gnostic traditions. Justin Martyr discusses fallen angels as having grosser bodies than good angels, combining the tradition of angels of nations and cities with the watcher tradition.[84] Irenaeus describes the devil as an angel, created good, but falling from grace into apostasy, rejecting the gnostic idea of the world as the product of an evil creator.[85] As late as Lactantius, the watcher myth still works into a complex story of primordial sin, fallen angels, and fallen humans. Jeffrey Burton Russell gives a rough chronology as follows: 1) creation of the spiritual world; 2) fall of Satan through envy of

[81] Ibid., 354.

[82] For general discussion of the devil in early Christian tradition, see Russell, *Satan*, and Forsyth, *Old Enemy*, 309–418.

[83] *Herm. Sim.* 6.3; *Ante-Nicene Fathers* 2.37.

[84] Justin Martyr, *Second Apology,* ch. 5; *ANF* 1:190.

[85] Irenaeus, *Against Heresies*. 4.37, 4.41, 5.21–24; *ANF* 1:518, 524, 548–54.

Christ, his "antecessor"; 3) creation of the material world, including human beings; 4) fall of humans; 5) fall of the other angels before the flood, through lust for women.[86]

As Christian theology moved from reacting to various heresies toward systematization, the mythic stories grew less useful. The watcher story became rare after Lactantius (ca. 240–320) and Methodius (d. ca. 311). Augustine makes no use of the watcher story and little of fallen angels. His theology of evil draws more from Aristotle and the concept of privation and the formal nonexistence of evil.

At the same time, the desert tradition turned the earlier absorption with persecution to an inner focus on the devil's persecution of the soul through temptation. The enemy is within but still personified as the enemy of Christ. The desert is the battleground, and Athanasius's popular *Life of Anthony* describes the pitched battles of the lone monastic with fierce animal passions and guides others toward an acute discernment of good and evil spirits.

From Augustine, the Christian tradition inherited a systematic, philosophical approach to the problem of evil. From the desert tradition, Christianity inherited a rich personal awareness of combat with the devil, who progressively grew more exotic in form, while, in the Augustinian tradition, retaining no existence in actuality.

Conclusion

These five typologies, narratives of the origin and nature of evil, are useful tools for the examination of the Iblīs story. Each narrative provides an angle of vision, a set of questions to bring to each of the seven versions of the story that we find in the Qur'ān. It does not matter whether a particular telling in, for instance, Sūrat al-Kahf or Sūrat al-Ḥijr, falls into one narrative type or another—that is not the purpose here. The purpose is to fine-tune our perception so that our reading is acute and astute, and the ingenuity of the text is disinterred. The knowledge that we gain is only as good as the questions that we bring. Putting the various types of explanations of evil in the Bible in comparison, one sees more and notices more.

We then become informed readers with a broad repertoire embracing the variety of narratives that have been used elsewhere to explain evil. With that knowledge we read each new narrative, testing whether it is a repetition of

[86] Russell, *Satan*, 156. See Lactantius, *Inst*. 2.9–15; *ANF* 7:52–64.

this type, a new twist on that type, or something entirely new. Like a student of English literature, who reads and discovers a multitude of devices that authors use to tell a story or describe a character, the point is not to develop a classification of types, but to be more aware of the way each author, and every new author one encounters, engineers the telling. It is all about asking the right questions, but even more it is about careful reading and rereading—letting the story reveal its layers and subtleties. To this work we now turn.

CHAPTER 4

Sūrah ṬāHā (20)

The first two versions of the Iblīs story we will consider, in this chapter and the next, are in Sūrah ṬāHā (20) and Sūrat al-Kahf (18). Both of these versions are short summaries of the Iblīs story with no dialogue, rendered as the direct discourse of God in the first person plural "We." All other versions of the Iblīs story are told by a narrator who describes the action from a neutral, third-party perspective, and most involve dialogue between Iblīs and God (15, 38, 7, 17, but not 2).

Structure

Sūrah ṬāHā consists of 135 *āyah*s, beginning with the mysterious letters that give it its name—Ṭā-Hā. Tradition ascribes this *sūrah* to the Meccan period, the 45th *sūrah* revealed, and associates it with the conversion of 'Umar. In his introduction to the *sūrah,* al-Qurṭubī tells the story according to Ibn Isḥāq, about a man who told 'Umar that some of his family had converted to Islam. 'Umar, at that time, was a fierce opponent of Muḥammad and returned to his house to tend to this shameful situation. Coming close to the house, he overheard his sister Fāṭima reciting Sūrah ṬāHā and was moved. When he entered, Fāṭima hid the sheet from which she was reciting, but he demanded to read it. She gave it to him, and he was moved to convert by the nobility of the words.[1] Al-Qurṭubī also relates a *ḥadīth* from al-Dārimī that "God recited (ṬāHā) and (YāSīn) a thousand years before he created the heavens and the earth, and when

[1] Al-Quråubï, *Al-Jāmi'a*, 11.85 (vol. 6) (translations mine). The story can also be found in Guillaume's translation of the *Sīra* of Ibn Isùäq, Ibn Hishäm, *Muhammad*, 156.

the angels heard the recitation they said, 'Blessed be the people to whom this is revealed and blessed be the breasts that bear this, and blessed be the tongues that utter this.'"[2] These traditions seem to testify to the significance of several verses that refer specifically to the Qur'ān itself, most importantly *āyah*s 113, which identifies the Qur'ān as "Arabic," and 114, which informs the hearers that the Qur'ān is not yet complete.

The *sūrah* displays a particular organic character that is unusual in the Qur'ān. It moves gradually and consistently from an irenic tone at the beginning to a stronger, more admonitory tone at the end.

One theme that pervades the *sūrah* is that of mystery and hiddenness, of private conferences and secrets; this emphasis is signaled by the very mystery of the initial letters, Ṭā-Hā. As the major story of the text unfolds, the story of Moses, we find a succession of plots on the part of Pharaoh, then his magicians, then Moses himself in his secret escape from Egypt, and finally the incident of the worship of the golden calf in Moses' absence. We will also find this theme picked up in the *sūrah*, in the al-Shayṭān story of the temptation in the garden. Related to this hiddenness is the earthy humanity of the characters presented here. Like characters in a novel, they stumble through their tasks with suspicion, boldness, fear, indecision and impulsiveness. The evil characters are often presented with some empathy, if not quite sympathy, and the noble characters show their deficiencies.

The Iblīs story is told in its most rudimentary form in this *sūrah*. It comes towards the end, in v. 116:

> *wa-idh qulnā li-l-malā'ikat isjudū li-ādama fa-sajadū illā iblīsa abā*
>
> And when we said to the angels, "Bow down to Adam," they bowed down—except Iblīs; he refused.

The text then moves directly to the al-Shayṭān story of the temptation in the garden, which is given in seven verses with subsequent commentary. How shall we interpret the meaning of so short a narrative of the Iblīs story?

Most Muslim commentary, as we have said, reads the narrative horizontally, combining it with other narratives in the Qur'ān, and commenting on the composite story as opposed to this particular narrative. On the other hand, a canonical and narrative reading seeks to understand the text in terms of

[2] Al-Qurṭubī, *Al-Jāmi'a,* 11.86 (vol. 6).

the surrounding narrative, particularly that narrative which dominates the *sūrah*, the story of Moses. Such a reading assumes that the Iblīs narrative in some way continues, modifies, or advances the meanings established by the preceding text. Particularly when the narrative is so brief, its importance must be referential, derivative from and supportive of the larger context. Hence, the bulk of this chapter will focus on the Moses narrative against which the Iblīs narrative will be read.

Introduction to the *Sūrah*

After the initial letters, Ṭā-Hā, which bear no explanation (though many have been proffered),[3] the text proceeds with words of comfort: "(2) we did not send to you the Qur'ān so that you should be distressed (*qur'ān li-tashqā*), (3) but (as) a reminder to those who fear (*li-man yakhshā*)." The assonance of two roots for "fear" *kh-sh-a* and *kh-w-f* and a root for "distress," *sh-q-'* and "hidden," *kh-f-'* is notable throughout the *sūrah*. Synonyms, such as *sirr,* "secret," and *kayd*, "plot," carry the theme further though the story.

Following doxological assertions of God's authority, verse 7 initiates the theme of secrecy: "if you proclaim aloud the word (*qawl*), then truly He knows the secret (*sirr*) and the more hidden (*akhfā*)." It is not clear if the declaration (*qawl*) referred to means the revealed *qur'ān* of verse 2 or to any declaration. Nor is it clear what is meant by that which is "secret" and that which is "more hidden." Hence the reference not only announces a mystery but dramatizes it.

The Moses Cycle

The Moses story occupies two-thirds of the *sūrah*, the longest version of the Moses narrative in the Qur'ān and one of the Qur'ān's longest stories altogether. This extended story gives us opportunity to explore the application of reader-response theory to the Qur'ān, and, at the same time, to outline the themes of the *sūrah* in order to understand the short Iblīs story within it. Like the Iblīs story, the Moses narrative exists in different versions. It differs from the Iblīs story in that Moses participates in several distinct narratives, portions of which appear in different *sūrahs*. We will see this when we look

[3] For an overview of interpretations of the "mysterious letters," see Massey, "Mysterious Letters," 3:471–76.

at Sūrat al-Kahf, which has a unique Moses story not included in the Moses cycle in Sūrah ṬāHā or elsewhere.

The story of Moses begins at v. 9 of Sūrah ṬāHā with the question that we have already noted in chapter 2, "Has the story of Moses come to you?" The expectation seems to be that the hearers should know the story. Towards the end of the Moses cycle, in v. 80, the *Banū Isrā'īl* are addressed. If they are the addressees of v. 9, then it would be expected that it is they who should know the story of Moses, but they are not mentioned prior to v. 80, so one cannot assume this.

The story is told by a narrator. The *pluralis maiestatis*, the "magisterial We," last appears in v. 2, after which the Moses story speaks of God in the third person. The first story is that of a fire (the "burning bush" of Exodus 3) which Moses investigates. A voice speaks from the fire, announcing God's presence and identity, and God's choice of Moses, though the purpose of the choice is held in suspense for several verses. First, God establishes Moses' obligations: to serve God and establish prayer. Then God warns that "the Hour" is coming, but God will "keep it hidden" (*ukhfīhā*). The word can also mean "to reveal," but that interpretation would both contradict the clear Qur'ānic idea that the timing of the Hour is not revealed[4] and also violate the theme throughout the *sūrah*, especially of v. 7.

Verses 17 through 23 give an account of two miracles—that of the stick turning into a snake and of Moses' hand turning white—which God, not Moses, performs in preparation for sending him to Pharaoh. The section ends with God's instruction to Moses to go to Pharaoh, for "he has transgressed the limit (*ṭaghā*)."

God's command to Moses unleashes a staccato series of requests—really commands—from Moses to God. This marks an abrupt change in the tone, since up to this time Moses has said very little. His only words to God have been in answer to God's question about his staff (v. 18). There Moses gives an answer of four clauses that also have a clipped quality. This gives force to Moses' complaint that he has an impediment of speech. In contrast to God's flowing prose, Moses' speech is awkward and abrupt. Mostly, he listens.

With God's command to go to Pharaoh, Moses carries on for eleven verses with seven requests, counting as three the request for aid from his family (29), that his helper be Aaron (30), and that God add to Moses' strength (31).

[4] See Q. 36:49f, 7:187, which refers not only to the unknown timing of the hour, but also to its suddenness, i.e., God will not reveal it ahead of time.

The verses are very short, breaking the pattern of the previous text. The rush of requests ends with a promise to praise God and a doxology. This provides a prelude to another theme that appears more clearly later in the *sūrah*, the theme of patience. Towards the end of the Moses cycle, Moses will "hasten" ahead of his people, providing the occasion, if not the cause, of his people's turning to the golden calf. In v. 114, the people are urged not to be impatient with the gradual unfolding revelation of the Qur'ān. In v. 130, the people are encouraged to be patient with those who disbelieve. Finally, in the last verse of the *sūrah*, v. 135, Muḥammad is instructed to say to the people, "All are waiting, so wait." Moses is depicted here as one given to haste. The tenor of his speech carries this sense of impatience and anxiety.

The subsequent section vv. 37–41, relates the story of Moses' birth, presented as a continuation of God's response to Moses' entreaties. As God responds patiently and positively to Moses' current litany of requests, God recalls two previous favors, his salvation from Pharaoh's death order (not mentioned) after birth and his salvation from trouble after murdering a man. There is little context given to the first story. Unless one is familiar with other versions, the listener has no idea why Moses' mother is being encouraged to throw Moses into a box and throw the box into the sea. The story implies a reader with a repertoire of knowledge beyond the text, perhaps that knowledge that is contained in Sūrat al-Qaṣaṣ, 28:4–7. The implied reader would have to notice what is absent in this telling. The people of Israel are strangely absent, the focus being entirely on Moses. The household of Pharaoh, or any indication that Moses is raised in an Egyptian household, or raised any differently from other Hebrews, or, for that matter, that he is a Hebrew and not an Egyptian—all these are not mentioned or are only vaguely intimated.

Sūrat al-Qaṣaṣ (28) gives a fuller version of the story of Moses which supplies most of these details. The implied reader, in Iser's sense, would likely be one familiar with the rest of the Qur'ān, at least once it was fully revealed, and so could have the background of Sūrat al-Qaṣaṣ as well as shorter anecdotes given elsewhere, such as in Sūrat al-'Arāf, 7:103–137, Sūrah Yūnus, 10:75–92, Sūrah Hūd, 11:96–99, Sūrat al-Shu'arā' 26:10–69, and Sūrat al-Nāzi'āt, 79:15–26. Yet the depiction of Moses is decidedly different in these other versions. Sūrat al-Shu'arā', for example, reflects the diffidence of Moses in the way we have found in Sūrah ṬāHā, but there his nobility comes strongly to the fore in confrontation with Pharaoh. In Sūrat al-Kahf, Moses also comes across as one who is unfailingly wrong, as we will describe in the next chapter. Here, in Sūrah ṬāHā, Moses is consistently hesitant and fearful.

Our study is an attempt to read this version of the narrative in isolation, noting its unique telling of the story, without presuming any particular repertoire of knowledge on the part of the reader/listener, yet aware that most readers will bring either some knowledge of the biblical story, or, more likely, knowledge of other Qur'ānic versions to their reading of the Moses cycle in Sūrah ṬāHā.

These stories are presented not as an original telling, but, as noted before, as a reminder (*dhikr*) of the story and an interpretation of it for didactic purposes. Because the implied reader is one seemingly expected to have a fuller story in mind (though what fuller story we cannot know), we should note what gaps and blanks are present. We cannot expect that those gaps and blanks will necessarily be filled with either the biblical version or the other Qur'ānic versions, or, for that matter, with the legends reported in the *qiṣaṣ al-anbiyā'* collections of al-Kisā'ī, al-Tha'labī, or others, or the histories of al-Ṭabarī, Ibn Kathīr, al-Diyārbakrī, and their colleagues. By reading *this* version carefully, we may be able to determine what the message of *this* rendering might be, with the particular shape that the narrator has given the story in *this* context.

This raises a particular question that should be addressed before proceeding further. Should we assume that the reader/listener would not automatically bring the rest of the inclusive Moses story, collected from all the different locations in the Qur'ān, immediately to bear in the reading of this story? We have already pointed out that some parts of the story—the casting of Moses into a box and then into the sea in v. 39 stands out—make little sense without the background which is provided in Sūrat al-Qaṣaṣ, 28:7. Should we consider modifying the Iserian notion of the implied reader that suggests that the reader may fill the gaps in the text with anything in his or her own repertoire, though the author has brought a particular repertoire to the writing of the text? Has the author assumed that, "of course," the reader will read this particular rendering of the Moses story along with the other renderings in the Qur'ān? Or, put more succinctly, are the other renderings of the Moses story *presumed*, by the author, to be present in the repertoire of the implied reader? This assumption would critically undermine any possibility that a particular telling—this telling in Sūrah ṬāHā—could possibly be read alone, as a carefully crafted, complete story in its own right.

This is a significant concern, since each *sūrah* ultimately does not stand alone, but is to be heard and read as part of the larger revelation. To be sure, Sūrah ṬāHā itself warns us, in v. 114: "Do not be impatient with the Qur'ān before its revelation to you has been completed, but say, 'Lord, increase knowledge for me.' " Here it is helpful to remind ourselves of the distinction that Iser makes between "gaps" and "blanks." A *gap* is a break in the story without great significance, simply because a narrator cannot tell all without boring the audience to somnolence. A *blank* is a break in the narrative that is designed to, or has the function of, inviting, even necessitating, the reader/listener to shape the narrative and thus enter into it. A blank wants to be filled, and by its presence indicates a particular intention on the part of the author. A gap will be filled in by the reader in order to allow visualization of the story, but it reflects no conscious intention on the part of the author.

While it may be most likely that other Qur'ānic versions will fill in the blanks in the story, we cannot assume that the missing information is missing only for the sake of convenience, perhaps to shorten the *sūrah*. It may be that blanks in the story serve to encourage or require a synthetic knowledge of the Qur'ān, in which one is constantly cross-referencing the various narratives to compose the amalgamated story. This would be a natural way of reading, even a traditional way of reading, but it is not the only way of reading. This synthetic reading strategy acts to diminish the effect of each particular telling since one would be, in one's mind, reading what Iser calls the "literary work," *this* story *plus* all the other stories combined into one, a *diatessaron*[5] of the Qur'ān. This approach would lessen the significance of each version since the assumption would be that the Qur'ān always intends the whole, the composite story. This also effectively belittles the value of the Qur'ān as a holy text in which each word and each passage are revelatory in their own right. Our approach to the Qur'ān directs us to the uniqueness of each formulation of the story and the precision of its expression and design.

We will proceed on the assumption that the blanks in *this* telling are there precisely to involve the reader/listener in the story, to convey a meaning or message in texts that could be classified as *mutashābihāt*. The blanks

[5] The *Diatessaron* was a compilation of the Gospel story in one continuous narrative, arranged by Tatian about 150–160 C.E. It was popular for several centuries, but gave way to the four separate Gospels. No copy has survived, but it is known through late translations, one surviving fragment, and early commentaries. See Petersen, *Tatian's Diatesseron*.

in *this* telling of the story reflect an authorial intention to shape the story in a particular way relevant to the theme of the particular *sūrah* in which it is found. There is, of course, missing information that cannot be filled by material in the Qur'ān but may still be part of the repertoire of the original and early readers. It is here that we will look to the legendary corpus in commentaries *bi-l-ma'thūr*, histories, and other literature.

We might also add a chronological dimension to this problem. According to the traditional Egyptian chronology, the Moses story in Sūrah ṬāHā is preceded only by the version in Sūrat al-'Arāf, 7.103–157, which presents the encounter with Pharaoh, the golden calf episode, and the giving of the tablets of the law. Most Western commentators put Sūrat al-'Arāf after Sūrah ṬāHā, making Sūrah ṬāHā the earliest version of the Moses story.[6] If the latter is true, then the first hearers of this revelation would not have had the fuller rendition of Sūrat al-Qaṣaṣ to explain the gaps. This may explain the counsel in v. 114, "Do not be hasty for the Qur'ān before its revelation is complete to you." The chronology is always uncertain, but the probability that the version of the Moses story in Sūrah ṬāHā precedes those other versions of the story that would explain it supports an approach that would read this version without filling in information from subsequently revealed *sūrahs*. It would initially have been read and heard on its own.

The Confrontation with Pharaoh

Verse 39 also introduces another term which will recur later, that of the "enemy," *'adūw*. The one who will retrieve Moses from the river is an enemy to God and an enemy to Moses, but God will protect Moses with his love (*maḥabbah*). He will be reared under the eye of God (v. 39), but also under the eye of his natural mother (v. 40). The two are set in parallel; God watches over Moses *through* his mother, but also *like* a mother. The story briefly chronicles Moses' murder of a "soul" (*nafs*) and his sojourn in (not flight to) Midian. God has afflicted or tested (*fatana*) Moses throughout. This is explained in v. 41: God has prepared (*aṣṭana'tuka*) Moses for his current work. The narrative returns us to the command to Moses to go to Pharaoh, first raised in v. 24. The intervening dialogue has provided background, but also established certain elements about the character of Moses: his uncertainty

[6] Nöldeke places the brief versions in *Sūrahs* 51:38–40 and 79:15–26 earlier than that in Sūrah ṬāHā; the traditional Muslim dating puts only Sūrat al-'Arāf earlier (Nöldeke, *Sammlung des Qorāns*, 104–5). See chart in Watt, *Introduction*, 206–11.

that provokes him to make demands upon God, his awkwardness of speech of which he is aware, his troubled life in which God has tested him, and God's protection of him that parallels the image of the watchful "eye" with the protection of his mother. The story then introduces a further tension in that, though Pharaoh is described as an enemy in v. 39, in v. 44 the possibility of his conversion is held forth: "Speak to him a gentle speech (*qawl^{an} layyin^{an}*), perhaps he will be reminded or fear (*yakhshā*)." The irenic tone established at the beginning of the *sūrah* continues; fear is qualified by gentleness.

The encounter between Moses (with Aaron, always included in the dual pronouns but never speaking or mentioned by name) and Pharaoh is respectful. Moses approaches Pharaoh with fear, however. More so than any other *sūrah*, here fear is a recurring element, both fear of God and fear of people and situations. Sūrat al-Nāzi'āt (79) also stresses the aspect of fear, but its focus is to emphasize the importance of fearing God and the last day, whereas Sūrah ṬāHā serves to assuage distress and fear of the words of the Qur'ān (v. 2), of Pharaoh (vv. 45–46), of Pharaoh's magicians (v. 67), and of Pharaoh's pursuit (v. 77). Other situations do not explicitly mention fear but convey the same feeling, such as the grief of Moses' mother at the loss of her child (v. 40).

Pharaoh inquires about the God of Moses with no indication that his questions are at all insincere. His second question concerns the condition of previous generations, to which Moses replies that only God has such knowledge. The hiddenness of God's knowledge is a point already made in v. 7. From this dialogue the text moves into a doxological statement about God's responsibility for creation, shifting from the narratorial voice to the magisterial "We." This provides a bridge to the next dialogue. Verse 56, still in the magisterial voice of God, gives an opening statement of what is to come: "We showed him our signs, all of them, then he rejected and he refused (*abā*)." The next verse records Pharaoh's question to Moses, though the position directly after God's magisterial statement makes it appear to be a response to God. A response to Moses, a messenger of God, *is* a response to God.

Pharaoh, responding to Moses' (and God's) reference to signs (*āyāt*) as proofs of God's authority and power, draws on his own ability to produce magicians who can perform signs, though the text never refers to the actions of Pharaoh's magicians as "signs." They are (merely) magic. Pharaoh also states that Moses' intention is to "drive us from our land." This is a surprise. There has been no mention of territorial dispute, or of threat to

Pharaoh's dominion. Moses has described the benefits of his Lord in terms of beneficence not to himself, but to Pharaoh, in vv. 53–54. Nevertheless, they set a meeting time for the contest of magic.

The recurrent theme of secrecy characterizes the account of the contest. Pharaoh makes a secret stratagem (*kayd*; v. 60), and the magicians dispute in secret (v. 62) and counsel Pharaoh that his sovereignty and government are under threat, so he should devise a stratagem. This information might have led Pharaoh to the conclusion given already in v. 57, yet it is seemingly only presented to him in v. 63. This discrepancy goes unremarked in the text. Al-Ṭabarī and al-Qurṭubī explain the earlier conclusion as a response to the signs, but do not address why Pharaoh might respond this way. Al-Zamakhsharī simply describes Pharaoh as trembling in fear.[7]

In v. 67 it is Moses who "becomes apprehensive in his soul with fear," the redundancy of the expression giving a sense of depth and pervasiveness to the feeling. Once again the Moses presented here is not the authoritative and noble messenger of God, but an uncertain servant, uncomfortable in the presence of Pharaoh, lacking confidence in the part he has been called upon to perform. God reassures him, the magisterial "We" returning, giving this reassurance intimacy and force, and making the subsequent actions of Moses a response to direct commands of God. It thus becomes God who performs the trick, with Moses as the physical instrument. The actual performance is passed over in silence, the text moving immediately to the awed reaction of the magicians, who prostrate themselves and make immediate confession to the "Lord of Aaron and Moses."[8] Pharaoh protests their change in allegiance and threatens them, but they answer boldly and at length, arguing that the proofs (*bayyināt*) establish God and His decrees as higher than those of Pharaoh.

The summary beginning in v. 74 compares those who come before the Lord as believers with those who come before the Lord as sinners. But there is another implicit comparison from the tenor of the story, between those who discover the Lord, convinced by proofs, and those who persist in their (dis-)belief. Though Pharaoh is the dominant figure in the story, it is the magicians who steal the show, first counseling Pharaoh concerning the dangers of Moses and his intentions, and then responding to Moses'

[7] Al-Qurṭubī, *Al-Jāmi'a,* 6.129; al-Ṭabarī, *Jāmi'*, 16.176 (vol. 9); and al-Zamakhsharī, *al-Kashshāf*, 3.71 (translations mine).

[8] The juxtaposition of Aaron and Moses here is notable, given that Aaron has nowhere been named in the preceding dialogue and planning. Moses is, however, given the prominent last position in order of naming.

demonstration with an immediate and comprehensive declaration of their own change of heart and allegiance.

Since the actual feat that Moses, or God through Moses, performs is not described (though the text implies that Moses throws his stick and it became a snake as per the demonstration at the encounter with the fire in v. 20), the emphasis of the narrative shifts away from the proof of magic and is directed towards signs that have been evoked throughout the text—the fact of creation and the fruitfulness and expanse of the earth. But even more, the attention of the story is on the changeableness of human character. The text initially presents Pharaoh as one who might possibly be convinced (v. 44), but then the magicians as ones who actually are convinced, against all expectations. There is no preparation at all for the sudden conversion and testimony of the magicians. On the other hand, the text describes Moses, the messenger of God, as vacillating, unsure, and requiring the constant encouragement of God. This is not presented in any way as a negative evaluation of Moses. He receives no criticism for his fit of fear in the face of Pharaoh's magicians. It is simply taken as a normal human response. Moses is one chosen (v. 40), watched (v. 39), prepared (v. 41) and equipped (vv. 25–36) by God, but never devoid of need for God's guidance. As we have mentioned before, this portrayal of Moses contrasts significantly with his image in other Qur'ānic narratives.

The next story in the Moses cycle is the story of the golden calf. Without going into detail, we may note two significant aspects. First, the overwhelming theme throughout this section is that of division. From the first verse, v. 83, Moses is separated from his people, absent from them. When he returns and questions the people, we have one group of people answering, but blaming another group of people who say of the golden calf, "This is your god" (v. 88). Aaron is divided from the people who will not obey his command (vv. 90–91), and he urges Moses not to accuse him of dividing the people (v. 94). The mysterious al-Sāmirī, who never appears elsewhere in the Qur'ān, divides the people by urging the creation of the golden calf, and then in turn is expelled from them by Moses. The people blame al-Sāmirī in v. 87, mentioning also their own limitation of power.

Second, the general impression in the story is that no one is fully capable. Moses is out of touch, both physically and mentally, with his people. Aaron presumes to command them, something that Moses does not do. Al-Sāmirī violates Moses' trust and is expelled. The people are divided in some way not described (v. 94) and vaunt their incapability of resisting the suggestions of al-Sāmirī, even as al-Sāmirī is incapable of resisting the suggestions of his own mind (v. 97). This vulnerability to suggestion echoes the similar helplessness of Moses when confronted by the Egyptian magicians (v. 67). All in all, the weakness of Moses as a character, upon which we have commented earlier, not only continues here but expands to include other leaders of Israel—Aaron and al-Sāmirī—and the people themselves.

The Moses cycle ends with a doxological section including a stronger reference to the day of judgment than we have seen before. This continues until v. 112, followed by an affirmation that the Qur'ān will explain to the believers what is necessary. Here we also have the reminder that the Qur'ān is, as yet, incomplete.

The Iblīs Story

This brings us, finally, to the short section dealing with Adam, Iblīs and al-Shayṭān. The transition is mysterious. The preceding doxology focuses on the Qur'ān as a reminder and a warning to the addressees of the *sūrah*. In v. 115, God, "We," mentions Adam as one with whom a covenant is made, but "he forgot, and we did not find in him a firm will." Adam, like Moses in the lengthy cycle before, is characterized as feeble. He forgets the covenant that God made with him. Further, he demonstrates a lack of resolve (*'azn)*. This should not surprise us. The *sūrah* as a whole has given the reader a litany of weak characters in responsible positions who fail in those positions: Moses conceiving fear before Pharaoh, Aaron failing to prevent the apostasy of the people, al-Sāmirī causing their apostasy, and, of course, the people themselves willingly following the counsel of al-Sāmirī. Now we have Adam, forgetting the covenant and weak in resolve. Since Adam is the first-born of humanity, his weakness is the paradigm of all human weakness.

All of this leads to the command of God to the angels to prostrate themselves to Adam. They do so, but Iblīs does not. He refuses:

> *wa-idh qulnā li-l-malā'ikati sjudū li-ādama fa-sajadū ilā iblīsa abā*
>
> And when we said to the angels, "Bow down to Adam," they bowed down—except Iblīs; he refused. (v. 116)

This is the extent of the Iblīs story, the core element that is in all seven versions of the story, but it comes as a surprise, a reversal. Given that Adam has just been portrayed as a forgetful and weak character, in the tradition of Moses, Aaron, and al-Sāmirī, it is not surprising that one might not want to be prostrate to such as him. The action of Iblīs seems entirely understandable in the face of the preceding verse, indeed in the face of the entire *sūrah*. Admittedly, the *sūrah* is quite clear that God has all authority. The presumption that one must obey a command of God is not weakened. Yet, at the same time, the command contrasts with the tenor of what has come before.

It is also entirely consistent with what has come before. Though Moses is presented as a fallible character, he is nevertheless the one chosen by God to confront Pharaoh and meet with God on the mountain. Though Adam is forgetful and weak of resolve, he is nevertheless chosen as one to whom the angels must prostrate themselves. This prostration is, the text clearly implies, not due to any special virtue of Adam, since it describes no virtue. Rather, the prostration is based solely on the command of God.

The artistry of the story presents no such argument or explanation. The contrast between the thorough censure of Adam and the subsequent expected adoration of him remains. The reader must draw his or her own conclusions.

There is also a confused sequence of actions here. The heedlessness of Adam would presumably refer to his eating from the tree that God had forbidden to him, but that event, in all other versions, comes *after* the Iblīs debacle. Clearly narrative order is not important here. The issue is obedience. Adam forgets, but Iblīs disobeys.

Iblīs, who appears in the *sūrah* only here, is neither condemned nor punished for this refusal. Like a similar refusal by Pharaoh in v. 56, also a refusal to believe signs or obey a direct command, this defiance goes without comment. Punishment is not the focus of the *sūrah*, weakness is.

The narrative goes directly into a different story, the account of Adam and his wife in the garden. Welch argues that the Iblīs story of the refusal to prostrate himself and the al-Shayṭān story of encounter in the garden are distinct stories that are combined late in the process of revelation.[9] Indeed, he uses this distinction as an element in his dating system. Those *sūrahs* in which the Iblīs story is associated with the al-Shayṭān/garden story (*sūrahs*

[9] Welch, "Pneumatology," 64–78.

2, 7, and 20) are for that reason later than those *sūrahs* in which the Iblīs story stands alone (*sūrahs* 15, 17, 18, and 38).

In our analysis, such a separation is not quite so clear. The al-Shayṭān account begins directly following the Iblīs verse, introduced with a *fa*, indicating continuation:

> *fa-qulnā yā ādamu inna hādhā ʻaduwun laka wa-li-zawjika fa-lā yukhrijannakumā min al-jannati fa-tashqā*
>
> Then we said, "O Adam, truly this is an enemy to you and to your wife, so do not let him get you two out of the garden so that you will be miserable."[10] (v. 117)

One would assume that "this" enemy refers to Iblīs. This is not necessarily so. Nowhere in the Qur'ān is Iblīs explicitly related to al-Shayṭān. The garden story is always associated with the Iblīs story, though not the other way around. Only here is there a hint that Iblīs is the enemy who tempts Adam and his wife in the garden.

Al-Shayṭān whispers to Adam, inviting him and his wife to eat of the tree of eternity. They follow al-Shayṭān's suggestion and their *sawā'*, "offense"—more specifically their private parts—becomes apparent to them, so they seek leaves in the garden to stitch together to make clothing. The narrator concludes:

> *wa-ʻaṣā ʻādamu rabbahu fa-ghawā*
>
> and Adam disobeyed his Lord and went astray. (v. 121)

This is likely the forgotten covenant of v. 115, though the chronology is still problematic. The human characters in the *sūrah* continue to be portrayed, with good reason, as fallible. God turns to Adam, chooses Adam, just as God chooses Moses (v. 13, using a different verb), and gives him guidance, but enmity continues to characterize human relations.

God's final comment, addressed directly to Adam and his wife, begins with a command ("Go down!") and continues on to assert that there will be mutual enmity. The text itself is unclear about the nature of the enmity. The command to "go down" (*ahbiṭā*) is in the dual, evidently addressed to

[10] The misery mentioned here recalls the misery in the very first verse of the *sūrah*: "We have not sent down the Qur'ān to make you miserable."

Adam and his wife. In that case the enmity would be between and among their progeny. However, the dual of "Go down!" is followed by *jamī'a* (altogether). This addition suggests that al-Shayṭān is also commanded to go down, which could mean that al-Shayṭān is the enemy of Adam and his wife, and indeed of all humanity.

Al-Ṭabarī and other commentators interpret the enmity to Adam and Eve as that of Iblīs and his progeny,[11] of Iblīs and the snake,[12] or of all humanity contending and warring in a general condition of disorder of the species. In general, the commentators prefer to interpret the enmity as that between humanity and the evil spirits—Iblīs, al-Shayṭān, the snake, and so forth—than as a state of conflict among people. Al-Bayḍāwī, however, sees this as enmity among all people.[13]

In truth, the various explanations are not mutually exclusive. Perhaps the fairest interpretation is "all of the above." Enmity, like fallibility, is a characteristic of humanity. Certainly enmity is rampant throughout the *sūrah*.

The commentaries address this question in terms of Iblīs, but in the garden story it is not Iblīs who tempts the first couple; it is al-Shayṭān. The presumption of the commentaries, and indeed of Muslim tradition throughout the generations, is that Iblīs and al-Shayṭān are one and the same. Yet, as already noted in chapter 2, Iblīs is never, in the Qur'ān, included in the garden story.

To examine the Iblīs story itself requires us to resist this elision of Iblīs and al-Shayṭān and focus on the narratives told explicitly about Iblīs. The al-Shayṭān/garden story, being always associated with the Iblīs, is of interest because of that association, but the garden story is not itself an Iblīs story, and must not be treated as such.

The *sūrah* ends with more exhortation to patience and a final *qul!* statement presumably addressed to Muḥammad that advises him that all are waiting for the fuller revelation that will identify those who are on the straight path.

Conclusion

Sūrah ṬāHā portrays its central characters, Moses, Aaron, al-Sāmirī, and finally Adam, as flawed individuals, much in need of guidance from God.

[11] Al-Ṭabarī, *Jāmi'*, 16.224 (vol. 9).

[12] Al-Qurṭubī, *Al-Jāmi'a*, 11.169 (vol. 6).

[13] Al-Bayḍāwī, *Tafsīr,* 2.60 (translations mine).

Iblīs plays a very small role, as an actor rather than a character.[14] Separate from the larger Qur'ānic context, the brief Iblīs narrative gives its attention to Adam, not Iblīs. There is no condemnation of Iblīs for the refusal to bow down to Adam. On the contrary, given the low regard for Adam's qualities, the refusal to show respect, much less adoration, is quite understandable. In later *sūrahs*, especially in Sūrat al-Ḥijr, we will see the theme of the unworthiness of Adam become clearer. Here it is only quietly implied through a careful, thematic reading of the whole *sūrah*. If Adam is as faltering as Moses, as helpless as al-Sāmirī, and/or as incompetent as Aaron, why should Iblīs prostrate himself to him? Such a question is not raised in the Iblīs story itself. The single verse is the barest skeleton of the narrative. If we read the story as a story about Iblīs, then we can read it as an example of the defiance of an angel (since there is no suggestion here that Iblīs is at all different from the congregation of angels that were commanded to prostrate themselves to Adam). However, if we read the Iblīs story as a part of the story of Adam, who is the subject of the verse before and the verses afterwards, then we can see that Iblīs's refusal to bow down to Adam is not primarily because of Iblīs's fallibility, but because Adam is described immediately before as forgetful of God's covenant, and immediately after as gullible and disobedient.

The *sūrah* as a whole tells a series of stories of encounter, each for the purpose of calling people to God's path. God sends messengers and messages. Moses encounters God at the burning bush and subsequently is commissioned and sent to Pharaoh and his minions, and to the Israelites. He brings a message not only from God, but also from creation. All the fullness of the earth is a message to Pharaoh and to all humanity. This message, variously delivered, ought to be utterly convincing, but humans are fallible—all of them—and the message is often rejected.

The *sūrah* escalates in the gravity and difficulty of accepting and following the command of God to believe. Moses has, perhaps, the easiest challenge. His first encounter with God begins with a sign, a fire that is unusual enough that he already knows it could be a source of guidance (v. 10). God presents Moses with a proposition—really a command. Before Moses can respond to God's directive, God provides proof of his power. God preempts Moses' possible, even likely, objections. Even with a bold demonstration of miracles—a staff turned into a serpent and back, a hand

[14] This is an exception to the rule. Normally it is Iblīs who performs as a character and al-Shayṭān who is simply a dynamic of evil. In this telling it seems the other way around.

diseased and then healthy—Moses squirms, bellyaches, and makes demands on God. But God is patient.

Moses then approaches Pharaoh in similar fashion, with command and proofs. It is not God who approaches Pharaoh but rather a messenger of God, a little less imposing than a burning bush. Moses is not presented in the *sūrah* as a very imposing figure. Pharaoh cannot have been much impressed. He nevertheless listens. Perhaps he might be convinced and turned (v. 44). This is somewhat surprising since he is described as an enemy of God and an enemy of Moses (v. 39). In the end Pharaoh refuses, but it takes a while.

The third case is that of the magicians. They play a surprisingly important role in the story. They arrive as Pharaoh's pride and joy, the ones who, at his bidding, will prove Moses and his claims to be empty. They plot and plan their assault on Moses, sure to crush him and his God. Instead it is they who are defeated. Not only do they fail in front of their ruler, but in an act of extraordinary boldness, they abandon their sovereign and convert in his very presence to the God of Moses. The magicians, in the end, are more decisive than Moses.

The fourth case is that of the people of Israel. They have seen the power of God that saved them from Pharaoh, but all of this associated with the leadership of God's messenger, Moses. When Moses leaves for the heights of Sinai, Aaron shows his inability to comprehend and keep the instructions of Moses, and al-Sāmirī steps in to deliberately mislead them. In the face of great pressure to erect the golden calf, the people of Israel fall victim, or at least that is how they represent themselves.

The Israelites have been called to the way of God and have seen some benefits from that, but God's presence has always been joined with the presence of Moses. When Moses leaves, it is as if God has left, and al-Sāmirī is there to fill the void. It is not clear from this story what their final disposition is.

The fifth case is that of Adam, or we might say Adam story #1. Adam makes a covenant with God and then forgets. He errs, but he does not disobey as do Pharaoh and the Israelites. On the other hand, with the brevity of the statement, there is an implication that Adam's forgetting is not an incident of forgetting, but a quality of forgetting. Adam is perpetually forgetful of his covenant with God.

Finally we come to Iblīs. As with Adam story #1, the narrative is brief. Unlike the previous Adam story, the text describes a specific incident. Yet, because of the context, the crime is the most serious of all. Iblīs is among the angels, no mere mortal. He needs no message or messenger because he lives in the presence of God. He needs no proofs, no burning bush or serpentine staff. God commands him directly. The command is quite simple, two words, *usjudū li-ādama* (bow down to Adam), and Iblīs, equally, simply and directly, refuses. Iblīs cannot even claim the excuse of temptation or human fallibility. He is a heavenly figure, an angel. The felony of defiance reaches into the very habitation of God. This crime is the most severe.

However, if the story is read not as a story about Iblīs, who quickly disappears from the scene, but as a continuation of the saga of Adam, the disobedience of Iblīs becomes almost incidental. The text actually does not characterize him as disobedient, but only describes an action—"he refused."

There is one final step in the story. Seemingly just another story of an encounter with God, a command, and a failure, Adam story #2, the temptation in the garden, is the only story of failure with a direct consequence. Not only are Adam and his spouse evicted from the garden, the two of them consequently enter into a new reality of enmity. However one might understand "you are enemies to one another," the result is seemingly perpetual conflict, suffering, challenge, and difficulty. Humanity is not simply fallible, but immersed in adversity.

Truly, the end of the story is the beginning. One might say that all of the difficulties that Moses, Pharaoh, the magicians, Aaron and the Israelites encounter derive from that initial error of Adam in that the consequence of his primal act is life in the turmoil of enmity for all future generations. The Iblīs story demonstrates that though God still believes in the worthiness of Adam and requires his angels to recognize that virtue, there are grounds, revealed by Iblīs, for coming to a different conclusion. Adam is *not* worthy of reverence, and Adam proves it again and again. The story is not about Iblīs and God, but about Iblīs and Adam. Which of the two is the stronger character? It is not Adam.

The focus of Sūrah ṬāHā seems to be a series of descriptions of human responses to God's command. Some obey and some consistently disobey, but most stumble along through the challenges of life, failing and achieving, erring and repenting. Are these, or the primordial ancestor of these, worthy of reverence? Iblīs, exercising independence of thinking, votes no. Other versions in other *sūrah*s expand on the Iblīs story, adding different meanings and complexities.

CHAPTER 5

Sūrat al-Kahf (18)

Sūrat al-Kahf (18) gives a longer rendition of the Iblīs story than that of Sūrah ṬāHā (20) previously considered, although still in a single *āyah* (v. 50). It will also add more to our understanding of Iblīs

Structure of the *Sūrah*

The general structure of Sūrat al-Kahf is based on three lengthy narratives: the story of the companions of the cave (*kahf*) or "Seven Sleepers" (vv. 9–26), the story of Moses and a mysterious "Servant of God" commonly understood to be Khiḍr (vv. 60–82), and the story of the equally mysterious Dhū al-Qarnayn (vv. 83–98). The first story emphasizes the confusion or lack of knowledge on the part of the companions and all who are around them. The second story of the travels of Moses and the Khiḍr-figure shows the lack of knowledge on the part of Moses, which here contrasts with the comprehensive knowledge of the servant. The third story, continuing the trend, shows the depth of knowledge and the supernatural power of Dhū al-Qarnayn. References to God's knowledge and power as creator throughout the *sūrah* support this first theme. In the case of the companions, their own ignorance is aggravated by the diversity of reports about them. A complement to this theme of limited mortal knowledge is a second theme of God's protection given to believers. This protection comes directly from God to the companions of the cave, and through the Khiḍr-figure and Dhū al-Qarnayn to various populations in the latter two narratives. Two shorter stories, a parable of two men and the Iblīs story, lie between the longer story of the companions of the cave and the two stories of Moses and Khiḍr and add dimensions to both themes.

A third theme that emerges periodically through the story is the issue of associating partners, particularly children, with God. That issue immediately raises the question of encounter with Christians who claim Jesus as the Son of God. Since the "companions of the cave" story is known in pre-Islamic times specifically as a Christian narrative, this clarification of a major disagreement with Christianity should not be surprising. But no evidence suggests that this story in the Qur'ān is revealed in the context of any actual encounter with Christians.

The three themes—limited mortal knowledge, divine protection, and the lack of partners for God—are closely entwined. Although the Khiḍr-figure and Dhū al-Qarnayn provide protection, they do not do so independently or as partners of God, but only as agents. At the same time, because of the weakness of the people, protection, either directly from God or through agents, is continuously necessary.

Therein lies the problem. It is easy to say that God is the only protector and that protection is based on God's knowledge (v. 26), but when one adds the factor of divine agents, one has introduced the issue of discernment. How does one know which person (using that term broadly) is a legitimate agent of God, a purveyor of God's protection? The *sūrah* examines a number of possibilities: a partner of God (No!); the companions of the cave (No), Iblīs (No), the knowledgeable attendant (Yes), Dhū al-Qarnayn (Yes). How might one discern the legitimate agent (*walīy*) from the imposter?

The Text

The *sūrah* begins, as most do through this period, with reference to the revelation (*al-kitāb*) in the first three verses. God sends down the Book to "his servant," whom we would normally take to refer to Muḥammad. In the context of the narrative in the *sūrah*, the Khiḍr-figure is also identified as a servant of God, and the presumption is clear that Dhū al-Qarnayn should also be so regarded. There is no claim, however, that they have received books or are given "revelation." In fact, the use of the term *kitāb* here, implying a written text rather than *qur'ān*, a recitation, clarifies the different roles of the recipient of the Book and of those other servants who also protect, but not by bringing textual guidance.

As if to clarify the status of all these servants in their various capacities, the reference to the Book is followed by the first warning against assigning to God a son (vv. 4–5). This assignment is identified as a falsehood and an invention. Those who believe such a thing (Christians) did not hear it from "their fathers," meaning the ancestors who retained the unaltered revelation to and through Jesus. The contemporary reader should not accept information from previous generations uncritically. The consequence of hearing this claim from the ancestors is likely to be anxiety—are the ancestors to be trusted?

The introductory passage ends with a reference to God's creative powers, put in the context of a test. God will test the people and can as easily produce a barren plateau as a lush landscape (vv. 7–8).

The Companions of the Cave

The story of the companions of the cave (vv. 9–26) has no referent in the Bible but draws on a widespread Christian tradition of the seven sleepers of Ephesus (imaginatively explored by Louis Massignon).[1] The populace threatens the companions of the cave at the time of their retreat to the cave and later upon their awakening (v. 20). God protects the youths in the cave, even turning them from time to time (v. 18). They are aroused in order to test the "two parties," who are not identified (v. 12). One might assume these to be the believers and unbelievers, but in verse 19 the companions are questioning each other.

The story makes several points. First, it provides a model for any community threatened by those who worship other than God (v. 16). For the beleaguered Muslim community in Mecca, the parallel must have been comforting. Ibn Isḥāq's *Sīra* of Muḥammad specifically cites the story in this vein.[2]

Secondly, God's protection and care of the companions is emphasized throughout. God covers their ears in the cave (v. 11) and warms the cave with sunlight (v. 17). In a touching and detailed passage, God turns them on their right side and then on their left, perhaps to protect them from cramps

[1] Massignon, "Les sept dormants," 59–112. Massignon's article is continued in seven subsequent sections in the same journal through 1962. See also the article in *EI²* (*Encyclopaedia of Islam*, 2nd ed.) by Rudi Paret, s.v. "aṣḥāb al-kahf," 1:691.

[2] Ibn Hishām, *Muhammad*, 137–39.

or bedsores during their long sleep. The dog stretches his forelegs over the mouth of the cave, and any passers-by are terrified.

Thirdly, the signs of God are constantly contrasted with the confusion of the youths (v. 19) and the bearers of the story (v. 22). The companions cannot figure out how long they have been asleep, and their speculations—a day, or part of a day—are wildly in error. Only God tells—or knows—the story in truth (vv. 13, 26). They have been asleep for 300 years. Those who report the story are uncertain as to the number of companions: Three? Five? Seven? Plus the dog? God warns against such controversies (v. 22) and urges that any plan be accompanied by *illa an yashā' allah* (unless God wills it; vv. 23–24). Human knowledge is limited. The stories passed down from the past are sometimes uncertain or flawed. Verse 26 sums up the themes of God's protection and privileged knowledge: "Say: God knows how long they remained; with him is the mystery (*ghayb*) of heaven and earth; he observes it and he hears it; they have no protector (*walīy*) apart from him; he does not share his rule (*ḥukmihi*) with anyone." This last element reflects the concern about a "son" raised in verse 4, but also raises questions and qualifications about the roles of Khiḍr and Dhū al-Qarnayn later in the text.

The design of the story of the companions of the cave reinforces the problems of relying on stories from the past. God introduces the story, asking not whether the listeners "remember" the story—the standard introduction for biblical stories—but rather whether the listeners consider this one of God's signs. God then tells the story in brief, in three verses (vv. 10–12). The next segment gives a commentary on the story, first giving detail as to the situation that forced their retreat to a cave (vv. 14–16), then detailing their sleep in the cave (vv. 17–18), and then describing their waking confusion (vv. 19–20). The text proceeds to describe the reception of the tale by the people who debate the details of the story (vv. 21–22). God makes the story known as a proof of the promise of God, specifically about the hour of judgment (which has not been raised earlier in the story), but the people want to make a place of prostration (*masjid*) over the companions. This last element would raise similar concerns about partnership with God. The text does not pursue this, although commentaries do.[3]

[3] Al-Ṭabarī reports, "God blinded those who discovered the place of the Companions of the Cave; they were not rightly guided. The *mushrikūn*, or idolaters, said: We built a structure for them; truly they are the sons of our fathers; we serve God in them. The Muslims say: Rather, we are truer than they. They are from among us. We will build a *masjid* for them [and] we will pray *ṣalāt* in it and we will serve God in it" (al-Ṭabarī, *Jāmi'*, 15.225 (vol. 9).

The Parable of the Two Men

The following passage begins like the normal beginning of a *sūrah*, with reference to revelation, *kitāb*, followed by exhortation to be patient and a *qul!* passage warning of the separate fates of reprobates (*ẓalimīn*) and those who believe in and do good works (vv. 27–31). This introduces the parable of the two men. This story stands apart from the three major narratives of the *sūrah*, being an anonymous parable rather than a story of a named person or group. It is also the longest parable in the Qur'ān:[4] a story of two men, one of whom has been given two abundant and reliable gardens and brags about his wealth and family power to his companion during an argument. He is described afterwards as a reprobate in his heart, who boasts that his gardens will last forever and that the hour of judgment will never come. His companion professes hope that God will give him something better later and that the Lord will destroy the first companion's garden. This second companion also vows that he will not associate anyone with God. The conclusion (vv. 42–43) skips to a point at which such destruction has somehow happened. The summary verse cites the importance of God's protection, reflecting a key theme of the *sūrah*. The companions present the ideal of those who trust their Lord implicitly. The parable offers the contrasting situation of one who has also benefited from the gifts of God but trusts in his own fortune, power, and wealth, and shows no gratitude to God.

The following section cites further parables (more typically short according to the Qur'ānic style) that reiterate the ephemeral nature of earthly provisions and the inevitability of a day of reckoning. Verse 49 concludes the section with another reference to the book (*kitāb*) that contains the summary of each individual's life, which will be given to them after the general resurrection, indicating their ultimate destination.

The Iblīs Story

This brings us to the Iblīs story, given in verse 50, as follows:

[4] The story of the messengers sent to a city, told in Sūrah YāSīn, 36:13–25, is of comparable length, but has more of the character of a historical story than a true parable, though it is introduced as a parable (*mathal*). All other *amthal* (pl. of *mathal*) in the Qur'ān are short—a single verse in length—and consist of similes.

wa-'idh qulnā li-l-malā'ikati usjudū li-ādama fa-sajadū illā iblīsā
kāna min al-jinni fa-fasaqa 'an amri rabbihi
a-fa-tattakhidhūnahu wa-dhurriyatahu awliyā' min dūnī
wa-hum lakum 'adūw^{un} bi'sa li-l-ẓālimīnā badal^{an}

And when we said to the angels, "Bow down," then they bowed down, except Iblīs;
He was one of the *jinn*; then he went astray from the command of his Lord.
Will you take him and his progeny as protectors and not me?
They are enemies to you. Evil is the compensation for the reprobates.

The first line above is identical to that found in Sūrah ṬāHā. In this *sūrah* Iblīs is identified as a *jinn*, and his error is defined as one of disobedience. One effect of the identification of Iblīs as a *jinn* is to distinguish him from the angels. This raises the controversial question as to the relationship between *jinn* and angels. As al-Ṭabarī points out in a long discussion on the issue, if Iblīs is not an angel, then the command to bow down should not apply to him. If he is an angel, then how can he disobey the command of his Lord?

The *Jinn*

Only in this telling is Iblīs specifically identified as a *jinn*. In Sūrat al-Ḥijr the *jinn* are also mentioned, but it is only implied that Iblīs is one of their number. What would the original hearers of this passage have understood from this association? What would the concept of "*jinn*" have meant to them? What would have been their repertoire of knowledge upon which they would have drawn to understand this reference?

The Jinn *in Commentary*

In commentaries, the issue of the nature of *jinn* is addressed primarily in comments on the Iblīs passage in Sūrat al-Baqarah (2:30–39), even though in that passage Iblīs is not identified as a *jinn*. The struggle to explain how Iblīs ended up in a crowd of angels results in a profusion and confusion of narratives and explanations. The following lengthy series of quotes is but a sample of what al-Ṭabarī includes in his commentary. Most, but not all, are initially reported by the master Qur'ān commentator, Ibn 'Abbās:

Iblīs was from one of the tribes of angels, which were called the *ḥinn*.[5] They were created from hot dry fire (*nār al-samūm*) among the angels. . . . His name was al-Ḥārith. . . . He was one of the custodians (*khuzzān*, can also mean "treasurer") of paradise. . . . The angels were created from light apart from this tribe. . . . The *jinn* who were mentioned in the Qur'ān were created from smokeless fire (*mārij min nār*), which is a tongue of fire that is at the tip of it when it flares up. The first to live on earth were the *jinn*, and they corrupted it and shed blood, and some killed some others . . . God sent Iblīs against them with an army of angels. They were this tribe that was called the *ḥinn*. And Iblīs and those who were with him killed them until he surrounded them on islands in the seas and the tops of mountains. When Iblīs did this he became proud in his soul. And he said, "I have done something which no one else has done" . . . then God was aware of this in his heart, but the angels who were with him were not aware of this. Then God said to the angels who were with him, "I am about to create on earth a vice-regent (*khalīfah*)". . . .[6]

Iblīs was from a tribe that committed disobedience among the angels; his name was 'Azāzīl.[7] He was one of the inhabitants of the earth, and he was one of the angels who strove the hardest and understanding (*ijtihād*), and the greatest of them in knowledge (*'ilm*), and this led him to pride. He was one of the tribe called the *ḥinn*[8] . . .

Iblīs was made the ruler (*malik*) over the lowest heaven (*samā' al-dunyā*, the "heaven of the world"),[9] and he was one of the tribes of angels, called the *jinn*; they were only called the *jinn* because they were custodians of Paradise, and Iblīs was a custodian with his own domain. [225-1] . . . Iblīs was one of the most eminent of the angels, from the noblest tribe of them . . . he was called a *jinn* only in that he was a custodian of it (Paradise), as one might call a man a Meccan, a Medīnan, a Kūfan or a Baṣran. [225-2]

[5] Some texts give this word as *al-jinn*. The difference is a mere dot. The correct form is *ḥinn*, who are defined as a lower class of *jinn*. See Kister, "Adam," 120 n. 40.

[6] Al-Ṭabarī, *Jāmi'*, 1.201 (vol 1). For the sake of brevity, I have removed most of the lists of transmitters and some repetitions of the same argument in this and the following quotes from al-Ṭabarī.

[7] 'Azāzil (or Azazel; also mentioned in Lev 16:8–10) is familiar from the watcher myth described in ch. 3. He is the angel sent to earth to watch over humanity, but he teaches them the secret heavenly arts such as metallurgy, ornamentation, and astrology.

[8] Al-Ṭabarī, *Jāmi'*, 1.224 (vol. 1).

[9] The notion that there are seven heavens is based on 65:12.

> . . . he used to sit between the heavens and the earth. [225-3] . . . it was Ibn Abbās who said: "If he were not among the angels, he would not have been commanded to bow down; he was one of the custodians of the lowest heaven. It was Qatādah who said: he hid (*janna*) from obedience to his Lord.[10] . . . the Arabs say: what are *jinn* but all those who conceal themselves and cannot be seen. . . but the angels conceal themselves and cannot be seen . . . the Quraysh say that the angels are daughters of God, but God says: "if the angels are my daughters, then Iblīs is among them, so they have made a relationship between me and Iblīs and his progeny." . . . the Arabs in their language deny that any conceal themselves except *jinn* . . . the Banū Adam are called humans (*al-ins*) in that they are visible and do not conceal themselves. Whatever is visible is human, and whatever conceals itself is *jinn*. . . . Others say: Iblīs was never for a moment one of the angels; he was the origin of the *jinn* just as Adam was the origin of humans.[11]

> Iblīs was one of the *jinn* whom the angels drove away. Some of the angels captured him and brought him to heaven. . . . the angels used to fight the *jinn*, then Iblīs was captured, and he was young. So he stayed with the angels and he served with them, and when they were commanded to bow down to Adam, they bowed down, and Iblīs refused. . . . one of the tribes of the angels were called the *jinn*; Iblīs was one of them. He governed what was between the heaven and the earth, then he disobeyed, so God transformed him into a stoned *shayṭān*. . . . Iblīs was the father of the *jinn*, just as Adam is the father of humans. The proof for those who say this is the text that God said in his book that he created Iblīs from hot fire, and from smokeless fire, and he did not say about the angels that he made them from something like this. And God said that he was one of the *jinn*. They say that it is not conceivable that one would recount something that God has not recounted. They say about Iblīs that he fathered children, but angels do not father or procreate. . . . God created creatures and said: Bow down to Adam. They said: We will not do it. So God sent fire upon them and destroyed them. Then he created another creature, and said: I am creating a man from clay; bow down to Adam. Then they refused. So he sent fire upon them and destroyed them. Then he created these, and said: Bow down to Adam. They said: Yes. Iblīs was among those who refused to bow down to Adam.[12]

[10] Al-Ṭabarī, *Jāmi'*, 1.225 (vol. 1).

[11] Al-Ṭabarī, *Jāmi'*, 1.225–226 (vol. 1).

[12] Al-Ṭabarī, *Jāmi'*, 1.226–227 (vol. 1).

Al-Ṭabarī then gives his own opinion in the matter:

> These reasons testify to the weakness of the knowledge of these people. This is that there is nothing to disprove that God has created varieties of angels among the varieties of things that he created. He created some from light, and some from fire, and some from other things. There is no word in what God revealed about what he created angels from, and the report about what he created Iblīs from requires that Iblīs would be outside the [scope of] meaning of it [the term, "angel"]. Thus it is conceivable that he created a kind of angel from fire, and Iblīs was one of them, and that he singled out Iblīs as one created from hot fire apart from the rest of the angels. Similarly, it is not precluded that he was one of the angels who could have family and children, because there arose in him passion and lust that were removed from the rest of the angels, since God willed disobedience for him.
>
> As for the word of God that "he was one of the *jinn*," it should not be dismissed that all things which conceal themselves from sight be called *jinn*, since we recall what was mentioned before in the poetry of 'Ā'isha, that there was Iblīs and the angels among them that avoided the sight of the Banū Adam.[13]

Al-Ṭabarī affirms the ambiguity of the Qur'ān, which says little about the character of either angels or *jinn*. He is unwilling to press the text to yield distinctions between the two.[14] Al-Bayḍāwī, not known to indulge in speculation on the basis of legend, nevertheless gives an intriguing and suggestive image of the relationship between *jinn* and angels:

> A'isha related that he (the prophet) said: The angels were created from light and the *jinn* from smokeless fire, because of the similarity, which we have mentioned: the sense of light is the essence of shining, and the fire is [also] like this—although the light is filled with swirls of smoke. One should beware of it because what is associated with it is an excess of heat and burning, but if it becomes cleansed and clear [*musfaha*] it would be pure light, although the initial condition

[13] Al-Ṭabarī, *Jāmi',* 1.226–227 (vol. 1).

[14] This ambiguity is summarized in MacDonald's article, "Malā'ika." On the other hand, Jadaane argues apologetically against such ambiguity, supporting the impeccability of angels based on Q. 16:49–50 and various commentators of this persuasion ("La place des anges"). Webb neglects the issue ("Angel"). For further discussion see Waugh, "Jealous Angels"; Ibrahim, "Questions of the Superiority of Angels," 65–75; and Murata, "Angels."

> [of smokiness] can return again and continue to increase until the light is extinguished and [only] the scattered smoke remains. This explanation is more accurate and appropriate for the separate texts.[15]

Al-Bayḍāwī's explanation, like al-Ṭabarī's, minimizes the difference between angels and *jinn*. It is a matter of the presence of "smoke" (i.e., impurity). The essential nature of both is light, whether in the form of pure light or of fire.

The Problem of Angels

Al-Ṭabarī's extensive comments on the origin of Iblīs are largely concerned not with Iblīs but with angels. He is making these comments as exegesis on the Iblīs passage in Sūrat al-Baqarah, which makes no mention of *jinn*. He is following the standard practice of the *mufasirūn* in commenting, at the first opportunity, on the composite story, which includes Sūrat al-Kahf's notation that Iblīs is a *jinn*. Iblīs disobeys God because that is what *jinn* often do. The problem is that Iblīs is in heaven as part of a congregation of angels, which implies that he is an angel. That is a problem because angels, as common messengers of God to humanity, must be reliable. Their message must be incontrovertibly a message from God, unimpaired by any freethinking on the part of angels. Separating Iblīs from the angelic community is necessary to preserve the reliability of the angels. In the comments above, al-Ṭabarī accepts that Iblīs and the *jinn* are angels, but angels of a particular type that are distinct—clearly and emphatically distinct—from the pure angels. He places Iblīs in the role of custodian of paradise, playing on the similarity of the word *jinn* to the word for paradise (*jannah*).

But in Sūrat al-Baqarah, maintaining the innocence of angels is not so easy a task for reasons that have nothing to do with Iblīs. Prior to the Iblīs story is this short narrative:

> And when your Lord said to the angels, "Behold, I will make (*jā'il*^{un})
> a vice-regent on earth;"
> They said, "Will you make someone who will cause corruption on
> it and shed blood, while we are glorifying you with praise?"
> He said, "I know what you do not know." (2:30)

The chapter devoted to Sūrat al-Baqarah will address this passage in greater detail, but the plain sense of the interchange here between God and the angels

[15] Al-Bayḍāwī, *Tafsīr*, 1.53.

is that the angels are indeed showing some independent thinking such as might compromise their willingness to convey God's will without any alteration or nuance. Thus the main concern of al-Ṭabarī and other commentators is to draw a clear line between fickle *jinn* and infallible angels.

Another factor may be at play here. We must also ask what the original hearers of passages concerning angels might have made of the concept. Although al-Ṭabarī is writing more than two centuries after the rise of the Islamic movement, and popular conceptions might be well-adapted and changed through such a long period of Islamic presence and influence, the question is still relevant. What did the pre-Islamic communities believe and know about angels? What repertoire, to use Iser's term, would they bring to the hearing and reading of this story?

In a word, little. In pre-Islamic times, the sources present little evidence for belief in angels in Arabia. They show ample evidence of *jinn* in a variety of subtypes—*ghūl*, *shiqq*, *si'lāh*, and others—which are prominent in pre-Islamic poetry, but there are few and only vague references to *malā'ika*. Jawād 'Alī, in his history of pre-Islamic Arabia, asserts the following:

> The belief in angels comes rather from Judeo-Christian sources than pure Arab sources. Except for those poets who were in contact with *'ahl al-kitāb* (The People of the Book), like the poet Umayya ibn abī al-Ṣalt, the rest of the Arabs at that point ignored the notion of angels.[16]

Although the Qur'ān makes reference to angels in passages such as Sūrat al-An'ām 6:8, dealing with unconverted Meccans,[17] thus showing belief in angels, pre-Islamic literature itself suggests that diverse roles of heavenly authority would have been fulfilled by *jinn* or gods, not angels. As the passage from al-Ṭabarī quoted above indicates, a major revision of pre-Islamic belief introduced by Islam was the affirmation of angels, which then became an obligation of the faith.[18] Angels by their nature—in Judaism, Christianity, and Islam—are beings in a heavenly hierarchy. They are messengers or servants of God. Such a role would make less sense in a universe populated by

[16] Jawād 'Alī, *al-Mufaṣṣal fī Tārīkh al-'Arab qabl al-Islām*, 6.738, quoted in El-Zein, "Jinn," 77–78.

[17] "They [the Meccans] say: Why was not an angel sent down to him [Muḥammad]? If we had sent down an angel, the matter would have been settled at once, with no respite for them."

[18] Belief in angels is one of the criteria of righteousness prescribed in Sūrat al-Baqarah 2:177.

diverse independent and ethereal beings. As Welch argues, the development of the Qur'ānic argument moves the Arab sense of the spiritual world from a pantheon of semi-independent spiritual beings to a strict hierarchy in which all spiritual beings operate at the command of God and lose their individuality in God.[19] Except Iblīs.

With reference to the "tribes" of angels, the Qur'ān subtly distinguishes between angels, referred to in the abstract, and the particular heavenly beings that are charged with the transmission of the revelation: the *qur'ān*. The Qur'ān never calls Gabriel an angel. Generic angels carry out a variety of errands for God, including giving extra-Qur'ānic instructions to humans from God. They are sometimes even recipients of revelation (8:12), but they are never the purveyors of the specific revelation that is the Qur'ān.[20]

The Community of Jinn

Al-Ṭabarī's additional concern, both here and elsewhere (such as in his discussion of Surāt al-Jinn, 72), is to address the issue of familial associations with God—whether *jinn* are children, daughters, or associates of God—a critical concern for the Muslim community. As the passage in Sūrat al-Kahf shows, this concern relates to the issue of *jinn* as protectors. This relationship is evident in the verse that follows the Iblīs story. After telling the story and identifying Iblīs as a *jinn*, the Qur'ān goes on in the following verse to comment on this fact:

> *mā ashhadtuhum khalqa al-samāwāti wa-l-arḍi wa-lā khalqa anfusihim wa-mā kuntu muttakhidha al-muḍillīna 'aḍud^an*
>
> I did not call on them to witness the creation of the heavens and the earth nor the creation of themselves, nor did I take those who lead astray as helpers. (v. 51)

After identifying Iblīs and his progeny as *jinn*, the Qur'ān goes on to reject their participation in God's acts of creation by declaring that God has not taken them as aides or partners in the fabrication of the heavens and the earth. Further, they themselves are created and did not self-create (an absurdity). Here partnership is identified not with protection but with creation, yet the

[19] Welch, "Allah."

[20] Rahman, *Themes*, 95.

flow of logic from one verse to the next does imply that the power to protect is ultimately a direct consequence of the power to create.

In the Iblīs story of Sūrat al-Kahf, the presumption of the story is that Iblīs, as a *jinn*, would break a command of his Lord. The conjunction between the identification of Iblīs as a *jinn* and the subsequent action of breaking the command is *fa*, which usually indicates either cause and effect or temporal sequence. Since the two clauses are not actions, the *fa* indicates that breaking the command is an effect of being a *jinn*. Throughout the comments of al-Ṭabarī, al-Bayḍāwī, and others, as well as the testimony of the Qur'ān, what holds constant is that *jinn* are fallible, impure creatures who, like humans, can and often do disobey God. Such commentary reveals a clear reluctance to identify *jinn* totally with demons. *Jinn* are like the humans with whom the Qur'ān associates them, capable of obedience and disobedience as well as faith and disbelief. Hence the commentators' understanding of the Qur'ānic description is not a cause and effect. The more precise meaning would be that, being a *jinn*, Iblīs was capable of disobeying, but being a *jinn* does not make him a demon, a *shayṭān*.

Is this how *jinn* should be generally understood? This presentation stands in tension with the pervasive Qur'ānic trend that associates *jinn* with humans in the common phrase *al-jinn wa-l-ins*. This phrase occurs with slight variations some fourteen times in the Qur'ān. The Qur'ān presumes a sharp separation between the earthly world of *jinn* and humans, on the one hand, and the heavenly world of angels and God, on the other. The human-*jinn* association is in accord with the popular tradition that is continuous from pre-Islamic times through the development of Islam and even to the present time.

On the other hand, Iblīs, although a *jinn*, is himself associated with a more celestial tradition. Being a creature of the Qur'ān, with no pre-Islamic appearances, Iblīs emerges as a narrative figure only in the context of the celestial confrontation with Adam and with God, and as a being among the angels. The commentators thus see him both as comparable and as contrastable with the angels. As soon as he is described as a *jinn*, as he is in Sūrat al-Kahf, however, a reader may well associate him with a terrestrial repertoire of tradition and legend that has rich roots in pre-Islamic Arabia. Hence the reader may have to negotiate a blending of repertoires: that of the Qur'ānic heavenly association with angels to which the commentators give their attention, and that of the rich *jinn* tradition of earth spirits who are often malicious but not uniformly or inevitably so.

Al-Ṭabarī and the lineage of commentators after him address *jinn* in the context of angels in the heavenly pantheon. They do not address *jinn* in the context of the earthly experience of a world potentially fraught with perils from unseen forces, which would be the predominant awareness of the early Muslim population and, arguably, is still the predominant association with *jinn* in the Muslim world. In that society, it is clear that *jinn* are commonly taken as protectors. The Qur'ān addresses this issue briefly but directly. Al-Ṭabarī does not.

The argument that I will develop here is that the commentarial tradition addresses a set of questions that ignore the common, even pervasive, popular legends and understandings of the nature of *jinn*. We have identified at least two traditions of interpretation: One, the Qur'ānic exegetical tradition, addresses celestial dimensions of the relationship among *jinn*, angels, and God. The second, the popular legendary tradition, exemplified by al-Damīrī, al-Jāḥiẓ, al-Majlisī, and others, preserves stories describing *jinn* as terrestrial figures usually in antagonistic relationships with humans. There is little overlap between the two traditions. This bifurcation of interpretive traditions raises the question as to which understanding of *jinn* the implied reader of the Iblīs narratives might bring to his or her encounter with the text and what difference this might make.

Terrestrial Jinn

The religion of pre-Islamic Arabia is not well understood but focuses primarily on local gods identified in the Qur'ān as "idols" (*ṭāghūt*), often installed in specific sacred precincts.[21] In addition, a large number and variety of spirits, often demonic, populated the world but not uniformly so. The community understands these spirits as various denominations of *jinn*. Like the pre-Islamic gods, they are attached to specific locales, although they may also range widely. According to Joseph Chelhod:

> They haunt wild places, ruins, cemeteries, dismal and dirty areas. They live in the soil, or even the underground. In the eyes of the Bedouin, they are virtual owners of the ground. This is why he does not dare set up a new tent, or build a house, without making a sacrifice to the "master of the place," *ṣāḥib al-maḥall*, that is to say the *jinni* who inhabits the ground on which he wants to establish himself. During the day, they hide from view, but at night, they scatter

[21] Serjeant, "Haram and Hawtah," 167–84

> among the trees which conceal them. The ancient Arabs greeted them saying, "you who find the darkness pleasant." Travelers who want to camp in a deserted place put themselves under the protection of the Master of the *Jinn*.[22]

Note particularly the last line in which the Master of the *Jinn* provides protection.

Al-Ṭabarī does make brief reference to this phenomenon. In his commentary on the Surāt al-Jinn (72:6), he gives several traditions in the vein of this one:

> A man in the time of *jāhiliyyah*, when he arrived at a *wādī* before Islam, he said: I seek refuge against the master of this *wādī*. And when Islam came they sought refuge in God and they [the *jinn*] left them alone.[23]

This description is the most explicit in differentiating between pre-Islamic custom and Islamic custom. Note that, unlike Chelhod's description above, here the Master of the *Jinn* is not protector, but adversary.

According to legend, *jinn* frequent abandoned or destroyed cities and wilderness areas. They also inhabit or appear in the form of various animals, especially snakes. The association of *jinn* and snakes receives a great deal of attention in some commentaries.[24] They can also associate with people in the form of demonic possession, informants, or lovers.[25] They are organized in the same fashion as humans. Chelhod writes:

> The social organization of the *jinn* is copied from that of the Arabs; they are also divided into tribes and clans. At their head are many kings which govern them and who conclude treaties of alliance with humans. Their conception of honor is similar to the latter. In particular, they respect the right of hospitality, so dear to the Arabs, protecting those who ask for their assistance, or come seeking refuge from their allies and if necessary to fight at their sides. Among them both solidarity and vengeance are *de rigueur*.[26]

[22] Chelhod, *Les stuctures* (translation mine).

[23] Al-Ṭabarī, *Jāmi'*, 14.109 (vol. 8).

[24] See, for instance, al-Qurṭubī, *Al-Jāmi'a*, 1.295–298 (vol. 1).

[25] See El-Zein, "Jinn," 108; Henninger, "Pre-Islamic Bedouin Religion," 3–22.

[26] Chelhod, *Les structures*, 75.

Kamāl al-Dīn al-Damīrī discusses the question of whether *jinn* can marry humans. While he gives several reports of people who have made claims to such a match, he dismisses them all and argues, on authority, that such relationships are impossible.[27] The *Fihrist* of Muḥammad Ibn al-Nadīm, however, includes an entire chapter recounting love affairs between humans and *jinn*.[28] El-Zein notes that the Qur'ān describes the virgins of paradise as those whom neither mortal nor *jinn* have touched.[29] Amira El-Zein presents the discussion of Badr al-Dīn al-Shiblī, who describes a number of such marriages and then raises the legal issues. He concludes that God wants humans to marry "from your own kind" (Q 30:21), and confirms this with a *ḥadīth* from the Prophet.[30] The existence of the argument indicates that *jinn* are not simply demonic presences in the world, but have a more benevolent dimension.

A final story, specifically relevant to Iblīs, is related by al-Damīrī.

> [Anas Ibn Mālik reports:] I was with the Messenger of God, leaving the mountains of Mecca when a Shaykh approached leaning on a staff. The Prophet said: [This is] the step of a *jinnī* and his sound." He said, "Indeed!" So the Prophet said, "From what *jinn*?" He said, "I am Hāmah bin al-Haym or Ibn Haym b. Lāqays bin Iblīs." The Prophet said, "I see only two fathers between you and Iblīs." He said, "Right." He said, "How old are you?" "I destroyed the world except for the littlest part of it. On the night that Cain killed Abel, I was a youth of some years and I used to look out upon the hills and bother the people." The Messenger of God said, "Evil work!" He said, "O Messenger of God, spare me the blame, for I am one who believed Noah and repented in front of him. When I scolded him about his mission, he cried and made me cry. He said, by God, that I am one of the repentant ones and I sought refuge in God lest I become one of the ignorant ones. I met Hūd and I believed in him and I met Ibrahīm and I was with him in the fire when he was cast into it, and I was with Yūsuf when he was cast into the well and I went before him to the bottom of it. I met Shu'ayb and Moses and I met Jesus, son of Mary and he said to me, "If you meet

[27] Al-Damīrī, *Ḥayāt*, 1.194 (translations mine).

[28] Al-Nadīm, *Fihrist*, 2.723–724.

[29] 55:56—"In them will be women chaste in their glances, deflowered by neither human nor *jinn* before them." See also 55:74.

[30] El-Zein, "Jinn," 300–5.

> Muḥammad, then say, 'Peace' to him from me." I have conveyed his message and I believe in you."
>
> So the Prophet said, "Peace be upon Jesus and upon you. What do you need, O Hāmah?" He said, "Moses taught me Torah and Jesus taught me the Gospel, so teach me the Qur'ān." So he taught him, and the story is that he taught him ten *sūrahs* from the Qur'ān.[31]

This is one of a small corpus of stories that connect earthly *jinn* with the original Iblīs, but this story indicates the malleability of the Iblīs character in contrast to the stark implications of the Qur'ānic story in Sūrat al-Kahf. Here, a direct descendent of Iblīs converts from evil activity to belief and faith well before the time of Muḥammad.

Jinn *as Protectors*

Sūrat al-Kahf goes on to cast the issue of Iblīs in terms of protection, a major theme of the *sūrah*. "Will you take him and his progeny as protectors and not me?" God protects the companions of the cave against a hostile community and against discovery and discomfort during their long sleep. The community then seeks to establish them as protectors (v. 21). We have also heard a parable about a man who believes that he needs no protection. We have examined at length the nature of *jinn*, as explained by the early commentators on the Qur'ān. We have also seen above that, although *jinn* are dangerous, especially in the night and outside the towns and cities, with their power they can equally be invoked as protectors. Now the reader/listener has the challenge of identifying the more reliable protector—God or the *jinn*.

Were the *jinn* beings *in* whom people sought protection or *from* whom people sought protection? The *sūrah* suggests the former, but popular legend gives evidence of both. Clearly *jinn* have power, power to harm and power to protect. The descriptions of pre-Islamic belief collected by El-Zein mostly depict *jinn* as beings from whom people might want protection.[32] They kidnap humans, frighten them with strange noises, chase them in the dark, possess their minds, and infect their bodies. They exist in the subgroups mentioned above, and the particular kinds of dangers they represent to humans identify them. The collection of stories in al-Damīrī and al-Jāḥiẓ add more evidence

[31] Al-Damīrī, *Ḥayāt,* 1.190.

[32] El-Zein, "Jinn," 54–122.

to this, although al-Damīrī in particular also relates a number of positive stories of *jinn*, most of them narratives of encounters with Muḥammad.[33] The solution to the dangers of *jinn* is to make a pact with them, although the nature and details of such pacts are not clear.

One finds occasional references to sacrifices made to *jinn* in the pre-Islamic period. Al-Damīrī notes:

> Abū ‘Ubaydah, in the book, *al-Amwal*, and al-Bayhaqī according to al-Zuhrī, from the Prophet, relate that he forbid sacrifices to the *jinn*. He said, “Sacrifices to the *jinn* are such that a man buys a house or opens up a spring or something like this and he kills a bird as a sacrifice to it.” This was in the time of *jāhiliyyah*. They said, if one does this the *jinn* will not harm its people. Then he abolished it and forbade it.[34]

El-Zein points out that sacrifices to gods are much more common.[35] The common response to *jinn* is to seek protection from them through the use of apotropaic amulets and charms. Strategies include hanging teeth or bones of animals, or the heel of a rabbit, around the necks of young children to protect them and rattling dry skin bottles. Incantations can also drive away a *jinn* from a person or place.[36]

The reports of Joseph Chelhod indicate that taking *jinn* as protectors was common. Travelers in secluded places seek the protection of the Master of the *Jinn*. They conclude treaties with humans and honor the tradition of hospitality, including the obligation to protect all who seek their assistance or ask for refuge. They are, in so many ways, just like humans.

In this context, the rhetorical question in verse 50 makes perfect sense, although none of the Qur’ānic commentators that we have examined capture this.

This raises an additional problem. The reports of pre-Islamic understanding of *jinn* show that they do, in effect, provide protection to humans at times. They follow unwritten but respected codes of honor. They are not avowed enemies of humans. The description of *jinn* in Surāt al-Jinn (72) confirm

[33] Al-Damīrī, *Ḥayāt*, 1.189–91.

[34] Ibid., 1.194.

[35] El-Zein, “Jinn,” 119.

[36] Ibid., 115.

that many *jinn* are believers who sit listening to the Qur'ān. Thus it would be wrong to say that the folly of Iblīs simply results from his *jinn* nature.

Surāt al-Jinn repeats the concern about enlisting *jinn* as protectors:

> *Wa-annahu kāna rijāl*[ūn] *min al-insi yaʿūdhūna bi-rijāl*[in] *min al-jinni fa-zādūhum rahaq*[an]
> *wa-annahum ẓannū kamā ẓanantum an lan yabʿatha allahu ahad*[an]
>
> And there were people among the humans who sought refuge in people among the *jinn*, and they increased them in folly.
> And they believed as you (pl.) believe: that God would never raise up a single one. (72:6–7)

Two other traditions exist describing positive roles of the *jinn*, both of which relate to the watcher myth described in chapter 3. One is the role of *jinn* in the inspiration of the seer (*kāhin*) and the poets. As in Sūrat al-Ḥijr, the *jinn* were known to listen in on the secrets of heaven and report to particular people (the diviners). This is helpful in discovering the future, which is planned in heaven. In several places the Qur'ān informs us that the *jinn* are excluded from such knowledge, but this itself suggests a popular belief that *jinn* are privy to heavenly secrets. It is possible to understand provision of knowledge as protection, but it is unreliable and cryptic. According to Michael Zwettler:

> What is clear is that whatever special knowledge the *jinn* or *shayāṭīn* (demons) might have communicated to poets and *kahhān* and however useful, pertinent, accurate, and wondrous it might on occasion have seemed, it was essentially a situation-specific, morally neutral kind of knowledge of relatively little practical value in ordering behavior, affairs, lives and communities of human beings over the long term. At their most prescriptive and normative, these mantic communications might take the form of cryptic advisories or warnings, aphoristic exhortations, bitter condemnations, affective appeals, satirical tirades, or idealized portrayals of exemplary conduct or character that could be adduced on an ad hoc basis to confirm or discredit something in terms of its conformity to established convention, received opinion, and shared experience. The discourse of *kahhān* and especially poets might have incorporated much that was true and valuable, and leaders—tribal chieftains and even kings—may have found it expedient to consult and patronize them; but certainly no one who operated under the control of such capricious, unreliable, antisocial, and often downright misanthropic powers as *jinn* and *shayāṭīn* could

> be expected to act dependably and consistently for the welfare of those who would follow his lead.[37]

A second gift of the *jinn*, also related to the watcher myth as expanded in *Enoch*, is their skill in the arts of working metal, particularly in sword-making. They are credited with a particular sword called a *ma'thūr*.[38] The next chapter will explore this more deeply.

The warning in Sūrat al-Kahf not to take Iblīs as a protector does not refer to any practice that was common among the hearers—there is no evidence of this. Rather, Sūrat al-Kahf is moving through a careful program of possibilities for protection. It upholds the companions of the cave as the ideal, trusting God throughout, even in their confusion. The parable of the two men demonstrates the danger of self-reliance. The protection of God is necessary, if not from earthly disaster, certainly in light of impending heavenly judgment. The spirit world, represented by the *jinn*, is also not capable of serving in this role. Even if they might convey the wisdom of heaven (and other Qur'ānic passages refute this possibility) they are not reliably honest, but culpable, vulnerable to evil. As the next *āyah* (v. 51) makes clear, God does not take as helpers those who might lead astray.

The reference to helpers (*'aḍuḍ*) brings together the theme of protection and the theme of the unity of God who has no partners. If Iblīs and his *jinn*-progeny are seen in their oracular function, however unreliable that may be, here it is denied that they are in any way helpers, confidants, or associates to God.

Iblīs and the Watcher Myth

The tension between Iblīs as a celestial figure related to angels and Iblīs as a terrestrial *jinn* calls to mind the watcher myth described in chapter 3. Gen 6:1–6 provides the watcher myth, and the book of *Enoch* expands upon it. It describes angels sent to earth to watch over humanity, but who become involved with mortal women (the Shemihazah version) and/or convey to humanity knowledge that belongs in heaven (the Azazel version). In al-Ṭabarī's commentary, various aspects of this story emerge. Most obvious is the name "Azazel." But add to this the oft-mentioned fact that Iblīs is a

[37] Zwettler, "Manic Manifesto," 79–80.

[38] Ibn Manẓūr, *Lisān al-'Arab*, 4.9; see also El-Zein, "Jinn," 103.

guardian and in charge of the *samā' al-dunyā*, the heaven of the earth, the domain of the watchers. Finally, he is associated with knowledge, as the greatest in *itjihād*. As in the situation of the watchers, the idea of heavenly beings who disobey is a challenge to exegetes.

In this *sūrah*, the parallel is to the Shemihazah version of the watcher story as narrated in *Enoch*. Spiritual beings on earth associate with mortals, sometimes taking them as wives. In the Shemihazah story, demons emerge as a consequence of these unholy unions. In popular Arab tradition, the *jinn* are also malicious spirits on earth. Their provenance is unclear, although al-Ṭabarī does describe them as primordial creatures on earth, created by God.

In this Arab tradition, evil comes from the terrestrial spirit world. One achieves protection from them through apotropaic devices—amulets, incantations, and so forth—or through pacts. In these cases *jinn* are protectors against other *jinn*. In the Azazel version of the watcher myth, the issue is knowledge. In both cases, the Shemihazah and the Azazel versions of the watcher myth, the respective issues of protection and knowledge are reflections of the themes of Sūrat al-Kahf. All this derives from the repertoire that the popular reader might be assumed to bring to his or her encounter with the text when Iblīs is identified as a *jinn*.

From the popular *jinn* legends, the troublesome issue of marriage between spiritual beings and humans stands out. We have also noted the role of the *jinn* in teaching secret knowledge, most specifically metallurgy, the making of swords. Finally, the *jinn* are those who bring secrets from heaven, knowledge of the future. The Azazel myth associates the watchers with astrology and the interpretation of heavenly signs.

We can see many points of contact between the watcher myth and the Iblīs story, particularly when we see that story in the context of *jinn* legends. At least some, perhaps many, of the readers and listeners of the Qur'ān would have this material in their own repertoire of knowledge. While the classical commentators give their attention to the heavenly conflict between *jinn* and angels, the context familiar to most hearers would be the terrestrial and local power of *jinn* and their ability to trouble human relationships and activities, demanding a certain fealty of those who share "their" property.

There is no suggestion in Sūrat al-Kahf that Iblīs directly challenges the authority of God, although some commentators do make that interpretive move based on other tellings of the story in other *sūrahs*. His *jinn* character is morally complex and not easily reduced to the evil of al-Shayṭān. While the spare, discursive presentation of the Iblīs story in Sūrat al-Kahf makes the strongest case for the evil of Iblīs, both the popular tradition of *jinn* and the commentarial tradition of the Qur'ānic exegetes tend to moderate this extreme staging. Here Iblīs can be interpreted as a petty competitor to God, ruler of his own patch of earth, like other *jinn*.

The following section of the *sūrah*, nestled between the short Iblīs story and the next lengthy narrative about Moses, returns to the third theme: that of contention. Against the clear guidance of God, the people still find reason to argue and dispute. God even takes responsibility for setting a "covering" (*akinnat*^{an}) over their hearts (v. 57).

Moses and Khiḍr

The story of Moses and Khiḍr (vv. 60–82) is fraught with mystery.[39] A brief account in which Moses travels with a servant to a rock to fetch a fish but forgets the fish when he arrives there precedes the story. There is not enough information in the Qur'ānic story itself to gain the sense of it. This leads to another story, not clearly related to the "fish" story, in which a knowledgeable servant of God, traditionally identified as Khiḍr, agrees to take Moses along on his rounds that Moses might learn understanding (*rushd*—right conduct, integrity). Khiḍr warns Moses that he will not understand much of what he sees, but Moses is confident that he will be patient in learning. They proceed through three events, each one of which elicits alarm and objection from Moses. He does not understand. Finally, Khiḍr explains the destiny and secret of each situation; he shows that what is apparently abusive—sinking a boat, killing a young man, and refusing food for work when they are hungry—serves a larger, beneficial purpose.

Here again, in ways that Moses, a messenger of God, could not possibly comprehend, God is protecting the righteous and punishing the unrighteous. Khiḍr here serves as a "helper," a servant of God, but he is identified specifically as "one to whom we have given our mercy, and whom we have taught knowledge which we possess." The diction emphasizes the first person

[39] On Khiḍr, see Augustinović, *"El-Khadr"*; al-Ṭabarī; *History;* Halman, "Where Two Seas Meet"; Omar, "Khidr"; Wensinck, "Al-Khadir"; and Wheeler, "Moses or Alexander?" Since Khiḍr is often associated with Dhū al-Qarnayn, sometimes as his servant, many of these references, especially Wheeler, include discussion of the latter. The Khiḍr story has been related to the Epic of Gilgamesh, the Romance of Alexander, and the story of Elijah and Rabbi Joshua ben Levi.

of God; the *-nā* suffix of the *maiestatis pluralis* occurs five times in a short verse of twelve words. Knowledge comes from one source, one alone.

Dhū al-Qarnayn

With no pause, another mystery, the story of Dhū al-Qarnayn (the Two-Horned One), follows the Moses-Khiḍr story. The identities of both Khiḍr and Dhū al-Qarnayn have inspired immense speculation. Many sources regard them as one and the same person. Some say that Dhū al-Qarnayn is Alexander the Great. Others identify him as a Himyarite king (variously named), or as the Lakhmid ruler al-Mundhir al-Akbar III b. Mā' al-Samā', or as Cyrus the Great.[40] Khiḍr became popular in Sufi accounts as a guide on the mystical path.[41] The text invites such speculation. The identity of such powerful guides is a compelling invitation for wonderment, only enhanced by the power of their interventions. More than angels, who deliver messages and occasionally do specific tasks at the divine bidding, both the unnamed servant of God in verses 65–82 and Dhū al-Qarnayn in verses 83–101 possess miraculous powers and engage in sustained intervention in human affairs. Both perform three feats, a triptych. They do, however, fulfill somewhat different roles. The Khiḍr-figure in the Moses story seldom engages with the populations that he affects. The one exception is a request for food in verse 77. Other than that request, he moves through the world unnoticed. The Khiḍr-figure's power is of a discreet sort. He is an invisible figure, more like the *jinn*.

Dhū al-Qarnayn, on the other hand, is quite visible and acts like the ruler he is so often assumed to be. He travels the world, like Khiḍr, but when he arrives at a place, the people call out to him with requests for help. He is a protector against the powers of evil. While the Khiḍr-figure's authority is located in his knowledge, given by God (v. 65), the authority of Dhū al-Qarnayn is invested in his power to accomplish physical feats. Both are peripatetic figures, unattached to any particular realm. In this they are unlike kings, although the aptness of the identification with Alexander the Great is clear here.

The final epilogue of Sūrat al-Kahf (vv. 102–10) rehearses the themes. Even though Khiḍr and Dhū al-Qarnayn have been depicted as protectors of people, God reiterates that they are not protectors apart from God. God

[40] Wheeler, *Moses or Alexander*, 199.

[41] Halman, "Where Two Seas Meet."

cannot be placed in competition with his servants. Moreover, not even a lifetime of good works is enough to confirm the destiny of people unless they recognize the signs of the Lord (i.e., the signs of his power and control) and the ultimate confirmation of that power: the day of judgment. Working righteous deeds is not enough. One must also believe.

The *sūrah* ends with two *qul!* verses: the first putting forward the rich image of a sea of ink, which would not suffice to write the words of God; and the second offering the final instruction to Moses, which encapsulates all of these themes into one:

> Say: I am only a man like you. It has been revealed to me only that your God is one, so whoever expects a meeting with his Lord, indeed, let him work a work of righteousness and not associate anyone in the worship of his Lord. (18:110)

Conclusion

The Iblīs passage in this *sūrah* serves to provide one instance among many of a claim by one other than God to be a protector. The grounds for such a claim are difficult to discern in the context of the Iblīs story as given in the *sūrah* itself. When read in the context of the likely repertoire of Arab tradition, however, the controversy becomes clear. The Iblīs story is entirely comprehensible in the context of the Arab custom of regarding *jinn* as: a) proprietors of various locales; b) adversaries, who need propitiation through apotropaic devices; and/or c) partners in pacts that then turn hostile *jinn* into protectors, perhaps even marriage partners.

Iblīs's identification as a *jinn*, uniquely stressed in this version of the Iblīs story, is the basis of his association with this legendary tradition. Stories of the progeny of Iblīs makes the association much closer.

Those whom the people might seek as protectors apart from, or associated with, God include saints (the companions of the cave), themselves (the rich garden owner), *jinn* (Iblīs and his progeny), spiritual guides (Khiḍr), powerful leaders (Dhū al-Qarnayn), and even Muḥammad himself. But there is no protector apart from God, and the day of judgment will be an unwelcome surprise for those who do not realize this.

Equally, the Iblīs story reflects and continues the other major theme of the *sūrah*: the issue of knowledge. In the verse following the Iblīs story,

God declares that the *jinn* did not witness the creation of the cosmos, the heavens and the earth, and they did not witness the creation of themselves. They are ignorant of such things. Not only does their power limit them, but their experience does as well.

In the present version of the *jinn* story, there is no discussion between God and Iblīs. In narrations of the story in the following chapters, God queries Iblīs about the reasons for his refusal to bow to Adam. This is true in Sūrat al-Ḥijr, Sūrah Ṣād, Sūrat al-Isrā', and Sūrat al-'Arāf (but not Sūrat al-Baqarah). Iblīs gives reasons, and in the interchange that follows, God curses Iblīs, or Iblīs promises God that he will pursue and tempt humanity, or both.

In this version, Sūrat al-Kahf, none of that happens. God does not curse Iblīs, nor does Iblīs speak at all. Rather, God identifies Iblīs as an enemy to humanity. This may be a small distinction. One may regard God's identification of Iblīs as an enemy to humanity as an implied curse, but given the parallel stories elsewhere, most of them likely later than this telling in Sūrat al-Kahf, the refusal of Iblīs to bow down to Adam does not imply a precipitating event to the evil and activity of Iblīs.

So why did Iblīs not bow down? No explanation is given. We do not even have a declaration that Iblīs refused. The understanding of the nature of *jinn* that we have developed indicates that the character of *jinn* is quite variable. They can be demonic, for sure. They can also be devout reciters of the Qur'ān. They can be masters of particular places. One can negotiate protection and passage with them, just as one might with any tribal leader. In short, what the term *jinn* tells us about Iblīs is that one cannot make any assumptions about his moral state. One cannot assume that because he is a *jinn*, it would be inevitable, or even likely, that he would disobey God.

This is especially true given al-Ṭabarī's description of Iblīs as a former treasurer of the divine realm in a fallen angel version of the Iblīs story. That myth is not what we have here, but the point is that the tension implicit in the fallen angel myth—that an angel, or a subset of angels, can be good and turn bad—is also applicable to *jinn*.

Because Iblīs is a *jinn*, his character is changeable, which is to say, unreliable. That is why he is unsuitable as a protector. We do not know whether Dhū al-Qarnayn or Khiḍr are reliable. As servants of God they would not presume to take on roles that are not specifically granted to them. Their protector roles are by God's permission. Presumably they are reliable in their understanding of their proper place in the hierarchy of God's servants.

In this narration, Iblīs fulfills no divine purpose. He is not a professional tempter or a heavenly prosecutor of humanity testing their devotion. No siblings, real or implied, are present, only progeny. Although al-Ṭabarī tells many stories of Iblīs's former responsibilities in heaven, in this telling in Sūrat al-Kahf, there is no trace of former glory. He is not the enemy of God. There is, in this version, no encounter at all between Iblīs and God.

In this story we see Iblīs as a figure hostile to humanity by choice—a choice that might be traced back to his roots in the *jinn* tribe. Al-Ṭabarī describes all the ways in which this origination might have come about. Just as in the watcher story, something happened in primordial times to produce a creature, even a tribe of creatures, whose nature is to be independent of humanity, often hostile, sometimes partnered, but never steadfast. God did not create them intentionally for any particular purpose. Indeed, God did not directly create them at all. Rather they come about through incidents of encounter between humans and some lesser divine figures, such as the watcher angels. An integral part of the narrative tradition of the watcher myth that fits well with this particular telling of the Iblīs story is the rich corpus of spirit-human marriages. The world of lesser spiritual beings and the world of humans have a complex relationship. The hostility between *jinn* and humans is changeable. Beyond the usual defensive mechanisms such as charms or prayers, there are strange and wonderful ways of resolving the conflict, the strangest of all being the covenant of marriage.

All of this gives an account of the origin of evil at odds with that given or implied in other Qur'ānic Iblīs narratives. Iblīs is an enemy to humanity because, as a *jinn*, he has chosen to be for some reason. The origin of evil is not at issue here. The unreliability of Iblīs as a protector is the issue. He is not like trustworthy and wise Dhū al-Qarnayn or Khiḍr.

As long as the Iblīs stories are read as a composite, such nuances are lost. Read separately, these stories have something unique to tell us about Iblīs. Because Iblīs is a *jinn*, he will not be a reliable protector. Equally, because Iblīs is a *jinn*, one may expect some stories, some situations, some times when Iblīs or his progeny might act in ways that are not hostile to humanity. Such a story appears in al-Damīrī. A similar story appears in Rūmī's *Mathnawi*, the story of Iblīs and Mu'āwiya.

This aspect of the nature of Iblīs cannot be adduced from the other tellings of the Iblīs story in the Qur'ān. Only here, in Sūrat al-Kahf, is the way left open to see the possibility that Iblīs, the *jinn*, might have choices and dimensions that are not unalterably, eternally, and thoroughly hostile to humanity.

In this *sūrah*, two points emerge. First, the description of *jinn* attempting to hear the secrets of heaven calls to mind the heavenly knowledge communicated to mortals by Azazel and his associates in a version of the watcher myth. Secondly, this Iblīs narrative casts Adam and Iblīs as participants in a sibling rivalry narrative. The first of these two mythic strands poses the question of evil in terms of knowledge—that particular knowledge that earthly beings seek but remains reserved for heavenly beings. Much of this knowledge has to do with the issue of fate or destiny, a theme throughout the *sūrah*.

The second theme, that of sibling rivalry, highlights an important aspect of the early presentation of Iblīs: that initially, he is not presented as the icon of evil. We saw in Sūrat al-Kahf that some interpreters wish to take Iblīs as a *jinn*-protector. Iblīs becomes an enemy of humanity, not inevitably but as a result of choice, a prerogative of all *jinn*. Here, Iblīs makes a reasonable argument for his superiority to Adam as a basis for declining to bow down to him. God is unswayed. As in the biblical stories of Cain and Abel, Isaac and Ishmael, Jacob and Esau, and the prodigal son, the relationship and destiny of the two siblings, relative to each other, has less to do with their inherent characteristics than with God's sovereign choice. God's choice reflects God's unique knowledge, even secret knowledge, which thus connects the second theme of sibling rivalry to the first theme of knowledge reserved to heaven.

Both of these themes, especially the second, are inherently narrative. The story of the relationship between siblings in the Bible, particularly in the Cain and Abel and the Jacob and Esau stories, is never told in a starkly moralistic tone. The characters are complex, as is the message of the story.

CHAPTER 6

Sūrat al-Ḥijr (15)

The *Sūrah*

In her analysis of Sūrat al-Ḥijr, Angelika Neuwirth notes a liturgical organization to the *sūrah*. The first verse gives the source and authority for this liturgy:

> *tilka āyātu al-kitāb wa-qur'ān^{in} mubīn^{in}*
>
> These are signs of the Book and a clarifying *qur'ān*.

In Neuwirth's interpretation, the *kitāb* or Book refers to the heavenly fixed text from which a variety of signs (*āyāt*) issue forth as revelation. These in turn are recited ceremonially and liturgically as *qur'ān*. Thus the initial verse announces the form and function of what follows. The rest of the *sūrah* follows a general pattern that the early Meccan community might have found in the other monotheistic communities. Neuwirth draws parallels between eastern Orthodox liturgy and a possible early Islamic liturgy. She divides the *sūrah* into four sections as follows:

1. Verses 2–25. *Ektenia*—a litany of pleas to God. Here they are God's response to the pleas, a promise of consolation.
   Part a. The rejecters of the Qur'ān will suffer a grievous fate. Their demands for evidence of the veracity of the Message ignore the evidence that God has already given to them.
   Part b. A recitation of the signs, literally a reading from the Book of signs (*āyāt*).

2. Verses 26–48. The mythic origins of the Message and the origin of confusion about the Message. This is the Iblīs story with a final section (41–48) that illustrates the two destinies, one for the righteous and one for those who allow themselves to be led astray by Iblīs. This is a reading from the Book of Salvation History, the heavenly section.

3. Verses 49–84. Continues the narration of the Book of Salvation History, a history of the conveyance of the Message, but this is the terrestrial section. This includes the stories of Abraham, Lot, the mysterious *aṣḥāb al-Ḥijr*, the "companions of the rocky area." This last is an ambiguous reference, but often identified with the tribe of Thamūd.[1]

4. Verses 85–99. A closing exhortation and *ektenia*, with instructions as to how to respond to the adversaries.[2]

Neuwirth places Sūrat al-Ḥijr early on the basis of several observations. It is the only *sūrah* that demonstrates consciousness of itself as a unit, what Neuwirth calls "self-referentiality." As described above, it shows evidence of a pre-textual, liturgical organization, placing its generation early in the process of community formation. It is the first *sūrah* to make conscious reference to itself as a portion of a larger text: "and we have given you seven repeated [verses?] and the mighty Qur'ān" (v. 87). It is the first to include a long narrative.[3] It also shows an emerging consciousness of a community: "Tell my servants (*'ibādī*)" (v. 49, with parallels in vv. 40, 42, and, as "guests," v. 68). In her view, the story of Iblīs is part of a larger cosmogonic focus that the *sūrah* reflects throughout, drawing in turn from the earlier, hymnic Sūrat al-Raḥmān, particularly 55:14–15.[4] With these characteristics in mind, Neuwirth places Sūrat al-Ḥijr not only as the first in the Iblīs passages but also at the heart of the Qur'ān.

[1] Al-Ṭabarī, *Jāmi'*, 14.49–50 (vol. 8).

[2] Neuwirth, "Referentiality and Textuality." Neuwirth gives a somewhat different division of the *sūrah* in the beginning, based on literary distinctions, but I find the liturgical arrangement more helpful.

[3] Prior to this, in her chronology, the longest was the story of the guests of Abraham (51:24–37). Elsewhere, narratives tend to be 2–3 verses in length.

[4] Neuwirth, "Negotiating Justice (Part I)," 31.

Kitāb and *Qur'ān*

Like so many of the *sūrahs* in the Middle Meccan period, a major theme in Sūrat al-Ḥijr is the rejection of the message. This appears in the first pericope after the introduction (vv. 2–3):

> *rubbamā yawaddu al-ladhīna kafarū law kānū muslimīna*
> *dharhum ya'kulū wa-yatamatta'ū wa-yulhimim al-amalu fa-sawfa ya'lamūna*
>
> Perhaps those who do not believe would wish that they had become Muslims.
> Leave them to eat and enjoy themselves, and be oblivious of hope; they will soon know.

A significant addition to this theme is the issue of destiny, which appears throughout the *sūrah*. In verses 4 and 5, it appears as follows:

> *wa mā ahlaknā min qaryat^{in} illā wa-lahā kitāb^{un} ma'lūm^{un}*
> *mā tasbiqu min ummat^{in} ajalahā wa mā yasta'khirūna*
>
> We never destroyed a village but that it had a known decree
> and the people cannot anticipate their term, nor delay [it].

The term *kitāb* mirrors the first verse: "these are the signs/verses (*āyāt*) of the Book/writing (*kitāb*) and a clear Qur'ān/recitation/proclamation (*qur'ān*)." One can read this verse in many ways. Three levels of reference to a canon of Scripture appear here: the verses, the Book, the Qur'ān. As Neuwirth points out, the canon was early in the process of formation at the time this verse was first heard. There is not yet a "Qur'ān" in the shape of a written text. But there is the beginning of a consciousness of being a worshipping monotheistic religious community.

But we also see an alternative level of reference to that to which the Qur'ān testifies: to the signs (*āyāt*) in the heavens, to the decree (*kitāb*) of God, and to the act of each revelation (*qur'ān*) as it comes to Muḥammad. The Book is both the Qur'ān text in the process of manifestation, and the written decree in heaven that governs human life and all creation. As Daniel Madigan puts it:

> [The Qur'ān] uses words derived from the root *k-t-b* mostly to refer not to the Qur'ān itself but to phenomena with which we are familiar from other religious contexts: the recording of all that is destined

> to happen (e.g., Q 3:145; 58:21); divine decrees binding either on humanity (e.g., Q 4:24) or on God himself (e.g., Q 6:12, 54); the inventory of all that exists (e.g., 10:61; 11:6); and the registers of each individual's good and evil deeds, written either by God himself (e.g., Q 3:181) or by heavenly agents (e.g., Q 10:21).[5]

In this sense the first verse, in the context of the sixth verse, adds the dimension of destiny to the questions of belief.

Madigan argues that throughout the Qur'ān the primary referent of *kitāb* is to the knowledge of God and to the authoritative divine will. He then states that 15:1 uses the terms *kitāb* and *qur'ān* interchangeably.[6] I would argue that this is not the case according to his own line of reasoning. The *kitāb* here is the content of that to which the signs point, the authority that sets the term of life, the *ajal* that verse 5 mentions. The *qur'ān* is an articulation of that knowledge, or more accurately, of only that portion of the heavenly knowledge that is revealed and recited to clarify those signs.

William Graham has pointed out that the basic meaning of the word *qur'ān* is "to proclaim aloud, to recite orally."[7] It refers to those particular revelations that are distinguished from other revelations that became *ḥadīth qudsī*, divinely inspired but not usable for the *ṣalāt* (i.e., not usable for liturgical purposes). Hence the term *qur'ān* cannot be applied to just any revelation or speech from God, but solely to the liturgical revelations that were eventually, most likely after the time of Muḥammad, gathered into the canon of the scriptural Qur'ān. This is particularly true if the Syriac Christian *qeryānā* has an etymological link to the term.[8] Hence the *qur'ān* is that portion of the *kitāb* that: (a) is to be revealed to humanity; and b) has a liturgical use. All *qur'ān* is *kitāb*, but not all *kitāb* is *qur'ān*.

This introduces, subtly to be sure, a distinction between the divine knowledge of God, which must be complete, and the divine knowledge of (in the possession of) humanity that is incomplete, but nevertheless sufficient to establish belief. Not all that is decreed in heaven (*kitāb*) is made known on earth (*qur'ān*). The superiority of God's knowledge and the willingness of humanity to believe on the limited but sufficient basis of signs (*āyāt*) and communications (*qur'ān*) form a leitmotif throughout the *sūrah*.

[5] Madigan, *Self-Image*, 4.

[6] Ibid., 15.

[7] Graham, "The Earliest Meaning of Qur'ān," 367.

[8] Graham, "The Earliest Meaning of Qur'ān," 365; Madigan, *Self-Image*, 129–30.

In the first verse, it is difficult to determine whether the *qur'ān*, the verbal communication, is the recitation of Muḥammad, or of the believer, or of God. In one sense, all three are the same. What God recites—or God through Gabriel—is then recited by Muḥammad. What Muḥammad recites is then recited by the Muslim community. The context suggests that the speech here is that of God, the meaning being, at least at one level, that these are the signs of what is declared in heaven and spoken clearly by God (through Gabriel) so that all who will may understand and believe.

Structure of the *Sūrah*

The first section, as Neuwirth has divided the *sūrah*, recapitulates the theme of many Middle Meccan *sūrahs*—that of the disbelievers who mock Muḥammad and his message. As elsewhere, the text makes reference to the long lineage of messengers whom people also mocked. The tales of old, the salvation history, provide antecedents for the contemporary community. Their situation is not new, not unexpected, and not without precedent. These same themes appear in the next *sūrah*: Sūrah Ṣād.

In verses 12–13a, God abets their intransigence: "we insert into the hearts of the miscreants that they should not believe in it." An example of the degree of their unwillingness to believe the signs that have been laid before them immediately follows: "were we to open a gate of heaven to them, and they would continuously ascend to it, they would say, 'our eyes have become drunk; indeed, we are a people bewitched.'" This again raises the question of destiny. Has God foreordained the disbelief of the miscreants? The nature and purpose of this prompting on the part of God is not explained. It simply raises the issue of God's predestination of human acts.

Thus the tension appears already set between two perceptions. On the one hand, the disbelievers willfully persist in their disbelief in spite of the array of evidence that God has placed before them: the signs of the zodiac, the messengers, the mountains of the earth, the rains, and the sufficient produce of the world. To this disbelief is added the knowledge that God has of their future persistence in disbelief, such that greater interventions would be futile. But, on the other hand, set against this knowledge is the subtle role that God has in creating precisely that intransigence that qualifies the degree of human choice in the matter. The tension is not resolved here, although it will command persistent and voluminous attention in subsequent Muslim theology.[9]

The theme of human willingness relates to, but is different from, the theme of knowledge, the knowledge that God has, and the knowledge that the disbelievers do not have but will have in the future, to their great regret (v. 3). This common Qur'ānic theme was developed in Sūrat al-Kahf. Here the knowledge is, in part, an awareness of their term of life (*ajal*), which is written in a divine compilation of decrees (*kitāb*). God sets the *ajal* not only of individuals but of settlements as well, a harbinger of the Lot story later in the *sūrah*. Such knowledge is never available to them, but the warning of the penalty for disbelief is available to them as the message, the reminder (*al-dhikr*) in verses 6 and 9.

This message is not only available through the prophet Muḥammad but is also displayed in the natural world that is appreciated throughout the Qur'ān: a sign (*āyah*) and demonstration of God's sovereignty and grace.[10] This message makes the rejection of the rejecters triply naïve. Not only have Muḥammad (v. 6), and his predecessors (v. 10) presented the message of God to them, but it is also manifest in creation, which is all around them and continually provides them with sustenance (v. 20). Just as the message has been preserved through repeated messengers (v. 9), it is also preserved from evil spirits (v. 17). The second part of this section mirrors the first but on a cosmological plane. The contrast between those mortals who would not believe even if they were to be given access to heaven (vv. 14–15), and evil spirits who attempt to gain such access to heaven and are prevented from doing so, provides the hinge between the two parts. The final pericope (vv. 23–25) provides a hymnic coda: all things come from God, and all things return to God (as an inheritance); all things are known to God, who will gather the eager and the hesitant and deal with all.

We will address verses 16–18, which mention the evil spirits (*shayāṭīn*) and the Iblīs story that occupies the second section according to this division, in detail below. The second section (vv. 26–48) contains the Iblīs story and continues the preceding attention to cosmology but moves the setting from the contemporary (or perhaps eternal) setting to the primordial. It continues the theme of God's creativity noted in the first section.

[9] See Watt, *Free Will*.

[10] Graham, "Winds," 25–34.

The Iblīs story ends with a brief description of the hell that is promised to those who go astray: the *ghāwīn* of verse 42. The reference to the seven gates of hell is unique, although several references to the seven heavens appear in the Qur'ān.[11] The division or classification of sinners is not specified here, but the idea of different groups reflects a previous reference to sects (*shiya'i*) in v. 10.

The description of hell with its plural gates contrasts with the promise of plural gardens and springs. Verse 47 reads: "and we (will) extract from their breasts what malice is therein; [they will be] brothers on thrones facing each other." The lack of regret here contrasts with the arousal of regret that will be the lot of those who do not accept the message of Muḥammad as described in verses 2–3, thus uniting the first fifty verses into a unity.

Verses 49–50 also provide a transition into a section of historical stories. The command "Tell!" links verse 49, "Tell my servants," which is a summation of the warning section, with verse 51, "Tell them about the guests of Abraham."

Another link between the Abraham story and the previous section is the greeting of peace. The faithful will enter into the gardens with peace and security (v. 46), and the guests greet Abraham with "Peace" and, in response to his fear, relieve his fear. The promise of peace is explicit, and that of security implicit. The earthly house of Abraham links with the heavenly garden.

A further parallel is the theme of the message. The first task of the messengers is to deliver good news, which Abraham first questions but then accepts. This contrasts with the disbelievers in the beginning of the *sūrah* and those in the story of Lot, who also receive signs of good news but do not accept it even when given further supporting evidence.

The final section (vv. 85–99) rehearses the theme of God's purposeful creation of the heavens and the earth. It mentions the "seven repeated," usually taken to refer to the seven *āyah*s of the Sūrat al-Fātiḥah and the *qur'ān al-'aẓīm*, which refers to the text of the Qur'ān, or at least to a corpus of passages already revealed. The addition of *al-'aẓīm* gives it an altogether different sense than the *qur'ān* mentioned in the first *āyah* of the *sūrah*.

Verses 87–91 of the final section refers to certain treatments of the text, but the commentators have widely differing views as to the exact meanings, all of which are speculative. However we might interpret the details of this last section, the larger message is similar to that at the end of Sūrah Ṣād.

[11] 2:29, 17:44, 23:86, 41:12, 65:12, 67:3, 71:15.

Verse 89 begins with a *qul!* instruction to Muḥammad to continue to preach the message of the Qur'ān (v. 94), in spite of opposition (v. 97). The final reference to joining those in prostration is a clear allusion to the angels, who prostrate themselves to Adam, and to Iblīs, who refuses.

The Evil Spirits

Verses 16–18 make brief reference to evil spirits (*shayāṭīn*; sing. *shayṭān*) from which the zodiacal signs have been guarded:

> *wa-la-qad ja'alnā fī al-samā'i buruj*^{an} *wa-zayyannāhā li-l-nāẓirīn*
> *wa-ḥafiẓnāhā min kuli shayṭān*^{in} *rajīm*^{in}
> *illā man istaraqa al-sam'a fa-atba'ahu shihāb*^{un} *mubīn*^{un}

> We made in the heaven the constellations and we made them adornments for the beholders,
> And we preserved them from every stoned evil spirit (*shayṭān*^{in} *rajīm*^{in}),
> But anyone who sneaks a hearing, a bright flame (*shihāb*^{un} *mubīn*) follows him.

The second of the two verses adds that these *shayāṭīn* seek to eavesdrop on the heavens, and a bright flame or meteor chases them.

The phrase *shayṭān rajīm* has become a common devotional preamble following the Qur'ānic instruction in Sūrat al-Naḥl, 16:98: "When you recite the Qur'ān, seek refuge (*f-asta'idh*) in God from *al-shayṭān al-rajīm*, the stoned Satan. This has come to mean "the accursed Satan," but this is an interpretation of the more literal "stoned," as Padwick points out.[12] Sūrat al-Naḥl is commonly understood to be later than the four *sūrah*s that contain the stoning myth,[13] and so the devotional refuge-seeking (*isti'ādha*) with specific reference to *al-shayṭān al-rajīm* is likely to be derived from the myth, but the general pattern of devotional *isti'ādha* is early, as evidenced by the last two *sūrah*s of the Qur'ān, Sūrat al-Falaq, and Sūrat al-Nās.[14]

The stoning myth appears in three other *sūrah*s—Sūrat al-Ṣāffāt, Sūrat al-Mulk, and Sūrat al-Jinn.

[12] Padwick, *Muslim Devotions*, 83–93.

[13] Sūrat al-Naḥl 37:6–10; 67:5; 72:6–10; and here, 15:16–18. See Watt, *Introduction*, 206–13.

[14] According to Nöldeke, Sūrah 16 is Medīnan (*Ursprung des Qorāns*, 145–47). The common Egyptian ordering puts it as 70th.

Sūrat al-Ṣāffāt (37) gives a further explanation in a passage that mentions the high council that we will also find in Sūrah Ṣād:

innā zayyannā al-samā'a al-dunyā bi-zīnat^in al-kawākibi
wa-ḥifẓan min kulli shayṭān^in mārid^in
lā yassamma'ūna ilā al-malā'i al-'alā wa-yuqdhafūna min kulli jānib^in
duḥūr^an wa-lahum 'adhāb^un wāṣib^un
illā man khaṭifa al-khatfata fa-atba'ahu shihāb^un thāqib^un

Truly we have adorned the heaven of the earth (the lowest heaven) with a decoration of stars (*kawākib*),
And (it is) a protection from all rebellious evil spirits (*shayṭān mārid*).
They will not listen to the high council (*al-malā'i al-'ala*) and be hurled down from every side,
Chased away; and for them will be a permanent torment;
Except those who seize something suddenly—then they are chased by a piercing flame (*shihāb thāqib*). (vv. 6–10)

This passage adds a quality of rebelliousness to the evil spirits and suggests that they are not listening to the high council. The last three verses imply that some spirits will be chased away, perhaps by angels, but it is those who snatch something, perhaps information, that a "piercing flame" (*shihāb thāqib*) chases. This last expression could refer to shooting stars or meteors.[15]

Sūrat al-Mulk (67) adds the following information:

wa-laqad ziyyannā al-samā'a al-dunyā bi-maṣābīḥa wa-ja'alnāhā rujūm^an li-l-shayāṭīni wa-a'tadnā lahum 'adhāba al-sa'īri

We have adorned the lowest heaven with lamps (*maṣābīḥ*), and we made them stones (*rujūm*) for the evil spirits (*shayāṭīn*), and we have prepared for them a torment of flame. (v. 5)

Here the stars (called "lamps" here and in 41:12) become the weapons that are aimed at the evil spirits. In Sūrat al-Ḥijr the constellations (*burūj*) guard the heaven, but in Sūrat al-Ṣāffāt it is the stars (*kawākib*) that guard.

Finally, Surāt al-Jinn (72) adds this comment:

wa-annahu kāna rijāl^un min al-insi ya'ūdhūna bi-rijāl^in min al-jinni fa-zādūhum rahaq^an
wa-annahum ẓanū kamā ẓanantum an lan yab'atha allahu aḥad^an

[15] See Welch, "Pneumatology," 83.

> *wa-annā lamasnā al-samā'a fa-wajadnāhā muli'at ḥaras*[an] *shadīd*[an] *wa-shuhub*[an]
> *wa-annā kunnā naq'udu minhā maqā'ida li-l-sam'i fa-man yastami'i al-ana yajid lahu shihāb*[an] *raṣad*[an]
> *wa-annā lā nadriy asharr*[un] *urīda bi-man fī al-arḍi am arāda bi-him rabbuhum rashad*[an]

> And there were people among the humans who sought refuge in people among the *jinn*, and they increased them in folly.
> And they believed as you (pl.) believe: that God would never raise up a single one.
> And we sought the heavens, but we found it filled with a strong guard and flames (*shuhub*).
> And we used to sit among them in seats to listen, but those who listen now find for him a watchful flame (*shihāb raṣad*).
> And we are not aware of the misfortune that is intended for those on earth or [if] their Lord wants for them right conduct. (vv. 6–10)

This *sūrah* begins in verse 1 with *jinn* listening to the Qur'ān and approving of what they hear. Then, speaking in the first person plural, the *jinn* acknowledge that some among them lie about God in verse 4. From the preceding verse (v. 3), it would seem that the lie concerns God's association with a female companion or a child. Verse 7 implies that the disagreement about God may be whether God will indeed bring the world to a final moment in which all are raised to judgment. This, in turn, provides the context for listening in verse 8. Unlike the versions of the story in Sūrat al-Ḥijr and Sūrat al-Ṣāffāt, there is no indication of stealth or secrecy in Surāt al-Jinn. Nevertheless, guards and flames defend the heavens, and here it is the flames (*raṣad*) that are in hiding.

The resistance of heaven to eavesdropping *jinn* is a new development. Verse 9 implies that sitting and listening to the counsels of heaven used to be a normal activity, but it is "now" (*al-an*) that the heavens are guarded. The text gives no indication as to what has changed, or why. Al-Ṭabarī's collection of primordial legends, especially those legends that have Iblīs as a guardian of the treasury of heaven and/or in the lower ranks of angels, may lie in the distant background here.

It is clear from verse 10 that the counsel, which used to be shared but now is not, has to do with the destiny of humanity. We see this concern in the earlier comment on the desire of mortals to know the term of their lives (*ajal*) in verse 5. A further piece of valuable information concerns which mortals will receive guidance (*rashad*) and which will not. This prohibition of active listening is enhanced by the use of the eighth form of the verb (*yastamiʿ*) "one who listens," in verse 9, which gives a slightly more passive sense to the listening. The same form is used in Sūrat al-Ḥijr for listening by stealth (*istaraqa*), which literally means, "to steal a hearing." Sūrat al-Ṣāffāt intensifies this aspect further by describing attempts to steal something (*khaṭifa al-khaṭfata*) from heaven: perhaps the information about the destiny of mortals to which Surāt al-Jinn refers.

The idea that certain knowledge in heaven is to be kept from humanity is one familiar from the Azazel or Asael version of the watcher myth, described in chapter 3. Here it is knowledge of metallurgy, ornamentation, alchemy, herbology, and astrology that are mentioned, but many of the fields of knowledge involve knowledge not simply of skills, but of destiny:

> Amasras taught incantation and the cutting of roots; and Armaros the resolving of incantations; and Baraqiyal astrology, and Kokarer'el (the knowledge of) the signs, and Tam'el taught the seeing of the stars, and Asder'el taught the course of the moon as well as the deception of man. And (the people) cried and their voice reached unto heaven. (*1 En*. 8:3–4)[16]

1 Enoch 8:6 gives the interpretation of the archangels Michael, Surafel, and Gabriel. They complain to God that Azazel has "revealed eternal secrets which are performed in heaven (and which) man learned." This still does not clarify whether these secrets are the secrets of skills or of foreknowledge.

Later chapters of *1 Enoch* emphasize the danger of this knowledge:

> And so to the Watchers on whose behalf you [Enoch] have been sent to intercede—who were formerly in heaven—(say to them), "You were (once) in heaven, but not all the mysteries (of heaven) are open to you, and you (only) know the rejected mysteries. Those ones you have broadcast to the women in the hardness of your hearts and by those mysteries the women and men multiply evil deeds upon the earth." Tell them, "Therefore, you will have no peace!" (*1 En*. 16:2–3)[17]

> The name of the first is Yeqon; he is the one who misled all the children of the angels, brought them down upon the earth, and perverted them by the daughters of the people. The second was named

[16] Charlesworth, *Old Testament Pseudepigrapha*, 1:16.

[17] Ibid., 1:47–48.

> Asb'el; he is the one who gave the children of the holy angels an evil counsel and misled them so that they would defile their bodies by the daughters of the people. The third was named Gader'el; this one is he who showed the children of the people all the blows of death, who misled Eve, who showed the children of the people (how to make) the instruments of death (such as) the shield, the breastplate, and the sword for warfare, and all (the other) instruments of death to the children of the people. Through their agency (death) proceeds against the people who dwell upon the earth, from that day forevermore. The fourth is named Pinem'e; this one demonstrated to the children of the people the bitter and the sweet and revealed to them all the secrets of their wisdom. Furthermore he caused the people to penetrate (the secret of) writing and (the use of) ink and paper; on account of this matter, there have been many who have erred from eternity to eternity, until this very day. For human beings are not created for such purposes to take up their beliefs with pen and ink. For indeed human beings were not created but to be like angels, permanently to maintain pure and righteous lives. Death, which destroys everything, would have not touched them, had it not been through their knowledge by which they shall perish; death is (now) eating us by means of this power.[18] (*1 En.* 69:4–11)

Ginzburg cites Jewish legend that "by means of the magic arts taught them by the angels Uzza and Azzael, they set themselves as masters over the heavenly spheres, and forced the sun, the moon, and the stars to be subservient to themselves instead of the Lord."[19] In his notes, Ginzburg conflates the two myths and comments on philological grounds that Shemihazah and Azzael (/Aseal/Azazel) and Uzza (and theophoric variations) are all the same. This may be arguable on linguistic grounds, but it is clear from the sources that the myths of Azazel and Shemihazah, which come together in *Enoch* and subsequent legend, are originally distinct.[20] Gen 6:1–4 draws only on the Shemihazah myth, but does not specifically name Shemihazah.

In the Qur'ānic *jinn* myth with which we are dealing here, there is significant similarity with the myth associated with Azazel, but no implication of the Shemihazah story in Sūrat al-Kahf. The Azazel story appears in the *Apocalypse of Abraham*. In fact, the Shemihazah myth is

[18] Ibid., 1:47–48.

[19] Ginzburg, *Legends*, 1:124.

[20] Nickelsburg argues that the Shemihazah myth is the earliest stratum, to which the first elements of the Asael myth were added: namely the teaching of knowledge—and finally the Asael figure appears (Nickelsburg, *1 Enoch*, 169–73)..

repeated in the Apocrypha in many places—*Jubilees* 4:15, 22; and 5:1, the *Testament of the Twelve Patriarchs* (*T. Reu*. 5:6, *T. Dan* 1:7, 3:6, *T. Naph*. 3:5). The *Clementine Homilies* (8:12–16) combines both once again but attributes the cause of evil in the world and the reason for the subsequent flood to the angelic involvement with human women.

The *Testament of Solomon* (probably third cent. C.E.) gives the most data relevant to this particular Qur'ānic story. Solomon has been given a ring by the archangel Michael that allows him to interrogate demons. One of those demons, Ornias, tells Solomon that a certain boy will die. Solomon asks him how he knows God's plan for the future:

> Then I ordered Ornias to be brought to me again and I said to him, "Tell me how you know that the young man will die in three days." He responded, "We demons go up to the firmament of heavens, fly around among the stars, and hear the decisions which issue from God concerning the lives of men. The rest of the time we come and, being transformed, cause destruction, whether by domination, or by fire, or by sword, or by chance." I asked him, "Tell me, then, how you, being demons, are able to ascend into heaven." He replied, "Whatever things are accomplished in heaven (are accomplished) in the same way also on earth; for the principalities and authorities and powers above fly around and are considered worthy of entering heaven. But we who are demons are exhausted from not having a way station from which to ascend or on which to rest; so we fall down like leaves from the trees and the men who are watching think that stars are falling from heaven. That is not true, King; rather, we fall because of our weakness and, since there is nothing on which to hold, we are dropped like flashes of lightning to the earth. We burn cities down and set fields on fire. But the stars of heaven have their foundations laid in the firmament."[21] (vv. 11–17)

In this version of the myth, the blazing flames are not the guardians of the heavens, but the falling demons themselves. This story, which parallels the Qur'ānic version closely, asserts that the information sought by the demons is that of future events. The text goes on to state that the boy does die; the information is accurate.

The Enochic versions of the Azazel story focus on the knowledge of illicit arts and crafts brought down from the celestial regions by the watcher angels in the antediluvian era. The *Testament of Solomon*, like the Qur'ānic myth,

[21] Charlesworth, *Old Testament Pseudepigrapha*, 1:983.

describes a regular practice of demonic spying on the heavenly counsels. The situation reported in the *Testament of Solomon* is that which no longer applies in the Qur'ān—the demons can no longer gain knowledge of heavenly plans and designs, according to 72:9, but they used to. Something has changed.

The Qur'ānic myth of the *jinn* spies in heaven, collated from four *sūrahs*, describes an effort on the part of the *jinn* to discover information about the destiny of humanity and, perhaps, of themselves, from the heavenly council. The effect of this narrative is to emphasize the barrier between what is known in heaven (*kitāb*) and what is revealed to earth (*qur'ān*). Unlike the narrative of the *Testimony of Solomon*, the Qur'ān implies that *jinn* efforts are normally unsuccessful. Heaven is carefully guarded.

There is another sense, investigated by Jaroslav Stetkevych, in which the presence of *jinn* marks the boundary between heaven and earth. He points out that the cairns (*rajam*) that pilgrims stone on the last day of the Hajj at Minā mark the boundary between the sacred precincts of Mecca and the world beyond.[22] There is little legendary explanation for the ritual of stoning these pillars, but popular belief associates these three stones with al-Shayṭān; as such, they require stoning. But prior to the establishment of the Islamic Hajj, pilgrims stoned the pillars of Minā on their day of departure, as described by Ibn Isḥāq, with no reference to any demon.[23] Here it is a ritual of separation. Stetkevych compares this to the pile of stones set up by Laban and Jacob to mark the boundary of their lands (Gen 41:44–52). The mound itself is a testimony to the contract, but it also has an apotropaic function that prevents either Laban or Jacob from passing beyond the limit to do harm. Stetkevych points out that the mound at Minā has a further relevance as a place where seventy men and one woman entered into a covenant accepting Muḥammad's prophethood, making it not only a boundary but a place of covenant similar to the dual function of the Laban-Jacob mound.

Given the popular association of *jinn* with the wilderness, such cairns might mark the boundary between the settled areas where humans have control and the wilderness areas that are the domain of *jinn*. Beyond the marker, humans must defend themselves with apotropaic means or conclude covenants with the *jinn* masters of the wild.

Stetkevych points out that the connection of the cairns with al-Shayṭān comes through the linguistic evidence of *wathan*, an Arabic word meaning

[22] Stetkevych, *Muḥammad*, 41–48.

[23] Ibn Hishām, *Muhammad*, 90–91.

a "set-up" idol with Sabaic roots meaning a boundary marker. He claims that there is a similar relationship between the *rajam* (stone cairns) and their current appellation (*jamarāt*), which literally means "live embers" but has come to mean a cairn with heaps of pebbles, the common description of the three pillars at Minā.

In the context of the *jinn* spies, it is startling that it is "live embers" (here the *shihāb* in its various forms—*thāqib*, *mubīn*, or *raṣad*) that most characterizes the myth. Whether the *jinn* are chased by the *shihāb* or actually are the *shihāb*, their light marks the boundary between the domain of the earth with its limited knowledge and the domain of the heavens with its unlimited knowledge. In the skies the watchful guardians stone them. On earth departing pilgrims stone them. In both places, they mark the boundary between the sacred and forbidden (*ḥarām*) precincts and the wider world.

The *jinn* spy myth sustains the theme of destiny in Sūrat al-Ḥijr as the separation between celestial knowledge and the limited human and *jinn* knowledge, as well as the limitation of human and *jinn* access to the secrets of the future.

The Iblīs Story

Adam and Iblīs

The Iblīs story, told at great length in verses 26 through 42 or 44, follows from a declaration of God, rendered in the first person plural "we," proclaiming the broad knowledge of God. Verse 26 continues the pronominal "we": "We created humanity from ringing clay (*ṣalṣāl*), from stinking black clay (*ḥamā' masnūn*)." This reference to the creation of humanity (*al-insān*) follows from verse 23, where God says, "Truly it is we who bring to life and we bring death." Two verses later, the description moves from the collective action of heaven to the individual action of God, from "we" to "I." Verse 28 parallels the announcement in Sūrah Ṣād (v. 71), except that the clay has become more specified. This specification indicates a new angle to the Iblīs story: the parallelism of Iblīs and Adam.

The beginning of the Iblīs story in Sūrat al-Ḥijr sets Iblīs and his race of *jinn* in contrast to Adam (not yet named here) and the race of humanity. The *jinn* are the first creation, but it is humanity that is mentioned first:

> and we created humanity from ringing clay, from stinking black clay; and the *jinn* we created before from the fire of scorching wind. (vv. 26–27)

The symmetry of the passage comes through better in the Arabic:

> *wa-la-qad khalaqnā al-insāna min ṣalṣal*^{in} *min ḥamā'*^{in} *masnūn*^{in}
wa-l-jinn khalaqnāhu min qablu min nāri-s-samūm^{in}

One can see the chiastic relationship in the beginning of the two verses:

> *khalaqnā al-insāna*
al-jinn khalaqnāhu

The creation of humanity is emphasized by being mentioned first, but the inversion of subject and verb in the second verse balances the emphasis, which gives prominence to the *jinn*. Paired *min*-phrases evenly balance the remainder of the two verses, the second of which have similar rhythms and sound patterns. Both of the final words, *masnūn* and *samūm*, are derivatives of geminate roots, *s-n-n* and *s-m-m*. There is also a near-symmetry of rhyme within the first verse: *insān* and *masnūn*.

The rest of the story sets off this poetic diptych in three ways. First, the verses continue the first person plural discourse of the previous verses of the *sūrah*, while the following verses mark the first break into a first person singular discourse. Secondly, *idh,* which normally marks the beginning of a literary unit, introduces the next verse (v. 28). Thirdly, the poetic nature of these two verses stands apart from what follows. What precedes them also has a similar rhyme and rhythm but is set apart from the introduction of the Iblīs story by the formulaic colophon in which God is identified by particular, multiple, divine names, in this case *hakīm* and *'alīm*, the wise one and the knowing one.

These two verses, therefore, have a signal role, setting the theme for what is to follow. The phrase *ṣalṣal*^{in} *min ḥamā'*^{in} *masnūn*^{in} is repeated twice more in the following text: once by God (v. 28) and then again by Iblīs (v. 33). They set up a contrast, but also a parallel, between the *jinn* and humanity, both identified in terms of their material creation. God creates both *jinn* and humanity. They are of common origin. *Jinn* and humanity are mentioned together often in the Qur'ān: both have evil spirits (*shayāṭīn*), which oppose prophets (6:112); they may assemble together (6:130); peoples (*ummam*) of each kind have passed into the fire in past times (7:38, 41:25) and will do so in the future (7:179, 32:13); they might be tempted to try together to produce the likes of the Qur'ān (17:88); both are created to serve God (51:56); both might be tempted to try to pass beyond the boundaries of heaven (55:33). Finally, and significantly, both are susceptible to the whisperings of the evil one (*al-waswās al-khannās*) in Sūrat al-Nās (114:4–6).

Through this constant parallelism, *jinn* and humanity share a common purpose—to worship God—and a common destiny—either paradise or the fire. Several passages mention *jinn* who will end up in the fire.[24] No passages specifically describe *jinn* in paradise, but the description of believing *jinn* in Surāt al-Jinn implies that this option is open. Later commentators discuss whether *jinn* may enter paradise and come up with various opinions. The predominant opinion is that *jinn* may, indeed, enter paradise. Al-Damīrī gives the flavor of the debate:

> It is said that among the *jinn* are favored ones and reverent ones, just as there are among humanity. According to this verse [55:46] the majority believe that the *jinn* of the believers will enter Paradise and will be recompensed as humans will be recompensed. But Abū Ḥanīfah and al-Layth disagree about this; they say the believers among them will be recompensed by being spared from the Fire. Most disagree with the two of them, even Abū Yūsuf and Muḥammad. Abū Ḥanīfah and al-Layth have no proof except the statement of God, "And he will deliver you from a severe torment," [46:31] and God's statement, "So whoever believes in his Lord shall not fear loss nor oppression [72:13]. But there is not mentioned in the two verses a recompense except the redemption from torment. The rejoinder is in two aspects: the first of the two is that there is silence about the recompense, and the second is that this is from the talk of the *jinn* and it is possible that they were not informed about the lofty [aspects] of this and what God has prepared for them concerning recompense is hidden from them. Some say that when they enter paradise they will not be with humans but rather they will be in an outlying section of it.
>
> In a *ḥadīth* from Ibn 'Abbās he said all creatures are in four kinds: creatures which are all in Paradise, and they are the angels; creatures all of whom are in the Fire, and they are the devils; creatures which are in Paradise and the Fire, and they are the *jinn* and the humans. For them are the recompense and the punishment. This is found in Ibn 'Abbās, the blessings of God on both of them and in it is

[24] 6:128; 7:38, 179; 34:12; 41:25; and 46:18.

> something which is that the angels will not be recompensed with good in Paradise.
> One of the peculiar [reports] is what is related by Aḥmad b. Marwān al-Mālikī al-Dīnawarī in the first part of Part Nine of Al-Majālisah according to Mujāhid, that he was asked about the *jinn* believers if they would enter Paradise and he said they would enter it but they will not eat in it and will not drink but rather will inspire praises and consecration and so will find in these two what the inhabitants of Paradise will find in the sweetness of the food and drink.[25]

Jacqueline Chabbi has introduced a novel understanding of the nature of *jinn*. She points out that in Arab culture fire (*nār*) is not valued negatively. At night fire provides warmth, protection from the wild, and a means for cooking. Hence *nār* as an agent of punishment would not be a natural association. During the day the fiery heat of the desert, however, a heat causing distortions on the horizon (the infamous mirages) might conjure images of spiritual beings especially associated with the scorching desert wind (*samūm*). Thus the *nār samūm* of verse 27, often translated as burning fire, really refers to scorching wind.[26]

The attention of the passage changes abruptly, announced with an *idh*. The narrator appears and describes the primordial encounter between God and the angels in which God announces his intention. This section parallels the language in Sūrah Ṣād but with added detail repeated from the poetic introduction:

> *wa-idh qāla rabbuka li-l-malā'ikati inni khāliqu basharan min ṣalṣālin min ḥamā'in masnūnin*
> *fa-idha sawwaytuhi wa-nafakhtu fīhi min rūḥī fa-qa'ū lahu sājidīna*

> And when your Lord said to the angels, "Truly I am creating a human from ringing clay, from stinking black clay.
> So when I have shaped him and blow into him [something] of my spirit, then fall down before him in prostration." (vv. 28–29)

Verse 28 repeats verse 26, except for the shift from *insān* to *bashar*. Both terms mean a human and may refer to male or female, but the connotations differ. The root *b-sh-r* has to do with the complexion of the skin. Lane (q.v.) cites the "Annotations on the Qamūs" of Muḥammad al-Fāsī that *bashar*

[25] Al-Damīrī, *Ḥayāt*, 1.186.

[26] Chabbi, *Le Seigneur*, 189–211.

refers to the human skin devoid of hair and wool.[27] *Insān* derives from *i-n-s*, meaning, "to be sociable." An *ins*, according to Lane (q.v.), is a sociable and enjoyable companion: a friend.[28] Hence *insān* refers to humanity in the social aspect, and *bashar* refers to humanity in the physical aspect. In verse 26, the use of *insān* implies the creation of the human race, the community or tribe of humans. In the second instance, verse 28, the context is more the physical construction into which God will subsequently breathe spirit and life.

The Refusal

The next section of the narrative gives the kernel of the Iblīs story, found, with slight alterations, in all seven narratives:

> *fa-sajada al-malā'ikatu kulluhum ajma'ūna*
> *illā iblīs abā an yakūna ma'a al-sājidīna*
>
> So the angels bowed down, all of them together,
> Except Iblīs; he refused to be with those who bowed down. (vv. 30–31)

Unlike several other versions, Sūrat al-Ḥijr does not evaluate the refusal to bow down. Iblīs is not accused of being haughty and an unbeliever (Sūrah Ṣād and Sūrat al-Baqarah) or a *jinn*, who breaks the command of his Lord (Sūrat al-Kahf). At this point in the story, with no other information, we might expect a reasonable explanation for such a refusal. God asks for such an explanation:

> *qāla yā-iblīsu mā laka allā takūna ma'a al-sājidīna*
> *qāla lam akun li-asjuda li-bashar^{in} khalaqtahu min ṣalṣāl^{in} min ḥamā'^{in} masnūn^{in}*
>
> He [God] said, "O Iblīs, what is with you that you are not with those who bow down?"
> He [Iblīs] said, "I am not one to prostrate myself to a human (*bashar*) whom you created from ringing clay, from stinking black clay." (vv. 32–33)

In Sūrah Ṣād, God specifies that the object of prostration is the handiwork of God, but here it is Iblīs who makes that specification. Further, it is the third

[27] Lane, *Arabic-English Lexicon*, 1:207–8.

[28] Ibid., 1:113–15.

repetition of the phrase *min ṣalṣāl[in] min ḥamā'[in] masnūn[in]* (from ringing clay, from stinking black clay). Why such an emphasis?

In Sūrah Ṣād, the emphasis is on the fact that it was God who created the creature (the *bashar*). Here, both *jinn* and *bashar* are creations of God, but the *bashar* is created from inferior elements. The classical commentaries give a great deal of attention to the exact nature of the clay from which the *bashar* is formed, although no attention at all to the implication of such definitions. Al-Ṭabarī reports some descriptions that put a noble spin on the phrase. Mujāhid describes the clay as *mithl al-khazzaf min al-ṭīn al-ṭayyib* (like ceramic of fine clay). But more common are terms such as *lāzib* and *lāziq* (sticky), *yābis* (dried), *muntin* or *munattan* (putrid, decayed), *sawād* (black), *raṭb* (moist), and *sanīn* (stinking).[29] Al-Qurṭubī, Ibn Kathīr, and al-Bayḍāwī give much the same list of equivalents and explanations.[30] I am not aware of any texts in Christian or Jewish traditions that describe the substance from which Adam was created in such negative terms.[31]

The text leads the reader into the irony of angels and *jinn* created of fire and scorching wind but bowing prostrate before a clinking, stinking form. The commentators attempt to undo the irony. Thus al-Qurṭubī reports from al-Quffāl:

> Truly part of the essence of clay is composure and tranquility, dignity and equanimity and forbearance and shyness and patience. This is what called Adam, after the good fortune that he had had before, to repentance and humility and supplication so it resulted in forgiveness, election and guidance for him. The essence of fire is fickleness, thoughtlessness, impetuosity, rising and disappearing and disruption. This is what called Iblis, after the misfortune that happened to him, to pride and willfulness, so that it gained for him destruction, agony, the curse and misery.[32]

[29] Al-Ṭabarī, *Jāmi'*, 14.27–29 (vol. 8).

[30] Al-Bayḍāwī, *Tafsīr*, 2.529; Ibn Kathīr, *Tafsīr*, 3.669; al-Qurṭubī, *Al-Jāmi'a,* 10.20–21 (vol. 5).

[31] Chipman, "Mythic Aspects," 16. Leigh Chipman surveys the legendary corpus in Judaism and finds no parallel. Early Christian writings occasionally describe the body as corrupted and corruptible, but this is not in terms of the creation of Adam, but rather in contrast to the purity, or neutrality, of the soul. See Ambrose, *On Belief in the Resurrection*, 10.177.

[32] Al-Qurṭubī, *Al-Jāmi'a*, 10.155 (vol. 5). Kamali, *Principles*, 197–228.

The power of the narrative, however, maintains the tension between the dynamic description of the *jinn* as fire or scorching wind and the repulsive description of the substance of humanity as sticky, slimy, and decaying mud.

Iblīs's complaint is entirely understandable. The commentators commonly accuse him here of being the first to use *qiyās*, reasoning by analogy. In Sunnī circles *qiyās* came to be considered an entirely legitimate source of law, but its use and abuse (in the eyes of the beholder/critic) was regularly subject to criticism.[33] This trajectory of explanation leads the commentators to miss the larger point of the story, particularly in the context of the *sūrah*.

A more trenchant understanding of the text's dynamic is accessible through the parallels with tales of sibling rivalry. As in the Cain and Abel and the Jacob and Esau stories, both from Genesis, the younger, less able child is chosen over the older child. Cain is a farmer, a nobler profession than Abel's shepherding, but Abel's offering is accepted. Esau is a hunter, while Jacob dawdles around the cooking pots, but it is through Jacob that the lineage of Israel passes. He supplants Esau. In the Qur'ān, Iblīs, the elder, made from purifying fire, is also supplanted and even commanded to prostrate himself before the new creation made from putrid mud.

In all three stories, the texts give no explanation for this violation of the Semitic pattern of primogeniture. In the two primordial stories, subsequent interpretation has seen in this reversal of the expected order the origin of human evil, an origin neither in the sin of pride, nor in that of malice, but in human jealousy, even justifiable jealousy. In this justification lies the tragic element. We can well imagine the anger and confusion of Cain that his offering is not accepted. We can understand the affront to Esau when his birthright and blessing are conned away. We can likewise understand the affront to Iblīs that he should bow down to this newer and lesser creation.

We have also seen that subsequent commentary on both primordial accounts justifies God's choice of the younger Abel and Adam over the older Cain and Iblīs. Most Christian interpretation and some Jewish commentary, such as that of Josephus, quoted in chapter 3, conjure up comprehensive descriptions of Cain's evil. Likewise we have seen similar arguments that Iblīs was always evil. These are attempts to convert a story that has essential tragic elements into a more familiar *shayṭānī* story of good versus evil: a combat myth.

That is not what the Qur'ān is presenting here. The elegance of the poetic diptych at the beginning of the narrative (vv. 26–27), repeated in the

[33] Hallaq, *History*, 82–107.

middle of the narrative, places Iblīs and Adam in fraternal relationship set in tension by God's action of reordering their relationship. That it is God who initiated this reordering of the expected relationship is a key point in the sibling rivalry.

This larger point becomes clearer in the final section in which Iblīs, having been ejected from heaven, blames God for his predicament and demands respite from the curse that God has pronounced upon him.

> *qāla fa-akhruj minhā fa-innaka rajīm^{un}*
> *wa-inna ʿalayka al-laʿnata ilā yawmi al-dīni*
> *qāla rabbi fa-anẓirnī ilā yawmi yubʿathūna*
> *qāla fa-innaka min al-munẓarīna*
> *ilā yawm al-waqti al-maʿlūmi*
> *qāla rabbi bi-mā aghwaytanī la-uzayyinanna lahum fī al-arḍi wa-la-ughwiyannahum ajmaʿīna*
> *illa ʿibādaka minhumu al-mukhlaṣīna*
>
> He [God] said, "Then get out from it, for truly you are cursed (lit. "stoned" *rajīm*).
> And truly a curse is upon you until the day of judgment."
> He [Iblīs] said, "My Lord, give me respite to the day they are raised."
> He [God] said, "Then truly you are among those given respite
> Until the day of the known time."
> He [Iblīs] said, "My Lord, because you have led me astray, I will lay out enticements for them on earth and I will surely lead them all astray
> Except your servants among them, the pure-hearted ones." (vv. 34–40)

Iblīs does not blame God in response to the curse. When God pronounces the curse upon Iblīs, his response is to move from the informal, even disrespectful explanation of his refusal (v. 33), to a more respectful demand or request for respite. He now addresses God as *rabbi*, "My Lord."

Only after having received this boon from God does Iblīs mention, more as explanation than retort, that since God has led him astray, he will lead others astray. The responsibility for Iblīs's divergent path lies firmly with God. The statement lacks any hint of the passion of accusation. Al-Ṭabarī even comments that God had given to Iblīs passion and lust from which other angels were free when God willed disobedience in him.[34] Neither does God

[34] Al-Ṭabarī, *Jāmiʿ*, 1.227 (vol. 1). Al-Ṭabarī's comment concerns arguments associated with the issue of whether Iblīs is an angel. He argues that just because Iblīs produces progeny (a process for which passion and lust are helpful) does not mean that Iblīs is not

refute this simple declaration in any way. It has all the marks of an agreement between Iblīs and God. The sentence begins with *bi-mā*, which does not have the sense of cause and effect, but rather a sense of giving a reason.[35] This is the destiny of Iblīs.

From the beginning of the *sūrah*, the chasm between what is known in heaven and what is revealed on earth has been established. Those on earth live in ignorance of the term decreed for them (vv. 4–5) but are not without sufficient indications to make the choice of belief, although God may even prompt disbelief at times (vv. 12–13). Now God has also led Iblīs astray. God has given Iblīs a term of life on earth that is both known and unknown. The rapid shift of terminology produces a promise with considerable uncertainty. God curses Iblīs until the "day of judgment"—the term *yawm al-dīn* is common and clear. Iblīs asks for respite until the "day on which they (the dead) are raised up." This also is clear, although it shifts the emphasis from the negative experience of judgment to the immediately preceding positive hope of resurrection. Iblīs wants to know his own *ajal*, the term of his life. God agrees, but shifts the language yet again to an entirely mysterious *yawm al-waqt al-ma'lūm* (the day of the time that is known). Of course, this time is known only to God and need not have anything to do with any eschatological events, so the term of Iblīs's respite (*ajal*) is as uncertain as ever. It is a promise without content. Iblīs is removed once again from heavenly knowledge, just as the rest of the *jinn* are kept at bay by the *shihāb* (v. 18).

The term *yawm al-dīn* is a general one, usually interchangeable with several other terms: *yawm al-qiyāma* (day of raising up), *yawm al-ḥisāb* (day of reckoning), *yawm al-ba'th* (day of resurrection) and *yawm al-jum'a* (the day of gathering).[36] The basic sequence of the eschaton is that first, at the soundings of the trumpet, the world will be annihilated in two stages, and then all will be resurrected in groups to stand before the judging angels. Some will then be condemned to the fire, and some will gain entrance into paradise.[37] On this understanding, there would be no significant difference between the

---

an angel, because God specifically wills those attributes in him. This, of course, begs the question whether God also wills an ability to disobey or an inclination to pride—Iblīs's point in raising the issue.

[35] Wright, *Grammar*, 2:160.

[36] Chittick, "Eschatology," 380. William Chittick points out that al-Ghazzālī lists over 100 names for this event in his *Iḥya 'Ulūm al-Dīn*.

[37] Smith and Haddad, *Islamic Understanding*, 63–97.

yawm al-dīn of which God speaks and the *yawm yab'athūna* to which Iblīs refers. In fact, the resurrection occurs prior to the moment of judgment.

The difference is not chronological, but rather one of emphasis. *Yawm al-dīn* is normally taken to refer to the whole day, which includes resurrection and judgment. Iblīs prefers to put the emphasis on resurrection, ignoring the issue of judgment. Perhaps he feels at this moment that by that time he will have done penance under the curse. Yet there is no tone of penance in his request, only, by the inclusion of the polite address, *rabbi*, an acknowledgment of God's greater authority and power.

Once again, divine knowledge confounds the plans of others. The "known time" leaves Iblīs without clarity. This knowledge compounds the disruption Iblīs has already experienced. Adam has been placed above him in contravention to the principle of primogeniture and the logic of material superiority. Iblīs will be reprieved, but for an indeterminate time. The greater must bow down to the lesser. Only God knows why.

The narrative supports the divine prerogative by steering clear of strong condemnation of Iblīs. Yet Iblīs is subject to a curse in verse 35 as is any other miscreant, human or *jinn*, who disobeys God. There is no hint of Iblīs as the origin of evil or as related in any way to al-Shayṭān. By being described as *rajīm* (stoned) in verse 34, his fate is associated with the *shayṭān* in verse 17, also so described. The concept of stoning applies not only to *jinn* and *shayāṭīn* but also to humans, such as to Abraham by his father in 19:46 (*yarjumu*), and potentially to Noah by his people in 26:116 (*marjūm*). The specific form, *rajīm*, however, is only applied to Iblīs, *shayāṭīn* and *al-shayṭān*.[38]

Iblīs takes upon himself a task of leading mortals astray. In this task he is acting no differently from God who led him astray, or who does at least not deny that charge. There are clear indications in the *sūrah* that God will lead some astray: "We insert into the hearts of the sinners that they should not believe in it (the message)" (vv. 12–13, see also 26:200). The larger emphasis of the *sūrah* is that God does provide signs clear enough that unbelievers can choose to believe. But God also knows beforehand who will go astray, such as the wife of Lot who will look back (v. 60). The signs given from heaven are adequate for belief, but the secrets of heaven, particularly the duration of life, are still kept from mortals and from *jinn*, and now, also from Iblīs.

In the latter half of this Iblīs narrative, the mythic theme of the fallen angel comes to the fore. It has not been present in the two *sūrahs* that we have

[38] In 3:36; 15:17; 15:34; 16:98; 38:77; and 81:25.

examined previously: Sūrah ṬāHā and Sūrat al-Kahf. It becomes dominant in Sūrat al-'Arāf and Sūrah Ṣād.

In al-Ṭabarī's catalogue of primordial myths of the origin of *jinn*, sampled in the last chapter, a number of them explain Iblīs's presence among the angels by according to him some prominent position in heaven: the ruler over the lowest heaven or the position of treasurer. This position does not quite achieve the adulation expressed for the king of Tyre in Ezekiel 28, but the sense of a privileged figure becoming arrogant and prideful, and for that reason cast down, is the essence of the fallen angel myth. The reference in Luke 10:18 to a falling angel recapitulates the story *in nuce*. There is surely no significance to the variant terminology of "falling" and being "cast out." It is unlikely that Satan somehow tripped.

The later and various accounts of the eviction of Satan from heaven found in *The Life of Adam and Eve* reflect most of the elements of the Iblīs story—the command to bow down to Adam, the refusal, and the resultant eviction. *The Life of Adam and Eve* includes a number of other details: the involvement of the angel Michael; the inclusion of other angels who also refused to bow and are evicted; and Iblīs's envy of Adam. What is absent from the various lives of Adam and Eve is any argument with God. But Satan argues with the angel Michael in terms similar to what we have found here in Sūrat al-Ḥijr, on the basis of his primogeniture.

The Christian story is set in a context of a conversation between Satan and Adam. In *The Life of Adam and Eve*, as well as in the account in Sūrat al-Ḥijr, Satan/Iblīs becomes, if not appealing as a figure, at least one deserving of some pity. But who should feel such pity? To whom is Iblīs making his case? In the Qur'ānic story, it is God with whom Iblīs argues. Adam is the subject of conversation but not part of the conversation. In *The Life of Adam and Eve*, Satan is making his case to Adam directly. God is absent from the conversation. There are other parallels.

In both narratives Iblīs/Satan is questioned as to why he did what he did. In Sūrat al-Ḥijr, God questions Iblīs about his reason for refusing to bow to Adam:

> He [God] said, "O Iblīs, what is with you that you are not with those who bow down?" (v. 32)

In the *Life of Adam and Eve*, Adam questions Iblīs about his reason for tempting Eve:

> "What have I done to you, and what is my blame with you? Since you are neither harmed nor hurt by us, why do you pursue us?" (12:2)

In both narratives Iblīs/Satan puts the blame on his conversation partner, Adam or God, respectively:

Sūrat al-Ḥijr

> He [Iblīs] said, "My Lord, because you have led me astray, I will lay out enticements for them on earth and I will surely lead them all astray
> Except your servants among them, the pure-hearted ones." (vv. 39–40)

Life of Adam and Eve

> And the devil sighed and said, "O Adam, all my enmity and envy and sorrow concern you, since because of you I am expelled and deprived of my glory which I had in the heavens in the midst of angels, and because of you I was cast out onto earth. (12:1)
>
> So with deceit I assailed your wife and made you to be expelled through her from the joys of your bliss, as I have been expelled from my glory. (16:3)

The *Life of Adam and Eve* begins with Adam and Eve arriving on earth. It does not itself include the story of Satan's refusal to bow down to Adam. Satan tells that story in retrospect. In this rendering, God is more distant. The angel Michael instructs Satan to bow down to Adam and rebukes him for refusing. Satan narrates all of this to Adam so that the main venue of action is on earth. Hence the dominant relationship is a personal one between Adam and Eve, and by implication their progeny, and Satan. Satan operates with a certain independence on earth, having committed himself to the task of tempting humanity.

Deal-Making

In the Iblīs story, the dominant relationship is between Iblīs and God. The locus of action is in heaven, before Iblīs is cast out. Iblīs's intention to become a tempter to Adam and Eve forms in the presence of God. Although God does not explicitly approve of this plan of Iblīs, God does, by implication, accept that Iblīs will, and may, tempt those who are not God's pure servants. This implicit permission comes close to implicating yet a third mythic theme: that of the divine prosecutor.

The story of Job in the Old Testament, the archetypal biblical expression of the heavenly prosecutor theme, also does not include any formal designation by God of Satan as prosecutor of humanity in the divine court. It is clear, though, that he has that role. That is equally true here in Sūrat al-Ḥijr. Both in Job and here, the action is set in heaven and is primarily a conversation between God and Satan/Iblīs. The conversation is more adversarial in Sūrat al-Ḥijr, evoking the effect, if not the content, of the combat myth. Yet it is clear that Iblīs is not, in the end, an opponent of God in the way that characterizes the combat myth. This is apparent in the negotiation that occurs between God and Iblīs, reserving the *mukhlasīn* (sincere servants of God) from exposure to the machinations of Iblīs.

God's authorization is essentially negative, agreeing with Iblīs that Iblīs will have no authority over the *mukhlasīn*, yet with one exception: those of the *mukhlasīn* who, of their own volition, choose to follow Iblīs as *ghāwīn*. By this interaction Iblīs himself excludes the *mukhlasīn* from the class that he will lead astray. God then affirms the sincerity of the *mukhlasīn* and excludes the *ghāwīn* from the class of *mukhlasīn*. The negotiation proceeds by exclusion: the identification of those with whom each is *not* concerned.

The *ghāwīn* are those who exclude themselves from the ranks of the *mukhlasīn*. How this happens is not clear. Iblīs has already declared that he will exclude the *mukhlasīn* from his work of temptation. God restates this, not in terms of exclusion from temptation, but in terms of authority. Iblīs will not be a *sultān*, an authority over them. This is several degrees short of declaring that he will not tempt them or arrange to place temptations in their paths. Here God is allowing Iblīs a degree of access to the *mukhlasīn* that is greater than Iblīs has previously demarcated for himself.

Conclusion

The story of Iblīs in Sūrat al-Ḥijr integrates three mythic narratives of the origin and nature of evil. The prelude to the Iblīs story itself presents a version of the Azazel story of the watcher myth. The extended first half of the Iblīs story itself presents a sibling rivalry narrative. Finally, the post-refusal negotiation between God and Iblīs has the character of a heavenly prosecutor story.

Drawing on three different themes in rapid sequence would seem necessarily to result in a confusion of consequential meanings, but this is not necessarily so. Set in the context of the larger themes of the *sūrah*, the shape of an argument begins to appear.

From the beginning, the *sūrah* discusses the disbelievers. For the present they disregard the message of Muḥammad, enjoying themselves with a false confidence, mocking messengers, ignoring every sign that is, or even could be, sent to them. This contrasts with Abraham and Lot, who welcome messengers from God. There are further brief examples of communities that ignore or reject the messengers.

Who has responsibility for such disbelief? The question hovers over the whole *sūrah*. The disbelievers fool themselves in the present, but God sets limits for them, the *ajal*, a limit to their opportunity for reprieve. Further, God makes "it" enter into the hearts of the evildoers (v. 12). "It" here may be the inclination to mock God's messengers in the preceding verse and exemplified in verses 6–7, or more generally their disbelief, cited in the following verse and exemplified at various points throughout the *sūrah*. In verse 12, God participates in some way in their disbelief. It is not entirely their own doing even if it is primarily their own choice. God gives them sufficient information, but not all the knowledge that God could have provided, such as the limits of their *ajal*. The *shayāṭīn* know to seek out this vital information, but the foolish disbelievers do not even try.

We come then to the Iblīs story. His *ajal* is indefinite. He was created long ago, even before Adam. God says, prior to the passage, that God knows those who have gone before and those who come after: the ordering of creation (v. 24). Iblīs did come before, and reminds God of this. God is unappreciative of this point. Not only the length of *ajal* but its quality are hidden in heaven. Even a late-created creature of stinking mud is more valuable than Iblīs. This is not logical or fair, but logic and reason are not sufficient, or perhaps are even deceptive, as means to determine faithfulness and priority in the eyes of God.

After being informed of this erroneous presumption, Iblīs argues further about his *ajal*, with unclear results. God will simply not be cornered into making clear commitments as to the destiny of any. This becomes clearer as God allows even the *mukhlisīn* to be subject to Iblīs's influence, if not his authority. God is all-knowing (v. 25); we are not. The last line of the *sūrah* (v. 99) captures the irony of all this:

> *wa-'abud rabbaka hattā ya'tiyaka al-yaqīn*
>
> Worship the Lord until there comes to you certitude.

What is certain? Everything and nothing. We can be certain of God, but God holds in the secret realms of heaven the identity of the *mukhlisīn*.

The sovereign prerogative of God and the exclusive knowledge of God disrupt human norms. The effect of this is that expected orderings of human or terrestrial relationships are arbitrarily upset by God, causing jealousy, anger, and further disorder in the terrestrial realm. The simple moral of this is that humans cannot predict the justice of God, a position that irritated the Mu'tazilites. The richer implication of the story is that the unpredictability of God's choices can be, in themselves, a source of human disorder and inexplicability. The consequence of such divinely ordained disorder is the tragic sensibility in which God has assured "absolutes like justice and order, but revealed a universe which promised neither and often dealt out the reverse."[39]

Iblīs has every reason to conclude that he, an individual experienced and established in the world as well as made of fire, should not be prostrating himself to one that all agree (God, narrator, and Iblīs himself) is made of stinking, decayed mud—the scum of the earth. It is a travesty of justice and reason that he should be asked to do so: Who is God to make such a demand?

The answer, of course, is that God is God. Constraints of justice do not apply to God. Nevertheless, Iblīs will undertake to prove God wrong, to prove that this creature, this mucky Adam, and his equally mucky descendants, are indeed not worthy of admiration, much less reverence. He will expose their human corruption, unreliability, deceits, and deceptions.

We, the readers, know that Iblīs will fail to change God's mind. Iblīs, however, tragic figure that he is, will strive against inevitability, asserting the superiority, not of himself, but of reason, fairness, and justice.

[39] Sewall, *Vision of Tragedy*, 46.

CHAPTER 7

Sūrah Ṣād (38)

Sūrah Ṣād, like Sūrat al-Ḥijr, shifts the story of Iblīs from the discursive form of a first-person declaration by God to a third-person narrative about God. The unifying theme of the *sūrah* is disputation among unbelievers and the rejection of Muḥammad. The theme of disputation is set up in the second verse: "But those who do not believe are in pride (*'izzah*) and dissension (*shiqāq*)." Verses 3–4 are commonly taken to refer to the visit of a group of Meccan notables to Muḥammad's uncle, Abū Ṭālib, urging him to restrain his nephew's preaching.[1] The theme is reinforced by reference to those who have rejected messengers before—the tribes of Noah and 'Ād, Pharaoh, and others (vv. 12–13). In verse 17, the text turns to the story of David, who is not presented as a messenger but as one who turned to God and was rewarded. The "story of the adversaries" (v. 21) is clearly related to the biblical story of Nathan's confrontation of David following David's affair with Bathsheba (2 Samuel 11–12), although the latter incident is not mentioned in the Qur'ānic text, and the story is not clear without that context. Nevertheless, that background connects the denial of Muḥammad's warning in verse 4 to David's heeding of a warning in verse 24 and his consequent reward (vv. 25–26).

After a summation in verses 27–29, the text turns to the story of Solomon, who is described as one of the rewards given to David for his repentance. Solomon is also tested (v. 34), but in a fashion difficult to discern from the text. The reference to a body that replaces Solomon on the throne calls to mind the rabbinic story in which Asmodeus, king of the demons, replaced

[1] Al-Ṭabarī, *Jāmi'*, 23.125 (vol. 12). See also the same story in Ibn Hishām, *Muhammad*, 118–21.

Solomon for three years as a punishment for his three sins of multiplying horses, wives, and silver and gold.[2] An Islamic variant of the story in al-Kisā'ī has Sakhr, the rebellious, taking Solomon's place temporarily on the throne and assuming his form.[3]

A third application of the theme is in the story of Job (41–44), although there is no clear narrative of temptation here. The reference to striking (a rock? the ground?) with the foot to produce water is unclear.[4] The story does, however, end with the same reference to turning, *abā*, as do the previous two stories (vv. 34, 40).

References to other prophets in verses 45–48 introduce another broad contrast of the promise of paradise and the threat of the fire (vv. 49–64). Verse 65 moves to a pair of direct instructions to Muḥammad, introduced by *qul!* (Say!), which assert the majesty of God and the limited knowledge of Muḥammad. They reflect Muḥammad's role as the conveyer of the message and not its originator. This instruction leads finally to the Iblīs story beginning with verse 71. The *sūrah* ends with a third and final *qul!* passage in verses 86–88, which again focuses on the message.

Overall, the *sūrah* has a four-part construction: 1) a complaint about those in Muḥammad's time who rejected the message (1–11); 2) stories of those who, in the past, have erred, or been tempted, and then turned (*abā*) to the Lord (12–48); 3) a statement of the message—the promise of paradise and the terror of the fire (49–64); and 4) a series of three instructions to Muḥammad, each introduced by *qul!*, that clarify that Muḥammad is a bearer of the message, not the knowing originator of the message.

The Iblīs story is placed after the second *qul!* passage as an interpolation. It does not fit with the rest of the *sūrah* in several ways. It breaks the symmetry of the three *qul!* passages (each 2–4 vv. long) with a passage introduced by *idh* (when) (15 vv. long). It departs from the direct address to Muḥammad in the *qul!* passages. Finally, it shifts from God as the first person narrator of the text to God as the third person subject of the text. This change is introduced in the first *āyah* by identifying the subject of *qāla*, "he said," as "your Lord." It is likely, then, that the final section of three *qul!* passages was already assembled before the Iblīs narrative was inserted to expand upon the divine council reference in verse 69.

[2] Ginzberg, *Legends*, 4:165–72.

[3] Al-Kisā'ī, *Tales of the Prophets*, 318–19.

[4] Perhaps this story relates to that of Moses striking a rock with his staff in Num 20:2–13.

How does the Iblīs story contribute to the overall theme of the text? It would have been more logical to introduce the Adam story, perhaps in the second section, as an example of a prophet or messenger who erred, but then turned to God. But the story of Adam's error is not raised here, and Iblīs does not turn to God in repentance.

What prompts the Iblīs story is the reference to *al-malāʾ al-aʿlā*, the high council (v. 69), which then relates to God's address to the angels (*malāʾikah*, v. 71) announcing his intent to create Adam. The reference in verse 69 is to the point of assuring the hearers that Muḥammad is not privy to the counsels in heaven: a central point in the *qul!* passages and in the rest of the *sūrah* (see the reference in vv. 7–9 concerning the accusation that the message has been invented by Muḥammad). The verb describing the interaction in the high council is *yakhtaṣimūna* (to dispute with one another). This is an odd usage—who is disputing in heaven? The only other citation of the high council is in 37:8 in the context of the *jinn* who are trying to overhear their deliberations.

In the Tanakh the heavenly council is mentioned in Psalm 82 where YHWH, the God of the Israelites, is one god among many, although one that emerges dominant.[5] The other gods are referred to in several places as *bĕnê hā-ʾĕlōhîm* or *bĕnê ʾĕlōhîm*, (Ps 29:1; 89:6–7; Deut 32:8 in the LXX, ἀγγέλων θεοῦ, but not the Masoretic text), and elsewhere as the "holy ones" (Deut 33:2; Job 5:1; Ps 89:6–7; Zech 14:5), which would include *haś-śāṭān* (Satan) based on Job 2:1.[6] In Job 38:7 these gods are associated with the stars or planets. The Israelites held this concept in common with Ugaritic and Mesopotamian tradition for whom the assembly of gods governed by a high god was normative.

The function of the divine council is primarily to dispense judgment, and thus they are related to prophecy in the Tanakh. In the rabbinic tradition, the composition of the divine council is understood to be angelic, not godly, and the council of angels retains the primary function of a judicial court. They arbitrate the final fate of mortals. For instance, Ahab is tried in the heavenly court. The accusing and defending witnesses exactly balanced each other until the spirit of Naboth—a man from whom he, or rather his wife Jezebel, had stolen a vineyard—arrive to accuse him and tip the balance.[7] The court

[5] Mullen, *Divine Council*, 226–44.

[6] Idem, "Divine Assembly," 275.

[7] Ginzberg, *Tales*, 4:187.

arbitrates in angelic disputes such as that between Michael and Sammael over Jacob and Esau, for whom they are, respectively, guardian angels.[8] God also consults the court in difficult decisions, such as the destruction of Pharaoh's army in the Exodus, where the court mediates between God and Uzza (the angels of the Egyptians).[9]

The concept of a heavenly council does not appear prominently in the writings of the early Christians. Augustine's commentary, *On the Psalms*, discusses the gods of Psalm 82, noting that the LXX uses συναγωγή (synagogue).[10] He interprets this term to refer to the people of Israel, since the congregation of the church is never called a synagogue. God is standing in the midst of Israel, whom he calls gods, for like the gods they have eternal life offered to them, but they "shall die like men" because they refuse the offer. Hence Augustine, like other patristic authors, rejects an understanding of Psalm 82 as referring to a divine council.

The *Lisān al-'Arab* identifies *malā'* as the nobles of a tribe and the prominent among them—those whose advice is consulted. Ibn Manẓūr then quotes a *ḥadīth*:

> "Is it fate that the High Council argues about? The angels want the favorites," and in the interpretation of al-'Azīz: "Do you not look towards the council?" and in [the ḥadīth] also: he said [concerning] the Council: he reported that the prophet (SAWT) heard a man from the Anṣār who had returned from the battle of Badr and he said: "We only killed the old bald ones." Muḥammad said: "These are the nobles of the Quraysh; if you had been involved in their activities (i.e., the nobles of the Quraysh), then you would despise your activity.[11]

From both the use of *malā'* elsewhere in the Qur'ān and the definition in *Lisān al-'Arab*, the high council would appear to refer to a regular gathering of the leadership of heaven. Ibn Manẓūr's reference above to the idea that the high council would be arguing about fate recalls our lengthy discussion of heavenly knowledge in the previous chapter on Sūrat al-Ḥijr. Presumably, these nobles in the high council would be angels, which would provide the connection to the Iblīs story.

[8] Ibid., 1:313. See also *Jubilees* 25:17.

[9] Ibid., 3:23–24.

[10] Augustine, *On the Psalms*, 82.1; *Post-Nicene Fathers* 8:395.

[11] Ibn Manẓūr, *Lisān al-'Arab*, 1.159 (parentheses mine).

The Iblīs Story

Annunciation

idh qāla rabbuka li-l-malā'ikati inni khāliq[un] *bashar*[an] *min ṭīn*[in]
fa-idha sawwaytuhu wa-nafakhtu fīhi min rūḥī fa-qa'ū lahu sājidīna

When your Lord said to the angels, "I am creating a human from clay. When I have shaped him and breathed my spirit into him, fall down in prostration to him." (vv. 71–72)

The Iblīs story is introduced by *idh* "When," which immediately notifies the reader of a shift. The same participle introduces the story of the disputants in verse 21 and the story of Solomon in verse 31. In all three cases, the preceding line is also preparatory to the story, so the introduction is not sudden. This pattern strengthens the connection between the second *qul!* text and the Iblīs story. Hence, although the Iblīs story interrupts the structure of the three *qul!* pericopes, it is joined to the preceding text in a way that has precedent in the *sūrah*.

Another transition is signaled by the phrase *qāla rabbuka*, "your Lord said." In Sūrah Ṣād, the predominant voice is that of the first person plural. God speaks in the royal, or conciliar, "we." This voice is reflected in *rabbuka* (your Lord). It is normal for the divine first person to switch between singular and plural. But here the verb *qāla* (he said) is in the third person, which indicates the shift that will persist throughout the Iblīs story. Up until this point in the *sūrah*, the reader has been directly and intimately addressed by God. We, the readers or hearers of the story, are party to God's words and thoughts. We sit, as it were, with God, and are addressed by God in the second person: "Has the story of the disputants reached you?" The *rabbuka* continues this voice, but then we are abruptly removed from such an intimate stance. Now God is described by a narrator semantically located at some distance from God. His interchange, first with the angels, then with Iblīs, is recorded and recounted. The reader's position is that of an observer, no longer an addressee. We sit back and watch, and listen, no longer involved.

We may know, although this possibility is nowhere raised, that the event we are watching is not a current event. We are watching, as if we were present, a sequence that we could never have observed, both because it is located in heaven, and because not even Adam was fully created at this time (although, as we shall see, this version of the story skips over the creation of Adam).

We are watching a movie, or a video, of a memory in the mind of God, but not one narrated by God. We are not only taken back in time but out of time.

This view is, of course, one of the indicators of myth. The grammar of the story tells us that this is a story in which God is an actor, and we are in the heavenly seat of an observer of God's action, far removed in time and space from the natural domain of human knowledge. To some degree it divinizes the hearers, or at least the teller, anonymous but close to the hearers, by making them, or him, privileged to watch the divine in action, beyond mortal space and time.

It would be unwarranted to make too much of this. After all, the story is still contained within the speech of God in the Qur'ān to us, the readers and hearers of the story. It is still God who is addressing mortals, giving guidance to humanity. But in the immediate and sudden shift, we are given to imagine ourselves as already transported, not to paradise, but to heaven itself, and given a vision, not just a telling, of a divine secret. In a sense, this vision violates the message just expressed in the second *qul!* pericope that Muḥammad does not have knowledge of the affairs of those on high, the heavenly council. In the Iblīs story, we not only have knowledge of heavenly affairs but are there, watching, hearing, and learning.

God announces to the angels, in this first verse of the story (v. 71), his intention to create a human from clay. God's declaration reads, "Truly I [am] a creator of a human being from clay." Since the high council was mentioned two verses before, we may assume that the context in which God is speaking to the angels is the high council, but this assumption is not required by the text. It could be that God always announces his intentions to the angels, as in Sūrat al-Baqarah (2:30). We do not know.

The sentence is a nominal sentence, without verb, so the assumption that it is a declaration of future intention comes from the context provided by the next verse, not the grammar of the current verse. The current verse indicates the identity of God as a creator, not the act of creating. The next verse moves to the action of creating. The information that God gives is that a new step in the creation process is about to be undertaken: that it will be a creation of a human being—the word *bashar* is genderless—and that the material used will be clay.

The material of human creation, clay, is specified here, as well as in Sūrat al-Ḥijr and Sūrat al-'Arāf. In Sūrat al-Ḥijr, the clay is further described as stinking, decayed matter (*min ḥamā'*^{in} *masnūn*^{in}). Here there is no such elaboration. Sūrat al-'Arāf describes God as shaping humanity but does not identify clay as the material. Clay is mentioned later in this passage in Iblīs's justification of his refusal. Thus in the "creation of Adam" story itself, Sūrat al-'Arāf mentions shaping but not clay; Sūrat al-Ḥijr mentions clay but not shaping; Sūrah Ṣād mentions both.

The use of *bashar* for a human says little about the nature of the creation, but the construction material—clay—says more. The construction of this human being will be a dynamic process. This being will be shaped by God, crafted by God. We will learn in verse 75 that God used his hands, which clarifies what is unspoken, but imagined, in verse 72. Shaping clay requires hands, effort, and getting dirty. It is hands-on work that we do not normally imagine of the majestic Lord of all creation.

The effect of this description of the shaping of the man is to create a feeling of great intimacy. While earlier we pointed out that the imposition of a narrator places the reader at some distance from God, at the same time the nature of the narration communicates intimacy. The presence of the narrator may enable such intimacy. The narrator may say of God what God would not say of himself. The narrator protects God's majesty while at the same time showing God in an act of deep tenderness.

The specific designation of clay as the ingredient of human construction is necessary to prepare for the argument of Iblīs in verse 76. Iblīs will argue that his own creation out of fire is superior to the human creation from clay.

The verb in verse 72 implies that the human will be made proportionate, perhaps meaning equalized bilaterally, with the right side matching the left side. Further, God will breathe into the human. As in Hebrew, the word *rūḥ* can mean "breath," "breeze" or "spirit." Thus the creation of the human involves both a lowly material—clay (common, simple, infinitely malleable)—and the personal involvement of God in shaping that clay, and finally, the insertion of God's breath, which is, at the same time, spirit.

The combination of opposite materials, clay and divine breath, has provided theologians and mystics with rich imagery for descriptions of the nature of humanity as both close to the divine and distant from the divine—containing opposites.[12] The contrast in Sūrat al-Ḥijr between the material of Iblīs (fire) and the material of Adam (clay) is made somewhat less stark here. Instead, our attention is drawn to the more subtle contrast between handled

[12] For instance, Rūmī, *Mathnawi*, 5.95–102 (vol. 3); *Knowledge of God*, 338–41.

clay and divine breath. Only here, of the seven narratives, is God's use of his hands mentioned.

The actual creation of the human is contained within a dependent clause. It is not the focus of the passage. While Iblīs's refusal to prostrate himself is the central element in all seven versions of the story, what varies is the elaboration of that refusal. In Sūrat al-Ḥijr, it is the sibling relationship—Iblīs versus Adam. Here it is Iblīs versus God, the intimate creator, who shaped this human by hand. What we will eventually know as Adam, the product of creation, is not important in this story. It is God's action as creator that is central. It is a prelude, a necessary introduction, to the story of Iblīs. Adam and Eve remain unnamed, and the actual creation is not described. Only the intention to create is described. The text jumps from the intention to the prostration of the angels to something—the human—which has already been created.

The intention behind the telling of this Iblīs story may be to present another narrative of warning like those of David, Solomon, and Job. The story of Iblīs differs from that of the historic prophets and messengers in that he does not "turn," does not repent. If the purpose of the story is not to provide history but to provide warning, then the warning is only effective if Iblīs is understood to be a human-like individual, a counterpart to the audience of the Qur'ān. The story is not placed among the other hortative stories in what I have designated as section 2 of the *sūrah*. Is this placement because the story is not admonitory, or because it is a negative example instead of a positive example? Or is there another reason? How does the story of Iblīs function, here? We are not yet ready to answer that question.

Refusal

fa-sajada al-malā'ikatu kuluhum ajma'ūna
illā iblīs astakbara wa-kāna min al-kāfirīna
qāla yā-iblīsu mā mana'aka an tasjuda li-mā khalaqtu bi-yadayy astakbarta am kunta min al-'alīn
qāla inā khayr[un] minhu khalaqtanī min nār[in] wa-khalaqtahu min ṭīn[in]
qāla fa-akhruj minhā fa-innaka rajīm[un]
wa-inna 'alayka la'natī ilā yawmi al-dīn

So the angels prostrated themselves, all of them together
Except Iblīs; he was puffed up and he was one of the unbelievers.
[God] said, "O Iblīs, what prevented you from prostrating yourself to what I created with my own hands? Are you puffed up or are you one of the high?"

> He said, "I am better than he is; you created me from fire and you created him from clay."
> [God] said, "Go out from it, and truly you are rejected (*rajīm*),
> And upon you is my curse until the day of judgment!" (73–78)

In obedience to God's command, the angels prostrate themselves. The object of their prostration is known from the previous line, the human that God has shaped. The emphasis on this act is increased by the addition of *kulluhum* (all of them) and further stressed with *ajma'ūna* (together). There is no reluctance indicated, no hesitation, but a unity of movement and response. The compounding emphasis of *kulluhum* and *ajma'ūna* not only intensifies the spectacle of masses of angels in synchronous prostration before Adam but also heightens and strengthens the pathology of Iblīs's refusal.

All the angels bow down to the human. Except Iblīs (v. 74a). The sentence of exception is short, abrupt, and communicates the startling violation of the previous uniform action. They *all* bow, except for one who does not. There is no indication here that Iblīs is not to be included in the collectivity of the angels. There is no suggestion that he is a *jinn*. The cause of his exception is given immediately: he is proud, puffed up, and one of those who reject the faith (the *kafirūn*, v. 74b).

The comment that Iblīs is puffed up, haughty, and one of the unbelievers is an insertion on the part of the unnamed narrator. Although the haughtiness is suggested by God in the next verse (v. 75), the conclusion that Iblīs is a *kāfir* is not confirmed directly by the text. We are reminded here of the different levels of perspective. God and God's speech are, in the immediate sense, the object of our observation and hearing. Had we readers been at that primordial time and place, we could have watched the spectacle of Iblīs's refusal to prostrate himself and the subsequent conversation that came to pass between Iblīs and God (vv. 75–86). The narrator occupies a perspective close to ours and describes what our eyes can see and our ears can hear. Up until now, everything that the text says could be confirmed by our own eyes and ears. In a sense, the authority of the scenario is our own potential witness to it. But this interpretation now provides information that we cannot confirm by our own senses. It comes only on the narrator's authority. In the larger sense of the Qur'ān as a whole, we understand that the authority is still the authority of God, as the Qur'ān as a whole is the speech of God. But here a narrative voice intrudes briefly, then returns us to the action of the story, to what we can witness "with our own eyes."

God questions Iblīs about his lack of participation in the group response (v. 75). There is a tension built into the question. The first part of God's query is less personal than one might expect. God does not ask "why did you not prostrate yourself?" with the emphasis on Iblīs himself and his intention, but "what was it that prevented you from prostrating yourself?" The question directs our attention to a thing, an objectified force that acts upon Iblīs, compelling him to do or not to do what he might otherwise have done. The effect is to depersonalize that act of Iblīs.

The question suggests, however subtly, that acts are influenced by outside forces. Iblīs does not "choose" to disobey God. He is prevented from doing so. One can take this as an allusion to the idea that humans are acted upon by outside forces—demonic forces, al-Shayṭān, and the *shayāṭīn*—that "whisper" suggestively into the human ear. This outside force is a characteristic of the evil spirits, most powerfully represented in the last two *sūrahs* of the Qur'ān:

> Say: I seek refuge with the Lord of the Dawn
> From the evil of created things
> From the evil of darkness as it gathers
> From the evil of the women who blow on knots
> From the evil of an envious one when he envies.
>
> Say: I seek refuge with the Lord of the people
> With the king of the people
> The God of the people
> From the evil of the slinking whisperer
> Who whispers into the breasts
> Among the *jinn* and the people. (113–14)

These two *sūrah*s are apotropaic prayers of protection against evil spirits and witchcraft that may prevent pious behavior.

The issue of free will and predestination is well beyond the bounds of our discussion, but the text raises a smaller question. The question in Sūrah Ṣād and in Sūrat al-'Arāf is: "What prevented you?" In Sūrat al-Ḥijr, the question is: "What is your reason?" The second formulation lays the emphasis on the free choice to disobey God. Iblīs has within himself the capacity to choose evil. This perspective forms the foundation of most of al-Ṭabarī's primordial legends of the *jinn*. *Jinn*, by definition, can choose evil. We discussed this perspective in the context of the identification of Iblīs as a *jinn* in chapter 5.

The idea that something prevents Iblīs from obeying the command to prostrate himself gives more insight into the psychology of disobedience. Pride is an element within the human/*jinn* composite. It can be isolated and identified as something that "makes" one do things that are contrary to God's will. This subtle externalization of impulse lays the groundwork for a subsequent psychology or theology in which Iblīs is an external tempter of humanity. But it also raises the question of the existence of demons, or al-Shayṭān, contemporaneous to Iblīs. Is there a "whisperer" coaxing Iblīs to disobey? There is no indication of such in the Qur'ān. But if not, then this odd formulation of God's question suggests that people can disobey with no external influence at all. Al-Shayṭān may be an instigator of disobedience, but we can manage to err quite on our own.

The second half of the question, however, personalizes the issue with respect to God. The offense of non-prostration is not an offense against the object of prostration, the human, but against the creator of that human, against God. The importance of the human is invested in the fact that God made it. Further, God made it with God's own hands. The human is mentioned in verse 75 only pronominally.

God goes on to question the motivation of Iblīs—"Are you proud?"—confirming the assessment of the narrator in verse 74. But then God asks, "Are you among the *'ālīn*, the 'high'?" which suggests a reference to the high council, the *al-malā' al-'alā* of verse 69; (*a'lā* and *'ālīn* are different formations of the same root). This question is unique to this telling of the story here in Sūrat Ṣād.

Is this a rhetorical question? If Iblīs is a member of the high council then his disputatiousness has already been established. His error, perhaps, would be that he goes beyond disputation to action. If Iblīs is not one of the high council, then the relationship between the Iblīs story and the beginning of the second *qul!* passage is in doubt. Are the angels, whom God addresses in verses 71–72, the members of the high council? If the answer is that they are, then the disputation of the high council is addressed, perhaps resolved, by God's declaration to the angels. This resolution, however, would make God's question to Iblīs irrelevant. God already knows that Iblīs is one of the *'ālīn*. Hence the angels, and Iblīs among them, are likely not part of the high council. They are a separate group that is expected to act differently. In this case the question that God asks makes sense: Are you not one of the loyal angels that do what I command, or are you one of the members of the high council, who like to argue and to exercise independent thinking? We will return to this question.

A third possibility is that *'ālīn* is simply a synonym for proud, but this connection is unlikely for three reasons. First, the use of this word repeats the earlier usage, which connects the Iblīs story to the beginning of the second *qul!* passage. Second, the synonymous meaning is redundant and would repeat *astakbarta*. This redundancy is unlikely because of the conjunction "or" between them that implies two possibilities. Thirdly, as noted above, *'ālīn* does not appear in any of the other six Iblīs stories. Its uniqueness here suggests a particular significance.

Iblīs responds with a clear argument for his superiority: "I am better than he. You created me from fire and you created him from clay." Here we learn more about Iblīs. He is also a creation of God and quite aware of this. We also learn that his noncompliance with God's order derives from a conscious decision on the part of Iblīs, based on a logical deduction—fire is superior to clay. From the point of view of Iblīs, he is not proud, but simply, factually superior. So he argues.

But the boldness and the simple declaration give no acknowledgment of inferior rank to God. Note that when God addresses Iblīs, he does so by name: "O Iblīs!" When Iblīs responds, there is no formal greeting, but a simple, stark declaration. Two relationships are being negotiated here. On the one hand, Iblīs argues that he is superior to the human, on the basis of material construction. His relationship to the human is the object of his comment. On the other hand, his unapologetic response to God suggests that he believes he is of a status to argue with God. He addresses God with no vocative particle of address, such as *ya rabbi*, "my Lord," which he will use later. He addresses God as an equal. His refusal to obey the command of God confirms his independence from God. He will make up his own mind about what he will do. His relationship to God is the real subject of his comment.

Here we begin to see a subtle relationship to the issues of the rest of the *sūrah*. The introduction of the *sūrah* (v. 2) describes the unbelievers, who cast doubt on the testimony and warnings of Muḥammad, as being in *'izzah* (root: *'-z-z*), power and pride, and *shiqāq* (root: *sh-q-q*), meaning to be separate or in dissent. The latter term appears six times in the Qur'ān.[13] In one instance (4:35), the reference is to a dispute between two people, but in the other five, the schism is between some people and the revelation of God. The primary

[13] 2:137; 2:176; 4:35; 22:53; 38:2; and 41:52.

meaning of *shiqāq* is separation. The unbelievers are those who have held themselves separate and aloof from the message, or the reminder.

Now Iblīs holds himself separate, capable of making his own judgments and not subservient to the command of God. The word *shiqāq* is not used here in the Iblīs story itself, but the implication is that Iblīs is primarily guilty of *shiqāq*. A further indication of this guilt is the parallel in the other attribute of the unbelievers: *'izzah* in verse 2 and *istakbara* in the Iblīs story. The first attribute refers to strength and honor but used here in a negative sense, which would be pride. The second derives from the root *k-b-r* (to be great), thus meaning "to think oneself great"; again, this meaning would indicate pride. Thus the common appellation of "unbeliever" is applied both to the dissenters from Muḥammad in the beginning of the *sūrah* and to Iblīs at the end of the *sūrah*.

Let us now return to the issue of the high council. Note that the high council is described in the second *qul!* pericope as disputing with one another, *yakhtaṣimūna* (v. 69—the same root is used to describe the disputants in the David story in vv. 21–24.) Disputatiousness is precisely the nature of *shiqāq*. This disputatiousness returns us to the possibility, explored earlier, that Iblīs, the disputer of God's command, may indeed be a part of the disputatious high council. God's rhetorical question to Iblīs, "Are you among the *'ālīn*, the 'high'?" (v. 75b), may then be turned around to mean, "Are you acting in the typically disputatious manner of the high council, but now instead of disputing with one another, you are disputing with God?" Disputation is not evil in itself. The disputants who approach David in verses 21–24 are not condemned for disputing. Only those who dispute with God or with God's revelation are condemned as unbelievers.

This interpretation helps to clarify the otherwise mysterious usage of *yakhtaṣimūna*, which appears unseemly for a heavenly council. It also would help us begin to understand a question, or two related questions, which trouble the Muslim commentators on the Qur'ān: How is it that the angels in 2:30 can argue with God in Sūrat al-Baqarah's parallel to verse 71 in Sūrah Ṣād? Secondly, how is it that Iblīs turns bad? The beginning of an answer here is that angels are not at all immune to dispute, nor, perhaps, to the reasoning process that leads to dispute, as different parties come to different understandings. The error of Iblīs is not that he disputes, but that he disputes with God. Is his error that he uses logic to arrive at his conclusion that he is superior to the human? This dispute is one of the elements of tragedy: to raise some principle to be higher or more fundamental than the prerogatives of the divine. The tragic figure holds justice, fairness, and principle to be absolute and constraining even for God. Iblīs's error is that he holds his own logic to be more authoritative than God's direct command. This principled action is also his tragedy. We have seen the same dynamic in the previous chapter, in Sūrat al-Ḥijr.

God's response to this effrontery is to evict Iblīs from "it," presumably heaven, and to pronounce that Iblīs is *rajīm* (v. 77). As was discussed before, the meaning of this word is generally taken to be "cursed," although literally it means "stoned," from the root *r-j-m* (to cast a stone). The word in Arabic script is identical to *r-ḥ-m* (to bless) except for a dot. Al-Raḥmān, "the merciful," from the same root, is a name for God and perhaps one of the earliest appellations for God.[14] A common variant form is *raḥīm*.[15] *Rajīm* and *raḥīm* stand in contrast as the cursed and the merciful.

Given the actual meaning, "one who is stoned," the likely reference is to the shooting-star myth discussed in the previous chapter, with reference to Sūrat al-Ḥijr. *Rajīm* connects the Iblīs myth with the *jinn*.

Deal-making

Qāla rabbi fa-anẓirnī ilā yawm yub'athūna
Qāla fa-innaka min al-munẓarīna
Ilā yawmi-l-waqti l-ma'lūmi
Qāla fa-bi-'izzatika la-ughwiyannahum ajma'īna
Illā 'ibādaka minhumu l-mukhlaṣīna
Qāla fa-l-ḥaqqu wa-l-ḥaqqa aqūlu
La-amla'anna jahannama minka wa-mimman tabi'aka minhum ajma'īna

[Iblīs] said, "My Lord, grant me respite until the day [the dead] are raised."
[God] said, "Truly you are one of those given respite
Until the day of the appointed time."
[Iblīs] said, "Then by your power I will pervert them all
Except your servants among them, the sincere ones."
[God] said, "Then it is confirmed [true], and the truth is what I say

[14] See 25:60, an early *sūrah* where al-Raḥmān seems to be the main identifier of God. The intent of the passage seems to be to argue that al-Raḥmān and Allah are the same God. See also 17:110: "Call upon Allah or call upon al-Raḥmān; whichever you call [it is the same] for to him belong the Beautiful Names."

[15] The two forms are found together in the "*bismallah*" found at the beginning of every *sūrah* except Sūrat al-Tawbah (9): *bi-ism allah al-raḥmān al-raḥīm.*

> That I will fill Gehenna with you and with those who follow you,
> all of them!" (vv. 79–85)

The final section of the Iblīs story is another interchange between God and Iblīs with the roles reversed. Iblīs is now the questioner and the supplicant. God speaks in the declarative mode. God's response in the first exchange, when Iblīs declares his logical deduction of his superiority, is mighty. In verse 78, God uses the emphatic *la* to highlight his curse, which will be on Iblīs until the day of judgment. Iblīs responds with an entreaty, this time preceded by a formal mode of respectful address (*rabbi*), "O my Lord." God has cursed him until the *yawm al-dīn* (judgment day). Iblīs asks for respite until the *yawm yub'athūna* (day of resurrection).

This exchange exactly parallels that in Sūrat al-Ḥijr. Iblīs requests respite (*anẓirnī*). The root of the word is "to look at, regard," the assumption being that if God truly regards an individual, God's mercy will overcome God's anger.[16]

His wish is granted, but in a way that removes God's active agency. Literally, "you are/will be among those given respite." The final promise of respite—until *al-yawm al-ma'lūm* (the known time)—further emphasizes the gap in authority between God and Iblīs. God knows the time of the eschaton; Iblīs does not. At this point Iblīs cannot even be sure that it is the eschaton to which God is now referring. The extent of Iblīs's respite is now totally subject to the will and whim of God. Once again, the exclusive nature of God's knowledge and God's sovereign will are made clear.

The final exchange shows Iblīs, with further but not absolute recognition of God's superior authority, declaring that he will lead "them" astray, all of them, except those whom God has set aside. Iblīs begins by acknowledging that his future action will be "by means of your power." God's power is in play here, since it is God who is the source of good and evil (7:168, 13:11), but nevertheless Iblīs makes the decision and declaration of intention to pursue evil. Here in a nutshell is one traditional Muslim understanding of the nature of evil. It cannot come about except by the power of God, yet it is the human (or *jinn*!) decision to utilize that power, and to utilize it for evil intents, that makes all evil the individual's responsibility.

Even here, one sees Iblīs overreaching. He declares that he will lead them *all* astray, but then, with a pause punctuated by an *āyah* division, he allows

[16] Lane, *Arabic-English Lexicon*, 2:2810–13.

an exception, a rather major exception—except the servants of God, those whom God has made *khalas* (pure, redeemed). The contrast between the "all" and the "excepted" parallels verse 73 where "all" the angels prostrate themselves, "except" Iblīs.

God's final response is to declare the arrangement true and proper with a double pronouncement: He says, "It is the truth (*ḥaqq*), and the truth, I say." (v. 84):

Qāla fa-l-ḥaqqu
wa-l-ḥaqqu aqūlu

The doublet, with another remarkable example of chiastic inversion, asserts both an objective affirmation—it is the truth—and a subjective affirmation—I say it is true. One might possibly understand this affirmation as the sovereign declaration: "It is true *because* I say it is true." It is succinct and punctive.

Those who follow Iblīs, whom Iblīs leads astray, will end up in hell. With this pronouncement of a satisfactory conclusion, the text returns from its digression to the third *qul!* passage. Here Muḥammad, in contrast to Iblīs's demand for respite and responsibility, declares his lack of interest in reward for delivering this message.

The structure of the Iblīs story in Sūrah Ṣād is twofold. The first four *āyahs* are descriptive and set the stage for a conversation between God and Iblīs. They keep the focus on God's intention, first God's professed intention to make a human being, then God's intention to have all the angels prostrate themselves before this creature. Adam is not named and is given no attention in his own right. The focus for the first section is on God the creator. Iblīs is only named in the last *āyah* of the first section.

The second section is a conversation, or more, a disputation, between God and Iblīs. One sees Iblīs move from a posture of an apparent claim to parity with God to a recognition of God's power and authority but still coupled with defiance of God. The conversation is both begun and ended by God, so God frames the discourse by a question (v. 75) and a declaration of truth (v. 84–85). This second section is the focus of the text, the first being necessary to set the stage.

The debate between Iblīs and God serves to illustrate the point made in the three *qul!* passages where Muḥammad repeats that he does not know more than is given to him to reveal. He does not even know the counsels of the chiefs of heaven. The Iblīs passage serves to show that not even the chiefs of heaven have full understanding. This limitation of knowledge is indicated first by God's revelation to the angels of his intention to create humanity. Even the angels only know what God tells them. But more importantly, Iblīs, who presumes himself equal in knowledge to God, is reduced to recognition of God's superior knowledge and power—knowledge in that only God knows the termination of Iblīs's respite, and power in that Iblīs's new livelihood depends on God's power. He can only lead astray by God's power, and he can only lead astray those whom God does not set aside.

Conclusion

The narrative in Sūrah Ṣād largely parallels that in Sūrat al-Ḥijr. In parts, they are exactly the same. In both the issue of God's knowledge has been prominent. The major difference is that in Sūrat al-Ḥijr, the focus is on the relationship between Adam and Iblīs, whereas here, in Sūrah Ṣād, Adam is not mentioned at all, and greater attention is given to God's creative activity, particularly with the unique mention of God's hands. The larger context of the *sūrah* also directs our attention to the theme of disputation. Iblīs's response to God's query as to his reasons for failing to prostrate himself is more contentious—"I am better than he," a declaration not found, although implied, in Sūrat al-Ḥijr. Further, the knowledge that Iblīs is created from fire, normally understood to be a noble element of the natural sphere, is a narratorial comment in Sūrat al-Ḥijr, but direct discourse in Sūrah Ṣād—"You created *me* from fire, and you created *him* from clay." This boast still reflects God's supremacy as the creator, but in a way that is almost accusatory—"*You* created me from fire, and *you* created him from clay [so how can *you* upset the clear implications of what *you* created.]" The sentence can be read both ways and perhaps should be read both ways to capture the subtlety of the narrative design.

Clearly, the versions of Sūrat al-Ḥijr and Sūrah Ṣād are closely related, but the differences between the two show a clear intent to tell the same story in two distinct ways to give two distinguishable angles on the issue of evil. In Sūrat al-Ḥijr, the dominance of the sibling rivalry motif de-emphasizes the characterization of either character as good or evil. The nature of evil arises from the disordering of creation due to God's sovereign interventions combined with human/*jinn* passions—a classic recipe for tragedy. Sūrah Ṣād uses essentially the same story but with enough variation to change the intonation of the character of Iblīs from one with a justifiable complaint against God to one who is haughty, puffed up with pride, and defiant of God. Iblīs's initial justification has a certain logic to it, but the tone here has shifted. Iblīs is more assertive, more defiant. Whereas in Sūrat al-Ḥijr the reader might be tempted to sympathize with Iblīs in his objection to God's command, here it is less easy to do so.

The Qur'ān tells the same story, but in different narratives with significantly different ranges of meaning. There is no reason to assume that any one version is intended to abrogate another. Rather, the Qur'ān intends to communicate the complexity of the issue of theodicy precisely by giving several different renditions of the issue. The message of Sūrat al-Ḥijr and that of Sūrah Ṣād are both true (*ḥaqq*): God says so.

CHAPTER 8

Sūrat al Isrā' (17)

The seventeenth chapter of the Qur'ān is commonly named for the event alluded to in its first verse: the *isrā'* and the related *mi'rāj*, which refer to Muḥammad's night journey to Jerusalem and subsequent ascent into heaven for the beatific vision of Allah.[1] This event has great importance in Islam, particularly in its Sufi expressions, and significant fascination for students of the history of religions.[2] However, except for this possible but veiled allusion here, in verse 1, the night journey story is otherwise unremarked on in this *sūrah*, indeed in the Qur'ān as a whole, unless verse 60 of this same *sūrah* is taken to refer to Muḥammad's vision of heaven in the *mi'rāj*.

The general characteristics that we will note about the *sūrah* are its particular way of characterizing the relationship between God and the individual, its emphasis on the nature of the Qur'ān as a text revealed piecemeal, and its attention to the role of the messenger. We will also examine a characteristic of the Qur'ān we have so far ignored: the pattern of assonance in the *sūrah*. Most *sūrahs,* including this one, exhibit a rhyming pattern that is relatively consistent from verse to verse. In Sūrat al-Isrā' all verses, except for the first and last, end with an indefinite accusative ending -^{an}.

God, the *Wakīl*

The early parts of Sūrat al-Isrā' follow a familiar outline. After an initial doxology praising God, who has shown signs to his servant, presumably

[1] In some places the *sūrah* is referred to as Sūrat Banī Isrā'īl.

[2] See Olson, "Heavenly Journeys," 233. She reviews the rich corpus of commentary on this event in both the Arabic and the Western sources.

Muḥammad, the *sūrah* moves directly into a historical account—here a description of the bestowal of the book to Moses and the subsequent twofold punishment of Israel for its failures to heed the book's warnings.

In this historical passage, God says to the *Banū Isrā'īl*, "Do not take a Trustee apart from me" (17:2). The term that I have translated here as "Trustee" is *al-Wakīl*, one of the ninety-nine names of God (*al-asmā' al-ḥusnā*), which means, according to Ibn Manẓūr, "He is the enduring guarantor (*al-muqīm al-kafīl*) of the provisions (*arzāq*) of the people (*'ibād*), and his essence is that he assumes the burden of the command entrusted (*mawkūl*) to him." Verses 54, 65, 68, and 86 repeat this term. This concept of God's trusteeship needs to be correlated with the text in verse 7 that emphasizes the responsibility of the *Banū Isrā'īl*, and all people, for their own conduct:

> *in aḥsantum aḥsantum li-anfusikum, wa-in asa'tum fa-lahā*
>
> If you did well, you did well to your own selves, and if you did evil, it is also to them [your own selves].

Verses 13–15 reaffirm this assertion of individual responsibility. This assertion has a different tone from that which most dominates the Qur'ān, (and is still present in Sūrat al-Isrā'): the absolute authority and power of God. While the Qur'ān generally accords to individuals full responsibility for their own actions, seldom does it state this as clearly as here in Sūrat al-Isrā'.[3] Here also is acknowledgment of an inherent flaw in human nature, for humanity is *'ajūl*[an] (hasty; v. 11). Although God has ultimate authority and power over all that comes to pass on earth, including human actions, each individual has immediate responsibility for his or her own actions: *wa-kulla insān*[in] *al-zamnāhu ṭā'irahu fī 'unuqihi* "we have attached each person's 'bird' to his (own) neck" (v. 13). The bird is a common omen of the future and here, a representation of one's works.[4]

This first section of the *sūrah* begins with an account from history and follows with a theological elucidation of that history. The *Banū Isrā'īl* are given the book and a warning. Unlike Noah, who is grateful, they err severely,

[3] Watt, *Free Will*, 13. Watt cites several passages, but not this one. These other passages refer to God allowing free will to humanity (18:29–31, 21:47, and 36:54). The verse under consideration here does not even include God in the equation.

[4] Al-Ṭabarī cites many authorities that equate *ṭā'ir* with *'amal*, "works." See al-Ṭabarī, *Jāmi'*, 15.50–51 (vol. 9).

twice, and are restored the first time and still might be the second time. God will punish corruption, and God will be merciful, but humanity is impatient (*'ajūl*[an]). Nevertheless, each person is solely responsible for his or her own fate. The lesson here is not only that each individual is responsible but also that the clan or tribe may not assume responsibility for the individual. This intercession may be that of other gods (the objects of worship already mentioned in verse 22 and elsewhere—gods taken *with* Allah, not instead of him), or it may refer to the intercession of Muḥammad as is suggested below with reference to verse 54.

In the next section of the *sūrah* (vv. 23–39), the Qur'ān cites a series of specific commandments having to do with social and personal relationships. This collection of commandments is identified as wisdom (*ḥikmah*) that is revealed (*awḥā*). The collection begins (vv. 22–23) and ends (v. 39) with warnings not to worship other gods. The sequence of commandments, having to do with respecting parents, caring for orphans, the poor, and the travelers, not killing children out of poverty, or cheating in business—all of these are based on the idea that God is *al-Wakīl*, a protector that will supply what one needs, such that one need neither hoard nor turn away those in need.

Verse 41 begins the first extended section that describes the Qur'ān as a text of explanation and reminding (vv. 41, 45) and a text of recitation (vv. 45–47). The text's attention then turns to an unidentified group of those who do not believe in the afterlife, *al-akhirah*. The afterlife has already been mentioned in the *sūrah* generally (vv. 8, 10, 19, 21), and specifically in the context of receiving the record of one's deeds (vv. 13–14). Both of these themes will be repeated later in the *sūrah*. This particular group of unbelievers doubts the possibility of resurrection (vv. 49–52). The response to this objection on the part of this unnamed group is not condemnation of them and warning of eventual, and surprising, punishment in store for them, but rather a *qul!* passage in which Muḥammad reassures the believers.

This unusual response, directed to the believers, but not those who have just addressed Muḥammad, again affirms God as *al-Wakīl*. In this first *qul!* passage of the *sūrah*, Muḥammad is specifically addressed, although not by name, as one who is *not* required to be a *wakīl* for the community (v. 54). That role is reserved for God (v. 55). This passage suggests that the previous assertions of individual responsibility are intended to refute the idea that Muḥammad is an intercessor for the community, their *wakīl*.

The Iblīs Story

The Iblīs passage (vv. 61–65) is the second of two *idh* passages. Both passages (vv. 60 and 61) begin with *idh qulnā li-* making the parallelism strong between the two. They contrast with each other, however, in their focal point. The second passage, addressed to no one in particular, begins the Iblīs story. The first passage addresses Muḥammad in terms of his own knowledge and experience:

> *wa-idh qulnā laka inna rabbaka aḥāṭa bi-nāsi*
> *wa-mā ja'alnā al-ru'yā alatī araynāka illā fitnat^an li-l-nāsi*
> *wa-l-shajarata al-mal'ūnata fī l-al-qur'āni*
> *wa-nukhawwifuhum fa-mā yazīduhum illā ṭughyān^an kabīr^an*

> When we said to you, "Truly your Lord has power over humanity;"
> And we only made the vision that we showed you as a trial to humanity,
> And the cursed tree in the Qur'ān.
> And we made them fear, but it only increases them in great transgression. (v. 60)

Al-Ṭabarī understands the first line above to mean that Muḥammad is protected from humanity, or the Arabs, until the Qur'ān is complete. This understanding would be consistent with the attention given later in the *sūrah* to the process of the revelation of the Qur'ān but is not immediately evident in the *āyah* itself. Al-Ṭabarī reports several understandings of the vision and its associated trial. Some interpreters take it to be the *isrā'* and *mi'rāj*, Muḥammad's miraculous night journey from Mecca to Jerusalem and then to heaven, and the *fitnah* is the disbelief of many upon hearing Muḥammad's account of that journey. Alternative interpretations are that this vision is of Muḥammad's entry into Mecca, or it is a dream of apes on Muḥammad's *minbar* (pulpit). Al-Ṭabarī favors the association with the *isrā'* and *mi'rāj*.[5]

The "cursed tree" in verse 60 is generally understood to be the tree of Zaqqūm, a tree producing bitter butter and dates, or sometimes a tree within a fire, or a parasitic dodder plant (*kashuth*), or, finally, one that comes into view like the heads of the demons (*shayāṭīn*).[6]

[5] Al-Ṭabarī, *Jāmi'*, 15.110–113 (vol. 9).

[6] Ibid., 15.113–115 (vol. 9).

If this *āyah* is a doublet with the following overture to the Iblīs story in verse 61, as is suggested by the similar *idh* introductions, what can we make of this? There is no obvious answer to this question from the commentaries on verse 60. We must push on into the Iblīs story itself and return to the question.

The Iblīs story in Sūrat al-Isrā' is told in five verses, rhymed throughout. The first verse (v. 61) begins directly with the command to the angels, their response, and Iblīs's refusal.

> *wa-idh qulnā li-malā'ikati-sjudū li-ādama*
> *fa-sajadū illā iblīsa*
> *qāla a'asjudu li-man khalaqta ṭīn*[an]
>
> When we said to the angels, "Bow down to Adam,"
> Then they bowed down, except Iblīs;
> He said, "Shall I bow down to one you created from clay?" (v. 61)

The first two lines are identical to the text in Sūrat al-Kahf (18:50) and close to the texts of Sūrat al-Baqarah (2:34), Sūrat al-'Arāf (7:11b), and Sūrah ṬāHā (20:116). This passage is the core of the story. In other versions, Iblīs's refusal is emphasized with *abā* (he refused): Sūrat al-Baqarah (2), Sūrah ṬāHā (20), and with further elaboration, Sūrat al-Ḥijr and Sūrat al-'Arāf (7); or explained by the narrator: "He was one of the *jinn*" in Sūrat al-Kahf (18); and "He was haughty" in Sūrah Ṣād (38). In other passages, God queries Iblīs as to his inaction—*mā mana'aka an tasjuda li-mā khalaqtu bi-yadayya* "What prevented you from bowing down to what I created with my hands?" (Sūrah Ṣād, v. 75, and parallels in Sūrat al-Ḥijr, v. 32, and Sūrat al-'Arāf, v. 12).[7]

But here all such elaboration and narrative explanation are absent. Having presented the basic narrative—God's command, the angels' obedience, and Iblīs's refusal—Sūrat al-Isrā' uniquely moves directly into Iblīs's defense of his act. The focal point is the dialogue between Iblīs and God. The narrator fades into the background, revealed only by the introductory *qāla* in the third line of verse 61 and at the beginning of verses 62 and 63. In each case the speaker can only be inferred from the nature of the dialogue. In fact, even to call this encounter a dialogue may stretch the term, since there is only Iblīs's defense of his non-act and God's rejoinder in verses 63–65.

[7] See Appendix A, the chart of Iblīs *sūrahs*, for a graphic and clearer comparison of the different texts.

In comparison with the other versions of the Iblīs story, the version here is the most confrontational. Iblīs does not wait for God to question him, or even notice that he has refused to prostrate himself to Adam as commanded. In other versions, Iblīs's explanation of his choice not to bow down is made in declarative form—God asks the question, and Iblīs replies. But here, in Sūrat al-Isrā', Iblīs questions God in a rhetorical form that ridicules the suggestion that he might be expected to bow down to one made of clay. He does not assert his own superiority due to his own creation from fire. Rather, with a perceptible intonation of incredulity, he asks, "Shall *I* bow down to one you created from clay?"

The inflection of *ṭīn*^{an} (clay) as an indefinite accusative is required by the pattern of rhyme throughout the *sūrah*. The grammatical effect of the change is to convert *min ṭīn*—the construction found in other versions of the Iblīs story and a description of the substance from which Adam was created—into a *ḥāl* (a condition describing the state of Adam's existence). A *ḥāl* is an accusative of state or condition that modifies the subject or object of its clause, not the verb. Therefore, the quality of "clayishness" describes not the manner of the verbal act of creating (*khalaqta*), but the one created (*man*), referring to Adam. Thus *min ṭīn* describes the original material from which Adam was made. The grammatical construction here (*ṭīn*^{an}) describes an enduring condition of the referent of the object of the clause: Adam; he is "clayish" in nature.[8]

This being so, in an ever so subtle fashion, the issue of Adam's original creation being inferior to that of Iblīs's creation from fire becomes an issue of Adam's continuing condition of inferiority. He is clayish. This condition may remind us that the *sūrah* has once before indicated a weakness in the nature of humanity, in another *ḥāl* in verse 11: *wa-kāna al-insānu 'ajūl*^{an} (man is hasty).

The discourse of Iblīs continues in verse 12, introduced by another *qāla*:

> *qāla ara'aytaka hādha alladhī karramta 'alayya*
> *la-in akhkhartani ilā yawmi al-qiyāmati*
> *la-aḥtanikanna dhurriyyatahu illā qalīl*^{an}

> He said, "Do you yourself see? This is the one you have honored over me.

[8] See Wright, *Grammar*, 2:114. As Wright points out, a *ḥāl* usually implies a transitory state, but this is most often when it is an adjective. Here the *ḥāl* is a noun and describes a continuing condition.

> Indeed, if you grant respite to me to the day of resurrection,
> Truly I will gain mastery over his descendents, except a few." (v. 12)

Iblīs continues his indignation. He refers to Adam as "this one," which God has honored above him. Inanimate clay characterizes Adam more than humanity. Iblīs's address to God is a challenge, with emphasis on the pronoun of address, "you." In the first clause of this continued speech, the phrase *ara'aytaka* (do you see?) is unique among the Iblīs passages. Like the previous sentence, it is a question directly addressed to God. The accusatory "you" is included twice: once as the subject of the sentence and again as the apparent object of the verb "to see," which becomes, as al-Qurṭubī and others point out, a pronoun of emphasis.[9]

Iblīs asks for respite, a request that is reflected in three of the other versions.[10] In all three other versions of the story, this request comes in response to God's angry command: *ukhruj*, "Get out!" Here that command is absent. The effect of this absence is to remove any hint of God's rejection of Iblīs from the story. Such rejection may be derived only from the reader's knowledge of other extant versions of the story. There is nothing here that indicates Iblīs's ejection from God's presence. The respite that Iblīs desires acknowledges that God's natural reaction might be some form of punishment and/or restriction, but says nothing of the nature of that response. The emphasis of the passage therefore shifts from God's eviction of Iblīs to Iblīs's intention to master the descendents of Adam. This intention is expressed in terms of a unique verb that receives a great deal of attention from the commentators: *aḥtanikanna*, an *af'ala* (IV) form of the verb *ḥ-n-k*, made doubly intensive by the doubling of the *nūn* at the end and the *la* at the beginning. Al-Qurṭubī gives a number of synonyms for the meaning of *ḥ-n-k*: *astawliyanna 'alayhum* (I will overwhelm them), *aḥtawiyannahum* (I will take control of them), and *uḍillunnahum* (I will lead them astray). Another image, however, is far more violent: an image of locusts (*jarād*) overcoming a field and destroying everything. Al-Zamakhsharī,[11] al-Bayḍāwī,[12] al-Bursawī,[13] and al-Ṭabarsī[14] repeat this image, but surprisingly, al-Ṭabarī does not.

[9] Al-Bayḍāwī, *Tafsīr*, 1.576; al-Qurṭubī, *al-jāmi'a*, 10.258 (vol. 5).
[10] 15.36; 38.79; and 7.14.
[11] Al-Zamakhsharī, *Al-Kashshāf,* 2.633.
[12] Al-Bayḍāwī, *Tafsīr*, 1.576.
[13] Al-Bursawī, *Tafsīr Rūh*, 5.180
[14] Al-Ṭabarsī, *Majma'*, 5–6.656.

God's response to Iblīs's promise confirms the sense of violence in Iblīs's assault on humanity. The first response is the typical prediction of *jahannam* (hell) for those that follow Iblīs. The second verse of God's response (v. 64) is an energetic encouragement for Iblīs to fulfill his promise to lead astray, even to scourge (*aḥtanikanna*), all those that he can.

> *wa-stafziz man istaṭa'ta minhum bi-ṣawtika*
> *wa-ajlib 'alayhim bi-khaylika wa-rajilika*
> *wa-shārikhum fi-l-amwāli wa-l-awlādi wa'idhum*
> *wa-mā ya'iduhum al-shayṭānu illā ghurūr^{an}*

> And incite those whom you can among them with your voice.
> And threaten them with your horses and your men.
> And associate with them in wealth and children, promising them.
> But what does Satan promise them but delusion? (v. 64)

Iblīs here has a tripartite assault on humanity. He incites with his voice, threatens with an army of horses and men, and inserts himself into human relationships with wealth and children. The second line bears multiple interpretations, particularly in the verb *j-l-b,* here translated as "assault," which appears only here in the Qur'ān.[15] Who are the cavalry and infantry, who are assaulting, and how do they assault? Some understand this cavalry as those men and *jinn* who went along with Iblīs in disobedience to God. This passage may refer to legends that Iblīs was the chief of an army of angels or *jinn* in primordial times.[16] The Qur'ān also refers to the hosts of Iblīs in Sūrat al-Shu'arā (26:95). Lane discusses this passage and offers several interpretations drawn from the lexicographers. In Ibn Hishām's *Mughnī al-Labīb*, the passage is rendered as "and raise confused cries against them." In al-Bayḍāwī's *Tafsīr*, the interpretation is, "cry out against them with a clamor, so it is a cry" (*wa-ṣah 'alayhim min al-jalabah, wa-hiya al-ṣiyāh*),[17] but in the *Tāj al-'Arūs* of Murtaḍā al-Zabīdī, the interpretation is, "and collect against them and threaten them with evil."[18]

In general, though, the Qur'ān speaks of Iblīs alone and only speaks of groups and hordes when speaking of al-Shayṭān. In this particular speech, the final reference is to al-Shayṭān, not Iblīs. The tripartite array of assaults

[15] It appears in a nominal form in 33:59, referring to a cloak.

[16] See al-Ṭabarī, *Jāmi'* 1.201 (vol. 1).

[17] Al-Bayḍāwī, *Tafsīr*, 1.576.

[18] Lane, *Arabic-English Lexicon*, 1:439; s.v. *j-l-b.*

is associated with the *shayṭānī* discourse, which here is brought into close association with the Iblīs story. In this narration, Iblīs is depicted in a more adversarial, accusatorial manner, and the entire story has been shifted in a *shayṭānī* direction. Although Iblīs and al-Shayṭān are still not identified with one another, this passage makes it easy to join the two identities into one.

God's speech ends (v. 65) with a reaffirmation of his role as *al-Wakīl*, which insulates his servants from the rule (*sulṭān*) of Iblīs.

> *inna 'ibādī laysa laka 'alayhim sulṭān*[un] *wa-kafā bi-rabbika wakīl*[an]

> Truly you will have no authority over my servants; your Lord is sufficient as a *Wakīl*. (v. 65)

The curious expression raises questions. Does Iblīs have *authority* over those who are not the servants of God? The previous verse depicts Iblīs, or al-Shayṭān, as seducing, clamoring, shouting, and involving himself in human wealth and family, but not ruling. On the other hand, the implication may be that these people have, perhaps unwittingly, accepted Iblīs, or al-Shayṭān, as their *wakīl*, a *wakīl* vested with authority as a trustee.

The Iblīs story, as told in Sūrat al-Isrā', edges toward the *shayṭānī* discourse of opposition. Although Iblīs makes an argument as to why he should not be made to bow down to Adam, the tone of his language, with its accusatory challenge to the rationality of God's command and its incredulity that God would command such an absurd act, steals the show. The story becomes not one of Iblīs's disobedience, or even of God's response to his disobedience, but rather one of the adversarial relationship between Iblīs and God and then between Iblīs/al-Shayṭān and humanity.

Returning to the question raised above—that of the suggestive parallelism between verse 60 and the Iblīs story beginning with verse 61— both passages beginning with *wa-idh qulnā*—a possible explanation emerges. Verse 60 begins with an expansive assertion that "your Lord encompasses humanity." The passage then introduces contrary information: trials for humanity, the existence of the tree of Zaqqūm, and fear and transgression. All of this contradicts the idea that God encompasses humanity as their *Wakīl*.

The second part of the doublet also begins with an affirmation of the importance of humanity—God commands the angels to bow down to Adam. This passage also introduces a contrary note of dissonance—Iblīs refuses, pointing out the essential clayish quality of Adam. In so doing, he emphasizes, particularly in his tone of address, his challenge to God's encompassing trusteeship. Hence, both passages begin with an expression of God's authority and the centrality of humanity in God's guardianship, and both passages then introduce a dissonant note that challenges that guardianship.

The argument of Iblīs, and God's affirmation of Iblīs's adversarial role, implicitly affirm God's authority, even over Iblīs's challenge itself. God also circumscribes Iblīs's influence, limiting it to an ambiguous "they"—those that follow Iblīs and accept him as their *wakīl*.

The role of God as *al-Wakīl* is further elaborated in a beautiful image of God guiding the ships at sea, calming the waves, and bringing those that call upon him back to the land (vv. 66–70). The image recognizes the storminess that characterizes even the life of the faithful. While God makes the ship sail smoothly (v. 66), nevertheless, distress will befall you (v. 67). The key to safety is not simply calling upon God, but gratitude, a recognition of God's enduring role as *al-Wakīl*.

Muḥammad—Messenger, not *Wakīl*

The second half of Sūrat al-Isrā' focuses on Muḥammad's role as the messenger of God and the Qur'ān as the inimitable guide for humanity. Beginning with verse 71, the *sūrah* addresses the temptations of Muḥammad. This is a reversal of the common pattern where humanity, or various tribes and groupings of humanity, are tempted astray. Here, those who have strayed are trying to tempt Muḥammad away from the revelation (v. 73). It is a serious temptation, as Muḥammad requires strength from God to resist (v. 74). Hence Muḥammad is not reliable as a *wakīl*.

Verses 78–81 comprise another interlude of direct command from God, similar to the legislation in verses 23–39. Here the subject is prayer: both the times of prayer and the content. The content of the prayer is a plea for a *sultān* as an aid. The answer to this prayer is given in the next section. It is not, as might be expected, Muḥammad. The *sultān* is instead the Qur'ān. The nature of its inspiration, which is to say the relationship between the Qur'ān and Muḥammad, is described in verses 85–93. The Qur'ān is inimitable (v. 88), a small piece of the knowledge of God (v. 85), but nevertheless containing explanation of all similitudes. Those who reject the Qur'ān look for a miraculous revelation (vv. 90–93), but Muḥammad is only a man, a mortal sent to mortals.

The last section of the *sūrah* (vv. 101–11) returns to the story of Moses as, in a sense, the *ur*-messenger to whom revelation was sent. Its truth did not adequately convince the Israelites, which is a historical lesson and a warning for contemporary doubters.

Conclusion

This chapter has proposed the notion of God as *al-Wakīl* as the binding concept for Sūrat al-Isrā'. This notion shapes the overall construction of the *sūrah* and, in particular, the nature and function of the Iblīs story. While the core of the story remains substantially unchanged from several other versions, the dialogue between Iblīs and God is dramatically revised to emphasize the adversarial relationship between them and between Iblīs and humanity. This moves the story in a decidedly *shayṭānī* direction. Indeed, the name al-Shayṭān emerges in the latter part of the story, with no accounting for the shift.

This story underscores a tension between the notion that God is *al-Wakīl*, who encompasses all of humanity, and the awareness that there are nevertheless competing claims for the fealty of humanity. In the Iblīs story, God affirms his own authority while giving Iblīs near-free rein to contest that authority. Iblīs's own recognition that this authority and opportunity is given to him and does not stem from his own existence by right is muted. The nature of Iblīs's bold discourse elevates his challenge to God in stronger terms than in any other version of the story. This is truly Iblīs, a *shayṭānī*, the enemy not only of humanity but of God. The menacing role of Iblīs makes the protection of God, the true *Wakīl*, abundantly necessary.

In mythic terms, Iblīs emerges here in a form close to that of the combat myth described in chapter 3. Even the imagery used, cavalry and infantry, call to mind a full-fledged assault on humanity. Although other Qur'ānic versions of the story of Iblīs may suggest a tragic figure worthy of some element of pity, there is no room for such here.

CHAPTER 9

Sūrat al-'Arāf (7)

The Iblīs story in Sūrat al-'Arāf is one of three that joins the eviction story of Iblīs with the garden story of al-Shayṭān; the others are Sūrah ṬāHā 20:116–21 and Sūrat al-Baqarah 2:30–36. This study did not give careful consideration to the temptation story in its analysis of Sūrah ṬāHā but will rectify that lack here.

Sūrat al-'Arāf is almost twice as long as any of the other *sūrahs* considered so far here. This length suggests that the *sūrah* could be a composite of elements revealed at different times. It also makes the task of charting an outline of the entire *sūrah* more difficult. The *sūrah* consists of 206 verses of irregular length. Most verses end with an accusative *fataḥ* ending, but this pattern of assonance is broken sixteen times. Toward the latter half of the *sūrah*, these breaks all fall at natural section endings that cite the names or qualifications of God, such as *raḥīm^{un}* (vv. 153 and 167). But earlier in the *sūrah*, the irregularities come in the middle of connected verses, such as *mubīn^{un}* in the midst of the Moses narrative (v. 107) and in the Adam temptation narrative (v. 22). We will explore some implications of this below.

Nöldeke outlines the *sūrah* in five sections:

1–56	The seduction of Adam and the admonishment of the Children of Adam
57–100	Sending of the other Apostles—Noah, Sālih, and Shu'ayb
101–73	Moses and the destiny of the Jews
174–85	Concerning an anonymous enemy of God
186–205	Concerning the Last Hour

Nöldeke also suggests that although no close relationships exist between the sections, Muḥammad might conceivably have associated them.[1]

Opening of the *Sūrah*

After the initial *muqaṭṭa'āt* (mystery letters), *a-l-m-ṣ*, the *sūrah* begins with references both to the book (*kitāb*) and to some experience of oppression on its account. Where other *sūrah*s focus initially on the disbelievers, here encouragement is given to the believers to persist. The implication is that this text is revealed at a time when a community of believers was established, though beleaguered. With this encouragement (vv. 2–3), the Qur'ān recites the salvation history and points out that God is never absent (v. 7), that disbelievers may be and have been destroyed suddenly (vv. 4–5), and that the final judgment will measure the deeds of each person and reward them accordingly.

Verse 10 begins a new section, which introduces the Iblīs story:

> *Wa-la-qad makkanākum fī al-arḍi*
> *wa-ja'alnā la-kum fīhā ma'āyisha qalīl*[an] *mā tashkurūna*
>
> We have indeed placed you on the earth.
> And we have made for you on it resources for living, [but] little thanks do you give. (v. 10)

This verse sets a theme of human living on earth that will be repeated at the end of the Iblīs story. Few commentaries treat the Qur'ānic text in sections, but some that do, for instance, al-Nasafī and the English rendering of Yūsuf 'Alī, include verse 10 with the previous verses.[2]

Sūrat al-'Arāf has a tone of violence through much of the text. After the Iblīs and garden stories plus several following verses of commentary, the *sūrah* raises up the issue of choice and the consequences of wrong choice in verses 34–58. Signs and messengers are sent to all people, and each of the people must choose. The text begins with the *Banū Isrā'īl* but moves on to other nations. The scope of address includes all the people of the earth and all the nations.

[1] Nöldeke, *Ursprung des Qorāns*, 158–59.

[2] 'Alī, *Meaning*, 346; al-Nasafī, *Tafsīr*, 1.404.

The contrast is set up as one between the companions of the fire and the companions of the garden. At times it becomes an exchange in which the companions of the fire and the companions of the garden call out to each other. The text also mentions the responsibilities of leaders. As the companions of fire and garden, respectively, are calling to each other, a herald passes between the two condemning those who bar access to God.

Beginning in verse 59, several examples are given of nations whose people choose one path or another. The first is Noah, a messenger. He warns his people, but few choose to follow. The rest are drowned. Then God sends Hūd as a messenger to warn the people of 'Ād. The rulers (*al-malā'*) resist. He and those who listen to him are rescued and those who choose not to listen are cut off. God sends Ṣāliḥ to warn the people of Thamūd. The *al-malā'* resist. Ṣāliḥ and most of his family are rescued. Earthquake and rain destroy those who choose not to listen. God sends Shu'ayb to warn the people of Madyan. The *al-malā'* resist, and an earthquake destroys those who choose to join that resistance.

The much longer story of Moses follows after these accounts. As in Sūrat Ṭā-Hā, the theme of the story is the warning to Pharaoh as the ruler. In this version of the Moses story, a group of *al-malā'* encourages Pharaoh to resist the entreaties of Moses. The Israelites escape, and the army of Pharaoh was drowned. The story of the golden calf at the mountain follows. Here there is a variation on the theme that echoes the storyline of the garden story. Those who disobey and manufacture the golden calf recognize their error and repent. The consequence for them in verse 152 is the anger of the Lord and debasement (*ḍillah*) in the world, a consequence not unlike that visited upon Adam. Moses selects a group of seventy who are subsequently destroyed by an earthquake (v. 155). After that, Moses speaks of God's own freedom to choose some people for destruction, some for redemption, and the time for each.

The Moses story ends with the division of the Israelite community into twelve tribes, also called communities (*ummah*s) (v. 160). God provides for all of them. Some are grateful and ask for forgiveness when they do wrong, but others, such as those in a village that defiantly disregard the Sabbath, transgress, and therefore are turned into apes and cast out.

The conclusion of the *sūrah* begins with verse 168, which recapitulates the division of Israel into communities (in verse 160), but gradually widens the scope of its attention to include all of history, beginning with the primordial covenant with God, the covenant of *alastu* in verse 172. In verse 175, Adam is cited, not by name but as "one to whom we gave our signs," emphasizing not his status as the first human but God's provision of signs from the beginning of time. Al-Shayṭān also reenters as the one who lures Adam into error. From this rehearsal of early human history, the last *āyah*s speak of the provisions of God for humanity and the importance of human choice:

> Among those we have created are a people (*ummah*) who guide by the truth and act justly by it.
> And those who lie about our signs, we will deal gradually with them in ways they do not know. (vv. 181–82)

The *sūrah* ends extolling those who worship God, praise him, and finally prostrate themselves to him. They do exactly what Iblīs refuses to do.

The Iblīs Story

Creation and Refusal

The core Iblīs story begins with verse 11. It repeats the initial construction of the previous verse: *wa-la qad khalaqnākum* (v. 11) compared with *wa-la-qad makkanākum* (v. 10). From the reminder of God's placement of humans on the earth and provisions for them, the next verse retreats to the previous action of God, to create and shape Adam, and then to provide for his honoring.

> *wa-la qad khalaqnākum thumma ṣawwarnākum thumma qulnā li-malā'ikati*
> *usjud li-adama, fa-sajadū illā iblīsa lam yakun min al-sājidīna*

> Indeed we created you; then we shaped you; then we said to the angels, "Bow down to Adam." So they bowed down, except Iblīs; he was not among the prostrators. (v. 11)

In keeping with the emphasis on God's sustenance for humanity, the creation is elaborated to distinguish a succession of stages, creating, shaping, honoring, placing, and provisioning. A similar pattern occurs in Sūrat al-Ghāfir with the same emphasis on the identity of the one responsible for this beneficence:

> God is the one who made the earth for you as a residence and the heavens as a canopy, and shaped you, then made your shape good, and provided for you good things; this is God, your Lord; so bless God, the Lord of the worlds. (40:64)

This addition to the core Iblīs story focuses the reader/listener's attention on the role of God. The end of the verse treats Iblīs's refusal to bow down in a descriptive but not accusatory fashion. He is simply not one of the prostrators. By minimizing the language in a fashion similar to that in Sūrat al-Ḥijr (15:31–32), but without the repetition of the description in that *sūrah*, attention is not diverted to Iblīs. He is not described as *refusing* to bow down, but simply as not being one of those who did bow down.[3]

Explanation

Verse 12 follows with God's questioning of Iblīs and Iblīs's answer. The story shifts to the narrator's perspective, from the "we" of the previous two verses to "he."

> *qāla mā mana'aka a-lā tasjuda idh amartuka*
> *qāla anā khary^{un} minhu khalaqtanī min nār^{in} wa-khalaqtahu min ṭīn^{in}*

> He [God] said, "What prevented you that you did not bow down when I commanded you?"
> He [Iblīs] said, "I am better than he; you created me from fire and you created him from clay."

The initiative and focus remains with God. Even Iblīs's response is phrased in terms of what God has done in creating both Iblīs and Adam. The question is posed as a double negative, combining the verb *m-n-'* (to prevent) with the negative particle *lā*: literally, "what prevented you from not bowing down?" This variant on Sūrah Ṣād (38:75), which does not include the *lā*, elicits a great deal of commentary, all of which concludes that it is for emphasis.[4] The effect of this double negative is to stress the lack of performance by Iblīs, but again, without judgment. Al-Zamakhsharī asks why God should even ask

[3] Note that in 'Alī's translation of the Qur'ān, Iblīs *is* described as *refusing* to bow down in this verse (see 'Alī, *Meaning*).

[4] Al-Qurṭubī, *Al-Ahkām*, 7.153–154 (vol. 4); al-Ṭabarī, 8.129 (vol. 5).

such a question, since God must have known the answer. He answers that this was to make Iblīs's stubbornness manifest.[5]

An alternative answer might be that this keeps the initiative with God, since Iblīs is reduced to replying, in minimal fashion, to God's query, a query with the added force of the double negative. This narrative style contrasts with that of Sūrat al-Isrā' (17), where Iblīs takes the initiative and guides the narrative, and with Sūrat al-Kahf (18), where the narrator shifts the attention to Iblīs. There the narrator claims control of the story, and identifies Iblīs as one of the *jinn* who break the command of his Lord. Sūrah Ṣād also adds a narrator's summation of Iblīs's motives prior to narrating God's query, essentially giving the answer before God has asked the question. In that telling the initiative of the story also lies with the narrator. But here in Sūrat al-'Arāf the initiative remains with God. The narrator has a minimal role since God even tells the core story in the first person.

The answer that Iblīs gives is also simple and direct. Missing is the accusatory tone of Sūrat al-Ḥijr: "I am not one to bow down to a man that *you* created from ringing clay, from putrid mud," or a similar tone with a hint of defensiveness in Sūrat al-Isrā': "Shall I bow down to one you created *clayish*?" Iblīs's response is a simple statement, a declaration: "I am better than he; you created me from fire, and you created him from clay."

But God's question is also shorn of an accusatory tone present in other versions. In Sūrah Ṣād, for instance, God asks the same question but, after emphasizing that this mortal was created with his own hands, quickly goes on to suggest answers to the question, "Are you puffed up, or are you one of the high [perhaps the high council]?" Even before God asks the question, the narrator has given his own answer, essentially preempting the question, "He was puffed up and became one of the unbelievers (*kāfirīn*)."

One final aspect of this verse invites investigation. As was mentioned before, Sūrat al-'Arāf is characterized by a pattern of assonance throughout, with verses ending in the accusative definite *fataḥ*. There are sixteen exceptions to this pattern, one of which falls in this verse. The word *ṭīn*^{in} breaks the pattern. Indeed, it is the first break of the pattern in the *sūrah*. As in Sūrat al-Isrā', other versions of the story render the same word differently in order to adapt to the pattern of assonance in that *sūrah*. Hence the phrase *min ṭīn*^{in} found here and in Sūrah Ṣād (38:76) became *ṭīn*^{an} (17:61) with a

[5] Al-Zamakhsharī, *Al-Kashshāf*, 2.86.

slight shift in meaning. Could there be significance in the break in the pattern of assonance here?

The variation in Sūrat al-Isrā' indicates no unwillingness on the part of the Qur'ān to change established wording in order to adapt to a pattern of assonance, so the explanation cannot be an unwillingness to change the rendering already established in Sūrah Ṣād (which most assume to be earlier).

An examination of the other fifteen incidents of irregularity in the pattern does not provide an easy answer. All but one of the irregular verse endings are indefinite, the exception being verse 195: *thumma kīdūni fa-lā tundhirūna*, "then deceive, and do not give me respite." This occurs as part of a *qul!* passage, which continues in the next verse. Since verse length is highly irregular in this *sūrah*, the assonance could have been maintained quite easily by joining this verse with that which follows.

All the other irregular verse endings are genitive or accusative indefinite endings. Among these a number of them are common formulaic compounds such as in verse 73, *'adhāb*^{un} *alīm*^{un}. This compound appears more than forty-five times throughout the Qur'ān. Similar to it in frequency is the *ghafūr*^{un} *raḥīm*^{un} (vv. 153 and 167). But other irregular verse endings are rare: *thu'bān*^{un} *mubīn*^{un} (v. 107) and *min rabbikum 'adhīm*^{un} (v. 141), or unique: *nāṣiḥ*^{un} *amīn*^{un} (v. 68). In short, there is no pattern at all to the breaks in the assonance pattern of Sūrat al-'Arāf.

The implication of this is that the use of *ṭīn*^{in} in verse 12 is likely to be simply a repetition of the wording in Sūrah Ṣād (38:76). The fact that it disrupts the pattern of assonance in Sūrat al-'Arāf should not surprise the reader, since the pattern is disrupted elsewhere for no discernible reason. There is a rough parallel to this in the comparison of verse 112, an element of the Moses story, which also breaks the pattern of assonance but is identically phrased in Sūrat al-Shu'arā' (26:34), *sāḥr*^{in} *'alīm*^{in} "knowledgeable sorcerers."

But these two examples also provide support for the later dating of Sūrat al-'Arāf, since it is more likely that the pattern of assonance is broken in these cases because an established phrasing of a story is repeated from an earlier source than that the assonance would be broken for no reason at all. Both Western and Muslim scholars commonly date Sūrat al-Shu'arā' in the Middle Meccan period.[6]

[6] Nöldeke puts it 56th in order, and the Egyptian dating has it as 47th. Bell also sees most of the *sūrah* as Meccan, with later Medīnan additions in the final verses (*Introduction*, 206–7).

Further, the lack of concern evidenced here for maintaining a pattern of assonance throughout the *sūrah* lends greater credence to the significance of the opposite trend in Sūrat al-Isrā' where the same established phrasing is changed apparently in order to conform with the pattern of assonance, and the result, *ṭīn*^{an} rather than *min ṭīn*^{in}, yields a subtle shift in meaning.

Ejection and Respite

The next section of the Iblīs story gives the account of his ejection and respite in six verses (vv. 13–18).

In general, the narrative follows the pattern in Sūrat al-Ḥijr and Sūrah Ṣād but with some differences from both. Most remarkable is the change in tone.

> *qāla fa-ahbiṭa min-hā fa-mā yakūna la-ka an tatakabbara fī-hā fa-akhruj innaka min al-ṣāghirīna*
> *qāla anẓirnī ilā yawmi yub'athūna*
> *qāla innaka min al-munẓarīna*
>
> [God] said, "Go down from it, for it shall not be for you to be puffed up about, so get out, and you are among the insignificant."
> [Iblis] said, "Give me respite until the day of resurrection."
> [God] said, "Indeed you are among those who have respite." (vv. 13–15)

While the narrative to this point has been free of the evaluation and accusation that appears in other versions of the story, here God provides assessment of Iblīs's character that has been absent up to this point. Iblīs is "puffed-up" (*tatakabbara*) and at the same time, "one of the insignificant" (*min ṣāghirīn*) (v. 13). The two terms present a contrast in meaning: the first based on the root *k-b-r* (to be big) and the second based on the root *ṣ-gh-r* (to be small).

Iblīs asks for respite (v. 14), which God grants (v. 15) but without the variation of terminology for the endpoint of that respite as noted in Sūrat al-Ḥijr and Sūrah Ṣād. Iblīs next announces his intention to lead humanity ("them") astray. As the rhetoric of God has moved from the simple declarative to the accusatory, so too, the rhetoric of Iblīs makes a similar shift. His speeches become longer, and, as in the other two *sūrah*s that parallel this version, Iblīs blames God for his eviction: *fa-bi-mā aghwaytanī* (because you have led me astray) (v. 16). The phrasing parallels that in Sūrat al-Ḥijr (15:39).

The language escalates further. Iblīs not only announces his intention to lead them astray but describes a complex approach:

> *Thumma la-atīyannahum min bayni aydīhim wa-min khalfihim wa-'an aymānihim wa-'an shamā'ilihim*
> *Wa-lā takhidu aktharahum shākirīna*
>
> Then indeed I will come at them from in front of them and from behind them and on their right side and on their left side,
> And you will not find most of them thankful. (v. 17)

The language does not have the military imagery of troops and cavalry as found in Sūrat al-Isrā', but here it is literally an encompassing threat. In the previous verse, Iblīs describes himself not as assaulting the targets of his efforts but sitting—*la-aq'udanna*—in wait for them. But he describes the place of his waiting as the *ṣirāṭaka al-mustaqīma*, "your straight path," a direct allusion to the "path" of God known to every Muslim from Sūrat al-Fātiḥah (1:6). Although Iblīs has been evicted from the proximity of God, he returns not only closer to humanity but closer to the path of God. In answer, God repeats the expulsion order and additionally describes Iblīs as *madh'ūm*^{an} and *madḥūr*^{an} (disgraced and banished). The application of these words to Iblīs is unique to this telling.

God's language escalates through the story. God's early response to Iblīs's offense is to call him insignificant (v. 13). The word used in the beginning of the same verse for the expulsion is *ihbiṭ* (descend!). This is the same word used to command Adam to leave the garden. By the end of the verse (and reiterated in v. 18), God's response is more forceful and angry. *Ihbiṭ* (Go down!) has become *ukhruj* (Get out!) and by verse 18, Iblīs is disgraced and banished. He has also made himself quite significant!

The Garden Story

In verse 19 an abrupt shift occurs. With no warning God's dialogue with Iblīs has become a command to Adam and his wife. The text has switched stories, although the direct discourse of God continues from the previous verse. Three *sūrahs*—Sūrah ṬāHā, Sūrat al-Baqarah, and here, Sūrat al-'Arāf—attach the garden story (to which Neuwirth refers as the transgression story) to the Iblīs story. The story was considered briefly in the study of Sūrah

ṬāHā, noting that in the context of the *sūrah*, the focus is on the fallibility of humanity, exemplified not only by Adam but also by Moses, Aaron, and the Israelites. In this telling of the story in Sūrat al-'Arāf, the focus shifts to the cunning of al-Shayṭān.

The story of Adam and his wife is a rich and popular one and well worth considerable attention. Focus, however, must remain on the Iblīs story itself, examining the garden story in that light, and avoiding temptations to ex-plore the wonderful intricacies of the narrative of al-Shayṭān, Adam, and his wife. The question raised here is how the garden story relates to the story of Iblīs.

The garden story begins with a direct address to Adam and, by reference, to his unnamed wife. It then describes al-Shayṭān's whispering and solicitations to them that result in their disobedient act of eating from the tree that God had forbidden to them. Their consequent shame leads them to sew garments for themselves. God rebukes them, and they turn to God asking for forgiveness. God does not clearly grant that forgiveness but does evict them from the garden. Here is a translation:

> "O Adam! Dwell, you and your wife, in the garden, and eat whatever you wish; and do not approach this tree or you will become one of the transgressors."[7]
> Then al-Shayṭān whispered to them in order to reveal to them the shame that was hidden from them, and he said, "Your Lord forbade you this tree lest you become two angels or that you become eternal."
> And he swore to them, "Truly I am for you both a sincere adviser."
> So he led them by deceit; then they tasted of the tree, their shame was revealed to them, and immediately they started sewing for themselves from the leaves of the garden.
> And their Lord called to them, "Did I not forbid you from that tree, and did I not tell you that al-Shayṭān is a clear enemy to you?"
> They said, "Our Lord, we have offended ourselves, and if you will not forgive us and have mercy on us, then we will be among the hopeless."
> He [God] said, "Go down, with some of you being enemies to others, and you will have on earth a dwelling-place and goods for a while."
> He said, "There you will live and there you will die, and from there you will be taken out." (vv. 19–25)

[7] Al-Ṭabarī, *Jāmi'*, 8:139 (vol. 5). Al-Ṭabarī notes a Basran interpretation that the last two clauses of this verse could be understood as two distinct clauses, two separate commands: *do not approach this tree, and do not become transgressors.*

The whole passage, Iblīs and garden stories combined, is framed by God's placement of humanity and provision for them. This frame begins with verse 10 in which God places "you" on earth and provides (*maʻāyisha*) means of living. It is reintroduced in the middle in verse 19, when God places Adam and his wife in the garden and instructs them to "eat whatever you wish," and ends with verses 24–25 when God sends Adam and his wife to earth with *matā*^{un} (provisions). A clear evolution, or more accurately a devolution, appears from the *maʻāyisha* of verse 10, which has the implication of living together, and verses 24–25 where humanity is living in enmity with one another.

The story of Adam and al-Shayṭān in the garden is followed by a commentary on the story that imaginatively extends the images of clothing and shame. When Adam and his wife taste from the forbidden tree, their "shame" becomes manifest. The word used here (*saw'āh*) can mean "shame, evil" or more specifically, "pudenda." The latter meaning is derived from the former, as Lane points out.[8]

Verse 26 immediately picks up the image:

> O children of Adam, we have bestowed upon you clothing [*libās*] to hide [*yuwarī*] your shame [*saw'ātikum*], and plumage [*rīsh*], and clothing [*libās*] of piety [*taqwā*] that is good.

Here clothing fulfills a double function: that of hiding the *saw'āh* and that of adornment, here given the colorful term (*rīsh*) literally meaning "feathers" but implying bright clothing. This physical description is then extended to the moral "clothing of piety." The next verse immediately reverses the application:

> O Children of Adam, do not let al-Shayṭān tempt you in the way that he caused your parents to leave the garden, stripping off from them their clothes [*libās*] in order to make visible their shame [*saw'ātihimā*]; truly he watches you, he and his tribe, from a place where you cannot see them; truly we made the devils [*shayāṭīn*] the friends for those who do not believe. (v. 27)

[8] *Saw'āh* means anything that one regards as an abomination, foul, or offensive. In Sūrat al-Mā'idah, 5:31, the meaning of the term may be an unburied corpse. See Lane, *Arabic-English Lexicon*, 1:1458.

The original garden story in verses 19–25 says nothing about al-Shayṭān stripping clothes off Adam and his wife. His action was to encourage them to eat, although the intention ascribed to him was to expose their shame (*saw'ātihumā*). But just as God clothes Adam and his progeny, now al-Shayṭān seeks to strip them of their clothing, clothing that now means a covering for "shame," God-sanctioned adornment, and *taqwā* (piety).

In the following verse (v. 28), the discussion of shame shifts from the term *saw'āh* to a synonym (*fāḥishah*), which also means "evil" and "abominable" but has implications of enormity and no particular associations with anatomy. Verse 31 picks up the image of clothing as God encourages *zīnah* (adornment) at places of prayer, although this is accompanied by a caution against excess. The final verses of this section of commentary on the garden story (vv. 32–33) continue the contrast between *zīnah* and *fāḥishah*.

How does the Iblīs story relate to the Adam story? A brief outline of contrasts may highlight the relationship:

Iblīs disobeys	Adam disobeys
Iblīs is questioned as to motive	Adam is not questioned as to motive
Iblīs himself decides to disobey	Adam is tempted
Iblīs expresses no regret	Adam asks for forgiveness
Iblīs gets reprieve	Adam gets no reprieve, but rather enmity on earth
Iblīs is evicted	Adam is evicted
Issue is disobedience	Issue is shame and indecency
Iblīs becomes tempter	Adam remains tempted

The two stories begin as narratives rooted in command and disobedience. The Iblīs story is a shorter, sparer narrative. For instance, the request for and granting of reprieve is simple and straightforward. The garden story has more elaboration, although there is little detail that does not directly bear on the meaning of the story.

The actions of al-Shayṭān provoke the disobedience of Adam. Although one must assume that Adam has free choice in the matter, he does not act independently. He is tempted and fooled. Iblīs, on the other hand, does act with independence. There is no al-Shayṭān for Iblīs, no tempter whispering in his ear. Yet Iblīs is given reprieve. Adam asks for forgiveness but is not forgiven. Iblīs asks for reprieve (although not forgiveness) and receives it immediately without the questioning and debate present in other *sūrahs*. Iblīs is shameless, literally, while for Adam shame becomes a crucial and enduring issue.

For Iblīs, eviction leads to a vocation that he chooses for himself: the vocation of tempter. This choice is based on an accusation that we have seen before in Sūrat al-Ḥijr: "Because *you* have led me astray." God is responsible. God is the tempter for Iblīs. No clear basis for this accusation is given in the text, but Iblīs claims this as the reason for, if not his act of disobedience, his decision to become the persistent and pervasive adversary of humanity.

God is furious. God hurls the eviction command at Iblīs again but with further notice of the ultimate consequences of his action. There is a subtle expansion noticeable in God's promise:

> *qāla akhruj minhā maḍ'ūm[an] madḥūr[an] laman tibi'aka minhum la'amla'anna jahannama minkum ajma'īna*
>
> He [God] said, "Get out from it, disgraced and banished; surely those who follow you from among them, indeed I will fill Gehenna from among you, all." (v. 18)

God says first that he will fill up Gehenna with all those who follow Iblīs, but then adds, "from among you, all together," which would include Iblīs. Thus not only the followers of Iblīs will end up in Gehenna but Iblīs himself will. About the interval between his eviction from heaven and his final destination in Gehenna, God says nothing. He does not agree to Iblīs's intention to become a tempter, nor does God qualify that agenda, as occurs in Sūrat al-Ḥijr and Sūrah Ṣād. God says nothing, but only here does God condemn Iblīs to the final destination of Gehenna.

For Adam the evolution is different. After his eviction from heaven and condemnation to life, death, and conflict on earth, Adam receives from God a sign of blessing and hope:

> *yā-banī ādama qad anzalnā 'alaykum libās[an] yuwārī saw'ātikum warīsh[an]*

> *wa-libāsu al-taqwā dhālika khayr*[un] *dhālika min 'āyāti allahi la'allahum yadhdhakkarūna*
>
> O children of Adam, We have sent down to you clothing to cover your private parts and as plumage and the clothing of piety—that is best; this is one of the signs of God that perhaps they will remember. (v. 26)

Once again the theme of God's provision appears.

The garden story, in its three versions, is exclusively associated with the Iblīs story. In fact, even the name "Adam" is seldom mentioned in the Qur'ān apart from the eviction and garden stories.[9]

Surveying the entire passage from the beginning of the Iblīs story through the commentary (vv. 10–33), one can see that the core Iblīs story itself, from the initial command and disobedience through the grant of respite, is *pro forma* and recited with some elaboration but no indication of hostility. The exchange of accusations (vv. 16–18) initiates an impassioned adversarial stance that sets up the garden story. The garden story then illustrates, or manifests, the implication of hostility between al-Shayṭān and God.

After Iblīs declares his intention to approach humanity and tempt them, al-Shayṭān (presumed to be the same as Iblīs but never identified as such) approaches Adam and his wife in the garden. He succeeds in tempting them away from God's command, but their request for forgiveness, indicating that they do not follow al-Shayṭān, displaces God's promise to "fill Jahannam" with them. The section from Iblīs's accusation against God (v. 16) through the garden story and the commentary upon it is characterized by hostility. The prior narrative, the core Iblīs story, is all preamble.

Conclusion

In this *sūrah* one sees the Iblīs story set alongside the garden story in order to contrast the different treatments of Adam and Iblīs. Iblīs is not identified as a *jinn* in this story, as he is in Sūrat al-Kahf, which may be an earlier rendering of the story. Nor is Iblīs set alongside Adam in a sibling rivalry story as in Sūrat al-Ḥijr. One gets the rudimentary comparison of Iblīs and

[9] The name "Adam" is mentioned twenty-five times in the Qur'ān. Of these, only five are in the *sūrahs* that do not include the Iblīs story (3:33, 3:59, 5:27, 19:58, 36:60).

Adam in verse 12, but this is enough to set up the grounds for comparison. Iblīs does this himself: "I am better than he."

Although both characters disobey, and both are consequently evicted, that sequence is the end of their similarity. Iblīs's response to disobedience is first defiant self-justification and then commitment to what is ultimately a life of disobedience. He will not only refuse to bow down to Adam; he will forever refuse to acknowledge any value in Adam or his descendants. He will continue to treat them with contempt. He knows nothing of repentance.

Adam, on the other hand, responds with an immediate confession and cry for forgiveness. He and his wife are nevertheless punished not only by eviction but also through the difficulties of life in the world, a life characterized by internecine hostility and a limited life span. Unlike the situation of Iblīs, characterized by stasis, the condition of Adam and his descendants is dynamic. They are not only consigned to difficult lives. They are also given the provisions that they need. Their shame is exposed but also hidden if they so wish. Their lives are characterized by choice. Iblīs, having chosen once, resolves to live with no choice. He has a job to do, with no apparent intention ever to change.

This contrast does not appear in the story of al-Shayṭān. Al-Shayṭān, although wily and deceptive, never demonstrates any independence of action. He is an actor, not a character. Iblīs, on the other hand, chooses to disobey, asks for reprieve, and then commits himself to a life of crime. He is a character who moves from a heavenly context to a new life situation on the basis of a sequence of choices. Iblīs, not al-Shayṭān, stands in complex contrast to Adam and Adam's choices. In theory, having chosen to be a tempter, Iblīs could reverse his decision. As described in chapter 1, there are numerous post-qur'ānic stories in which Iblīs actually considers such a reversal. In none of them, though, does he follow through. In Sūrat al-'Arāf, there is no hint of any desire to reconsider.

One might, in addition, draw a contrast on the basis of shame and the covering of shame and see the earthly life and mission of Iblīs as a shameful one. It is not, however, presented as such. God condemns Iblīs to hell but makes no attempt to stop Iblīs from his chosen path, or even to dissuade him. Iblīs has freedom of choice. So does Adam.

One of Iblīs's choices is to ask for reprieve. Reprieve from what? Iblīs suffers no punishment other than eviction. He is sent "down," but to what sort of life? Adam's life is characterized by limited life span and continuing societal conflict. No evidence suggests that Iblīs has a limited life span. Given the discussion of the termination of reprieve in Sūrat al-Ḥijr and Sūrah Ṣād, the reprieve could be a suspension of such a limit. Also no hint emerges that Iblīs will be the victim of hostility. He is certainly the producer of hostility toward humanity, but he is free of its effects, at least until the day of judgment.

The hostility between God and Iblīs in Sūrat al-'Arāf is greater here than in any other Iblīs story. Only here in verse 18, do we get such an enraged condemnation of Iblīs:

> Get out from it [heaven], disgraced and banished; surely those who follow you from among them—I will indeed fill Gehenna with you, all [of you]. (v. 18)

God and Iblīs go their separate ways. All that may be left between them is fuming fury. This is in the character of the combat myth. God and Iblīs are opposed to each other with no reconciliation in sight, and consequently Iblīs and humanity are similarly opposed. Opposition is total. Iblīs will attack humanity frontally, from the flanks, and secretly from behind. Further, his attacks on humanity are indirectly attacks on God, for he will dissuade mortals from gratitude toward God.

Adam's situation is a contrast to this. God and the descendants of Adam are in constant relationship. God provides consolation to all of humanity—clothing to cover their shame, signs to lead them to piety, the greatest of remedies for shame. God's guidance is ever present, not only for the remittance of shame but for protection from Iblīs and his putative successor, al-Shayṭān. In true combat form, the lines of opposition are set and inflexible. Human beings have to choose which side they are on: the side of God or the side of al-Shayṭān.

CHAPTER 10

Sūrat al-Baqarah (2)

Sūrat al-Baqarah, the longest *sūrah* in the Qur'ān, is commonly identified as early Medīnan and the latest of the seven *sūrahs* under consideration here. Medīnan *sūrahs* are characterized by long verses, by a shift from polemical language toward exhortation and didactic legislation, and by more attention to the relationship—contemporary and historical—to the People of the Book.

Structure

With its lengthy and composite nature, Sūrat al-Baqarah may elude summary but in fact does show a coherent structure. David Smith suggests that the *sūrah* is organized around an "Allah–Qur'ān–Muḥammad authority structure."[1] He elaborates this by pointing out that the history of revelation in the first 167 verses shows the failure of the children of Israel and those who have rejected the prophets to understand either the revelation or the success of Abraham and Muḥammad in receiving it. Smith divides this portion into three sections: verses 2–39 establish the authority of the Qur'ān and Muḥammad; verses 40–118 rehearse the failure of the children of Israel to follow the prophets; and verses 119–67 connect the authority of the Qur'ān and Muḥammad to the Abrahamic tradition. The second half of the *sūrah* (from v. 168 to the end) elaborates on legislation that is the substance of the revelation, punctuated regularly by reaffirmations of the failure of the children of Israel and the success of Muḥammad to accept the divine revelation.[2]

[1] Smith, "Structure of al-Baqarah," 121.

[2] Verses 211–12 and 253 recall the failure of the children of Israel to accept the divine revelation. Verses 252 and 285 affirm the authority of Muḥammad.

Neal Robinson locates the key to the *sūrah* in verse 143, "We have made you an *ummat*[an] *wasat*[an]—a community in the middle; a balanced community—that you might be witnesses to the people." Thus the *sūrah* as a whole places Islam as a legitimate tradition in its own right with its own regulations and legal code. It is the true religion of Abraham, ancestor to both Christianity and Judaism and correcting the errors and exaggerations of each.[3]

I propose a somewhat different schema for the initial section. The prologue, a series of exhortations, ends with verse 29. The salvation history begins at verse 30, not verse 40, with God's announcement of a divine intention to create a vice-regent on earth. There is no reason to separate what might be called the primordial history—the sequence of events that occurs extraterrestrially, in heaven and in the garden—from those events that we might regard as more historical, the stories of the *Banū Isrā'īl*, beginning with verse 40. It is all an account of salvation history.

Further, this division clarifies that the key issue in Sūrat al-Baqarah is the issue of knowledge. This will become abundantly clear in the examination of the Iblīs story itself, but can be seen in the prologue as well.

Prologue

The first substantive verse, ignoring for the moment the *muqaṭṭa'āt*, declares "That[4] is the Book; (there is) no doubt that in it is guidance *(hud*[an]) to the God-fearers." The Book, here referring to an established, though as yet incomplete, written text of the Qur'ān, contains a guiding knowledge for the faithful. One should note that the recitation indicators (*'alāmāt al-waqf*) give two alternative meanings to this declaration. The reciter may pause after *al-kitāb*, giving the meaning as I have interpreted above, "That is the Book; (there is) no doubt that in it is guidance to the God-fearers." The semicolon indicates the pause (*waqf*). The *'alāmāt al-waqf* indicate that one may also pause after *lā rayb* ("no doubt"), rendering the meaning, "That is the Book without doubt; in it is guidance for the God-fearers." The *'alāmāt al-waqf*

[3] Robinson, *Discovering the Qur'ān*, 201–2.

[4] Usually translators have "This" here, though the Arabic, *dhālika*, is properly translated as "That." Commentators give a number of reasons for the unexpected *dhālika*. See al-Qurṭubī, *Al-Jāmi'a*, 1.153–154 (vol. 1); Ibn Kathīr, *Tafsīr*, 53–54. The effect of "that" is to put the speaker at greater distance and separation from the object of reference. The "Book" becomes a more independent entity.

indicate that one may stop in either place, but not both. The latter reading gives more emphasis to the guidance (*hud^{an}*).[5]

The next two verses parse two aspects of this guidance. Some of this knowledge is belief in the unseen (*al-ghayb*). The mysterious letters themselves are often taken as examples of this.[6] Some of this knowledge is belief in "that which is sent down to you" (*mā unzila ilayka*), and "that which was sent down before you" (*mā unzila min qablika*). Verse 5 reiterates that this is guidance, *hud^{an}*. Verses 6–7 describe the determined rejecters. Their rejection is itself within the knowledge of God. Much greater attention is given to the hypocrites, the *munāfiqīn*, in verses 8–20. God's knowledge is aware of their deceit and responds accordingly.

The final section of the prologue (vv. 21–29) is addressed generally to the "people" (*nās*), a formula typical of Medīnan *sūrah*s. This passage describes the beneficence of God, the tension between knowledge and doubt, the usefulness of God's similitudes, and the importance of maintaining the covenant with God. Throughout the prologue references to God's knowledge and human knowledge abound. There are four citations of the root *'-l–m* (know):

v. 13 *wa-lākin lā ya'lamūna.*
v. 22 *wa-antum ta'lamūna.*
v. 26 *fa-ya'lamūna annahu al-ḥaqqu min rabbihim.*
v. 29 *wa-huwa bi-kulli sha'^{in} 'alīm^{un}.*

v. 13 But they (the hypocrites) do not know.
v. 22 And you (believers) know.
v. 26 They know that it is truth from their Lord.
v. 29 And he is in everything knowledgeable.

Three of these occurrences are at natural endings of passages (vv. 13, 22, and 29). The last terminates the prologue. That there is no such reference to the divine name in verse 39 gives further weight to the assertion that the Iblīs story ought to be included in the salvation history.

[5] Nelson, *Reciting*, 27–28; Ibn Kathīr, *Tafsīr,* 1.54. Ibn Kathīr expresses a preference that recitation put the *waqf* before *lā rayb,* not after.

[6] See, for example, al-Qurṭubī, *Al-Jāmi'a* 1.154–155 (vol. 1).

The Story of Iblīs

The story of Iblīs found within a four-part section in Sūrat al-Baqarah. In addition to the core Iblīs story and the garden story, there is the addition of two "prequels": first, a story of a conversation between God and the angels concerning God's intention to create a *khalīfah*, a vice-regent or deputy on earth, and secondly a story of Adam's naming of all things. These four stories comprise an extended narration that describes the essential nature of humanity. Humanity, with Adam as its representative progenitor, is both superior in knowledge to the angels and vulnerable to error. One may describe these stories as four parts of the Iblīs story, but this is not quite accurate, since Iblīs himself figures in only one story. It is more accurate to consider them as a primordial cycle, since all stories occur in primordial time, in an extraterrestrial sphere. It might be even more accurate to describe these stories as the primordial story of Adam in which Iblīs has a bit part in the third scene.

The Angels' Complaint

The first story, unique here in the Qur'ān but with parallels in Jewish midrash,[7] has evoked a great deal of commentary among the *mufassirīn*.

> *wa-idh qāla rabbuka li-malā'ika*
> *innī jā'il^{un} fī al-arḍi khalīfat^{an}*
> *qālū ataj'alu fī-hā man yasfiku fī-hā wa-yufsiku al-dimā'a*
> *wa-naḥnu nusabbiḥu bi-ḥamdika wa-nuqaddisu la-ka*
> *qāla innī a'lamu mā lā ta'lamūna.*

> And when your Lord said to the angels, "Truly I am making on the earth a vice-regent,"[8] they said, "Are you making on it one who will cause corruption on it and shed blood, while we glorify you with praises and sanctify you?" He said, "Truly I know what you do not know." (v. 30)

[7] See Ginzberg, *Legends*, 1:52–54; Katsh, *Judaism and the Koran*, 26–29.

[8] The proper translation for *khalīfah* is significant. It means both a successor (raising the question of whom Adam might be succeeding) and a representative or deputy, hence "vice-regent." The latter translation is correct, but fails to capture the sense of successorship that became the predominant sense when applied to the Caliphs, successors to Muḥammad as leader of the Muslim community.

At issue is the nature of angels and their knowledge. How did the angels know that this being that God would create would cause corruption on earth and shed blood? Further, how could angels, who are presumed to be models of obedience to God, question God's plan?

Al-Ṭabarī explores these questions at length.[9] Concerning the knowledge of the angels, al-Ṭabarī recites a lengthy legend of the prehistory of Iblīs, to wit, that Iblīs has been a member of a tribe of angels assigned to guard the garden. *Jinn* are created before humans and inhabit the earth. The *jinn* fight with one another, shedding blood and corrupting the earth, so Iblīs is sent at the head of an army to destroy them. Iblīs's success leads to his pride. This story, says al-Ṭabarī, is reported by Ibn 'Abbās through al-Ḍaḥḥāk. A second story, also reported by Ibn 'Abbās, but through Ibn Mas'ūd, reports that God assigns Iblīs to rule over the lowest heaven, the *samā' al-dunyā*. He is custodian (*khāzin*) of the garden (*jannah*), which is why his tribe is called the *jinn*. This assignment leads to Iblīs's pride. Here, a more extended conversation occurs:

> God said to the angels, "I am making on the earth a vice-regent." They said, "Our Lord, what will this vice-regent be?" He said, "He will have progeny that will cause corruption on the earth and will envy each other and some will kill some others." They said, "Our Lord, are you making on [earth] one who will cause corruption there and shed blood, while we glorify with your praises and sanctify you?" He said, "Truly I know what you do not know."[10]

Al-Ṭabarī concludes that the second story makes less sense.

Further stories of the gathering of clay from the earth to make Adam, which also have their parallels in midrash, accompany both of these stories.[11] Given that the Iblīs story in Sūrat al-Baqarah occurs first in the bound order of the Qur'ān, it is on this passage that the bulk of the commentators on the Iblīs legends expend their energies. I have related many of these stories in previous chapters.

Al-Ṭabarī cites further legends and explanations of the conundrum. A legend reported by Qatādah says that the angels' concern about the creation of Adam is not based on knowledge of the past, but rather on the likelihood

[9] Al-Ṭabarī, *Jāmi'*, 1.201–202 (vol. 1). See partial translations, 121–23.

[10] Ibid., 1.203 (vol. 1).

[11] See Ginzberg, *Legends*, 1.54–55.

of future bloodshed on earth, but that God knows of the coming of prophets, messengers, and righteous people. God knows what they do not. Ḥasan al-Basrī and others reports similar narratives.

The story of God's pronouncement of intention to the angels shifts the emphasis of the entire Adam/Iblīs segment from a narrative focusing on obedience and disobedience to one focusing on knowledge. God announces an intention, a notification of future action, to the angels. This announcement does not require any sort of response on the part of the angels, but nevertheless they do respond with their own knowledge. They "know" that what God creates on earth will, or likely will, create corruption and bloodshed. Their knowledge appears to compete with God's knowledge. God's reply simply asserts that the divine knowledge is more complete, or more accurate, than angelic knowledge. The fact that the angels do possess knowledge but that their knowledge is deficient necessitates commentarial intervention. The narrative character of the story also deserves attention. Although the Medīnan *sūrah*s are not known for their poetic features, this story does show rhythm and pattern. Consider the following analysis:

wa-idh qāla		
rabbuka li-malā'ika	ending i-a	
qālū ataj'alu fī-hā	ending i-ā	8 syllables
man yufsidu fī-hā	ending i-ā	6 syllables
wa-yasfika al-dimā'a	ending i-ā'a	7 syllables
wa-naḥnu nusabbiḥ bi-ḥamdika	ending i-a	11 syllables
wa-nuqaddisu laka	ending a-a	7 syllables
qāla innī a'lamu mā lā ta'lamūna	ending u-a	

The reply of the angels to God builds a rhythm and momentum that follows three lines, all ending in an *i-ā* pattern, describing the corruption of the earth. These three lines flow easily from one to another, with 6–8 syllables. The three imperfect verbs—*ataj'alu*, *yufsidu*, and *yasfika* (roots: *f-'-l*, *f-s-d*, and *s-f-k*)—amplify the poetic assonance.

The next line, in which the discourse shifts to the angels' own contrasting vocation of praise, breaks this pattern with two lines ending with *-ka*. The first line of this second pattern is longer—eleven syllables, which also signals the shift. The angels' effusive praise may dispel the impression that their earlier query represents the kind of heavenly tension found in Sūrah Ṣād (38:69–71). The passage here is reminiscent of the Sūrah Ṣād passage in which God also declares an intention to create humanity, although there is no mention in Sūrah Ṣād specifically of a *khalīfah*.

> When your Lord said to the angels, "I am creating (*innī jā'il*^{un}) on the earth a vice-regent" (2:30)

> When your Lord said to the angels, "I am creating (*innī khāliq*^{un}) a human from clay" (38:71)

In Sūrah Ṣād, the verbal element *khāliq*, an active participle, refers specifically to the act of creating, whereas in Sūrat al-Baqarah the verbal element *jā'il*, also an active participle, refers more generally to acting with no specific reference to creating. This suggests that the focus of the narrative is not on God's creation but on God's action. The following verses will bear this out, as the creation of Adam is entirely absent from the story.

Finally, God's response disrupts the pattern. All the previous phrases show a diversity of voweling, mixing the *ḍammah,* "u," the *kasrah*, "i" and the *fatḥah*, "a" in lively variety. The last phrase of verse 30, God's response, is vocalized mostly with *fatḥah*, "a," in a sequence of a-a-i-i-a-a-u-a-a-a-u-a. This gives a more declarative, assertive tone to God's declaration, "I know what you do not know." The verb *'-l-m* (to know) is used twice here.

The omniscient narrator mainly reports dialogue here, giving no reference to time or place. The indicator *idh* and the movement from the narrator's direct speech throughout the prologue to reported speech is one marker of the break from the previous section, the prologue of the *sūrah*. The narrator makes no comment in this first narrative, simply reporting the interaction between God and the angels. However, a continuity between the prologue and the long salvation history is provided by the reference to God as *al-'Alīm* (the Knower) in the last line (v. 29) of the prologue, and God's statement, "I know what you do not know," in the last line of the first verse (v. 30).

Teaching Adam the Names

The second prequel further develops the focus on knowledge. Here God gives Adam knowledge superior to that of the angels.

wa-'allama ādama al-asmā'a kullahā thumma 'araḍahum 'alā al-malā'ikati
fa-qāla anbi'ūnī bi-asmā'i hā'ulā'i in kuntum ṣādiqīna.
qālū subḥānaka lā 'ilma lanā illā mā 'allamtanā innaka anta al-'alīm al-ḥakīm.
qālā yā-ādamu anbi'hum bi-asmā'ihim
fa-lammā anbā'ahum bi-asmā'ihim qāla alam aqul lakum
innī a'lamu ghayba al-samāwāti wa-l-arḍi
wa-a'lamu mā tubdūna wa-mā kuntum taktumūna

And he taught Adam the names, all of them; then he presented them to the angels; then he said, "Tell me the names of these, if you are truthful."
They said, "Glory to you; we have no knowledge except what you have taught us; truly you, you are the Knowing, the Wise."
He said, "O Adam, tell them their names." When he had told them their names, he said, "Did I not tell you that I, I know the unseen of the heavens and the earth, and I know what you reveal and what you have concealed?" (vv. 31–33)

This second section, leading up to the Iblīs story, has a parallel in Gen 2:19–20 in which Adam names the creatures. The Genesis version does not describe this as a contrast to the deficiency of angelic knowledge, but Jewish midrash does make this comparison.[12]

Here the narrator takes a stronger role than in verse 30, describing God's act of teaching all the names, or the names of all things, to Adam, and then placing "them" before Adam. The second clause implies that *kullahā*, "all of them," refers not to the names but to the named, the same referent to which "these" refers in God's command. But the three verses of this story, longer than the first story, still consist mostly of dialogue.

The primary characters in this story are still God and the angels. Although Adam is featured, Adam is silent; it is only God and the angels who speak. As before, the angels are effusive in praise of God. Here they offer no questions, no objections. This story is a continuation of the previous story. Having claimed superior knowledge, God goes on to ensure that even Adam has knowledge superior to the angels. This knowledge is, of course, not natural to Adam. God must teach him the names.

There is an element of the sibling rivalry story here, although the adversaries are not Adam and Iblīs but Adam and the angels. Yet it is not

[12] Ginzberg, *Legends*, 1:61–62; Katsh, *Judaism and the Koran*, 30–31.

truly a sibling rivalry pattern. First of all, no generative relationship is claimed, unlike Sūrat al-Ḥijr where the createdness of both Adam and Iblīs is placed in parallel. Although the angels are active in the first story in raising objections, or at least questions, about this new creation, Adam is entirely passive in the story. The focal point remains God, who takes the initiative throughout. God first announces an intention, then squelches the objection, then not only proves his own superior knowledge but actively generates Adam's superior knowledge. Elements of sibling rivalry are here, but the narrator puts the emphasis elsewhere.

The narrator conspires in Adam's silence. Where we might have expected Adam to speak after God commands him, "O Adam, tell them their names," the narrator intrudes and informs us that Adam did so. This intrusion silences Adam's voice and diminishes his role in the story, or rather prevents it from resurfacing. The focus shifts directly back to God. The angels speak only, although not briefly, in praise of God and God's knowledge, and in deprecation of their own knowledge.

The Core Iblīs Story

When we move to the Iblīs story proper (v. 34), the core narrative instruction to the angels now appears as a continuation of an ongoing chronicle. The command to the angels to bow down is a logical extension of the previous two anecdotes, further addressing the relationship between the angels and Adam. The first anecdote defends the creation of humanity, and by implication Adam, in the abstract. The second anecdote establishes the superior knowledge of Adam, superior to the angels. Their response is to claim their lack of knowledge. This third anecdote demands a more physical expression of their inferiority to Adam: they are commanded to bow down. The import of this further command is that what we have seen in other narrations as an introduction to the Iblīs story becomes here a continuation of the story of the demotion of the angels. It is not about Iblīs at first. It is about the angels. Iblīs is a sidebar.

The command to the angels to bow down to Adam is, of course, the first element of the core Iblīs story present in all seven versions of the story in the Qur'ān, with little variation. This particular version of the core story begins in the same fashion as do the versions in *sūrahs* 17, 18, and 20. It then summarizes other elements of the story.

> *wa-idh qulnā li-malā'ikati sjudū li-ādama fa-sajadū illā iblīsa abā wa-stakbara wa-kāna min al-kāfirīna*
>
> And when we said to the angels, "Bow down to Adam," then they bowed down, except Iblīs; he refused and was proud. And he was one of the unbelievers. (v. 34)

Just as the narrator denies Adam a voice in the previous story, so Iblīs receives similar treatment here. The narrator summarizes and describes his refusal to bow down, but Iblīs himself never speaks.

The narrator, however, has switched positions, drawing closer to the action. Whereas the narrator tells the first two stories from an observer position, *qāla*, "He said," the narrator tells the next two stories from the companion position, *qulnā*, "We said." It is possible that the difference between the two sets of stories is temporal, but it is difficult to see what would be the significance of the small gap in time between teaching Adam the names and instructing the angels to bow down to him. It is more likely that the text is drawing on the pattern of the majority of the previous versions of the story: four other Iblīs passages use *qulnā* here,[13] while one uses *qāla*,[14] and one is expressed in the first person singular.[15] The consistency of the shift suggests something more. The narrator is placing himself at some distance from the two stories that focus on the angels. The third story, the Iblīs story, begins with focus on the angels, but shifts immediately to Iblīs himself. Does the shift in narratorial position indicate a particular stance toward the angelic community, such that when angels are entirely in accord with God, the narrator closes ranks with them?

As Welch has pointed out, the Medīnan passages in the Qur'ān, those that are post-Badr, show angels increasingly as extensions of God's will, showing less independence of action.[16] This subtle change of diction may indicate just such a shift. The angels in the first two stories are in some degree of discord with God. They express profuse praise of God, so this discord is not rebellion, but clearly they show some independence of will. The third story, however, shows the angels in full obedience to God, and it is Iblīs, and in the garden

[13] 7:11, 17:61, 18:50 and 20:116.

[14] 15:28

[15] 38:72

[16] Welch, "Allah," 746-9.

story Adam and al-Shayṭān, who are separate from God. The narrator then looks together with God upon all who disobey and transgress.

This third story of the primordial cycle summarizes previous versions of the Iblīs story. It adds nothing not seen before in various Meccan versions:

wa-idh qulnā li-malā'ikati sjudū li-ādama	= 17:61; 18:50; 20:116
fa-sajadū illā iblīsa	= 17:61; 18:50; 20:116
abā	= 20:116; 15:28
[*wa*]-*stakbara wa-kāna min al-kāfirīna*	= 38:74

In content, this text adds nothing unnecessary, such as the repetition for emphasis in 7:11—*lam yakun min al-sājidīn*. It is spare and lean, describing: 1) the initial circumstance—the command to prostrate oneself, 2) what Iblīs does—he refuses, 3) an explanation for his refusal—he is proud, and 4) the implication of his refusal—he is among the unbelievers. All of this is expressed tersely but lucidly.

The inclusion of *idh* in the beginning is narratively surprising since the *wa-idh* combination usually indicates the beginning of a new section of the text. Its inclusion here may underscore that this language is simply repeated from previously revealed versions of the story, not (re-)constructed in a particular way for this occurrence.

It is important to note what is *not* here, that is, the blanks. There is no mention of *jinn*. There is no mention of the creation of Adam, much less of the materials of his creation. There is no mention of Iblīs's own defense of his actions, or God's questioning of him. There is no mention of his eviction from heaven, or his bargaining for respite from God's curse. Finally, there is no mention of his intention to lead humanity astray. This last is somewhat surprising, since it would establish the basis for the connection with the garden story. Sūrat al-'Arāf, which includes Iblīs's expressed intention to assault "them" in 7:16–17, followed by a lengthy version of the temptation in the garden (vv. 19–25), does imply, although does not clearly establish, such a connection. However, the intention to deceive humanity is found in Sūrat al-Ḥijr (15:39–40), Sūrah Ṣād (38:82–3), and Sūrat al-Isrā' (17:65) without the garden story.

The version here bears some similarity to that in Sūrah ṬāHā (20:117–21), which also gives the garden story without an account of Iblīs's intention to deceive. Like the Sūrat al-Baqarah version, Sūrah ṬāHā has a brief summary of the core Iblīs story—even briefer than that here. The garden story is presented, as we noted in chapter 4 on Sūrah ṬāHā, as a continuation of the Iblīs story, connected by a *fa-* indicating sequence or consequence. Here in Sūrat al-Baqarah, the conjunction is *wa-*, a weak indicator of continuity.

The same conclusion is appropriate here as in the consideration of the Iblīs story in Sūrah ṬāHā. This is an Adam narrative in which Iblīs has a bit part. Because Iblīs is not at the center of attention—indeed, here, is an actor rather than a character—the Iblīs story itself is reduced to its bare minimum. Indeed, one might even say it detracts from the larger narrative, taking attention away, for a moment, a verse, from the central theme of God's creation and care of Adam. The interjection of the Iblīs story makes no contribution to this, unless one conflates Iblīs with the al-Shayṭān story of the subsequent garden encounter, to which we now turn.

The Garden Story

The fourth and final story of the primordial cycle is the story of al-Shayṭān and Adam in the garden. The version here is shorter than those in Sūrah ṬāHā and Sūrat al-'Arāf. As in the previous three primordial stories, the narrator assumes a major role. The story begins with God's instruction to Adam and his wife to dwell in the garden, where there is bountiful provision, and to stay away from the specified tree. Then the narrator tells us that al-Shayṭān causes them to err, and thus they are evicted. The text then switches back to God's direct speech, telling them to descend to earth and dwell as enemies to one another, with the provisions available there, for a period of time.

wa-qulnā yā-ādamu skun anta wa-zawjuka al-jannata
wa-kulā minhā raghad[an] *haythu shi'tumā*
wa-lā taqrabā hadhihi al-shajarata
fa-takūnā min al-ẓālimīna

fa-azallahumā al-shayṭānu 'anhā
fa-akhrajahumā mimā kānā fīhi
wa-qulnā hbiṭū ba'ḍukum li-ba'ḍ[in] *'adūw*[un]
wa-lakum fī al-arḍi mustaqarr[un]
wa-matā'[un] *ilā hīn*[in]

And we said, "O Adam, dwell, you and your wife, in the garden;
And eat from it of the bounty as you wish;
And do not go near this tree

> Or you will become one of the transgressors."
>
> So al-Shayṭān made them slip from it
> And made them depart from the manner in which they were.
> And we said, "Go down, some of you being enemies to others,
> And you will have on earth a dwelling and supplies for a time."
> (vv. 35–36)

Commentary on this story in the *tafsīr* literature is rich and extensive. Much of it we have already reviewed. Our interest is mainly in its narrative character and its relationship to the rest of the primordial cycle. As we have noted with the Iblīs story, this text is the first instance of the garden story in order of bound text, although the last in order of revelation. The commentaries treat it as the first telling, but we will approach it as the last telling. This raises the question: What has been added or left out in this latest version of the garden story? The version in Sūrat al-Baqarah summarizes the earlier versions. All three renditions contain the basic elements of the story:

1) Command to dwell in the garden	2:35, 7:19
2) Presence of bounty in the garden	2:35, 7:19, 20:118
3) Command not to go near the tree	2:35, 7:19
4) Appearance of al-Shayṭān	2:36, 7:20, 20:120
5) Command to "go down"	2:36, 7:24, 20:123
6) Announcement of enmity among people	2:36, 7:24, 20:123
7) Provision on earth	2:36, 7:24–25
8) Adam's repentance	2:37, 7:23

As is clear from this chart, Sūrat al-Baqarah tracks Sūrat al-'Arāf most closely. Sūrah ṬāHā includes a preliminary warning to Adam prior to al-Shayṭān's appearance, and gives al-Shayṭān a prominent role, even voice. In that version, al-Shayṭān is a focal point, even to the point of passing over God's warning to avoid the tree.

The situation is similar in Sūrat al-'Arāf, where al-Shayṭān also has voice (7:20). The extensive attention given to Iblīs's expression of intention to lead astray (7:16–17) leads the reader to understand Adam's failure in that context. Sūrat al-Baqarah merely mentions al-Shayṭān as the cause of the eviction of Adam and his wife. The focal point is Adam, and the narrative hurries toward the ultimate disposition: that Adam and his wife dwell on earth in a situation of enmity.

The reason for this becomes apparent when we see this in the context of the whole primordial cycle. The final disposition of Adam and his wife is reminiscent of the angel's question in the first story, "Are you making on [earth] one who will cause corruption in it and shed blood?" (2:30). Although corruption and blood-shedding are not specifically mentioned here, we now understand that the angels were not wrong in their concerns about God's intentions. This is further confirmed in the next verse:

fa-talaqqā ādamu min rabbihi kalamāt[in]
fa-tāba 'alayhi
innahu huwa al-tawwābu al-raḥīmu

Then Adam learned from his Lord words,
Then he turned to him;
Truly he is the One Who Turns, the Compassionate. (v. 37)

As the materialization of enmity on earth reflects the angels' concern in the first primordial story, so the teaching of words to Adam reflects the second primordial story. In that story Adam is taught the names of things (v. 31). Here Adam is taught other words, perhaps words of repentance or words of faith, since the result is that the Lord as the compassionate one turns to him. The garden story ends with a contrast between those who accept the guidance from God, and those who reject it:

qulnā hbiṭū minhā jamī'[an]
fa-immā ya'tiyannakum minnī hud[an]
fa-man tabi'a hudāya
fa-lā khawf[un] *'alayhim wa-lā hum yaḥzanūna*
wa-la-ladhīna kafarū wa-kadhdhabū bi-āyātinā
awlā'ika aṣḥābu al-nāri
hum fīhā khālidūna

We said, "Go down all from it,
And if there comes to you guidance from me,
Then whoever follows my guidance
Will have no fear on them, and they will not grieve.
And those who disbelieve and lie about our signs,
These will be the companions of the fire.
They will be in it eternally." (vv. 38–39)

The beginning of verse 38 repeats the command in verse 37, moving the narrative back in time to the ejection from the garden. The adverb, *jamīʿan* (all of you), added in this repetition of the command, emphasizes that while all of the previous discourse about Adam and his wife is in the grammatical dual mode, addressed to two people, the command to "go down" is in the plural. Commentators differ about whether this applies to Adam, his wife, and al-Shayṭān, or whether this applies to all of the future progeny of Adam. It is curious, though, that this phrase is repeated from verse 36:

2:36	*wa-qulnā hbiṭū baʿḍukum li-baʿḍin ʿadūwun*
2:38	*qulnā hbiṭū minhā jamīʿan*

Compare with:

7:24	*qāla uhbiṭū* *baʿḍukum li-baʿḍin adūwun*
20:123	*qāla uhbiṭā minhā jamīʿā* *baʿḍukum li-baʿḍin ʿadūwun*

The phrasing in Sūrat al-Baqarah draws from both previous versions, except that the narrator has drawn closer to the speaker, using "we." In Sūrah ṬāHā, the collective, *jamīʿā* (all; altogether), stands in tension with the dual case of *uhbiṭā*.[17] God commands Adam and his wife to "Go down" and then extends the effect of the command to *jamīʿā*. One explanation of this in the commentaries is that the command applies to Adam and Hawā, and then extends to include Iblīs.[18] Another explanation is that this includes the children of Adam and Hawā.[19] A third explanation is that Adam and Hawā are sent down, but the enmity is with the offspring of Iblīs.[20] Clearly the text is ambiguous.[21]

[17] The dual *uhbiṭā* contrasts with the plural *uhbiṭū*.

[18] Al-Bayḍāwī, *Tafsīr*, 2.60; al-Qurṭubī, *Al-Jāmiʿa*, 11.169 (vol. 6).

[19] Al-Nasafī, *Tafsīr*, 2.77; al-Suyūṭī, *Jalaylayn*, 418; al-Zamakhsharī, *Al-Kashshāf*, 3.94.

[20] Al-Ṭabarī, *Jāmiʿ*, 16.224 (vol. 9).

[21] Al-Bursawī, *Tafsīr*, 16.440–441 (vol. 5). Al-Bursawī turns the meaning around, suggesting that the descent is a rejection in its appearances (*al-ʿitābu wa-al-lawmu fī al-ṣūrati*) but a perfection and ennoblement on the path of self-discipline (*qahr*) in that it reminds the

The duplication in Sūrat al-Baqarah, drawing separately from the two previous versions, is curious. Al-Ṭabarī does not comment on this. Al-Qurṭubī writes that this repetition makes the command emphatic, even "rough" (*taghlīẓ*), but he adds that some say that this is to avoid making every commandment to Adam and his wife dependent on the ruling of the other command.[22] Al-Bayḍāwī distinguishes between the intention of the first command to "Go down" as a descent to the abode of tribulation (*dār balīya*) in which they will contend with one another but not remain forever, and the second command as descent to obligation such that those who follow guidance will be saved. The two together encourage fear, which will, in turn, produce receptivity to the guidance. In particular, al-Bayḍāwī suggests that the first command emphasizes the division of humanity, being enemies to one another, and the second command emphasizes the coming together: *jamīʿan*.

The division between those who will follow the guidance from God and those who will not reaches back to the prologue and its discussion of divine guidance, beginning in verse 2. It also provides a connection to the Iblīs story itself within the primordial cycle in the identification of Iblīs in verse 34 as an unbeliever, one of the *kāfirīn*.

---

individual of the fear of God, but also of other things that have come down—the Qur'ān, the angels, the rain, and so on.

[22] Al-Qurṭubī adds the following stories: "Some say that the first descent is from the Garden to heaven and the second from heaven to earth. This is said to be an indication that the Garden is in the seventh heaven, as the report of the night journey has it. . . . Wahb b. Munabbih said: when Adam descended to earth, Iblīs said to the wild animals, if this is enmity for you, then destroy him. So they met together and appointed him a leader. When Adam saw this he was dismayed by this. Gabriel came to him and said, "Stroke the head of the dog with your hand." He did so. When the beasts saw that the dog had become intimate with Adam, they scattered. The dog was faithful to him, and Adam was faithful to [the dog], and he remained with him and with his children. . . . If he were pelted with dirt-clods, he would flee like a fugitive and then return to be intimate with him. In him [the dog] is a portion of Iblīs and in him is a portion from the rubbing of Adam. He is part Iblīs when he barks and growls and attacks for blood, and he is of the rubbing of Adam when his heart becomes deadened until he is humble and he obeys and is intimate with him and his son and guards them" (al-Qurṭubī, *Al-Jāmiʿa,* 1.308 (vol. 1).

Conclusion

The series of four primordial stories is a true cycle with its own intertextual references. The narrator assumes a major role, keeping the focus throughout on God as the primary speaker, initiator of action, and steward of knowledge. The last two verses recall a primary theme of the prologue, indeed of the Qur'ān as a whole—the contrast between believers and unbelievers.

The Iblīs story itself is a bare summary of previously revealed versions, as is the garden story. Whereas in Sūrat al-'Arāf, the Iblīs story sets a foundation for a lengthy garden story in which al-Shayṭān and his malice are the focal points, in Sūrat al-Baqarah, neither Iblīs nor al-Shayṭān is the focal point. The reader's attention is directed not to the presence of evil characters and tempters, but to the vulnerability of humanity. The subject at hand is human character.

Looking at the larger picture, the prologue has provided a basic typology of belief and disbelief. There are those who believe, those who disbelieve, and those who pretend to believe, but do not. Why is this so? The answer is provided through a historical narrative that shows: a) that angels and God have some foreknowledge of human vice; b) that God gifts humanity with knowledge superior to that of angels; c) that humanity has that knowledge only because of the intervention of God; and d) that humanity is nevertheless vulnerable to error. The consequence is that humanity has to choose to believe, and choose again after each failure. Human knowledge has come from God. What mortals do with that knowledge—that is a matter of choice. This is the primordial pattern that Adam establishes.

In this story, both Iblīs and al-Shayṭān are reduced to minimal roles in the narrative. The issue of evil, while not removed from the involvement of al-Shayṭān, and by implication, Iblīs, shifts more to the arena of human choice. Iblīs's role diminishes in favor of al-Shayṭān, who comes to dominate the Medīnan discourse. Iblīs does not appear again in any Medīnan *sūrah*. Whereas in Sūrat al-Ḥijr we saw Iblīs presented in a fashion that recalls the sibling rivalry motif, and in Sūrat al-'Arāf, we saw the combat archetype as more prominent, here we see nothing of the former, and only hints of the latter. Iblīs himself is identified simply as an example of those who reject the faith: the *kāfirūn*. Al-Shayṭān fits more into the heavenly prosecutor role here, but not perfectly. There is no sense that he acts at the direction of God. There is no mention of any interaction between al-Shayṭān and God here at all.

On the other hand, like the *śāṭān* of the Tanakh—in Job, Zechariah and elsewhere—al-Shayṭān is clearly an adversary to humanity, represented here by Adam, although al-Shayṭān is not in this story identified directly with evil. His function is causative.

The entire tenor of the primordial cycle in Sūrat al-Baqarah affirms God's foreknowledge and direction of the unfolding of history. This theme is introduced in the prologue, where God "sets a seal on their (the unbelievers') hearts and on their ears." (2:7). Although God's foreknowledge of, and control of, all events is an ongoing theme in the Qur'ān, it is a particular emphasis of the primordial cycle.

CHAPTER 11

Conclusion

This study has had two foci. On the one hand, we have experimented with the application of narratological approaches to Qur'ānic narrative—a methodological task. On the other hand, we have been exploring various narrative interpretations of the origin and nature of evil—a theological task. Having examined the seven narratives of the Iblīs story in the Qur'ān, we must now assess whether narratology has contributed to theology. This conclusion proceeds in three steps. The first will be methodological, asking whether and how the narratological approach to the Iblīs stories has contributed to an understanding of Qur'ānic expression. Given this evidence, we will make some comments on the chronology of the various versions of the Iblīs story. The second will be an examination of modern literature in which Iblīs figures, especially four works: a poem by Muhammad Iqbal, two novels by Egyptians Naguib Mahfouz and Nawal Saadawi, and a short story by another Egyptian, Tawfīq al-Hakīm. These will demonstrate a range of interpretation that ultimately traces back to the, albeit narrower, range of interpretation found in the Qur'ān. The third will be a theological excursus on Iblīs as a tragic character.

The Narratological Enterprise

In chapter 2 we described how many commentators, most with some background in the Bible, have found Qur'ānic narrative to be comparatively dry and "wooden." Using literary tools to examine the seven narratives of the Iblīs story, we have found these narratives to be complex and nuanced. There is a common story, but seven versions of the story, each different enough to present a particular angle, reflecting a theme of the *sūrah* in which it is found. In exposing these differences, the tool of narratology has proven to be useful and revealing.

The Seven Versions

In Sūrah ṬāHā (ch. 4), we found a brief version of the Iblīs story tucked between two portions of the Adam story. This version emphasizes the feebleness of Adam, in continuity with Moses, Aaron, and others, and the willingness of God to choose and then sustain the weak in confrontation with human enemies—Pharaoh, the magicians, and al-Sāmirī, for instance. Iblīs is simply another flawed and disobedient character, not particularly exceptional here. We might assume, from the pattern of the *sūrah*, that Iblīs might at some point reform and become a believer: a possibility held out for Pharaoh, who does not, and the magicians, who do. Repentance is always an option (vv. 70–76).

We concluded, though, that here the Iblīs story is almost incidental, a part of the Adam story but having no independent value in and of itself. The Adam story carries the theme of the whole *sūrah*. The Iblīs encounter falls in line with this theme in that Iblīs resists and defies the command of God, but the real story is that of the resistance of Adam. The Iblīs story, told in a single verse in its most rudimentary form without elaboration or explanation, sets the scene for the garden story with the encounter of Adam and al-Shayṭān.

As in Sūrah ṬāHā, the Iblīs story in Sūrat al-Kahf (ch. 5) is short, a single though longer verse. Uniquely, Iblīs is presented here as a *jinn* in competition with God for the role of protector. (It is implied, but not stated, that Iblīs is a *jinn* in Sūrat al-Ḥijr.) This Iblīs story comes after that of the companions of the cave in which God protects and cares for seven believers during their long sleep and confused awakening, and before the mysterious stories of Khiḍr and Dhū al-Qarnayn who are, as well, God's protectors of the people. Iblīs competes with God as a protector.

He is a *jinn*, an identity that we explored in the context of the time of the revelation of the Qur'ān. Certain aspects of the story reflect the watcher angel motif of divine beings associating with mortals. Iblīs chooses to be an enemy to humanity, but because he is a *jinn*, he can always choose a different path. He could repent. He cannot be permanently an actor, a one-dimensional scion of evil, a proto-Shayṭān. He remains one who can choose, even if the choice he makes is that of enduring enmity. This alternative view of *jinn* accords with the existence of many stories about Iblīs in which he is not an evil figure, but a pious believer, a repentant, or a teacher of the faithful.

Set within the context of the likely repertoire of the earliest reader/hearers of the Qur'ān, the *sūrah* argues that *jinn* are not to be taken as protectors (*wakīl*) from misfortune; only God is a *Wakīl*. Indeed God is the only *Wakīl*, *al-Wakīl*, though subordinates—Dhū al-Qarnayn and Khiḍr—may act as protectors on God's behalf. The task of distinguishing between true protectors and false or ineffective protectors continues throughout the *sūrah*.

Sūrat al-Ḥijr (ch. 6) presents a rather startling view of Iblīs that we have analyzed in terms of the sibling rivalry motif. Here Iblīs, the fiery primogenitor, is placed alongside, and in contrast to, Adam, the mortal made from stinking, decayed matter: *ḥamā' masnūn*. Iblīs uses *qiyās*, analogical reasoning, a controversial but often acceptable tool in Islamic jurisprudence, to explain to God why he should not be required to prostrate himself to Adam. The logic of his argument is coherent. It is easy to sympathize with Iblīs. We know this dynamic. We have seen it before in the biblical stories of Cain and Abel, Jacob and Esau, and other sibling stories in the biblical record. The elder is resentful of God's inexplicable choice, and no good can come from the unfairness of it.

Iblīs determines, by *qiyās*, that injustice has been done to him—by God, no less. God, who is al-'Adl, the Just (Q 6:115), ought to act according to the logic of justice. But God is also God, the Hidden, al Bātin (Q 57:3). Iblīs is determined to demonstrate to God the error of his ways. Iblīs says, "Because you have put me in the wrong, . . . I will put them (humanity) in the wrong," thereby proving that the foul creature made of stinking, decayed mud will have similarly decayed morals. Iblīs is determined to prove himself in the right, however fruitless any argument with God may prove. Here is the essence of the tragic character: tilting against God. Though the sibling rivalry motif is represented strongly, the story does not end on that note. Iblīs's response is to become a tempter on earth, but one who himself sets limits—he will not assail those who are sincere believers. He comes to agreement with God as to his own role on earth, a conclusion seemingly satisfactory to both. Iblīs ends with a role not unlike that of the public prosecutor, a servant of God rather than an adversary of God. Yet his goal remains to prove God wrong, to show God that he, God, has erred, violated his own justice, and therefore needs to restore the right order of nature, where—who knows?—it might be Adam who bows to Iblīs.

Sūrah Ṣād (ch. 7) parallels the narrative in Sūrat al-Ḥijr to a great degree but focuses not on the relationship between Iblīs and Adam, but rather on God's creative activity in making humanity, and on Iblīs's disputation with God. Iblīs is haughty and defiant in this version of the story. Where we might sympathize with Iblīs in the Sūrat al-Ḥijr version, it is less easy to do so here in Sūrah Ṣād.

Uniquely in this *sūrah*, Iblīs commits himself to pursuing those who are not servants of God "by your power." By this consideration, Iblīs sets himself not in confrontation with God, but in servitude to God. It is not by his power but by God's that he sets about his task of temptation on earth. God confirms this by replying, *fa-al-ḥaqq*, "it is right." Because of this, the myth that most informs this narrative is that of the heavenly prosecutor, one who operates contrary to God's benevolence but in accordance with God's command, or at least God's agreement.

In Sūrat al-Isrā' (ch. 8), the story of Iblīs takes a decidedly darker turn. The enmity of Iblīs to humanity dominates the narrative. The first part of the narrative, the refusal to bow down to Adam and Iblīs's explanation, is given in two verses. This part is followed by three verses in which God *commands* Iblīs not only to tempt humanity but also to assemble armies and use every deceit to lead all but the servants of God astray. Only here is Iblīs closely associated with al-Shayṭān. The background myth is the combat myth. Iblīs is denied authority over the servants of God, which implies that he is given authority over everyone else. God has abandoned the gullible to the dominion of Iblīs. It is all-out war, played out on the fields of the earth, but reflecting the opposition between Iblīs/al-Shayṭān and God.

The fact that God commands all this would suggest that Iblīs acts as God's emissary, similar to the role of the heavenly prosecutor, but the violence of Iblīs's task is more consonant with the combat myth.

In Sūrat al-'Arāf (ch. 9), as in Sūrah ṬāHā and Sūrat al-Baqarah, the Iblīs story is associated with the garden story of the temptation of Adam. Here the garden story is lengthy, yet, unlike the narratives in Sūrah ṬāHā and Sūrat al-Baqarah, the Iblīs story is not abbreviated.

As in Sūrat al-Isrā', Iblīs's future role on earth is to assault humanity. Unlike Sūrat al-Isrā', it is not God who commands this but rather Iblīs who volunteers. He says he will assault humanity from all sides. God's disgust with Iblīs is such that he orders Iblīs out of heaven not once, but twice. The combat myth comes to mind again. The anger between God and Iblīs is palpable.

Finally, in Sūrat al-Baqarah (ch. 10), we find a complex, four-part story of the creation of Adam. After the discussion between God and the angels about the creation of humanity, and the narrative in which God teaches the "names" to Adam, we find the Iblīs story in rudimentary form. It is followed by the garden story. As in Sūrah Ṭāhā, the Iblīs story here is merely transitional, a part of the Adam saga but not the focus of attention. Iblīs is not a character here but an actor with a bit part.

The Diversity of Readings

Throughout our examination of the seven versions of the Iblīs story, the tools of narratology have shown themselves to be useful. We have uncovered subtle points of difference between the various versions of the Iblīs story. The semantic breadth makes Iblīs a character in the terms that we raised in the first chapter. Whereas al-Shayṭān is an actor with a fixed function in the divine drama, Iblīs shows diversity in his role even within the Qur'ānic corpus.

Some versions align themselves with different classical myths of the origin and nature of evil. Sūrat al-Ḥijr is a sibling rivalry story that culminates in more of a divine prosecutor mode. Sūrat al-Isrā' and Sūrat al-'Arāf conform to the combat motif, but the former shows elements of the heavenly prosecutor myth. Sūrat al-Kahf is a combat story as well, though expressed in less strident language. Sūrah Ṣād conforms more to the heavenly prosecutor myth. In Sūrat al-Baqarah and Sūrah Ṭāhā, the Iblīs narrative is subordinated to the Adam story and does not in itself contain enough substance to relate to any myth of the origination of evil.

Although the watcher myth and the fallen angel myth are not clearly represented in the Qur'ān, they are present in Qur'ānic commentary, especially in the commentary of al-Ṭabarī (described in ch. 3). The watcher myth gives insight into the nature of *jinn*, which would have been part of the interpretive repertoire of the early readers/hearers of the Qur'ān, and of many contemporary readers/hearers as well.

We have followed a single story, the eviction of Iblīs from heaven, through seven readings. In every version of the story, Iblīs refuses to bow down to Adam, after being commanded to do so. In every version of the story, he is evicted from heaven. In some versions he defends his action, but those defenses do not differ substantially from one another. There are elements of the story in one version and not in another, but there are no elements that directly contradict another version of the story in the Qur'ān. Iblīs is not described in one version as a *jinn* and in another version as an angel, or in one version claiming that he is made of fire and in another that he is made of light.

Yet, examined narratologically, we do find that inclusions and omissions in various versions do expand the range of interpretation such that, while one can understand Iblīs as a tragic figure in Sūrat al-Ḥijr, such an understanding is not possible in Sūrat al-ʻArāf. The story is the same, but the version of the story is different and the location of the story within an extensive range of interpretation shifts with each version.

The Diversity of Readers

The approach of narratology requires some transparency on the part of the initial reader, in this case, the author of this study. Reader-response theory, certainly in Iser's articulation of it, argues that the meaning of the text is located in part in the mind of the actual reader and in each instance of reading. As an actual reader of the Iblīs story, I read and reread the story many times, sometimes finding what seemed to be the correct questions or keys to a passage by accident. Is such a discovery the result of a forced effort of interpretation, or is it the result of a struggle to bring to conscious level what lurks in my subconscious—and lurks in the text itself?

As I reread what I have written, I flag portions that seem, in retrospect, possibly over-read. At other times, even well into the editing process, I see something in the text, even something quite significant, that has eluded me through previous months, even years of reading. These new insights derive in mysterious ways from some new frame of mind, shaped by the fabric of experience and thinking of that particular moment, a particular reading history, even the accident of picking up this particular book in a library and finding this particular story, legend or analysis that becomes suggestive of an aspect of the Iblīs story that I had missed.

This will, of course, be true for every reader. Readings are idiosyncratic, as diverse as the number of readers, each with his or her own particular repertoire of expectation, experience, and skill. Hence the intended value of this study is not so much to assert the correctness of these particular readings of each version of the Iblīs story but to assert the value of these particular approaches to the process of reading.

The particularity of my own readings, however, is not mine alone. Iser claims that the meaning of the text is not only in the reader's mind but also in the text itself. Narratological interpretation is not simply a record of one individual's idiosyncratic reading, but an analysis of real aspects of the received text. Therefore my own readings also indicate a range of possibilities that do exist in the text. They are not reducible to, or wholly an expression of, my own repertoire. My readings do not exhaust the range of possibilities in the text, and some readers may find a particular reading of mine is, in their view, outside the range of reasonable possibilities.

The first two chapters of this study claimed that the Qur'ān tells stories as reminders of the salvation history that, as the Qur'ān presumes, are part of the necessary or helpful knowledge base of the believer. Further, in the Qur'ān itself there is justification for multiple readings and allusive readings, in the difference between the *muḥkamāt* and the *mutashābihāt* described in Sūrat al-'Imrān 3:7. These terms, particularly *mutashābihāt*, have been subject to varying interpretations through Islamic history. Among these interpretations are ones that affirm not only variable understandings of Qur'ānic verses, but also understandings that may vary according to the reader. This comes close to Iser's understanding of the application of the reader's repertoire to the meaning of the text. One possible understanding of the *mutashābihāt* of the Qur'ān is that the very nature of narrative requires each actual reader to engage the fixed text with the variability of his or her own repertoire, yielding a range of meanings. Narrative passages encourage a "wandering viewpoint," a range of possibilities left open by the blanks and gaps that are inherent in story more so than in the parænetic passages of the Qur'ān.

Chapter 2 also discussed the issue of the collection of the Qur'ān, noting the uncertainty surrounding the question of how the longer *sūrah*s were assembled. The ambiguities about the occasions of revelation (*asbāb al-nuzūl*) and the divisions between separate revelations might have led Muslim commentators to comment on the Qur'ān atomistically, verse by verse, rather than on larger units of narration. Nothing in the Qur'ān itself, however, imposes such a limitation, and recent commentaries such as those discussed by Mustansir Mir have been more willing to look at *sūrah*s as thematic wholes. The examination of narrative, the thematic whole par excellence, invites a different relationship from that normally used in Muslim commentaries on the Qur'ān, a relationship between the details of each verse and the larger units of each *sūrah* or the *sūrah* as a whole. It is this kind of approach that we have utilized in the examination of the seven Iblīs stories.

What is diminished in this approach is the sense that the Qur'ān is a single univocal text, and therefore that the Iblīs narrative is also a single collective story. The normative approach in Muslim commentaries is to treat the Qur'ān as a single text, thereby minimizing, if not eliminating, attention to the differences between various versions or versions of the same story. If the Qur'ān is a single univocal text, then all versions of a story can be combined into a single composite narrative for purposes of commentary, which is exactly what al-Ṭabarī, al-Qurṭubī, and others do. The approach of this study does not deny that the Qur'ān is a single text, but it does present a complementary alternative, giving greater emphasis and greater value to the distinctiveness of each version of a story, and thus to the internal diversity of the Qur'ān.

The Qur'ān, in its message, is both univocal and multivocal. The Qur'ān, by telling stories differently in different places, embraces a range of interpretation, making space for a wandering viewpoint that not only allows but affirms a range of meaning. Because of this we find that Iblīs displays a different nature in different versions of the story—the mark of a character as opposed to an actor—and these in turn suggest a range of ways to understand the nature of evil, each secured in a reading of a particular Iblīs story. This suggestive capacity of the Qur'ān to embrace such a versatility of expression, encouraging a range of meaning, is an aspect of its *'ijāz*, its inimitability.

A Chronology of the Qur'ānic Iblīs Story

A chronological ordering of *sūrah*s cannot be based on the Iblīs story alone, but the variations in the narration of the Iblīs story provide a significant contribution to chronological analysis.

As demonstrated in the discussion of chronology in chapter 2, there is considerable disagreement about the chronological order of the various *sūrah*s with Iblīs stories. The single point of agreement among the various scholars included and the traditional Egyptian dating is that the latest of these is Sūrat al-Baqarah. In that rendering the Iblīs story is told in cursory fashion within an extended narrative about Adam, ending with the garden story. The Iblīs story itself adds nothing to the larger narrative. It is an accessory to the Adam story.

The discussion in chapter 2 charts the chronological placement of the Iblīs stories according to several analyses, including the dating system based on the 1924 Egyptian, or King Fu'ad, printed edition of the Qur'ān which has become widely accepted among Muslims.[1] Of these, Welch gives specific attention to the Iblīs passages, but does not give detailed justification for his chronological ordering. Neuwirth, on the other hand, gives extensive

[1] Böwering, "Chronology," 322–26; Albin, "Printing," 272.

attention to the chronological ordering of the Iblīs narratives. Her argument demands careful attention.

Neuwirth begins by describing a process of canonization through which an oral, liturgical *qur'ān* becomes a fixed, textual *kitāb*.[2] Seen as part of a canonical process, the various cosmogonic narratives—the Iblīs and garden stories in particular—should not be seen as mere repetitions but as stages of the growth of the canon and the community of hearers and believers.

Neuwirth characterizes the Iblīs narrative as the "bargain" story, "[t]he divine election of man to become God's chosen creature and the forecast of the chosen community as contrasted with those who reject the divine-human covenant."[3] What I have identified as the garden story is, for Neuwirth, the "transgression" or "test" story, in which the obedience of Adam and his wife are tested. From this foundation, Neuwirth proceeds to examine each occurrence of the two narratives.

She begins with Sūrat al-Ḥijr (15), the earliest of the Iblīs accounts. Drawing on an earlier work of mine,[4] she parallels the story with that of Job in the Old Testament, since both act with the explicit permission of God. This study sees a closer parallel with the biblical sibling rivalry theme, not considered in the earlier work, as Iblīs seeks to argue for his own superiority and then, with God's permission, to prove that humanity will act in an inferior fashion and thus be undeserving of adulation. Neuwirth understands this story as speaking to the early Meccan Muslim community, one that had successfully resisted the temptations of Iblīs but was surrounded by those who had not. The Iblīs story was, for them, one of consolation.

In Neuwirth's chronology of development, the account in Sūrah Ṣād (38) was revealed soon after, building on the nucleus of the first but giving more emphasis to the arrogance of Iblīs as a prototype of the arrogance of Muḥammad's Meccan detractors. The narrator intrudes to make clear that Iblīs is both prideful and an unbeliever. God is described not in terms of the role of creator, but in terms of omniscience. The contrast between Iblīs, representing the opponents in Mecca, and the believers, is drawn in stronger terms.

Sūrah ṬāHā (20) presents a brief, one-verse account of the Iblīs story. The *sūrah* is dominated by a Moses narrative that sets the scene for later references to Jewish practice—the direction of prayer, specifically—which

[2] Neuwirth, "Negotiating Justice (Part I)," 25–28.

[3] Ibid., 30.

[4] Bodman, "Stalking Iblīs," 253.

are found in Sūrat al-Isrā'.[5] The focus of the passage is on the instability of human commitment to God. The Iblīs story is followed by an extensive account of the garden story that demonstrates mortal fragility graphically. The Iblīs story here draws on elements of that found in the chronologically preceding Sūrah Ṣād.

Neuwirth places Sūrat al-Isrā' (17) next in chronological order, describing Iblīs in the full fury of violence against the believers.[6] This parallels the growing animosity between the Muslim community of Mecca and the rest of the Quraysh tribe. The words of God to Iblīs, "Surely you shall have no authority over my servants," affirms the independence of the Meccan believers.

In the fifth *sūrah* in order of revelation, Sūrat al-Kahf, the Iblīs story is reduced to reminiscence, a single verse (18:50) with no debate between God and Iblīs, but only a pronouncement about the nature of Iblīs. He is a *jinn* and a *fāsiq* (corrupter) unsuited as a protector for humanity. The story replicates that in Sūrat al-Isrā' closely, the term *fāsiq* effectively summarizing the evil of Iblīs that is more graphically related there.

The final two renderings of the Iblīs story are in Sūrat al-'Arāf and Sūrat al-Baqarah. Both recount the garden story at length. The first of the two, Sūrat al-'Arāf, also tells the Iblīs story in detail, drawing on elements of the versions of the previous *sūrah*s. In Sūrat al-Baqarah, the Iblīs story is reduced to a skeletal account of the story, tucked into a unique narration of contestation between the angels and Adam, mediated by God.

This chronology of the Iblīs stories is based not only on a concept of canonical development, but also on an analysis of other elements of the applicable *sūrah*s. A full examination of Neuwirth's analysis is beyond the scope of this study. Some observations are still relevant. It is important to maintain more distance between Iblīs and al-Shayṭān than Neuwirth allows. Although it is clear in each of the seven renderings of the Iblīs story that Iblīs is an adversary of humanity, and shares that role with al-Shayṭān, we have argued that the character of Iblīs demonstrates a much broader range of interpretation. The distinction between the two is vital.

There is also a general trend in the sequence of narrations, moving from a focus on Iblīs to a focus on Adam. In the earliest version, Sūrat al-Ḥijr, Iblīs is the focus, and Adam is merely an object of discussion, evaluated

[5] Neuwirth, "Negotiating Justice (Part II)," 1.

[6] Ibid., 1–3.

negatively entirely according to the substance of his manufacture. In the last version, Sūrat al-Baqarah, Adam is the focus of attention, evaluated negatively by the angels due to his predicted behavior, but positively affirmed, guided, and sustained by God. Between these two narratives, Sūrah Ṣād, the second rendering, does not even mention Adam by name, keeping the focus on Iblīs. As Neuwirth points out, Iblīs here is a somewhat stronger adversary to humanity than in Sūrat al-Ḥijr but arises to full violence and malice in Sūrat al-Isrā'. We thus see a trajectory in the stories of Iblīs as he becomes presented in progressively darker hues.

It is tempting to try to develop a chronology of the development of *iblīsī* theology based on an apparent evolution from Iblīs as a tragic figure, challenging God to live up to the highest standards (as judged by Iblīs) of justice and fairness, to a progressively adversarial, *shayṭānī* Iblīs, and then to relative oblivion as the focus shifts to the authority and divine commission of Adam. One might see in this an evolution of the early Muslim community, from a small congregation raising fundamental questions about the nature of God, especially a God that seems inattentive to their own suffering in Mecca to the increasing assaults upon them that necessitate their flight to Medīna, and finally to a community come into its own, confident under the leadership of a *khalīfah*.

It is necessary, however, to be cautious about such a program, since, as we have seen, each Iblīs narrative fulfills a purpose tied into the themes of the *sūrah* in which it is located. Therefore no chronology can be attempted without accounting for the messages of each *sūrah* as a whole, a task beyond the boundaries of this study.

The Consequence: Retelling the Story of Iblīs

Because Iblīs is a character, capable of change and evolution (and devolution), there is no end to the Iblīs story. It is as the proto-Shayṭān that Iblīs is most commonly rendered in the texts of the authoritative Islamic tradition, in particular the canonical *ḥadīth* collections. Yet we have seen that recognition of his other personae persist in the classical commentaries, especially those with higher tolerance for *isrā'īliyyāt*—al-Ṭabarī in particular, but also al-Qurṭubī and others. Sufi literature, as Awn describes, is particularly fertile ground for alternative readings of the story. The *qiṣaṣ* literature further expands the range of interpretation. Because Iblīs is a character, not an actor, his story emerges in new contexts, contexts in which there is some reason to challenge God, or more accurately, to challenge particular notions of God. Iblīs serves still as a medium through which established theologies may be challenged.

Iblīs in Modern Writing

To the extent that modern stories and poetry involve the character of Iblīs, they, too, can be considered commentary on the Qur'ān since Iblīs is a Qur'ānic character. None of the literature considered here intends or pretends to be *tafsīr*, but all are intentional as commentaries on Islamic society, that is, on societies shaped by Islam. To this purpose, they utilize the mythic and literal vocabulary of Islam, in our cases, the vocabulary of Iblīs.

These literary works are chosen because they explore or use the character of Iblīs in novel ways. They are all written by well-known and respected modern authors. They represent instances of modern writing from Islamic contexts that draw on aspects of the Iblīs figure that are within the range of Qur'ānic expression but are outside of the authoritative textual interpretation. The dominance of the traditional characterization of Iblīs in a *shayṭānī* form is demonstrated by the fact that in two of the three texts that use the name Iblīs in the original Arabic or Urdu, those by al-Hakīm and Iqbal,[7] the English translations render Iblīs as Satan. In el-Saadawi's novel, the character in the novel is Eblis, but the translator has rendered the title as *The Innocence of the Devil*. This mistranslation obfuscates the fluidity of the character of Iblīs that we have illustrated. Modern literature, drawing from the Islamic fount, continues to inscribe Iblīs into new contexts that reinterpret the root Qur'ānic story.[8]

Muhammad Iqbal

We begin with the case of Muḥammad Iqbal, a South Asian writer whose concerns are profoundly religious. His poem, *A Message from the East*,[9] was inspired by Goethe's *West-östlicher Diwan*, a critique of Western materialism.

[7] In Mahfouz's *Children of Gebelaawi*, the Iblīs character is called Idrees.

[8] Khalil Shaikh has explored a number of early modern Arab novels in detail. The texts explored here are not covered in his work. In particular, he gives a detailed analysis of the writings of Tawfiq al-Hakim. See Shaikh, *Der Teufel*.

[9] Iqbal, *Message*. See also Kiernan, "Iqbal and Milton," 231–41.

The series, "Reflections," includes "The Conquest of Nature" describing the creation of Adam. The second section of that poem is "The Refusal of Iblīs":

I am no creature of mere light
That I should bow to man.
He is a base-born thing of dust,
And I am of fire born.
The blood in the veins of the world
Is lit up by my flame.
The tearing speed of wind is mine,
And mine is thunder's boom.
I forge the atom's harmony,
The elements' concourse.
I burn, but also shape: I am
The fire that makes the glass.
The things I make I break to bits
And scatter in the dust,
In order to create new forms
From fragments of those lost.
This restless revolving sky
Is a wave of my sea;
And in my throbbing substance dwells
The shape of things to be.
The stars' bodies were made by You;
I am their motive force.
I am the substance of the world.
I am life's primal source.
The body draws its soul from You.
But I arouse the soul.
While You waylay with blissful peace,
I lead with action's call.
I never begged obedience
Of slaves who always pray.
I rule without a Hell: I judge
Without a Judgment Day.
That low-born creature of earth, man,
Of mean intelligence,
Though born in Your lap, will grow old
  Under my vigilance.[10]

[10] Iqbal, *Message*, 47–49.

In this surprising verse, Iblīs is the spirit of the world, of human endeavor, of curiosity, and of industry and art. His is the creative energy to take the stuff of God's original creation and to transform it into the material of civilization. He brings the fire that forges glass, "the atom's harmony, the elements' concourse." He brings the world that allows humanity to flourish. But he claims too much for himself—lordship over this world. He is dismissive of human character, which is a "base-born thing of dust," and "of mean intelligence." He asserts that it is he, not God, who supervises the energy of the world. His gifts to humanity evolve from and nurture his own hubris, yet the product of his mind and hands are not benefits that most mortals would reject. His flaw, his *hamartia*, does not come from malice, but from pride.

Iqbal sees the industry of the West and the thrall of intellectual striving as an alluring temptation that leads the people away from God. Iblīs's call to action is a temptation to Adam:

> Good and evil, virtue and sin
> Are myths created by your Lord.
> Come taste the joy of action and
> Go forth to seek your due reward.[11]

Standing before God on the day of judgment, Adam says:

> I took Your ocean and poured it
> Into canals made by my art.
> My pickaxe brought forth streams of milk
> And honey from the mountain's heart
> . . .
> I was deflected from the path
> Of virtue by Iblīs' fraud.
> Forgive my error and accept
> My humble penitence, O God!
>
> One cannot subjugate the world
> Unless one yields to its allure;
> For Beauty's wild pride is not tamed
>   Until it falls into Love's snare.[12]

[11] Ibid., 49.

[12] Ibid., 51–52. Hussain's translation renders Iblīs as either "Satan" or "the Devil." After checking the original Urdu and finding that the word is "Iblīs" and not "al-Shayṭān," I have

Iqbal presents Iblīs as an advocate of human industry and creativity that is fatal to the spiritual life. Indeed, Iblīs even rejects the concepts of "good and evil, virtue and sin." Adam confesses his seduction by the dynamism of Iblīs. Clearly Iblīs here is in the familiar role of the adversary of humanity. What is different is that the temptations that Iblīs places before us are, in many cases, not what we would normally consider to be evil. Is activity to be scorned and passivity embraced? Do we not treasure the canals that carry the cargo and the mountain's products? Can Iblīs be dismissed here as merely malicious and evil? Is he *shayṭānī*?

The role of Iblīs here can be seen as a muted example of the combat myth, as Iblīs is the ruler of this world. A close corollary would be the rabbinic concept of the *yēṣer hā-ra'* described in chapter 3. Recall the explanation from the Talmud:

> Three good conditions the Holy One, Blessed be He, created in this world. They are the evil yetzer, envy, and mercy. If there is no evil yetzer, no man occupies himself with the duty of propagating the human race. If there is no envy, no man occupies himself with planting. If there is no mercy, the world does not endure.
>
> (Gen. R. 9.7). R. Nachman said, in R. Samuel's name, "Behold, it was very good." (Gen. 1.31) refers to the good yetzer, and "And behold, it was very good" to the evil yetzer. Can the evil yetzer be very good? That would be extraordinary. But for the evil yetzer, however, no man would build a house, take a wife and beget children. And thus said Solomon, "Again I considered all labor and all excelling in work, that it is man's rivalry with his neighbor" (Eccl. 4.4).[13]

In Iqbal's poem, the arrogance of Iblīs is on full display. He rejects both the rulership of God over all earthly creativity and the centrality of virtue to human life. Iqbal has pointed out the deepest temptations of the modern world, that the very aspects that most represent our conquest of the world are, in fact, the world's conquest of us.

This is not the tragic Iblīs, but this is Iblīs in a form more complex than a simple opposition of good and evil, mercy and malice. Iblīs has arrived in the modern world.

---

made that one correction to Hussain's translation. The rest is as he renders it.

[13] Cohen Stuart, *Struggle*, 19.

Naguib Mahfouz

Naguib Mahfouz, the Egyptian Nobel Laureate novelist, caused a furor in Egypt and much of the Muslim world with the publication of *Awlād Hāratinā*, "The Children of Our Quarter," translated into English as "Children of Gebelaawi."[14] The novel was initially serialized in the Egyptian newspaper *Al Ahrām* in 1959.

Pierre Cachia points out that this novel is one of the few pieces of modern Arab literature that directly addresses contentious religious issues. He summarizes the novel as representing in the popular understanding the three great Semitic religions as successive attempts to curb social abuses, with science as their modern inheritor.[15] The narrative follows a family in a neighborhood of Cairo, an allegory of the human family. Gebelaawi, the patriarch of the quarter, represents God. The six major chapters represent the major prophets sent to humanity according to Islam: Adham (Adam), Gebel (Moses), Rifaa (Jesus), and Qaasim (Muḥammad), and then Arafa, who may be regarded as representing scientific modernism. The Iblīs character is rendered as Idrees.

The story opens when the father, Gebelaawi, calls his five sons into his presence and announces that Adham will manage the trust in the future. Idrees, the eldest, whom all expected to be assigned this task, is shocked and angered. He spits out:

> – *Me and my full brothers are sons of a real lady, the best of women. As for this creature, he's the son of a black slave.*
> Adham's brown face paled, but he sat quite still. Gebelaawi shook his fist and warned:
> – *Mind your manners, Idrees!*
> Idrees was wild with fury. He roared:
> – *He's the youngest of us, too; give me one reason why you should prefer him to me, or is this the age of servants and slaves?*
> – *Hold your tongue, you idiot, for your own sake!*
> – *I'd rather die than be humiliated.*
> Radwaan looked up and said very gently:
> – *We're all your sons, and we have a right to be upset if we lose your favour. You have the last word in any case. . . we just want*

[14] Mahfouz, *Children of Gebelaawi*. On aspects of the controversy around this work, see Abu-Haidar, "Awlād Ḥāratinā," 119–31; Mehrez, *Egyptian Writers*, 17–38; and Najjar "Islamic Fundamentalism," 145–61.

[15] Cachia, "In a Glass Darkly," 37.

to know the reason. . . .
Gebelaawi turned to Radwaan, keeping calm for some reason, and said:
– Adham is familiar with the tenants and knows most of them by name. He's also learnt writing and arithmetic.
Idrees and his brothers were amazed by their father's words. Since when had knowing the masses been a distinction for which a man was preferred? And going to school—was that too a distinction? Would Adham's mother have sent him to school unless she had despaired of him succeeding in the world of strongmen? Idrees said bitterly:
– Are those the reasons for humiliating me?
Gebelaawi waved this aside angrily.
– It's my decision, all you have to do is to hear and obey. (He turned sharply towards Idrees's brothers.) *What do you say?*
Abbaas could not bear his father's gaze; he said heavily:
– I hear and obey.
Jaleel was quick to speak, staring at the floor.
– It's your decision, Father.
Radwaan swallowed hard.
– At your service!
Idrees laughed angrily and his face was horribly twisted. He thundered:
– Cowards! All I could expect from you was despicable defeat. Because you're such cowards this son of a black slave will push you around.
Gebelaawi thundered:
–Idrees!
But Idrees was out of his mind and shouted:
– What sort of a father are you? You were born to be a bullying strongman, and all you know is how to be a bullying strongman. You deal with us 'your sons' the same way as with all your other victims.
Gebelaawi took two ponderous steps forward and said quietly:
– Hold your tongue!
But Idrees went on:
– You're not going to frighten me; you know I can't be frightened. And if you want to raise that son of a slave above me, I shan't give you any sweet nonsense about hearing and obeying.
– Don't you know what impudence leads to, you damned idiot?
– The real damned idiot is that son of a slave.
The father's voice grew louder and more rasping.
– She's my wife, you fool. Now behave yourself or I'll floor you.
The other brothers were terrified, Adham as much as any of them, for they knew the violence of their despotic father. But Idrees thought no more of danger. He shouted:
– You hate me. I didn't realize, but there's no doubt that you hate me. Perhaps it was that slave girl who made you hate us; you are master of the desert, Founder of the Trust, the dreaded strongman,

> *but a slave girl can play with you. Tomorrow people will be saying all sorts of amazing things about you, lord of the desert!*
> – *I told you to hold your tongue, damn you!*
> – *Don't insult me for blacky Adham's sake; even the rocks will protest against that and curse him. Your crazy decision is going to make us the laughing-stock of all the neighborhood.*
> Gebelaawi shouted in a voice so loud that it was heard all over the garden and in the women's quarters:
> – *Get out of my sight!*
> – *This is my home and my mother's home, and she is its true mistress.*
> – *You shan't be seen here again—ever.*[16]

Idrees is evicted from the house. We then get the narrator's interpretation. The brothers and the people of the alley blame Adham for the unfairness of the assignment to manage the trust:

> Yes. The blame fell on him though he was innocent. Whenever people were sorry for Idrees, they cursed Adham. He went to the gate, opened it quietly, and slipped out. He saw Idrees not far off, reeling round in circles and rolling his eyes. His hair was tangled, and the front of his jellaba was open showing his hairy chest. When his eye fell on Adham he sprang to the attack, like a cat that has sighted a mouse; but drink had befuddled him and he fell to the ground. He filled his hand with soil and threw it at Adham, hitting him on the chest and dirtying his coat. Adham called gently to him:
> – *Brother!*
> Idrees raved as he swayed:
> – *Shut up, you dog, you son of a bitch! You are not my brother, and your father is not my father, and I am going to bring down this house over your heads.*
> Adham said with true affection:
> – *You are the finest and noblest son of this house.*
> Idrees laughed a hollow laugh and shouted:
> – *Why did you come out, son of a slave girl? Run back to mummy and take her down to the servants' quarters!*
> Adham spoke as warmly as ever:
> – *Don't get carried away by anger, and don't close the door to your friends.*
> Idrees shook his fist and said:
> – *Damned house! Only cowards can be happy in it—people who accept scraps humbly and love being crushed. I will never return to a house in which you are master. Tell your father I am living in the*

[16] Mahfouz, *Children of Gebelaawi*, 6–8.

> *desert he came from, and that I have become a bandit like he was, and a bad, quarrelsome crook like he is. Wherever I go, smashing things up, people point to me and say 'Gebelaawi's son.' And so I shall drag you through the mud, you who think you're lords when you're really robbers.*
> *– Stop, dear brother! Don't say things you'll be sorry for. The way is not closed to you. I swear things will go back to what they were.*
> Idrees came one step towards him, as slowly as if he were walking against a gale:
> *– What will you swear by, son of a slave?*
> Adham looked at him carefully.
> *– By brotherhood!*[17]

Here Adham and Idrees are half-brothers—no mention of *jinn*—and the sibling rivalry theme is dominant in much the same terms as we find in Sūrat al-Ḥijr. Adham is a younger son. He is born of a black slave, an echo of the biblical story of Hagar but here also a sign of unworthiness. Idrees describes Adham himself as "blacky," as if he were made of putrid black mud.

Gebelaawi gives a reason for his selection of Adham over Idrees to manage the trust, derived from the Iblīs story in Sūrat al-Baqarah. Adham has learned the names of all the tenants. In Sūrat al-Baqarah God teaches Adam the names of all creatures, knowledge that He does not impart to the angels. Because of this knowledge Adam is chosen over the others to be *khalīfah* (vice-regent) on earth.

The garden story emerges when Idrees persuades him to steal a look at their father's will, a book that Gebelaawi keeps in a special room. This calls to mind the legend of *jinn* listening at the edges of heaven to catch some of the discussions of human destiny reflected in Sūrat al-Kahf. Encouraged by his wife, Umayma, Adham steals a glance at the book and Gebelaawi catches him. He and Umayma are then also evicted from the house of Gebelaawi.

Idrees's resentment, not only of the position of his brother, but also of Adham's kind innocence, drives him further to drink and deception. At times Idrees is remorseful, but it is difficult to determine whether this remorse is a ruse or genuine. Mahfouz maintains this ambiguity.

Perhaps the most important aspect of Mahfouz's interpretation of the Iblīs story is the use of reason. Idrees demands of Gebelaawi a reason for his choice. Another brother, Radwan, supports the reasonableness of wanting justification for the choice. Recall that the angels in Sūrat al-Baqarah (v. 30)

[17] Mahfouz, *Children of Gebelaawi*, 13.

also assert themselves to question God. God dismisses the angels' concerns with a curt, "I know what you do not know." Here Gebelaawi responds angrily, "It is my decision, all you have to do is hear and obey!" The brothers, including Radwan, quickly accede to their father's will, affirming their obedience, just as the angels in Sūrat al-Baqarah respond to God's rebuke with effusive praise.

Idrees does not respond this way. He wishes to put reason, or at least his own reasoning, as the fundamental test for any decision. Until this is resolved, he will continue to defy his father and the will of his father, rejecting the "despotism" of his father. Leaving the house, Idrees accuses all who live there of cowardice. Only he will stand up for principle. For this heroic commitment, Idrees is evicted, condemned, and eventually becomes a drunken vagabond in the desert. Not even Adham's generous entreaties can bring him home.

Idrees is a tragic character, at once bold in his insistence on rationality and excessive in that same insistence. His reasoning does not include the virtue of brotherhood, that supreme value by which Adham swears, and for which Adham is willing to invite him back to the family. But for Idrees, a family that tolerates despotism and the violence that accompanies it is not a place where true brotherhood can thrive. He chooses to have no brotherhood at all rather than a brotherhood founded on a falsehood.

He challenges his father, Gebelaawi, even though he knows that such a challenge can never be successful. Nevertheless, he cannot refuse what his conscience, however flawed it may be, dictates. Gebelaawi asserts only authority, an authority founded on no discernible justification. It is despotic. The modern tragic figure rejects a God who is not accountable. No God deserves to be worshipped who relies solely on authority.

Nawal el-Saadawi

A compatriot of Mahfouz, Nawal el-Saadawi, also presents Iblīs in a tragic mode. Her novel, *Jannāt wa Iblīs*, translated as *The Innocence of the Devil*, is something of an Egyptian feminist version of Ken Kesey's *One Flew Over the Cuckoo's Nest*.[18] It is a difficult and complex tale. The main character is Ganat, a woman confined to an insane asylum, reminiscing about the

[18] El Saadawi, *Innocence*. See Saiti, "Paradise," 152–74. Ken Kesey wrote *One Flew Over the Cuckoo's Nest* (Viking Press, 1962), similarly a critique of society, using the context of an asylum to suggest that those confined in a mental institution are saner than those outside.

various times when she and other women in her family were deprived of opportunities to fulfill their abilities and often beaten by various men in their families and beyond. For her own objection to this injustice, and her refusal to adapt to the roles that a patriarchal society (in the persons of male family members as well as various officials) would assign to her, she is judged to be insane. Her life is entwined with others in the asylum, with the head nurse, who she suspects is her childhood friend Narguiss, with Nefissa whose younger brother is nicknamed Eblis (Iblīs), and with God, never named as such, who generally hides behind a tree on the grounds. Eblis is now also an inmate in the asylum, and also sometimes hides behind a tree on the grounds.[19] The identities of Eblis and God sometimes seem to merge.

Throughout the story, Ganat and other characters remember instances of assault on their character in the past, and experience further assaults at the hands of the director and the head nurse in the asylum.

God is an inmate in the asylum. In that role, he is quiet and reflective. This is not so outside of the asylum. At one point God reflects on his image in the eyes of others. In their eyes he is one who gives orders, who shouts out that he is the greatest and wears rows of medals on his chest, and horns and the disk of the sun above his head. He is Pharaoh, Ra, and a general combined. He sends soldiers to their destruction.[20]

Like God, Eblis has multiple identities. Outside of the asylum, he is the brother of Nefissa, a gentle and joyful child, but, like the women, treated harshly by his father and others.

Towards the end of the story there is a trial scene. Ganat protests her innocence,

> *I am Ganat . . . . I am not afraid. You who shed blood and sow corruption on the earth. You who hold a stick and demand obedience. I do not hide my face. I am not ashamed of my body.*

The judge is a composite of various male figures in her life—her grandfather, the director of the asylum, the king, her teacher Sheikh Bassiouni, and Zakaria, her husband. She is carried out of the asylum in a wooden box—free. Eblis watches, remembering a poem she had written to him just the night before:

[19] El Saadawi, *Innocence*, 8–9.

[20] Ibid., 222–24.

I love you
Because you are the only one amongst the slaves
Who refused to kneel
Who said no
I saw you walk
With your head upright and your hair so dense, so black
Covering distances in the dark
Amidst the desert storm
And smiling
No one can take your smile away from you
Nor take away your slim outline
Your body never bends
Your head never bends down, too.[21]

Here Eblis's original defiance becomes a model for all women who defy the patriarchal system, who refuse to bow down. He confesses, though, that he is not the devil, only Nefissa's brother.

As Ganat is being carried out of the asylum, Eblis tries to follow over the barbed wire fence. He is cut deeply, and bleeds to death on the asylum lawn. The next morning, the director, a God-figure, finds the body of Eblis. His eyes fill with tears:

How can you leave me alone like this? *O my son!* . . .
You made the world so rich for me, Eblis." . . .
Forgive me, my son. I know I used to wake you up so often from your sleep, and tell you to get up immediately, to go around whispering in people's ears. I wrote three books against you, and denied you the right to answer them. . . .
I am responsible for our defeat, my son!
He who has authority is responsible.
But the world was upside down.
He who is responsible for what happens is made out to be innocent.
And the people who are under our rule are put on trial.
The generals get medals.
The soldiers die. . . .
In the court they declared me innocent and made you the scapegoat. . . .
Forgive me, my son.
You are innocent. . . .
The word innocent dropped on to the white marble slap shining like a white piastre, and ringing loudly in the silence with a sound like silver.

[21] El Saadawi, *Innocence*, 216–17.

Innocent![22]

In Sūrat al-'Arāf (v. 16) and Sūrat al-Ḥijr (v. 39), Iblīs accuses God of leading him astray, an accusation God does not deign to answer. As noted in the first chapter, some Sufi interpretations suggest that Iblīs is unjustly accused. While he does not obey God's command to prostrate himself to Adam, he follows God's greater imperative to worship none but God alone. Here, el-Saadawi expands on that idea to assert that all those who refuse to bow to unjust commands are, like Iblīs, the victims of a religious system gone awry. In the final analysis, it is God who is responsible for the wrong in the world, not Iblīs. Society, in the name of God, gives commands that defy the supreme divine imperative to justice for all God's people, women not excepted.

The English title of the translation of *Jannāt wa-Iblīs* is given as *The Innocence of the Devil*, a title which would obscure for many the root metaphor of the story. The introduction, written by Sherif Hetata, does not give enough background to those unfamiliar with the Iblīs legend and its interpretation to provide a basis for understanding the relationship between the accusation against Iblīs and the position of women in Egyptian society that el-Saadawi is making. In a review of the book by Connie Lamb, the lack of awareness of the subtleties of the Qur'ānic Iblīs story leads her to miss the heart of the metaphor.[23]

Like the Qur'ānic Iblīs, el-Saadawi's Eblis never bows and never bends. He has been charged by the director to be the constant tempter, the savage and seedy adversary of all humanity. He is the divine prosecutor, the unholy servant of the holy. For all this he has been condemned by the director himself in Torah, Gospel, and Qur'ān. Commanded and condemned in one breath, denied voice and defense, he does not bend or break.

Naguib Mahfouz and Nawal el-Saadawi both employ the story of Iblīs as a critique of modern society. One might say, broadly, that as the medieval mystics used the Iblīs story to criticize an Islamic faith in which devotion is less that total, Mahfouz and el-Saadawi criticize an Islamic society in which justice is less than total. Neither Mahfouz nor el-Saadawi can be considered primarily religious writers.[24] Their use of Islamic imagery recognizes that the

[22] El Saadawi, *Innocence*, 229–31

[23] Lamb, "Review," 547–49.

[24] This is a point that Pierre Cachia stresses (see "In a Glass Darkly," 37–40).

audience they are addressing is one steeped in Islamic tradition. The story of Iblīs will be well-known and understood. He has found a place outside of the domain of religious thought, yet not entirely dissociated from it.

Tawfiq al-Hakīm

Tawfiq al-Hakīm has penned perhaps the most profound modern religious presentation of Iblīs in the context of religion, even though al-Hakīm himself could not be considered a religious author.

The story is *The Martyr*, written in 1954. It is Christmas. Iblīs[25] visits the Pope in the Vatican seeking to enter "the haven of faith," repentant, desiring to be called "the Accursed" no longer. He says, "My subjects are everywhere, even within these walls. . . . But what use is my fabled kingdom as long as I feel only deprivation? Save me, in the name of your God!" The Pope refuses. Why? Because the edifice of the church, the articles of faith, the day of judgment, and the surety of the Bible, all depend on the existence of evil.

Iblīs then consults the Grand Rabbi, with the same result. Then he goes to the Sheikh of El Azhar, again with the same result. Confused and dejected, Iblīs wanders the streets, crying out. His pain is heard in heaven, prompting Gabriel to appear to him.

> "What is it that you seek?"
> "Forgiveness."
> "At this time?"
> "Am I too late?"
> "On the contrary, you are too early. This is not the time to change the established order. . . . The order of creation must not be upset by mercy and forgiveness."

Like the religious leaders before him, Gabriel argues for the continuation of the balance of good and evil, each being necessary for the other. Iblīs cannot be allowed to abandon his role as the purveyor of evil. Hearing this, Iblīs weeps, alarming Gabriel:

> "Steady now, steady. They are raining down upon the faithful, who do not deserve to suffer this." Even the tears of [Iblīs] turn into catastrophe for others. He cannot be allowed to weep.

[25] The Arabic Iblīs is rendered in English as "Satan." For accuracy and consistency I will use "Iblīs" and make the appropriate substitution in direct quotes. See al-Hakim, *Arinī Allāh*, 13.

Gabriel tells him to do his duty, without rebelling, to which Iblīs replies:

> Rebelling? If I had really wanted to rebel I would have revolted, broken my loyalty, defied my orders. . . . But I love, and I seek not to revolt; my love for God is the secret strength by which the structure He has made of earth holds together. It is the secret of the harmony of His laws and His order.

Gabriel is unsympathetic, and Iblīs continues:

> He who dies in battle in the name of God is enrolled in His book as a martyr. But for Him I suffer more than death. I wish it were a battle. . . . I must exist to disobey the One I love: I despise myself, and I curse every instant of my being.

Gabriel still insists that Iblīs do his duty on earth. The story ends with these words:

> And he left heaven submissively and descended upon earth. But a stifled sigh burst out from him as he winged his way down through space; instantly, it was re-echoed by every one of the stars as though all were joining with him to cry out in agony:
> "I am a martyr—I am a martyr."[26]

Iblīs is committed to obedient disobedience to God, though this obedience does not bring joy, mercy and consolation, but rather suffering and self-hatred. He fulfills the role that he has been allotted, a role of opposition to both God and humanity, even if his heart and soul have turned fully to love. He can be the repentant, seeking restoration to the company of the faithful, but refused and destined to be a martyr to God's mission.

Other Voices

Such is the range of interpretation of the Iblīs character suggested by the Qur'ān. He can be the engine of human creativity and industry, although luring Adam and his progeny away from the simple love of God. He can be the bitter, rejected older brother whom Naguib Mahfouz describes. He can be the abused and wronged servant of a God who has allowed himself

[26] Al-Hakīm, "Martyr," 36–46.

to be, on earth, dictatorial, described by Nawal el-Saadawi. Iblīs is any of these, all of these, and more.

There are other examples worthy of attention. For instance, Ṣādiq al-'Aẓm discusses Iblīs in "The Tragedy of Iblīs," an essay in which he links the Qur'ānic story with Greek tragedy, modern existentialism, and the state of the modern Islamic world.[27] A poem by Amal Dunqul, "Weeping before Zarqa' al-Yamama," includes this verse:

> Praise be to Satan, adored by the winds
> Who said "no" in the face of those who said "yes"
> Who taught man the tearing of nothingness,
> Who said "no" and did not die
> And remained a spirit of eternal grief.[28]

The character of Iblīs is gaining some notice beyond the Islamic world as well. In the popular American science fiction TV and book series, *Battlestar Galactica*, one of the stories, "The War of the Gods," pits Commander Adama and his company against the mysterious Count Iblīs, a savior figure with Seraphs as angelic brothers, who is gradually revealed to have been a rebellious angel with nefarious designs on the Galactica fleet.[29] He is also a terrifyingly evil and destructive character in the "Sonic the Hedgehog" video game for Playstation 3.[30]

Iblīs, a Tragic Figure?

As explored in chapter 1, the tragic character, whether hero or not, pursues clarity in the midst of ambiguity and some sense of rightness in a world that wants conformity.

The unorthodoxy of a tragic interpretation of Iblīs reflects the unorthodoxy, in Islam, of the concept of tragedy. Shabbir Akhtar, a modern British Muslim philosopher of religion, expresses what most Muslims would affirm when he says:

[27] Al-'Aẓm, "Ma'sātu al-Iblīs," 55–87.

[28] Quoted in Wild, "Koran," 153.

[29] Larson and Yermakov, *Battlerstar Galactica 7*. There is also an Iblīs Trilogy in the Stargate science fiction TV and book series.

[30] http://sonic.wikia.com/wiki/Iblis. Accessed 13 May, 2011.

> Orthodox Islamic thought has always, by contrast [with Christianity], been characterized by its almost total freedom from the tragic instinct. Indeed, it is no exaggeration to say that for both modern and classical Islam, tragedy remains a foreign category of reflection . . . the resolute determination to guard against the temptation to tragedy is Islam's distinctive contribution to religious anthropology.[31]

Moshe Piamenta, in his analysis of aphorisms in everyday Arabic speaking, demonstrates that resignation to the will of God is a common theme in daily speech.[32] Likewise Dalya Cohen-Mor shows that such resignation is a common theme in modern Arabic literature.[33] Numerous speakers at a conference on the concept of the tragic in Arabic literature conclude similarly that the tragic sensibility is alien to Islam, and exists in Arabic literature only to the extent that it has been imported from the West.[34]

A more positive expression of this attitude is a complete trust in God. A corollary to this is indicated by the common expression, *Allahu ʿālam*, "God only knows." This phrase is used by al-Ṭabarī whenever he has presented a number of interpretations of a passage and has no reason to choose one over the other. *Allahu ʿālam* implies something different from predestination, though not opposed to it. It stresses the position of quiescent unknowing.

Against this attitude of acceptance, Iblīs represents resistance and defiance. In traditional Islamic teaching, this is resistance against God, but the tragic Iblīs is not one opposed to God, but one who seeks the highest truth. In the Sufi formulation, it is a deeper monotheism. In modern Arabic literature, it is commonly a resistance to the acceptance of injustices otherwise tolerated in Muslim societies, and justified in the name of Islam. In contrast to an attitude of religious resignation, a willingness to accept that "God only knows," the tragic Iblīs does not accept unknowing, for not to know is to evade responsibility.

In the core Iblīs story, God commands all the angels to bow down to Adam. God gives no reason or justification for this command. The angels, without question, obey. Presumably, if God commands this, it must be the

[31] Akhtar, *Faith*, 160. Akhtar is speaking of Sunni Islam only, as we have throughout this study. Akhtar considers Shiʿa Islam to be a heresy.

[32] Piamenta gives a comprehensive survey of various pious expressions and their usages in his *Islam in Everyday Arabic Speech*.

[33] Cohen-Mor, *Fate*.

[34] Decreus and Kolk, *Rereading Classics*.

right thing to do. Iblīs does not accept this logic. He refuses to bow down. God's command is not sufficient in and of itself. There must be explanation. There must be reason.

This is the Mu'tazilite understanding. God is rational, and would not command something that is unjust.[35] There must be a reason for that which God commands, a reason discernible to the mind. Hence the Mu'tazilites affirmed *qiyās*, analogical reasoning, as an acceptable, even a necessary method to determine the will of God.

The Mu'tazilite, however, never questioned that God had reasons for every divine command, and that the reasons were justifiable. Iblīs, however, asserts that his own reasoning is valid enough to require of God adequate substantiation for the justice of divine action and command. His *qiyās* justifies action—or in this case inaction—seemingly in direct contradiction to God's command to bow. The implication is not that God is rational in his command, but that God is wrong in his command. Where Iblīs says to God in Sūrat al-Ḥijr, "since you have put me in the wrong," the implication is actually that Iblīs has put God in the wrong, exposing the irrationality or incorrectness of God's command.

This, of course, is an unacceptable conclusion for a Muslim. Mortals, even *jinn*, cannot put God in the wrong. Yet, as we have shown, there is a certain reasonableness to Iblīs's discreet accusation that is suggested in some of the earlier renderings of the Iblīs story. Hence Iblīs cannot simply be dismissed as proud and defiant. He *is* proud and defiant, but there is more afoot here.

Al-Ḥallāj, al-Aṭṭār, and others resolve this in a way that maintains both the rightness of God and the rightness of Iblīs. Al-Ḥallāj distinguishes between God's command and God's will. God's command is that all bow down to Adam. God's will, his intention, is to test Iblīs and lead him to a greater purity of devotion.

> I serve him now more purely, in a more empty moment, in a more glorious memento; for I served Him absolutely for my own happiness, and now I serve Him for His.[36]

[35] Massignon, *Teaching of al-Hallāj*, 306–16.

[36] Ibid., 312.

Al-Ḥallāj does not claim that Iblīs makes the right choice. He does claim that Iblīs's motives are the highest and purest. Iblīs chooses. He may have chosen wrongly, but he has not chosen wrong. That is the tragic dilemma—first the courage to choose, and the possibility, perhaps even the inevitability, to make the wrong choice for the right reasons. Alternatively, the tragic figure makes *a* right choice, perhaps the better, more noble choice, and the consequences of that choice are pain and suffering. That is the case with Iblīs, according to al-Ḥallāj.

Iqbal's Iblīs is not a tragic figure. He represents a model in which the temptation that Iblīs places before humanity is one that has both negative and positive dimensions. Iqbal is in no doubt that Iblīs draws humanity away from God, and does so with a dismissive attitude towards humanity and defiance of God. Iblīs represents, indeed, is modernity, secularism. The tragedy is that of modern humanity that so easily loses God in the quest for progress.

Modern authors such as Mahfouz and el-Saadawi depict a genuinely tragic Iblīs. Mahfouz's Idrees confronts his father, rejecting both the tyranny of his decisions—"All you have to do is hear and obey"—and the rationale for his decision—Adham's familiarity with the tenants and his knowledge of writing and arithmetic. Idrees also berates his brothers for their meek submission to the father, even after they recognize that his decision is questionable. Finally, Idrees rejects Adham's appeal to brotherhood as a reason to accept a questionable decision. A society must be willing to accept a degree of rebellion and conflict if true justice and true religion are to be lived.

Like the Qur'ānic Iblīs, Idrees questions authority. In this questioning his motives are mixed. On the one hand, he does not want to be humiliated. On the other hand, tyranny and submission to tyranny are something that must be opposed. In this Mahfouz is criticizing a society that submits to an interpretation of Islam that requires unquestioning obedience. The Islam of Iblīs demands thought, choice, and the risks that accompany such independence of thinking. Mahfouz argues for *qiyās*. In his writing, he also demonstrates the courage of *qiyās*, a willingness to challenge his compatriots to think critically—hence the strong reaction against his novel.

Likewise, el-Saadawi highlights the willingness of Ganat to reject the traditional patriarchy of Egyptian society, a patriarchy justified in the name and by the authority of Islam. For this rebellion she is declared insane and removed from family and public, confined to an asylum in which the social construct is not different from that outside the walls. Here, though, she is given a platform to declare herself, "I am not afraid. . . . I am not ashamed of my body." Iblīs, like Ganat, is also one who "refuses to kneel." Both are innocent, but innocent of what? They are guilty of defying the commands of Islam as interpreted by the religious authorities. They are guilty of defying the apparent command of God. They are innocent, as is confirmed in the final paragraphs, of disobeying the will of God. The tragedy is that they suffer pain and death for their defiance, but it is only tragedy because of their courage to choose and the nobility of their motives.

Finally, the repentant Iblīs of al-Hakīm reveals the sickness of institutionalized religion. Islam, Christianity, and Judaism, which purport to offer the means of redemption to all who come to their doors, deny this to Iblīs, not because he is undeserving, but because the teaching of the church, the mosque, and the synagogue require a representation of evil in order to sustain their roles in society. How could there be a day of judgment with no Satan?

To the religious authorities Iblīs himself is not important. Only the needs of humanity, even the need of God, to have an adversary is important. They require a demonic force against which the church, the synagogue and the mosque can preach, each from its own argument, and from which humanity can flee and be saved. For others to be saved—if indeed it is truly salvation—Iblīs must remain lost, a martyr to the needs of religion. As the angel Gabriel says, "He who loves must endure his sufferings."[37]

While most Muslims may deny that the Islamic tradition countenances any concept of tragedy, the human condition dictates otherwise. Theology aims to chart the clear course towards salvation, redemption, and the good life; it cannot avoid the reefs of human experience, especially where the ideals of religion seem to conflict with the ideals of God. Likewise, Iblīs represents that untamable voice that questions whether, as al-Ḥallāj would put it, the apparent command of God is truly the will of God.

Iblīs in his various guises captures many dimensions of the tragic. In this he represents not himself, but all of humanity who struggle to determine the nature of righteousness and justice in a world that exemplifies neither. In this, religion both guides and misguides.

The evil of al-Shayṭān is simple and clear; one knows to reject it even if one does not. If humanity had been created with neither will nor reason, al-Shayṭān would be sufficient to reveal the boundaries of the straight

[37] Al-Hakīm, "Martyr," 45.

path. But mortals were not so formed. The burdens of discernment and the power of desire, even desire for God, lead mortals into a wilderness of God's own design. Although will and righteousness direct us towards the final destination, that same will and righteousness also lead us astray. Like al-Ḥallāj's Iblīs, we cannot assume that God's command, often interpreted through human medium and contextualized in time and space, with God's will, which is eternal, are the same. The very recognition that there is a difference is the fertile soil of tragedy. We choose, discern, reason, decide, and suffer the consequences, trusting in God's mercy.

While it is tempting, in the human search for the straight path, to dismiss tragedy as a failure of faith in God's good mercy, in fact it is in the tragic that we recognize that the straight path is not well lit. We choose, and suffer the consequences. That *is* the path.

Introduction

Sūrah ṬāHā	Sūrat al-Ḥijr	Sūrah Ṣād	Sūrat al-Isrā'	Sūrat al-Kahf	Sūrat al-'Arāf	Sūrat al-Baqarah
	26. And we created humanity from ringing clay, from stinking black clay. 27. And the *jinn* we created before from the fire of scorching wind.				11. Indeed we created you; then we shaped you.	30. And when your Lord said to the angels, "Truly I am making on the earth a vice-regent," They said, "Are you making on it one who will cause corruption on it and shed blood While we glorify with your praises and sanctify you?" He said, "Truly I know what you do not know." 31. And he taught Adam the names, all of them; then he presented them to the angels; then he said, "Tell me the names of these, if you are truthful." 32. They said, "Glory to you; we have no knowledge except what you have taught us; truly you, you are the Knowing, the Wise." 33. He said, "O Adam, tell them their names." When he had told them their names, he said, "Did I not tell you that I, I know the unseen of the heavens and the earth, and I know what you reveal and what you have concealed?"

Command and Response

Sūrah ṬāHā	Sūrat al-Ḥijr	Sūrah Ṣād	Sūrat al-Isrā'	Sūrat al-Kahf	Sūrat al-'Arāf	Sūrat al-Baqarah
116. And when we said to the angels, "Bow down to Adam," they bowed down,	28. And when your Lord said to the angels, "Truly I am creating a human from ringing clay, from stinking black clay; 29. So when I have shaped him and blow into him [something] of my spirit, then fall down before him in prostration," 30. Then the angels bowed down, all of them together,	71. When your Lord said to the angels, "I am creating a human from clay; 72. When I have shaped him and breathed my spirit into him, fall down in prostration to him," 73. Then the angels prostrated themselves, all of them together,	61. When we said to the angels, "Bow down to Adam," then they bowed down,	50. And when we said to the angels, "Bow down," then they bowed down,	(11.) Then we said to the angels, "Bow down to Adam." So they bowed down,	34. And when we said to the angels, "Bow down to Adam," then they bowed down,

Refusal and Explanation

Sūrah ṬāHā	Sūrat al-Ḥijr	Sūrah Ṣād	Sūrat al-Isrā’	Sūrat al-Kahf	Sūrat al-‘Arāf	Sūrat al-Baqarah
(116.) except Iblīs; he refused.	31. Except Iblīs; he refused to be with those who bowed down. 32. He [God] said, "O Iblīs, what is with you that you are not with those who bow down?" 33. He [Iblīs] said, "I am not one to prostrate myself to a human (*bashar*) whom you created from ringing clay, from stinking black clay."	74. Except Iblīs; he was puffed up and he was one of the unbelievers. 75. [God] said, "O Iblīs, what prevented you from prostrating yourself to what I created with my own hands? Are you puffed up or are you one of the high?" 76. He said, "I am better than he is; you created me from fire and you created him from clay."	(61.) except Iblīs; he said, "Shall I bow down to one you created from clay?" 62. He said, "Do you yourself see? This is the one you have honored over me.	(50.) except Iblīs; he was one of the *jinn*. Then he went astray from the command of his Lord.	(11.) except Iblīs; he was not among the prostrators. 12. He [God] said, "What prevented you that you did not bow down when I commanded you?" He [Iblīs] said, "I am better than he; you created me from fire and you created him from clay."	(34.) except Iblīs; he refused and was proud. And he was one of the the unbelievers.

Curse and Bargaining

Sūrah Ṭāhā	Sūrat al-Ḥijr	Sūrah Ṣād	Sūrat al-Isrā'	Sūrat al-Kahf	Sūrat al-'Arāf	Sūrat al-Baqarah
	34. He [God] said, "Then get out from it, for truly you are cursed (lit.'stoned' *rajīm*). 35. And truly a curse is upon you until the day of judgment." 36. He [Iblīs] said, "My Lord, give me respite to the day they are raised." 37. He [God] said, "Then truly you are among those given respite 38. Until the day of the known time." 39. He [Iblīs] said, "My Lord, because you have led me astray, I will lay out enticements for them on earth and I will surely lead them all astray 40. Except your servants among them, the pure-hearted ones."	77. [God] said, "Go out from it, and truly you are rejected (*rajīm*), 78. And upon you is my curse until the day of judgment!" 79. [Iblīs] said, "My Lord, grant me respite until the day [the dead] are raised." 80. [God] said, "Truly you are one of those given respite 81. Until the day of the appointed time." 82. [Iblīs] said, "Then by your power I will pervert them all 83. Except your servants among them, the sincere ones."	(62.) [Iblīs:] "Indeed, if you grant respite to me to the day of resurrection, Truly I will gain mastery over his descendents, except a few."		13. [God] said, "Go down from it, for it shall not be for you to be puffed up about, so get out, and you are among the insignificant." 14. [Iblis] said, "Give me respite until the day of resurrection." 15. [God] said, "Indeed you are among those who have respite." 17. [Iblīs:] "Then indeed I will come at them from in front of them and from behind them and on their right side and on their left side, And you will not find most of them thankful." 18. [God:] "Get out from it, disgraced and banished; surely those who follow you from among them, indeed I will fill Gehenna from among you, all."	

The Garden

Sūrah ṬāHā	Sūrat al-Ḥijr	Sūrah Ṣād	Sūrat al-Isrā'	Sūrat al-Kahf	Sūrat al-'Arāf	Sūrat al-Baqarah
117. Then we said, "O Adam, truly this is an enemy to you and to your wife, so do not let him get you two out of the garden so that you will be miserable."					19. "O Adam! Dwell, you and your wife, in the garden, and eat whatever you wish; and do not approach this tree or you will become one of the transgressors." 20. Then al-Shayṭān whispered to them in order to reveal to them the shame that was hidden from them, and he said, "Your Lord forbade you this tree lest you become two angels or that you become eternal." 21. And he swore to them, "Truly I am for you both a sincere adviser." 22. So he led them by deceit; then they tasted of the tree, their shame was revealed to them, and immediately they started sewing for themselves from the leaves of the garden. And their Lord called to them, "Did I not forbid you from that tree, and did I not tell you that al-Shayṭān is a clear enemy to you?" 23. They said, "Our Lord, we have offended ourselves, and if you will not forgive us and have mercy on us, then we will be among the hopeless."	35. And we said, "O Adam, dwell, you and your wife, in the garden. And eat from it of the bounty as you wish. And do not go near this tree Or you will become one of the transgressors." 36. So al-Shayṭān made them slip from it, And made them go out from the way they were in it.

Epilogue

Sūrah ṬāHā	Sūrat al-Ḥijr	Sūrah Ṣād	Sūrat al-Isrā’	Sūrat al-Kahf	Sūrat al-‘Arāf	Sūrat al-Baqarah
		84. [God] said, “Then it is confirmed [true], and the truth is what I say, 85. That I will fill Gehenna with you, and with those who follow you, all of them!”	64. [God:] “And incite those whom you are able among them with your voice, And threaten them with your horses and your men, And associate with them in wealth and children, promising them. But what does al-Shayṭān promise them but delusion?”	(50.) Will you take him and his progeny as protectors and not me? They are enemies to you. Evil is the compensation for the reprobates.	24. He [God] said, “Go down, with some of you being enemies to others, and you will have on earth a dwelling-place and goods for a while.” 25. He said, “There you will live and there you will die, and from there you will be taken out.”	(36.) And we said, “Go down, some of you being enemies to others; And you will have on earth a dwelling and supplies for a time.”

Bibliography

Abu-Haidar, Jareer. "Awlād Ḥāratinā by Najīb Maḥfūẓ: An Event in the Arab World." *Journal of Arab Literature* 16 (1985) 119–31.

Adang, Camilla. *Muslim Writers on Judaism and the Hebrew Bible: From Ibn Rabban to Ibn Hazm*. Islamic Philosophy, Theology, and Science 22. Leiden: Brill, 1996.

Akhtar, Shabbir. *A Faith for All Seasons: Islam and the Challenge of the Modern World*. Chicago: Ivan R. Dee, 1990.

Albayrak, Ismail. "Isrā'īliyyāt and the Classical Exegetes' Comments on the Calf with a Hollow Sound Q.20:83–98/7:147–155 with Special Reference to Ibn 'Aṭiyya." *Journal of Semitic Studies* 47 (2002) 39–65.

Albin, Michael W. "Printing of the Qur'an." In vol. 4 of *Encyclopedia of the Qur'ān*, edited by Jane Dammen McAuliffe et al., 264–76. 5 vols. Leiden: Brill, 2001–2006.

'Alī, 'Abdullah Yūsuf. *The Meaning of the Holy Qur'ān*. New Edition with Revised Translation and Commentary. Brentwood, Md.: Amana Corporation, 1992.

Ali, Ahmed. *Al-Qur'ān: A Contemporary Translation*. Princeton, N.J.: Princeton University Press, 1993.

Alter, Robert. *The Art of Biblical Narrative*. New York: Basic Books, 1981.

Ambrose. *On Belief in the Resurrection*. In *St. Ambrose: Select Works and Letters*. Vol. 10 of *The Nicene and Post-Nicene Fathers*. Series 2. Edited by Philip Schaff and Henry Wace. 1890–1900. 14 vols. Repr., Peabody, Mass.: Hendrickson, 1994.

Andersen, Francis I. "2 (Slavonic Apocalypse of) Enoch: A New Translation and Introduction." In vol. 1 of *The Old Testament Pseudepigrapha*, edited by James H. Charlesworth, 91–221. 2 vols. Garden City, N.Y.: Doubleday, 1983–1985.

Anderson, Gary A. and Michael E. Stone, eds. *A Synopsis of the Books of Adam and Eve*. 2d rev. ed. Early Judaism and Its Literature 17. Atlanta, Ga.: Scholars Press, 1999.

Ante-Nicene Fathers, The. Edited by Alexander Roberts and James Donaldson. 1885–1887. 10 vols. Repr., Peabody, Mass.: Hendrickson, 1994.

Asad, Muhammad. *The Message of the Qur'ān*. Bristol, U.K.: Book Foundation, 2003.

Arberry, Arthur J. *The Koran Interpreted*. New York: Macmillan, 1955.

'Attār, Nayshābūrī, Farīd al-Dīn. *The Conference of the Birds*. Translated by C. S. Knott. Berkeley: Shambala, 1971.

———. *Gadhkirat Al-Awliyā'*. Edited by Dr. Muhammad Isti'lāmī. Tehran: Zawār, 1346 A.H.

Auerbach, Erich. *Mimesis: The Representation of Reality in Western Literature*. Translated by Willard R. Trask. Princeton, N.J.: Princeton University Press, 1953.

Augustine. *On the Psalms*. In vol. 8 of *The Nicene and Post-Nicene Fathers*. Series 1. Edited by Philip Schaff. 1886–1889. 14 vols. Repr., Peabody, Mass.: Hendrickson, 1994.

Augustinović, A. *"El-Khadr" and the Prophet Elijah*. Translated by Eugene Hoade. Studium Biblicum Franciscanum. Collectio Minor 12. Jerusalem: Franciscan Printing, 1972.

Awn, Peter J. *Satan's Tragedy and Redemption: Iblīs in Sufi Psychology*. Studies in the History of Religions 44. Leiden: Brill, 1983.

Ayoub, Mahmoud. *The Qur'an and Its Interpreters*. Albany, N.Y.: SUNY Press, 1984.

al-'Aẓm, Sādiq. "Ma'sātu al-Iblīs." In *Naqd al-Fikr al-Dīnī*, 55–87. Beirut: Dār al-Ṭalī'ah l-il-Ṭibā'ah wa-al-Nashr, 1969.

Bal, Mieke. *Narratology: Introduction to the Theory of Narrative*. 2d ed. Toronto: University of Toronto Press, 1997.

Bamberger, Bernard J. *Fallen Angels*. Philadelphia: Jewish Publication Society of America, 1952.

Barker, Margaret. *The Great Angel: A Study of Israel's Second God*. Louisville, Ky.: Westminster/John Knox, 1992.

———."Some Reflections upon the Enoch Myth." *Journal for the Study of the Old Testament* 15 (1980) 7–29.

Bateman, Herbert W. *Early Jewish Hermeneutics and Hebrews 1:5–13: The Impact of Early Jewish Exegesis on the Interpretation of a Significant New Testament Passage*. American University Studies Series 7. Theology and Religion 193. New York: Peter Lang, 1997.

al-Bayḍāwī, Nāsr al-Dīn Abī Sa'īd Abdullah Ibn 'Umar Muḥammad al-Shīrāzi. *Tafsīr al-Bayḍāwī*. Beirut: Dār al-Kutub al-'Ilmiyyah, 1988.

Beentjes, Pancratius C. *Tradition and Transformation in the Book of Chronicles*. Studia Semitica Neerlandica 52. Leiden: Brill, 2008.

Bell, Richard. *A Commentary on the Qur'an*. Edited by C. Edmund Bosworth and M. E. J. Richardson. 2 vols. Journal of Semitic Studies Monograph 14. Manchester: University of Manchester, 1991.

———. *The Qur'ān: Translated, with a Critical Re-Arrangement of the Surahs*. 2 vols. Edinburgh: T&T Clark, 1937–1939.

Bewley, Abdalhaqq and Aisha Bewley. *The Noble Qur'an: A New Rendering of Its Meaning in English*. Norwich: Bookwork, 2005.

Blachère, Régis. *Le Coran. Traduction selon un essai de réclassement des sourates*. 3 vols. Islam d'Hier et d'Aujourd'hui 3–5. Paris: Maisonneuve, 1947–1950.

Bodman, Whitney S. "Stalking Iblis: In Search for an Islamic Theodicy." In *Myths, Historical Archetypes and Symbolic Figures in Arabic Literature: Towards a New Hermeneutic Approach*, edited by Angelika Neuwirth, Brigit Embalo, Sebastian Gunther, and Maher Jarrar, 247–70. Stuttgart: Steiner, 1999.

Boullata, Issa J., ed. *Literary Structures of Religious Meaning in the Qur'an*. Curzon Studies in the Qur'an. Richmond, Surrey: Curzon, 2000.

Böwering, Gerhard. "Chronology and the Qur'ān." In vol. 1 of *Encyclopedia of the Qur'ān*, 316–35. Edited by Jane Dammen McAuliffe et al. 5 vols. Leiden: Brill, 2001–2006.

Bowker, John. *The Targums and Rabbinic Literature: An Introduction to Jewish Interpretations of Scripture*. Cambridge, U.K.: Cambridge University Press, 1969.

Boyce, Mary, ed. and trans. *Textual Sources for the Study of Zoroastrianism*. Textual Sources for the Study of Religion. Manchester, U.K.: Manchester University Press, 1984.

Brock, Sebastian P. "Two Syriac Dialogue Poems on Abel and Cain." *Le Museon* 113 (2000) 333–75.

Budge, E. A. Wallis, trans. *The Book of the Cave of Treasures: A History of the Patriarchs and the Kings, Their Successors, from the Creation to the Crucifixion of Christ*. London: Religious Tract Society, 1927.

Bulka, Reuven. "To Be Good or Evil: Which is More Natural?" *Journal of Psychology and Judaism* 14 (1990) 53–71.

al-Bursawī, Ismā'īl Haqqī. *Tafsīr Rūḥ al-Bayān*. Beirut: Dār Iḥyā' al-Turāth al-'Arabī, 1985.

Burton, John. "Collection of the Qur'ān." In *Encyclopedia of the Qur'ān* Edited by Jane Dammen McAuliffe, 351–61. Leiden: Brill, 2001.

———. *The Collection of the Qur'ān*. Cambridge, U.K.: Cambridge University Press, 1977.

Butler, Jean. "Iblīs in the Qur'ān: His Origin and Nature. Selected Interpretations from Muqatil to Ibn Kathīr." Ph.D. diss., University of Copenhagen, 2000.

Byrne, Brendan J. *Sons of God, Seed of Abraham: A Study of the Idea of the Sonship of God of All Christians in Paul against the Jewish Background*. Analecta Biblica 83. Rome: Biblical Institute, 1979.

Cachia, Pierre. "In a Glass Darkly: The Faintness of Islamic Inspiration in Modern Arab Literature." *Die Welt des Islams* 23–24 (1984) 26–44.

Camus, Albert. "Lecture Given in Athens on the Future of Tragedy." In *Lyrical and Critical*, translated by Philip Thody, 177–87. London: Hamish Hamilton, 1967.

Carter, Michael. "Foreign Vocabulary." In *The Blackwell Companion to the Qur'ān*, edited by Andrew Rippin, 120–39. Malden, Mass.: Blackwell, 2006.

Chabbi, Jacqueline. *Le seigneur des tribus. L'Islam de Mahomet*. Paris: Noêsis, 1997.

Charlesworth, James H., ed. *The Old Testament Pseudepigrapha*. 2 vols. Garden City, N.Y.: Doubleday, 1983–1985.

Chelhod, Joseph. *Les structures du sacré chez les Arabes*. Islam d'Hier et d'Aujourd'hui 13. Paris: G.-P. Maisonneuve et Larose, 1965.

Chipman, Leigh N. P. "Mythic Aspects of the Process of Adam's Creation in Judaism and Islam: In Memorium Hava Lazarus-Yafeh." *Studia Islamica* 93 (2001) 5–25.

Chittick, William C. "Eschatology." In vol. 1 of *Islamic Spirituality: Foundations*, edited by Seyyed Hossein Nasr, 378–409. 2 vols. World Spirituality 19. New York: Crossroads, 1987.

Cohen-Mor, Dalya. *A Matter of Fate: The Concept of Fate in the Arab World as Reflected in Modern Arabic Literature*. Oxford: Oxford University Press, 2001.

Cohen Stuart, G. H. *The Struggle in Man between Good and Evil: An Inquiry into the Origin of the Rabbinic Concept of Yeser Hara*. Kampen: J. H. Kok, 1984.

Cook, Michael. *Commanding Right and Forbidding Wrong in Islamic Thought*. Cambridge, U.K.: Cambridge University Press, 2000.

Cooke, Gerald. "The Sons of (the) God(s)." *Zeitschrift für die alttestamentiche Wissenschaft* 76 (1964) 22–47.

———."The Israelite King as Son of God." *Zeitschrift für die alttestamentliche Wissenschaft* 73 (1961) 202–25.

al-Damīrī, Kamāl al-Dīn Muḥammad Ibn Mūsa. *Ḥayāt al-Ḥayawān al-Kubrā*. Beirut: Dār al-Qāmūs al-Ḥadīth, 1970.

Davidson, Maxwell J. *Angels at Qumran: A Comparative Study of 1 Enoch 1–36, 72–108 and Sectarian Writings from Qumran*. Journal for the Study of the Pseudepigrapha Supplement Series 11. Sheffield: JSOT, 1992.

Day, Peggy Lynne. *An Adversary in Heaven:* śāṭān *in the Hebrew Bible*. Harvard Semitic Monographs 43. Atlanta, Ga.: Scholars, 1988.

Decreus, Freddy, and Mieke Kolk, eds. *Rereading Classics in "East" and "West": Post-Colonial Perspectives on the Tragic*. Gent: Documentatiecentrum voor Dramatische Kunst Gent, 2004.

Delaney, David Kevin. "The Sevenfold Vengeance of Cain: Genesis 4 in Early Jewish and Christian Interpretation." Ph.D. diss., University of Virginia, 1996.

Dirksen, Peter B. *1 Chronicles*. Translated by Antony P. Runia. Historical Commentary on the Old Testament Series. Leuven: Peeters, 2005.

Donner, Fred M. *Narratives of Islamic Origins: The Beginnings of Islamic Historical Writing*. Studies in Late Antiquity and Early Islam 14. Princeton, N.J.: Darwin, 1998.

Duri, Abd al-Aziz. *The Rise of Historical Writing among the Arabs*. Translated by Lawrence I. Conrad. Modern Classics in Near Eastern Studies. Princeton, N.J.: Princeton University Press, 1983.

Early Islamic Mysticism: Sufi, Qur'an, Mi'raj, Poetic and Theological Writings. Edited and translated by Michael A. Sells. Preface by Carl W. Ernst. Classics of Western Spirituality 86. New York: Paulist, 1996.

Eichhorn, David Max. *Cain: Son of the Serpent: A Midrash or Homiletical Narration of the Fourth Chapter of the Book of Genesis*. New York: Whittier Books, 1957.

Elliott, James K., ed. *The Apocryphal New Testament: A Collection of Apocryphal Christian Literature in an English Translation*. Oxford: Clarendon Press, 1993.

El Saadawi, Nawal. *The Innocence of the Devil*. Translated by Sherif Hetata. Literature of the Middle East. Berkeley, Calif.: University of California Press, 1994.

El-Zein, Amira. "The Evolution of the Concept of the Jinn from Pre-Islam to Islam." Ph.D. diss., Georgetown University, 1995.

Firestone, Reuven. *Journeys in Holy Lands: The Evolution of the Abraham-Ishmael Legends in Islamic Exegesis*. Albany, N.Y.: SUNY Press, 1990.

Fish, Stanley E. *Is There a Text in This Class?: The Authority of Interpretive Communities*. Cambridge, Mass.: Harvard University Press, 1980.

———. "Literature in the Reader: Affective Stylistics." In *Reader-Response Criticism: From Formalism to Post-Structuralism*, 70–100. Edited by Jane P. Tompkins. Baltimore, Md.: Johns Hopkins University Press, 1980.

Fishbane, Michael. *Biblical Interpretation in Ancient Israel*. Oxford: Clarendon Press, 1985.

Fletcher-Louis, Crispin H. T. "The Worship of Divine Humanity as God's Image and the Worship of Jesus." In *The Jewish Roots of Christological Monotheism: Papers from the St. Andrews Conference on the Historical Origins of the Worship of Jesus*, edited by Carey C. Newman, James R. Davila, and Gladys S. Lewis, 112–28. Supplements to the Journal for the Study of Judaism 63. Leiden: Brill, 1999.

Forsyth, Dan W. "Sibling Rivalry, Aesthetic Sensibility, and Social Structure in Genesis." *Ethos* 19 (1991) 453–510.

Forsyth, Neil. *The Old Enemy: Satan and the Combat Myth*. Princeton, N.J.: Princeton University Press, 1987.

Fossum, Jarl. "Son of God." In vol. 6 of *The Anchor Bible Dictionary*, edited by David Noel Freedman et al., 128–37. 6 vols. New York: Doubleday, 1992.

Fox, Everett. "Stalking the Younger Brother." *Journal for the Study of the Old Testament* 60 (1993) 45–68.

Frye, Northrop. *Anatomy of Criticism: Four Essays*. Princeton, N.J.: Princeton University Press, 1957.

———. *The Great Code: The Bible and Literature*. New York: Harcourt Brace Jovanovich, 1982.

Fudge, Bruce. "The Men of the Cave: Tafsīr, Tragedy and Tawfīq al-Ḥakīm." *Arabica* 54 (2007) 67–93.

Gadamer, Hans-Georg. *Truth and Method*. Translation edited by Garrett Barden and John Cumming. New York: Seabury, 1975.

Gaylord, Harry E. "How Satanael Lost His '-El.'" *Journal of Jewish Studies* 33 (1982) 303–9.

Gibson, John C. L., ed. *Canaanite Myths and Legends*. Originally edited by G. R. Driver. 2d ed. Edinburgh: T&T Clark, 1978.

Ginzberg, Louis. *The Legends of the Jews*. Translated by Henrietta Szold. 7 vols. Philadelphia: Jewish Publication Society of America, 1909–1938.

Glenthøj, Johannes Bartholdy. *Cain and Abel in Syriac and Greek Writers (4th–6th Centuries)*. Corpus Scriptorum Christianorum Orientalium 567. Subsidia 95. Lovanii: Peeters, 1997.

Graham, William A. "'The Winds to Herald His Mercy' and Other 'Signs for Those of Certain Faith': Nature as Token of God's Sovereignty and Grace in the Qur'an." In *Faithful Imagining: Essays in Honor of Richard R. Niebuhr*, edited by Sang Hyun Lee, Wayne Proudfoot, and Albert Blackwell, 19–38. Scholars Press Homage Series 19. Atlanta, Ga.: Scholars, 1995.

———."The Earliest Meaning of 'Qur'ān'." *Die Welt Des Islams* 23–24 (1984) 361–77.

———. "Those Who Study and Teach the Qur'an." In *International Congress for the Study of the Qur'an: Australian National University, Canberra, 8–13 May 1980*, edited by Anthony. H. Johns, 9–29. Canberra City: South Asia Centre, Faculty of Asian Studies, Australian National University, 1981.

Greenspahn, F. E. "Primogeniture in Ancient Israel." In *Go to the Land I Will Show You: Studies in Honor of Dwight W. Young*, edited by Joseph Coleson and Victor H. Matthews, 69–80. Winona Lake, Ind.: Eisenbrauns, 1996.

Greimas, Algirdas Julien. "Narrative Grammar: Units and Levels." *Modern Language Notes* 86 (1971) 793–806.

al-Hakīm, Tawfīq. "The Martyr." In *Arabic Short Stories, 1945–1965*, edited by Mahmoud Manzalaoui, 36–46. Cairo: American University in Cairo Press, 1985.

Hallaq, Wael B. *The Origins and Evolution of Islamic Law*. Themes in Islamic Law 1. Cambridge, U.K.: Cambridge University Press, 2005.

———. *A History of Islamic Legal Theories: An Introduction to Sunnī Uṣūl al-Fiqh*. Cambridge, U.K.: Cambridge University Press, 1997.

Halman, Hugh Talat. "'Where Two Seas Meet': The Quranic Story of Khidr and Moses in Sufi Commentaries as a Model for Spiritual Guidance." Ph.D. diss., Duke University, 2000.

Hammad, Ahmad Zaki. *The Gracious Quran: A Modern-Phrased Interpretation in English*. 2 vols. Lisle, Ill.: Lucent Interpretations, 2007.

Hanson, Paul D. "Rebellion in Heaven, Azazel, and Euhemeristic Heroes in 1 Enoch 6–11." *Journal of Biblical Literature* 96 (1977) 195–233.

Heidel, Alexander. *The Babylonian Genesis: The Story of the Creation*. 2d ed. Chicago: University of Chicago Press, 1951.

Hennecke, Edgar, and W. Schneemelcher, eds. *New Testament Apocrypha*. Translation edited by Robert McL. Wilson. 2 vols. Trowbridge: SCM, 1973.

Henninger, Joseph. "Pre-Islamic Bedouin Religion." In *Studies on Islam*, edited and translated by Merlin L. Schwarz, 3–22. New York: Oxford University Press, 1981.

Hick, John. *Evil and the God of Love*. Rev. ed. New York: Harper & Row, 1978.

Hirschberg, Harris H. "Eighteen Hundred Years Before Freud: A Re-Evaluation of the Term Yetzer Ha-Ra." *Judaism* 10 (Spring 1961) 129–41.

Humphreys, R. Stephen. "Qur'anic Myth and Narrative Structure in Early Islamic Historiography." In *Tradition and Innovation in Late Antiquity*, edited by Frank M. Clover and R. Stephen Humphreys, 271–90. Wisconsin Studies in Classics. Madison, Wis.: University of Wisconsin Press, 1989.

Ibn Hishām, 'Abd al-Malik. *The Life of Muhammad: A Translation of Ishaq's Sirat Rasul Allah*. Translated by Alfred Guillaume. London: Oxford University Press, 1955.

Ibn Kathīr, Abū al-Fidā' Ismā'īl. *Tafsīr al-Qur'ān al-'Aẓīm*. Beirut: Dār al-Fikr, 1994. Ibrahim, Lutpi. "The Questions of the Superiority of Angels and Prophets between az-Zamakhsharī and al-Bayḍāwī." *Arabica* 28 (1981) 65–75.

Ibn Manẓūr, Muḥammad Ibn Mukarram. *Lisān al-'Arab*. Beirut: Dār Ṣāder, 1990.

Ibn al-Nadīm, Muḥammad Ibn Isḥāq. *The Fihrist of al-Nadīm: A Tenth-Century Survey of Muslim Culture*. Edited and translated by Bayard Dodge. 2 vols. Records of Civilization, Sources, and Studies 83. New York: Columbia University Press, 1970.

Iqbal, Muḥammad. *A Message from the East: A Translation of Iqbal's* Payām-i *Mashriq into English Verse*. Translated by M. Hadi Hussain. 2d ed. Lahore: Iqbal Academy Pakistan, 1977.

Irenaeus. *Against Heresies*. In vol. 1 of *Ante-Nicene Fathers*. Edited by Alexander Roberts and James Donaldson. 1885–1887. 10 vols. Repr., Peabody, Mass.: Hendrickson, 1994.

Iser, Wolfgang. *The Act of Reading: A Theory of Aesthetic Response*. Baltimore, Md.: Johns Hopkins University Press, 1978.

Jadaane, F. "La place des anges dans la theologie cosmique musulmane." *Studia Islamica* 41 (1975) 23–61.

Jalāl al-Dīn Rūmī, Maulana. *The Mathnawī of Jalālu'ddīn Rūmī*. Edited and Translated by Reynold A. Nicholson. 8 vols. E. J. W. Gibb Memorial Series: New Series 4. Cambridge, U.K.: Gibb Memorial Trust, 1925–1940. Repr., Lahore: Islamic Book Service, 1989.

Japhet, Sara. *The Ideology of the Book of Chronicles and Its Place in Biblical Thought*. 2d rev. ed. Frankfurt am Main: P. Lang, 1997. Repr., Winona Lake, Ind.: Eisenbrauns, 2009.

Jarick, John. *1 Chronicles*. Readings, A New Biblical Commentary. London: Sheffield Academic, 2002.

Johns, Anthony H. "Narrative, Intertext and Allusion in the Qur'anic Presentation of Job." *Journal of Qur'anic Studies* 1 (1999) 1–25.

———. "In Search of Common Ground: The Qur'an as Literature?" *Islam and Christian-Muslim Relations* 4 (1993) 191–209.

———. "Joseph in the Qur'an: Dramatic Dialogue, Human Emotion and Prophetic Wisdom." *Islamochristiana/Dirasat Islamiya Masihiya* 7 (1981) 29–55.

Josephus. *Judean Antiquities 1–4*. Translation and commentary by Louis H. Feldman. Vol. 3 of *Flavius Josephus: Translation and Commentary*. Edited by Steve Mason. Leiden: Brill, 2000.

Justin Martyr. *Second Apology*. In vol. 1 of *Ante-Nicene Fathers*. Edited by Alexander Roberts and James Donaldson. 1885–1887. 10 vols. Repr., Peabody, Mass.: Hendrickson, 1994.

Kalivoda, Robert. *Der Marxismus und die moderne geistige wirklichkeit*. Frankfurt: Suhrkamp, 1970.

Kamali, Mohammad Hashim. *Principles of Islamic Jurisprudence*. Cambridge, U.K.: Islamic Texts Society, 1991.

Kappler, Claude. "Le dialogue d'Iblis et de Mo'âwiye dans le daftar II du *Masnavi* de Mowlavi, beyts 2604–2792: Une alchemie du coeur." *Studia Iranica* 16 (1987) 45–99.

Katsh, Abraham I. *Judaism and the Koran: Biblical and Talmudic Backgrounds of the Koran and Its Commentaries*. New York: Barnes & Co., 1962.

———. *Judaism in Islam: Biblical and Talmudic Backgrounds of the Koran and Its Commentaries; Suras II and III*. New York: New York University Press, 1954.

Kaufmann, Walter. *Tragedy and Philosophy*. Princeton, N.J.: Princeton University Press, 1968.

Khadduri, Majid. *Al-Shāfi'īs Risāla: Treatise on the Foundations of Islamic Jurisprudence*. Cambridge, U.K.: Islamic Texts Society, 1987.

Khalidi, Tarif. *The Muslim Jesus: Sayings and Stories in Islamic Literature*. Convergences. Cambridge, Mass.: Harvard University Press, 2001.

———. *The Muslim Jesus: Sayings and Stories in Islamic Literature*. Convergences. Cambridge, Mass.: Harvard University Press, 2001.. *Arabic Historical Thought in the Classical Period*. Cambridge Studies in Islamic Civilization. Cambridge, U.K.: Cambridge University Press, 1994.

Khoury, Raif Georges, ed. *Wahb b. Munabbih*. Codices Arabici Antiqui 1. Wiesbaden: Otto Harrassowitz, 1972.

al-Khū'ī, Abū al-Qāsim Ibn 'Alī Akbar. *The Prolegomena to the Qur'an*. Translated by Abdulaziz A. Sachedina. New York: Oxford University Press, 1998.

Kiernan, V. G. "Iqbal and Milton." In *Iqbal: Commemorative Volume,* edited by Ali Sardar Jafri and K. S. Duggal, 231–41. New Delhi: All India Iqbal Centenary Celebrations Committee, 1980.

Kinberg, Leah. "Muḥkamāt and Mutashābihāt (Koran 3/7): Implications of a Koranic Pair of Terms in Medieval Exegesis." In *The Qur'an: Formative Interpretation*, edited by Andrew Rippin, 283–312. Formation of the Classical Islamic World 25. Aldershot, U.K.: Ashgate, 1999.

al-Kisā'ī, Muḥammad Ibn 'Abd Allāh. *Tales of the Prophets*. Edited by Seyyed Hossein Nasr. Translated by Wheeler M. Thackston, Jr. Great Books of the Islamic World. Chicago: Kazi, 1997.

Kister, M. J. "Adam: A Study of Some Legends in Tafsir and Hadith Literature." *Israel Oriental Studies* 13 (1993) 113–74.

———. "Ḥaddithū 'an Banī Isrā'īla Wa-Lā Ḥaraja: A Study of an Early Tradition." In *Studies in Jāhiliyya and Early Islam*, edited by M. J. Kister, 215–39. London: Variorum Reprints, 1980.

Klein, Ralph W. *1 Chronicles: A Commentary*. Edited by Thomas Krüger. Hermeneia. Minneapolis, Minn.: Fortress, 2006.

Knibb, Michael A. "Interpreting the Book of Enoch: Reflections on a Recently Published Commentary." *Journal for the Study of Judaism* 33 (2002) 437–50.

Knowledge of God in Classical Sufism: Foundations of Islamic Mystical Theology. Translated and Introduced by John Renard. Preface by Ahmet T. Karamustafa. Classics of Western Spirituality. New York: Paulist, 2004.

Krieger, Murray. "The 'Imaginary' and Its Enemies." *New Literary History* 31 (2000) 129–62.

Kugel, James L. *In Potiphar's House: The Interpretive Life of Biblical Texts*. San Francisco: Harper, 1990.

LaCocque, André. *Onslaught against Innocence: Cain, Abel and the Yahwist*. Cambridge, U.K.: James Clarke, 2008.

Lamb, Connie. "Review of Nawal el-Saadawi, Innocence of the Devil." *International Journal of Middle Eastern Studies* 32 (2000) 547–49.

Lane, Edward William. *An Arabic-English Lexicon*. 2 vols. London: Williams & Norgate, 1863-1893. Repr., Cambridge, U.K.: Islamic Texts Society, 1984.

Larson, Glen A., and Nicholas Yermakov. *Battlerstar Galactica 7: War of the Gods*. New York: Berkley, 1982.

Leaman, Oliver. *Evil and Suffering in Jewish Philosophy*. Cambridge Studies in Religious Traditions 6. Cambridge, U.K.: Cambridge University Press, 1995.

Leder, Stefan. "Conventions of Fictional Narration in Learned Literature." In *Story-Telling in the Framework of Non-Fictional Arabic Literature*, edited by idem, 34–60. Wiesbaden: Harrassowitz, 1998.

———, ed. *Story-Telling in the Framework of Non-Fictional Arabic Literature*. Wiesbaden: Harrassowitz, 1998.

Lee, Hindishe. "In the Shadow of Amalek." *Dor Le Dor* 17 (1988) 44–49.

Levenson, Jon D. *Creation and the Persistence of Evil: The Jewish Drama of Divine Omnipotence*. San Francisco: Harper & Row, 1988.

Lowry, Richard. "The Dark Side of the Soul: Human Nature and the Problem of Evil in Jewish and Christian Traditions." *Journal of Ecumenical Studies* 35 (1998) 88–100.

MacDonald, Duncan B., and W. Madelung. "Malā'ika." In vol. 6 of *Encyclopaedia of Islam,* edited by P. Bearman et al., 216. 12 vols. 2d ed. Leiden: Brill, 1960–2005.

Madigan, Daniel A. *The Qur'ān's Self-Image: Writing and Authority in Islam's Scripture*. Princeton, N.J.: Princeton University Press, 2001.

Mahfouz, Naguib. *Children of Gebelaawi*. Translated by Philip Stewart. Revised augmented ed. Colorado Springs, Colo.: Three Continents, 1995.

Majlisī, Muḥammad Bāqir Ibn Muḥammad Taqī. *Bihār al-Anwār*. Beirut: Mu'asasat al-Wafā', 1983.

Martin, Richard C. "Structural Analysis and the Qur'ān: Newer Approaches to the Study of Islamic Texts." *Journal of the American Academy of Religion Thematic Studies* 47 (1979) 665–83.

Massey, Keith. "Mysterious Letters." In vol. 3 of *Encyclopedia of the Qur'ān*, edited by Jane Dammen McAuliffe et al., 471–76. 5 vols. Leiden: Brill, 2001–2006.

Massignon, Louis. *The Teaching of al-Hallāj*. Vol. 3 of *The Passion of al-Hallāj: Mystic and Martyr of Islam*. Translated by Herbert Mason. 4 vols. Bollingen Series 98. Princeton, N.J.: Princeton University Press, 1982.

———. "Les sept dormants d'Éphèse en islam et en chrétienté." *Revue des études islamique* 22 (1954) 59–112.

McAuliffe, Jane Dammen. "Qur'anic Hermeneutics: The Views of al-Tabarī and Ibn Kathīr." In *Approaches to the History of the Interpretation of the Qur'an*, edited by Andrew Rippin, 46–62. Oxford: Clarendon Press, 1988.

McGinn, Bernard. *Antichrist: Two Thousand Years of the Human Fascination with Evil*. San Francisco: HarperSanFrancisco, 1994.

Mehrez, Samia. *Egyptian Writers between History and Fiction: Essays on Naguib Mahfouz, Sonallah Ibrahim, and Gamal al-Gitani*. Cairo: American University of Cairo Press, 1994.

Mellinkoff, Ruth. *The Mark of Cain*. Quantum Books. Berkeley, Calif.: University of California Press, 1981.

Mir, Mustansir. "The Sūra as a Unity: A Twentieth Century Development in Qur'ān Exegesis." In *Approaches to the Qur'ān*, edited by Gerald R. Hawting and Abdul-Kader A. Shareef, 211–24. Routledge/SOAS Series on Contemporary Politics and Culture in the Middle East. London: Routledge, 1993.

———. *Coherence in the Qur'an: A Study of Iṣlāḥī*'s *Concept of Naẓm in Tadabbur-i Qur'ān*. Indianapolis, Ind.: American Trust, 1986.

Mohamed, Yasien. "The Interpretations of Fitrah." *Islamic Studies* 34 (1995) 129–51.

Momen, Moojan. *An Introduction to the Shi'i Islam: the History and Doctrines of Twelver Shi'ism*. New Haven, Conn.: Yale University Press, 1985.

Motzki, Harald. "Alternative Accounts of the Qur'ān's Formation." In *The Cambridge Companion to the Qur'ān*. Edited by Jane Dammen McAuliffe, 59–75. Cambridge, U.K.: Cambridge University Press, 2006.

Mullen, E. Theodore. "Divine Assembly." In vol. 2 of *The Anchor Bible Dictionary*, edited by David Noel Freedman et al., 214–17. 6 vols. New York: Doubleday, 1992.

———. *The Divine Council in Canaanite and Early Hebrew Literature*. Harvard Semitic Monographs 24. Chico, Calif.: Scholars, 1980.

Murata, Sachiko. "Angels." In vol. 1 of *Islamic Spirituality: Foundations*, edited by Seyyed Hossein Nasr., 324–44. 2 vols. World Spirituality 19. New York: Crossroads, 1987.

Murphy, Roland E. "*Yēṣer* in the Qumran Literature." *Biblica* 39 (1958) 334–44.

Muslim Ibn Ḥajjāj al-Qushayrī. *Ṣaḥīḥ Muslim*. Beirut: Dār Iḥya' al-Turāth al-'Arabī, 2000.

Najjar, Fauzi M. "Islamic Fundamentalism and the Intellectuals: The Case of Naguib Mahfouz." *British Journal of Middle East Studies* 25 (1998) 145–61.

al-Nasafī, ʿAbd Allāh Ibn Aḥmad. *Tafsīr al-Nasafī*. Beirut: Dār al-Kutub al-ʿIlmiyyah, 1995.

Nelson, Kristina. *The Art of Reciting the Qur'an*. Modern Middle East Series 11. Austin: University of Texas Press, 1985.

Neuwirth, Angelika. "Du Texte de Récitation au Canon en Passant par le Liturgie." *Arabica* 47 (2000) 194–229.

———. "Negotiating Justice: A Pre-Canonical Reading of the Qur'anic Creation Accounts (Part I)." *Journal of Qur'anic Studies* 2, no. 1 (2000) 25–41.

———. "Negotiating Justice: A Pre-Canonical Reading of the Qur'anic Creation Accounts (Part II)." *Journal of Qur'anic Studies* 2, no. 2 (2000) 1–18.

———. "Referentiality and Textuality in Sūrat al-Ḥijr: Some Observations on the Qur'ānic 'Canonical Process' and the Emergence of a Community." In *Literary Structures of Religious Meaning in the Qur'an*, edited by Issa J. Boullata, 143–72. Curzon Studies in the Qur'an. Richmond, Surrey: Curzon, 2000.

———. "Qur'ānic Literary Structure Revisited: *Sūrat al- Raḥmān* between Mythic Account and Decodation of Myth." In *Story-Telling in the Framework of Non-Fictional Arabic Literature*, edited by Stefan Leder, 388–420. Wiesbaden: Harrassowitz, 1998.

Newby, Gordon D. "Tafsīr Isrā'īliyāt: Qur'an Commentary in Early Islam in Its Relationship to Judaeo-Christian Traditions of Scriptural Commentary." *Journal of the American Academy of Religion Thematic Studies* 47 (1979) 685–97.

Newman, Carey C., James R. Davila, and Gladys S. Lewis. *The Jewish Roots of Christological Monotheism: Papers from the St. Andrews Conference on the Historical Origins of the Worship of Jesus*. Supplements to the Journal for the Study of Judaism 63. Leiden: Brill, 1999.

Newsom, Carol A. "The Development of 1 Enoch 6–19: Cosmology and Judgment." *Catholic Biblical Quarterly* 42 (1980) 310–29.

Nickelsburg, George W. E. *1 Enoch: A Commentary on the Book of 1 Enoch*. Edited by Kaus Baltzer. Hermeneia. Minneapolis, Minn.: Fortress, 2001.

Nielsen, Kirsten. *Satan the Prodigal Son?: A Family Problem in the Bible*. The Biblical Seminar 50. Sheffield, U.K.: Sheffield Academic, 1998.

Nöldeke, Theodor. *Die Sammlung des Qorāns*. Vol. 2 of *Geschichte des Qorāns*. Edited by Friedrich Schwally. Leipzig: Dieterich'sche, 1919.

———. *Über den Ursprung des Qorāns*. Vol. 1 of *Geschichte des Qorāns*. Edited by Friedrich Schwally. Leipzig: Dieterich'sche, 1909.

Noth, Albrecht. *The Early Arabic Historical Tradition: A Source-Critical Study*. In collaboration with Lawrence I. Conrad. Translated by Michael Bonner. 2d ed. Studies in Late Antiquity and Early Islam 3. Princeton, N.J.: Darwin, 1994.

Olson, Brooke Elise. "Heavenly Journeys, Earthly Concerns: The Legacy of the Mi'rāj in the Formation of Islam." Ph.D. diss., University of Chicago, 2002.

Omar, Irfan. "Khidr in the Islamic Tradition." *Muslim World* 83 (1993) 279–94.

Padwick, Constance E. *Muslim Devotions: A Study of Prayer-Manuals in Common Use*. London: SPCK, 1961.

Page, Hugh R. *The Myth of Cosmic Rebellion: A Study of its Reflexes in Ugaritic and Biblical Literature*. Supplements to Vetus Testamentum 65. Leiden: Brill, 1996.

Pagels, Elaine. *The Origin of Satan*. New York: Random House, 1995.

Palmer, Richard H. *Tragedy and Tragic Theory: An Analytic Guide*. Westport, Conn.: Greenwood, 1992.

Paret, Rudi. "Aṣḥāb al-Kahf." In vol. 1 of *Encyclopaedia of Islam,* edited by P. Bearman et al., 691. 12 vols. 2d ed. Leiden: Brill, 1960–2005.

Patrides, C. A. "The Salvation of Satan." *Journal of the History of Ideas* 28 (1967) 467–78.

Patton, Corrine L. "Adam as the Image of God: An Exploration of the Fall of Satan in the Life of Adam and Eve." *Society of Biblical Literature Seminar Papers* 33 (1994) 294–300.

Petersen, William L. *Tatian's Diatesseron: Its Creation, Dissemination, Significance, and History in Scholarship*. Supplements to Vigiliae Christianae 25. Leiden: Brill, 1994.

Philo of Alexandria. "On the Birth of Abel and the Sacrifices Offered by Him and by His Brother Cain (*De Sacrificiis Abelis et Cain*) ." In *The Works of Philo: New Updated Edition*, 94–111. Peabody Mass.: Hendrickson, 1993.

Piamenta, Moshe. *Islam in Everyday Arabic Speech*. Leiden: Brill, 1979.

Pickthall, Marmaduke William, ed. and trans. *The Meaning of the Glorious Koran*. New York: New American Library, 1953.

Porter, F. C. "The Yecer Hara: A Study in the Jewish Doctrine of Sin." *Yale Bicentennial Publications*. New York: Scribner's Sons, 1901.

Pritchard, James B., ed. *The Ancient Near East: An Anthology of Texts and Pictures*. Translated and annotated by W. F. Albright et al. Princeton, N.J.: Princeton University Press, 1958.

Qara'i, 'Ali Quli. *The Qur'an with a Phrase-by-Phrase English Translaition*. Elmhurst, N.Y.: Tahrike Tarsile Qur'an, 2006.

Qur'ān, The. Translated by Alan Jones. [Cambridge, U.K.]: Gibb Memorial Trust, 2007.

Qur'ān, The. Translated by George Sale. London: Frederick Warne and Co., 1909.

Quinones, Ricardo J. *The Changes of Cain: Violence and the Lost Brother in Cain and Abel Literature*. Princeton: Princeton University Press, 1991.

Qummī, 'Alī Ibn Ibrahīm. *Tafsīr al-Qummī*. 2 vols. Beirut: Mu'ssasa al-'Ulami l-Matbu'at, 1991.

al-Qurṭubī, Abī 'Abdallah Muḥammad b. Aḥmad al-Ansārī. *Al-Jāmi'a Li-Aḥkam al-Qur'ān*. 20 books in 10 volumes. Beirut: Dār al-Fikr, 1993.

Rahman, Fazlur. *Major Themes of the Qur'an*. 2d ed. Minneapolis, Minn.: Bibliotheca Islamica, 1989.

Rasmussen, Anne K. *Women, the Recited Qur'an, and Islamic Music in Indonesia*. Berkeley: University of California Press, 2010.

Riddell, Peter G., and Tony Street, eds. *Islam: Essays on Scripture, Thought and Society: A Festschrift in Honour of Anthony H. Johns*. Islamic Philosophy, Theology, and Science 28. Leiden: Brill, 1997.

Ringgren, Helmer. *Studies in Arabian Fatalism*. Uppsala: Lundequistska Bokhandeln, 1955.

Rippin, Andrew. "Iblis." In vol. 2 of *Encyclopedia of the Qur'ān*, edited by Jane Dammen McAuliffe et al., 473. 5 vols. Leiden: Brill, 2001–2006.

Robinson, Neal. *Discovering the Qur'an: A Contemporary Approach to a Veiled Text*. London: SCM, 1996.

Rosenberg, Shalom. *Good and Evil in Jewish Thought*. Translated by John Glucker. Tel-Aviv: MOD Books, 1989.

Rubin, Uri. *Between Bible and Qur'ān: The Children of Israel and the Islamic Self-Image*. Studies in Late Antiquity and Early Islam 17. Princeton, N.J.: Darwin, 1999.

———. *The Eye of the Beholder: The Life of Muḥammad as Viewed by the Early Muslims: A Textual Analysis*. Studies in Late Antiquity and Early Islam 5. Princeton, N.J.: Darwin, 1995.

Rūmī Jalāl al-Dīn. *The Mathnawi of Jalalu'ddin Rumi*. Edited with critical notes, translation and commentary by Reynold A Nicholson. 8 vols. London: Luzac and Co., 1925–1940.

Russell, Jeffrey Burton. *The Devil: Perceptions of Evil from Antiquity to Primitive Christianity*. Ithaca, N.Y.: Cornell University Press, 1977.

———. *Satan: The Early Christian Tradition*. Ithaca, N.Y.: Cornell University Press, 1981.

Sagi, Avi. "The Punishment of Amalek in Jewish Tradition: Coping with the Moral Problem." *Harvard Theological Review* 87 (1994) 323–46.

Sailhamer, John H. *Introduction to Old Testament Theology: A Canonical Approach*. Grand Rapids, Mich.: Zondervan, 1995.

Saiti, Ramzi. "Paradise, Heaven and Other Oppressive Spaces: A Critical Examination of the Life and Works of Nawal el-Saadawi." *Journal of Arabic Literature* 25 (1994) 152–74.

Schenck, Kenneth. "A Celebration of the Enthroned Son: The Catena of Hebrews 1." *Journal of Biblical Literature* 120 (2001) 469–85.

———. "Keeping His Appointment: Creation and Enthronement in Hebrews." *Journal for the Study of the New Testament* 66 (1997) 91–117.

Schultz, Joseph P. "Angelic Opposition to the Ascension of Moses and the Revelation of the Law." *Jewish Quarterly Review* 61 (1971) 282–307.

Schwarzbaum, Haim. *Biblical and Extra-Biblical Legends in Islamic Folk-Literature*. Beiträge zur Sprach- und Kulturgeschichte des Orients 30. Walldorf-Hessen: Verlag für Orientkunde H. Vorndran, 1982.

Serjeant, Robert B. "Haram and Hawtah, the Sacred Enclave in Arabia." In *The Arabs and Arabia on the Eve of Islam,* edited by Francis E. Peters, 167–84. The Formation of the Classical Islamic World 3. Brookfield, Vt.: Ashgate, 1998.

Sewell, Richard B. *The Vision of Tragedy*. 3d ed. New York: Paragon House, 1990.

Shāfiʿī, Muḥammad Ibn Idrīs. *Risāla fī uṣūl al-fiqh: Treatise on the Foundations of Islamic Jurisprudence*. Translated by Majid Khadduri. 2d ed. Cambridge, U.K.: Islamic Texts Society, 1987.

Shaikh, Khalil. *Der Teufel in der modernen arabischen Literatur. Die Rezeption eines europäischen Motivs in der arabischen Belletristik, Dramatik, und Poesie des 19. und 20. Jahrhunderts*. Islamkundliche Untersuchungen 118. Berlin: Schwarz, 1986.

Shnizer, Aliza. "Sacrality and Collection." In *The Blackwell Companion to the Qur'ān,* edited by Andrew Rippin, 159–71. Malden, Mass.: Blackwell, 2006.

Ṣiddīqī, Muḥammad Zubayr. *Ḥadīth Literature: Its Origin, Development, and Special Features*. Edited and revised by Abdal Hakim Murad. Rev. ed. Cambridge, U.K.: The Islamic Texts Society, 1993.

Smith, David E. "The Structure of al-Baqarah." *Muslim World* 91 (2001) 121–36.

Smith, Jane I., and Yvonne Y. Haddad. *The Islamic Understanding of Death and Resurrection*. Albany, N.Y.: SUNY, 1981.

Sokol, Moshe. "Is There a 'Halakhic' Response to the Problem of Evil?" *Harvard Theological Review* 92 (1999) 311–23.

Sosevsky, Moshe Chaim. "Sha'ul and Amalek: Anatomy of a Sin." *Jewish Thought* 2 (1993) 37–56.

Speyer, Heinrich. *Die biblischen Erzählungen im Qoran*. 1931. Repr., Hildesheim: G. Olms, 1961.

Steenburg, Dave. "The Worship of Adam and Christ as the Image of God." *Journal for the Study of the New Testament* 39 (1990) 95–109.

Steiner, George. *The Death of Tragedy*. New York: Knopf, 1961.

Sternberg, Meir. *The Poetics of Biblical Narrative: Ideological Literature and the Drama of Reading*. Indiana Literary Biblical Studies. Bloomington, Ind.: Indiana University Press, 1985.

Stetkevych, Jaroslav. *Muḥammad and the Golden Bough: Reconstructing Arabian Myth*. Bloomington, Ind.: Indiana University Press, 1996.

Stokes, Ryan E. "The Devil Made David Do It . . . Or *Did* He? The Nature, Identity, and Literary Origins of the *Satan* in 1 Chronicles 21:1" *Journal of Biblical Literature* 128 (2009) 91–106.

Stone, Michael E. *A History of the Literature of Adam and Eve*. Early Judaism and Its Literature 3. Atlanta, Ga.: Scholars, 1992.

Stuckenbruck, Loren T. *Angel Veneration and Christology: A Study in Early Judaism and in the Christology of the Apocalypse of John*. Wissenschaftliche Untersuchungen zum Neuen Testament 2/70. Tübingen: J. C. B. Mohr, 1995.

Suyūṭī, Jalāl al-Dīn ʻAbd al Raḥmān Ibn Abī Bakr, and Jalāl al-Dīn Muḥammad Ibn Aḥmad al-Maḥallī. *Tafsīr al-Imāmayn al-Jalāyn*. Beirut: Dār al-Ma'rifah, 1990.

Syamsuddin, Sahiron. "Muḥkam and Mutashābih: An Analytical Study of al-Ṭabarī's and al-Zamakhsharī's Interpretations of Q.3:7." *Journal of Qur'anic Studies* 1 (1999) 63–79.

al-Ṭabarī. *The Children of Israel*. Vol. 3 of *The History of al-Tabari*. Translated by William M. Brinner. SUNY Series in Near Eastern Studies. Albany, N.Y.: State University of New York Press, 1991.

———. *Jāmiʻ al-Bayān ʻan Ta'wīl Ay al-Qur'ān*. 30 books in 15 volumes. Beirut: Dār al-Fikr, 1988.

Ṭabarsī, Abū 'Alī al-Fadl b. al-Hasan. *Majma' al-Bayān fi Tafsīr al-Qur'ān*. 5 vols. Beirut: Dār al-Ma'rifa, 1986.

Targum Pseudo-Jonathan: Genesis. Translated by Michael Maher. The Aramaic Bible 1B. Collegeville, Minn.: Liturgical, 1992.

Thiselton, Anthony C. *New Horizons in Hermeneutics: The Theory and Practice of Transforming Biblical Reading*. Grand Rapids, Mich.: Zondervan, 1992.

Van Ess, Josef. "The Beginnings of Islamic Theology." In *The Cultural Context of Medieval Learning: Proceedings of the First International Colloquium on Philosophy, Science, and Theology in the Middle Ages—September 1973*, edited by John E. Murdoch and Edith D. Sylla, 87–103. Boston Studies in the Philosophy of Science 26. Synthese Library 76. Dordrecht, Holland: Reidel, 1975.

Van Wolde, Ellen. "The Story of Cain and Abel: A Narrative Study." *Journal for the Study of the Old Testament* 52 (1991) 25–41.

VanderKam, James C. *Enoch and the Growth of an Apocalyptic Tradition*. Catholic Biblical Quarterly Monograph Series 16. Washington, D.C.: Catholic Biblical Association of America, 1984.

von Grunebaum, Gustave E. "Observations of the Muslim Concept of Evil." *Studia Islamica* 31 (1970) 117–34.

———. *Medieval Islam: A Study in Cultural Orientation*. Oriental Institute Essay. Chicago: University of Chicago Press, 1946.

Waldman, Marilyn Robinson. "New Approaches to the 'Biblical' Materials in the Qur'an." *Muslim World* 75 (1985) 1–16.

———. *Toward a Theory of Historical Narrative: A Case Study in Perso-Islamicate Historiography*. Columbus, Ohio: Ohio State University Press, 1980.

Watt, W. Montgomery. *The Formative Period of Islamic Thought*. Edinburgh: Edinburgh University Press, 1973.

———. *Bell's Introduction to the Qur'ān*. Islamic Surveys 8. Edinburgh: Edinburgh University Press, 1970.

———. *Free Will and Predestination in Early Islam*. London: Luzac, 1948.

Waugh, Earle H. "Jealous Angels: Aspects of Muslim Religious Language." *Ohio Journal of Religious Studies* 1 (1973) 56–72.

Webb, Gisela. "Angel." In vol. 1 of *Encyclopedia of the Qur'ān*, edited by Jane Dammen McAuliffe et al., 84–92. 5 vols. Leiden: Brill, 2001–2006.

Weiss, Bernard G. *The Search for God's Law: Islamic Jurisprudence in the Writings of Sayf al-Dīn al-Āmidī*. Salt Lake City, Utah: University of Utah Press, 1992.

Welch, Alford. "Allah and Other Supernatural Beings." *Journal of the American Academy of Religion Thematic Studies* 47 (1979) 733–58.

———. "The Pneumatology of the Qur'ān." Ph.D. diss., University of Edinburgh, 1969.

Wensinck, A. J. "al-Khaḍir (al-Khiḍr)." In vol. 4 of *Encyclopaedia of Islam,* edited by P. Bearman et al., 902. 12 vols. with indexes and etc. 2d ed. Leiden: Brill, 1960-2005.

———. *The Muslim Creed: Its Genesis and Historical Development*. Cambridge, U.K.: Cambridge University Press, 1932.

Wensinck, A. J., and L. Gardet. "Iblis." In vol. 3 of *Encyclopaedia of Islam,* edited by P. Bearman et al., 668. 12 vols. 2d ed. Leiden: Brill, 1960–2005.

Wheeler, Brannon M. "Moses or Alexander? Early Islamic Exegesis of Qur'an 18:60–65." *Journal of Near Eastern Studies* 57 (1998) 191–215.

White, Hayden. *Tropics of Discourse: Essays in Cultural Criticism*. Baltimore, Md.: Johns Hopkins University Press, 1985.

Whitney, K. William. *Two Strange Beasts: Leviathan and Behemoth in Second Temple and Early Rabbinic Judaism*. Harvard Semitic Monographs 63. Winona Lake, Ind.: Eisenbrauns, 2006.

Wild, Stefan, ed. "The Koran as Subtext in Modern Arabic Poetry." In *Representations of the Divine in Arabic Poetry*, edited by Gert Borg and Ed de Moor, 139–60. Orientations 5. Amsterdam: Rodopi, 2001.

———. *The Qur'an as Text*. Islamic Philosophy, Theology, and Science 27. Leiden: Brill, 1996.

Wilson, Leslie S. *The Book of Job: Judaism in the 2nd Century BCE: An Intertextual Reading*. Studies in Judaism. Lanham, Md: University Press of America, 2006.

Wintermute, Orville S. "Jubilees." In *The Old Testament Pseudepigrapha*, edited by James H. Charlesworth, 35–142. 2 vols. Garden City, N.Y.: Doubleday, 1983–1985.

Wright, William. *A Grammar of the Arabic Language*. Revised by W. Robertson Smith and M. J. de Goeje. 3d ed. Beirut: Librairie du Liban, 1974.

al-Zamakhsharī, Maḥmūd Ibn 'Umar. *Al-Kashshāf*. Beirut: Dār Iḥyā' al-Turāth al-'Arabī, 1997.

Zimmermann, Johannes. "Observations on 4Q246: The 'son of God.'" In *Qumran-Messianism: Studies on the Messianic Expectations in the Dead Sea Scrolls*, edited by James H. Charlesworth, Hermann Lichtenberger, and Gerbern S. Oegema, 175–90. Tübingen: Mohr Siebeck, 1998.

Zwemer, Samuel M. "The Worship of Adam by Angels (with Reference to Hebrews 1:6)." *The Moslem World* 27 (1937) 115–27.

Zwettler, Michael. "A Mantic Manifesto: The Sūra of 'The Poets' and the Qur'ānic Foundations of Prophetic Authority." In *Poetry and Prophecy: The Beginnings of a Literary Tradition*, in 75–119. Myth and Poetics. Edited by James L. Kugel. Ithaca, N.Y.: Cornell University Press, 1990.

Index of Foreign Terms

Index of Subjects

Aaron, 100, 105–9, 111–14, 212, 238. *See also* Moses
Abraham, 41, 53, 144, 149, 166, 169, 219–20; *Apocalypse of,* 154
Abū Bakr, 54–56
Abu Hanifah, al-Nu'mān b. Thābit, 159
Abū Nuwās, 2
Abū Ṭālib, 173
actor, 18–19, 51, 112, 178, 217, 230, 238, 241, 244, 248; angels and *jinn* as, 51; God as, 178; Iblīs as, 18, 112, 230, 238, 241, 244, 248; al-Shayṭān as, 18, 217, 241. *See also* character
'Ād, 173, 205
Adam (and Eve), authority on earth of, 81, 222n8, 247, 255, 262; in Christianity, fall of, 10, 84; clothing of, 213–14; as created clayish, 196–97, 199, 208; created of clay, 81, 171, 179–80, 223; enmity on earth of, 110–11, 213–14, 218, 231–34; in *Enoch*, 75; with Eve and Iblīs, 12–13, 76–79, 167–68; fallibility of, 10, 84, 108–9, 112–14; as father of humans, 122–23; forgiveness of, 162, 212, 214–17, 251; in garden story, 109–11, 114, 211–17, 229–31; God teaches names to, 7, 225–28, 232, 241, 255; Iblīs at grave of, 16; in Jewish tradition, 68, 84, 86n60; as judge of souls, 88n66; in *Life of Adam and Eve*, 76–79, 167–68; as made in image of God, 77–80, 89; as made of ringing clay (*ṣalṣāl*), 157, 161; as made of stinking clay (*ḥamā' masnūn*), 24, 157–62, 171, 239, 255; and narrative of creation, 80, 178, 224–25; repentance of, 217, 232, 250–51; shame of, 212–18; as sibling, 5, 141, 162–63, 226–27, 239, 255; with wife, 211–14, 216, 233–34. *See also* God, creates Adam; Adam story; *Life of Adam and Eve*; garden; al-Shayṭān
Ahab, Naboth and Jezebel, 175
Akhtar, Shabbir, 263
'Alī, Jawād, 125
'Alī, Yūsuf, 44–45, 204, 207n3
Alter, Robert, 3
Amalek, 63–64
Andersen, Francis I., 75
angels, Abel as a judge of, 88; in Bible, 2, 67–70, 74–75; challenging God, 7, 12, 25, 68–69, 125, 185; changing roles of, 50–51;

Qumran, 61, 64, 75
Qur'ān, assonance in, 99, 191, 203, 208–10, 224; chronological order of, 50–54, 104, 244–47; collection of, 52, 54–56, 243; as *dhikr* (reminder), 41; divine authorship of, 37, 56; Egyptian Edition of, 244; as guide for humanity, 200, 220–21; *'ijāz al–qur'ān*, 46, 56, 200; inner–textuality in, 49; intertextuality in, 49; linear reading of, 50, 55–56; as liturgy, 53; mystery letters in, 45, 97–99, 204, 221; occasions of revelation of, 48, 56, 58, 243; parænetic nature of, 31–33, 41, 44–45, 53, 243; quality of stories of, 39–40; as *qur'ān*, 53, 116, 143–46, 149, 156, 245; relationship to previous scriptures of, 30, 32, 41, 49; repertoire of, 30; as *sultān*, 200; unity of *sūrah*s in, 58, 243; 'Uthmānic codex of, 54–55. *See also* chronology
Quraysh, 122, 176, 246
al-Qurṭubī, Abī 'Abdallah, 38, 97–98, 106, 162, 197, 234n22, 244, 248
Qutb, Sayyid, 38, 58

rabbinic thought, 175; on Cain and Abel, 85–86; and divine council, 175; and good and evil inclination, 62–63, 251; and Solomon, 173–74
Rahman, Fazlur, 18
Ramadan, 55
range of interpretation, 33
Raphael, David D., 21–22
al-Rāzī, Fakr al-Dīn, 45–46, 49
reader, author as, 242–43; implied and actual, 4–6, 30–31; passive, 32; repertoire of, 4, 30–31, 34
reader-response criticism, 7, 28, 47–49. *See also* narratology
reasoning (*qiyās*), 23–25, 163, 186–87, 239, 256, 264. *See also* Mu'tazilite
recitation (*tajwīd*), 29–30, 48, 55, 97, 116, 145–46, 193, 220
reminder (*dhikr*), 41, 50, 99, 102, 148, 185, 243, of Adham, 255
renunciation (*zuhd*), 14
repertoire, 28–35, 242–43 ; Biblical, 4–5, concerning *jinn*, 128–41; of Qur'ān, 41–44, 102–4
response–inviting structures, 31, 33
Revelation to John, 11n6
Richards, I. A., 23
Riḍā', Rashīd, 38
Riddell, Peter, 39
Robinson, Neal, 220
Rubin, Uri, 39, 49n37
Rūmī, Jalāl al-Dīn, 14–17, 19, 25–26, 140
Russell, Jeffrey Burton, 93
Ruth, Book of, 48

al-Saadawi, Nawal, 38, 237, 248, 256–60, 262, 265–66
Ṣāliḥ, 205
al-Sāmirī, 107–9, 111–13, 238. *See also* Moses
Sanā'ī, Ḥakīm Abū al-Majīd, 14, 20

Harvard Theological Studies

64. Nasrallah, Laura, Charalambos Bakirtzis, and Steven J. Friesen, eds. *From Roman to Early Christian Thessalonikē: Studies in Religion and Archaeology*, 2010.
63. Short, J. Randall. *The Surprising Election and Confirmation of King David*, 2010.
62. Bodman, Whitney S. *The Poetics of Iblīs: Narrative Theology in the Qur'ān*, 2011.
61. Schifferdecker, Kathryn. *Out of the Whirlwind: Creation Theology in the Book of Job*, 2008.
60. Luijendijk, AnneMarie. *Greetings in the Lord: Early Christians and the Oxyrhynchus Papyri*, 2008.
59. Yip, Francis Ching-Wah. *Capitalism As Religion?A Study of Paul Tillich's Interpretation of Modernity*, 2010.
58. Pearson, Lori. *Beyond Essence: Ernst Troeltsch as Historian and Theorist of Christianity*, 2008.
57. Hills, Julian V. *Tradition and Composition in the* Epistula Apostolorum, 2008.
56. Nickelsburg, George W. E. *Resurrection, Immortality, and Eternal Life in Intertestamental Judaism and Early Christianity.* Expanded Edition, 2006.
55. Johnson-DeBaufre, Melanie. *Jesus Among Her Children: Q, Eschatology, and the Construction of Christian Origins*, 2005.
54. Hall, David D. *The Faithful Shepherd: A History of the New England Ministry in the Seventeenth Century*, 2006.
53. Schowalter, Daniel N., and Steven J. Friesen, eds. *Urban Religion in Roman Corinth: Interdisciplinary Approaches,* 2004.
52. Nasrallah, Laura. *"An Ecstasy of Folly": Prophecy and Authority in Early Christianity*, 2003.
51. Brock, Ann Graham. *Mary Magdalene, The First Apostle: The Struggle for Authority,* 2003.
50. Trost, Theodore Louis. *Douglas Horton and the Ecumenical Impulse in American Religion*, 2002.
49. Huang, Yong. *Religious Goodness and Political Rightness: Beyond the Liberal-Communitarian Debate*, 2001.
48. Rossing, Barbara R. *The Choice between Two Cities: Whore, Bride, and Empire in the Apocalypse*, 1999.
47. Skedros, James Constantine. *Saint Demetrios of Thessaloniki: Civic Patron and Divine Protector, 4th–7th Centuries C.E.*, 1999.
46. Koester, Helmut, ed. *Pergamon, Citadel of the Gods: Archaeological Record, Literary Description, and Religious Development*, 1998.
45. Kittredge, Cynthia Briggs. *Community and Authority: The Rhetoric of Obedience in the Pauline Tradition*, 1998.
44. Lesses, Rebecca Macy. *Ritual Practices to Gain Power: Angels, Incantations, and Revelation in Early Jewish Mysticism*, 1998.

43. Guenther-Gleason, Patricia E. *On Schleiermacher and Gender Politics*, 1997.

42. White, L. Michael. *The Social Origins of Christian Architecture* (2 vols.), 1997.

41. Koester, Helmut, ed. *Ephesos, Metropolis of Asia: An Interdisciplinary Approach to its Archaeology, Religion, and Culture*, 1995.

40. Guider, Margaret Eletta. *Daughters of Rahab: Prostitution and the Church of Liberation in Brazil*, 1995.

39. Schenkel, Albert F. *The Rich Man and the Kingdom: John D. Rockefeller, Jr., and the Protestant Establishment*, 1995.

38. Hutchison, William R. and Hartmut Lehmann, eds. *Many Are Chosen: Divine Election and Western Nationalism*, 1994.

37. Lubieniecki, Stanislas. *History of the Polish Reformation and Nine Related Documents*. Translated and interpreted by George Huntston Williams, 1995.

– Davidovich, Adina. *Religion as a Province of Meaning: The Kantian Foundations of Modern Theology*, 1993.

36. Thiemann, Ronald F., ed. *The Legacy of H. Richard Niebuhr*, 1991.

35. Hobbs, Edward C., ed. *Bultmann, Retrospect and Prospect: The Centenary Symposium at Wellesley*, 1985.

34. Cameron, Ron. *Sayings Traditions in the Apocryphon of James*, 1984. Reprinted, 2004.

33. Blackwell, Albert L. *Schleiermacher's Early Philosophy of Life: Determinism, Freedom, and Phantasy*, 1982.

32. Gibson, Elsa. *The "Christians for Christians" Inscriptions of Phrygia: Greek Texts, Translation and Commentary*, 1978.

31. Bynum, Caroline Walker. Docere Verbo et Exemplo*: An Aspect of Twelfth-Century Spirituality*, 1979.

30. Williams, George Huntston, ed. *The Polish Brethren: Documentation of the History and Thought of Unitarianism in the Polish-Lithuanian Commonwealth and in the Diaspora 1601–1685*, 1980.

29. Attridge, Harold W. *First-Century Cynicism in the Epistles of Heraclitus*, 1976.

28. Williams, George Huntston, Norman Pettit, Winfried Herget, and Sargent Bush, Jr., eds. *Thomas Hooker: Writings in England and Holland, 1626–1633*, 1975.

27. Preus, James Samuel. *Carlstadt's* Ordinaciones *and Luther's Liberty: A Study of the Wittenberg Movement, 1521–22*, 1974.

26. Nickelsburg, George W. E. *Resurrection, Immortality, and Eternal Life in Intertestamental Judaism*, 1972.

25. Worthley, Harold Field. *An Inventory of the Records of the Particular (Congregational) Churches of Massachusetts Gathered 1620–1805*, 1970.

24. Yamauchi, Edwin M. *Gnostic Ethics and Mandaean Origins*, 1970.

23. Yizhar, Michael. *Bibliography of Hebrew Publications on the Dead Sea Scrolls 1948–1964*, 1967.

22. Albright, William Foxwell. *The Proto-Sinaitic Inscriptions and Their Decipherment*, 1966.

21. Dow, Sterling, and Robert F. Healey. *A Sacred Calendar of Eleusis*, 1965.

20. Sundberg, Jr., Albert C. *The Old Testament of the Early Church*, 1964.

19. Cranz, Ferdinand Edward. *An Essay on the Development of Luther's Thought on Justice, Law, and Society*, 1959.

18. Williams, George Huntston, ed. *The Norman Anonymous of 1100 A.D.: Towards the Identification and Evaluation of the So-Called Anonymous of York*, 1951.

17. Lake, Kirsopp, and Silva New, eds. *Six Collations of New Testament Manuscripts*, 1932.

16. Wilbur, Earl Morse, trans. *The Two Treatises of Servetus on the Trinity: On the Errors of the Trinity, 7 Books, A.D. 1531. Dialogues on the Trinity, 2 Books. On the Righteousness of Christ's Kingdom, 4 Chapters, A.D. 1532*, 1932.

15. Casey, Robert Pierce, ed. Serapion of Thmuis's *Against the Manichees*, 1931.

14. Ropes, James Hardy. *The Singular Problem of the Epistles to the Galatians*, 1929.

13. Smith, Preserved. *A Key to the Colloquies of Erasmus*, 1927.

12. Spyridon of the Laura and Sophronios Eustratiades. *Catalogue of the Greek Manuscripts in the Library of the Laura on Mount Athos*, 1925.

11. Sophronios Eustratiades and Arcadios of Vatopedi. *Catalogue of the Greek Manuscripts in the Library of the Monastery of Vatopedi on Mt. Athos*, 1924.

10. Conybeare, Frederick C. *Russian Dissenters*, 1921.

9. Burrage, Champlin, ed. *An Answer to John Robinson of Leyden by a Puritan Friend: Now First Published from a Manuscript of A.D. 1609*, 1920.

8. Emerton, Ephraim. *The* Defensor pacis *of Marsiglio of Padua: A Critical Study*, 1920,

7. Bacon, Benjamin W. *Is Mark a Roman Gospel?* 1919.

6. Cadbury, Henry Joel. 2 vols. *The Style and Literary Method of Luke*, 1920.

5. Marriott, G. L., ed. Macarii Anecdota*: Seven Unpublished Homilies of Macarius*, 1918.

4. Edmunds, Charles Carroll and William Henry Paine Hatch. *The Gospel Manuscripts of the General Theological Seminary*, 1918.

3. Arnold, William Rosenzweig. *Ephod and Ark: A Study in the Records and Religion of the Ancient Hebrews*, 1917.

2. Hatch, William Henry Paine. *The Pauline Idea of Faith in its Relation to Jewish and Hellenistic Religion*, 1917.

1. Torrey, Charles Cutler. *The Composition and Date of Acts*, 1916.

Harvard Dissertations in Religion

In 1993, Harvard Theological Studies absorbed the Harvard Dissertations in Religion series.

31. Baker-Fletcher, Garth. *Somebodyness: Martin Luther King, Jr. and the Theory of Dignity*, 1993.
30. Soneson, Jerome Paul. *Pragmatism and Pluralism: John Dewey's Significance for Theology*, 1993.
29. Crabtree, Harriet. *The Christian Life: The Traditional Metaphors and Contemporary Theologies*, 1991.
28. Schowalter, Daniel N. *The Emperor and the Gods: Images from the Time of Trajan*, 1993.
27. Valantasis, Richard. *Spiritual Guides of the Third Century: A Semiotic Study of the Guide-Disciple Relationship in Christianity, Neoplatonism, Hermetism, and Gnosticism*, 1991.
26. Wills, Lawrence Mitchell. *The Jews in the Court of the Foreign King: Ancient Jewish Court Legends*, 1990.
25. Massa, Mark Stephen. *Charles Augustus Briggs and the Crisis of Historical Criticism*, 1990.
24. Hills, Julian Victor. *Tradition and Composition in the* Epistula apostolorum, 1990. Reprinted, 2008.
23. Bowe, Barbara Ellen. *A Church in Crisis: Ecclesiology and Paraenesis in Clement of Rome*, 1988.
22. Bisbee, Gary A. *Pre-Decian Acts of Martyrs and* Commentarii, 1988.
21. Ray, Stephen Alan. *The Modern Soul: Michel Foucault and the Theological Discourse of Gordon Kaufman and David Tracy*, 1987.
20. MacDonald, Dennis Ronald. *There Is No Male and Female: The Fate of a Dominical Saying in Paul and Gnosticism*, 1987.
19. Davaney, Sheila Greeve. *Divine Power: A Study of Karl Barth and Charles Hartshorne*, 1986.
18. LaFargue, J. Michael. *Language and Gnosis: The Opening Scenes of the Acts of Thomas*, 1985.
12. Layton, Bentley, ed. *The Gnostic Treatise on Resurrection from Nag Hammadi*, 1979.
11. Ryan, Patrick J. *Imale: Yoruba Participation in the Muslim Tradition: A Study of Clerical Piety*, 1977.
10. Neevel, Jr., Walter G. *Yāmuna's* Vedānta *and* Pāñcarātra*: Integrating the Classical and the Popular*, 1977.
9. Yarbro Collins, Adela. *The Combat Myth in the Book of Revelation*, 1976.
8. Veatch, Robert M. *Value-Freedom in Science and Technology: A Study of the Importance of the Religious, Ethical, and Other Socio-Cultural Factors in Selected Medical Decisions Regarding Birth Control*, 1976.

7. Attridge, Harold W. *The Interpretation of Biblical History in the* Antiquitates judaicae *of Flavius Josephus*, 1976.

6. Trakatellis, Demetrios C. *The Pre-Existence of Christ in the Writings of Justin Martyr*, 1976.

5. Green, Ronald Michael. *Population Growth and Justice: An Examination of Moral Issues Raised by Rapid Population Growth*, 1975.

4. Schrader, Robert W. *The Nature of Theological Argument: A Study of Paul Tillich*, 1976.

3. Christensen, Duane L. *Transformations of the War Oracle in Old Testament Prophecy: Studies in the Oracles Against the Nations*, 1975.

2. Williams, Sam K. *Jesus' Death as Saving Event: The Background and Origin of a Concept*, 1972.

1. Smith, Jane I. *An Historical and Semantic Study of the Term "Islām" as Seen in a Sequence of Qur'an Commentaries*, 1970.